THE NEW CAMBRIDGE HISTORY OF AMERICAN FOREIGN RELATIONS, VOLUME 4

Challenges to American Primacy, 1945 to the Present

Since their first publication, the four volumes of *The Cambridge History of American Foreign Relations* have served as the definitive source for the topic, from the colonial period to the Cold War. This new fourth volume explores the conditions in the international system at the end of World War II, the American determination to provide leadership, and the security dilemma each superpower posed for the others. It incorporates recent scholarship and revelations, carrying the narrative into the administration of Barack Obama. The author points to the nature of the Stalinist state, with its secrecy and brutal dictatorship, to explain the course of the Cold War. The character of the American political system, including the separation of political powers and the role of interest groups, prompted American leaders to exaggerate dangers abroad to enhance their domestic power. The book also provides fresh insight on Chinese and Soviet actions during the Korean War, the Taiwan Strait crises of the 1950s, and the Cuban missile crisis. It explains the rise and fall of détente in the 1970s, describes how imperial overreach strained both the United States and the Soviet Union in the 1980s, and reflects on what the Cold War has meant for the world.

Warren I. Cohen is University Distinguished Professor Emeritus at Michigan State University, the Distinguished University Professor Emeritus at University of Maryland, Baltimore County, and Senior Scholar at Woodrow Wilson International Center for Scholars. Professor Cohen has published nineteen books, the best known of which is *America's Response to China* (2010). In addition to scholarly publications, Professor Cohen has written for the *Atlantic*, the *Baltimore Sun*, *Christian Science Monitor*, *Dissent*, *Foreign Affairs*, *International Herald Tribune*, the *Los Angeles Times*, *Nation*, the *New York Times*, the *Times Literary Supplement*, and the *Washington Post*. He has served as the president of the Society for Historians of American Foreign Relations and chairman of the U.S. Department of State Advisory Committee on Historical Diplomatic Documentation. Professor Cohen has also been a consultant on Chinese affairs to the Senate Foreign Relations Committee, the CIA, the Department of State, two governors of Michigan, and three directors of the Michigan Department of Commerce.

The New Cambridge History of American Foreign Relations

Warren I. Cohen, Editor

THE NEW CAMBRIDGE HISTORY OF AMERICAN FOREIGN RELATIONS, VOLUME 4

Challenges to American Primacy, 1945 to the Present

WARREN I. COHEN

University of Maryland, Baltimore County
and
Woodrow Wilson International Center for Scholars

CAMBRIDGE
UNIVERSITY PRESS

CAMBRIDGE UNIVERSITY PRESS
Cambridge, New York, Melbourne, Madrid, Cape Town,
Singapore, São Paulo, Delhi, Mexico City

Cambridge University Press
32 Avenue of the Americas, New York, NY 10013-2473, USA

www.cambridge.org
Information on this title: www.cambridge.org/9780521763622

© Cambridge University Press 2013

First published 2013

Printed in the United States of America

A catalog record for this publication is available from the British Library.

Library of Congress Cataloging in Publication Data
The new Cambridge history of American foreign relations.
      p.   cm.
Includes bibliographical references and index.
ISBN 978-1-107-03183-8 (hardback set) – ISBN 978-1-107-00590-7 (hardback v. 1) –
ISBN 978-0-521-76752-1 (hardback v. 2) – ISBN 978-0-521-76328-8 (hardback v. 3) –
ISBN 978-0-521-76362-2 (hardback v. 4)
   I. United States – Foreign relations.   I. Weeks, William Earl, 1957–
   II. LaFeber, Walter.   III. Iriye, Akira.   IV. Cohen, Warren I.
   V. Title: New history of American foreign relations.
         E183.7.N48   2012
      327.73–dc23   2012018193

ISBN 978-1-107-00590-7 Volume 1 Hardback
ISBN 978-0-521-76752-1 Volume 2 Hardback
ISBN 978-0-521-76328-8 Volume 3 Hardback
ISBN 978-0-521-76362-2 Volume 4 Hardback
ISBN 978-1-107-03183-8 Four-Volume Hardback Set

In Loving Memory
of Nancy Bernkopf Tucker
My Beautiful Young Wife
1948–2012

CONTENTS

LIST OF MAPS

GENERAL EDITOR'S INTRODUCTION

My goal for *The Cambridge History of American Foreign Relations*, published in 1993, was to make the finest scholarship and the best writing in the historical profession available to the general reader. The response of readers and reviewers was gratifying. Then, as now, I had no ideological or methodological agenda. I wanted some of the leading students of diplomatic history, regardless of approach, to join me, and I was delighted to have my invitations accepted by the first three to whom I turned.

When I conceived of the project nearly thirty years ago, I had no idea that the Cold War would end suddenly, that the volumes would conclude with a final epoch as well defined as the first three. The collapse of the Soviet Empire, just as I finished writing Volume 4, astonished me, but allowed for a sense of completion those volumes would have lacked under any other circumstances.

Twenty years have passed since the publication of those volumes. Most obviously, additional chapters were needed to bring the story to the present. In addition, we were aware of the need to incorporate new scholarship, fresh insights into the works. *The New Cambridge History of American Foreign Relations* offers our most recent thoughts.

The first volume of the 1993 series was written by Bradford Perkins, then the preeminent historian of late-eighteenth- and early-nineteenth-century American diplomacy and doyen of active diplomatic historians. Brad's death necessitated a search for a successor to write the initial volume of *The New Cambridge History of American Foreign Relations*. With the concurrence of my colleagues Akira Iriye and Walter LaFeber, I chose William Earl Weeks as this generation's finest student of early American diplomacy.

Weeks has written persuasively, sometimes provocatively, on a broad range of subjects, focused primarily on American expansion. Like Perkins, he stresses the building of an empire and sees a pattern of imperial behavior that existed before the creation of an independent United States. He sees men such as Ben Franklin promoting a vision of a great nation, an empire of freedom that would stretch across the continent. Again, like Perkins, he notes the persistent effort of presidents to dominate policy, contrary to the intent of the participants in the Constitutional Convention. In particular, Weeks raises the stature of James Monroe, portraying him as the first "hidden hand" president, foreshadowing methods Dwight Eisenhower perfected more than a century later. He is equally impressed with the audacity of James Polk as he contributed mightily to the nation's self-declared expansionist mission. He describes how Polk's role in acquiring an empire on the Pacific provided an enormous stimulus to continental expansion. Weeks argues that the concept of Manifest Destiny was applicable to the entire forty years' period preceding the Civil War. He demonstrates that American leaders did not hesitate to eliminate all obstacles to the creation of the early American Empire. He details their brutal treatment of Native Americans as the nation satisfied its lust for land on which various tribes had lived for hundreds of years. And finally, he takes a fresh look at the issue of slavery as a cause of the Civil War.

Walter LaFeber, author of the second volume, is one of the most highly respected of the so-called Wisconsin School of diplomatic historians, men and women who studied with Fred Harvey Harrington and William Appleman Williams and their students, and were identified as "New Left" when they burst on the scene in the 1960s. LaFeber's newly revised volume covers the last third of the nineteenth century and extends into the twentieth, to 1913, through the administration of William Howard Taft. He discusses the link between the growth of American economic power and expansionism, adding the theme of racism, especially as applied to Native Americans and Filipinos. Once again, his rejection of the idea of an American quest for order is striking. He argues that Americans sought opportunities for economic and missionary activities abroad and that they were undaunted by the disruptions they caused in other nations. A revolution in China or Mexico was a small price to pay for advantages accruing to Americans, especially when the local people paid it. His other inescapable theme is the use of foreign affairs to enhance presidential power.

The third volume, which begins on the eve of World War I and carries the story through World War II, is again written by Akira Iriye, past president of the American Historical Association and our generation's most innovative historian of international relations. Japanese-born, educated in American universities, Iriye has been fascinated by the cultural conflicts and accommodations that permeate power politics, particularly as the United States has confronted the nations of East Asia. Iriye opens his book with a quick sketch of the international system as it evolved and was dominated by Europe through the seventeenth, eighteenth, and nineteenth centuries. He analyzes Wilsonianism in war and peace and how it was applied in Asia and Latin America. Most notable is his discussion of what he calls the "cultural aspect" of the 1920s. Iriye sees the era about which he writes as constituting the "globalizing of America" – an age in which the United States supplanted Europe as the world's leader and provided the economic and cultural resources to define and sustain the international order. He notes the awakening of non-Western peoples and their expectations of American support and inspiration. In his conclusion he presages the troubles that would follow from the Americanization of the world.

Much of my work, like Iriye's, has focused on American–East Asian relations. My friend Michael Hunt has placed me in the "realist" school of diplomatic historians. Influenced by association with Perkins, LaFeber, Iriye, Ernest May, and younger friends such as John Lewis Gaddis, Michael Hogan, and Melvyn Leffler, I have studied the domestic roots of American policy, the role of ideas and attitudes as well as economic concerns, the role of nongovernmental organizations including missionaries, and the place of art in international relations. In the final volume of the series, *Challenges to American Primacy, 1945 to the Present*, I also rely heavily on what I have learned from political economists and political scientists.

I begin Part I of the book in the closing months of World War II and end it with the disappearance of the Soviet Union in 1991. I write of the vision American leaders had of a postwar world order and the growing sense that the Soviet Union posed a threat to that vision. The concept of the "security dilemma," the threat each side's defensive actions seemed to pose for the other, looms large in my analysis of the origins of the Cold War. I also emphasize the importance of the two political systems: the paradox of the powerful state and weak government in the United States and the secrecy and brutality of the Stalinist regime. Throughout the volume, I note the importance of the disintegration of prewar colonial empires, the appearance of scores of newly independent states in Africa, Asia, and Latin America, and the turmoil caused by American and Soviet efforts to force them into an international system designed in Washington and Moscow. Finally, I conclude Part I with the reemergence of Germany and Japan as major powers, the collapse of the Soviet Union, and the drift of the United States, its course in world affairs uncertain in the absence of an adversary.

In Part II, two chapters focus on the American role in world affairs since the end of the Cold War. I write of the struggle of political leaders and public intellectuals in the United States to find a new lodestar after the collapse of the Soviet Union rendered containment obsolete. George H. W. Bush and William Jefferson Clinton were hampered by a public tired of efforts to pacify an unruly world, demanding attention to domestic affairs. Not until the al Qaeda attacks on American soil on September 11, 2001, was a new foreign policy goal, articulated by George W. Bush, "the War on Terror," widely accepted – with grim consequences in Iraq and Afghanistan. But in the twenty-first century, it was quickly apparent that the principal challenge to American primacy would be the resurgence of Chinese power. As I write, Barack Obama has disposed of Osama bin Laden, but American troops remain in Afghanistan, Iran and North Korea taunt the American president, and he rebalances his nation's defensive forces across the Pacific.

There are a number of themes that can be followed through these four volumes, however differently the authors approach their subjects. First, there was the relentless national pursuit of wealth and power, described so vividly by Weeks and LaFeber. Iriye demonstrates how Americans used their wealth and power when the United States emerged as the world's leader after World War I. I discuss America's performance as hegemon in the years immediately following World War II, and its response to perceived threats to its dominance through the Cold War – and after.

A second theme of critical importance is the struggle for control of foreign policy. Each author notes tension between the president and

Congress, as institutionalized by the Constitution, and the efforts of various presidents, from 1789 to the present, to circumvent constitutional restraints on their powers. The threat to democratic government is illustrated readily by the Nixon-Kissinger obsessions that led to Watergate, Reagan's Iran-Contra fiasco, and the deceptions of the Bush-Cheney administration that led to the invasion of Iraq.

Finally, we are all concerned with what constitutes American identity on the world scene. Is there a peculiarly American foreign policy that sets the United States off from the rest of the world? We examine the evolution of American values and measure them against the nation's behavior in international affairs. And we worry about the impact of the country's global activity on its domestic order, fearful that Thomas Jefferson's vision of a virtuous republic has been forgotten, boding ill for Americans and for the world they are allegedly "bound to lead."

Warren I. Cohen

ACKNOWLEDGMENTS

My thanks go first to Akira Iriye, Walt LaFeber, and Bill Weeks for join-ing me in this project and to Eric Crahan for inviting us to prepare this new series. Nancy Bernkopf Tucker examined every sentence I wrote with excruciating care. She *usually* failed to intimidate me and will have to settle for the dedication.

Most of the work for the 1993 volume was undertaken during a sabbatical leave from Michigan State University. I am grateful to MSU for its consistent support over the thirty years when I taught there. I was a fellow at the Woodrow Wilson International Center for Scholars, 1990–1, where Mary Bullock, Rob Litwak, Sam Wells, and Lindsay Collins looked after me, providing all the support one hopes for from a residential program. Sergo Mikoyan's comments on a paper I presented at the Center in June 1991 were most helpful. I revised and expanded Volume 4 in the leisure of retirement after a delightful fifteen years of teaching at UMBC, the most promising upcoming public institution in the country.

A work of this kind rests heavily on the research and writing of many other scholars, most of whom are mentioned in my notes and bibliographic essay. I benefited also from conversations over the years with many of those cited and with British, Chinese, German, Japanese, Korean, and Soviet colleagues at a wide range of international confer-ences. Equally rewarding has been the teaching of my students. Listening to Qing Simei probably delayed completion of the first manuscript by a year. Many of the insights in Part II, covering the years 1991 to 2010, derive from discussions with policymakers in Washington and abroad.

PART I

THE COLD WAR

PRELUDE

The late 1940s marked the origin of what the journalist and political philosopher Walter Lippmann called, in 1947, the "Cold War," denoting the emerging confrontation between the United States and the Soviet Union.[1] The term remained in use as a shorthand description of Soviet-American relations and an explanation of most of American foreign policy until 1989 or 1990. Culminating in the reunification of Germany, the events of those two years signaled the Soviet Union's surrender of much of what it had struggled to achieve, allowing the United States to proclaim itself the victor – and requiring American leaders to find a new rationale for the use and abuse of American wealth and power.

World War II ended in the summer of 1945, and the Korean War began in the summer of 1950. The United States and the Soviet Union spent much of the intervening five years defining their postwar relationship. Each nation pursued its vision of world order, exploring the possibilities of cooperation in achieving its goals, and testing the limits of the other's tolerance in pursuit of unshared goals. Each exploited the extraordinary opportunity to extend its influence in the vacuum created by the defeat of Germany and Japan and the decline of British power. Each found important allies, although much of the rest of the world proved less malleable than leaders in Washington and Moscow had imagined. They succeeded, nonetheless, in achieving most of their principal objectives, including a rough settlement of the major issues that divided them, and they provided for themselves whatever might

---

[1] First use of the term *cold war* is usually credited to Herbert Bayard Swope, a publicist employed by Bernard Baruch.

3

pass for security in a world over which hung the shadow of nuclear holocaust. They maintained an uneasy, but hardly threatened, peace between them. And they might well have devoted their energies in the 1950s and afterward to much-needed internal improvements, had Soviet adventurism in Korea not intensified the fears and reinforced the arguments of those American leaders who insisted that preparation for a military resolution of Soviet-American differences was essential.

I

AT WAR'S END

Visions of a New World Order

Allied forces returned to France in June 1944 and were soon battling their way inland from the Normandy beaches. In Washington, President Franklin D. Roosevelt knew that the defeat of Germany was on the horizon, the fall of Japan not far beyond. His thoughts and those of other American leaders, in and out of government, turned increasingly to the postwar world: What legacy would he leave the American people? How could he and his associates ensure an enduring peace and a prosperous America? What lessons could be learned from past failures, especially those that had followed World War I: the inability to stop the economic misery and aggressive violence of the 1930s?

Roosevelt and his colleagues expected the United States to emerge from the war as the greatest power on earth. And after this war, unlike the aftermath of World War I, they were determined to assert American leadership. This time they would create a world order conducive to the interests of the United States, a world order that would allow it to increase its wealth and power and carry its values to every corner of the globe. There would be no shirking of the responsibilities of power. The United States would provide the leadership necessary to create a liberal international economic order, based on free trade and stable currency-exchange rates, providing a level of prosperity the peoples of the world had never known. The United States would provide the leadership necessary to prevent the resurgence of German or Japanese power or the rise of others who might emulate Hitler and the Japanese militarists.

Typically, Roosevelt left the details of implementation to others, especially technical economic details. The balance among his economic advisers had shifted from the nationalists who had dominated in the dark days of 1933 to Cordell Hull at the Department of State and Henry Morgenthau at the Treasury. Hull, Morgenthau, and their aides were committed to the vision of the French philosophers of the Enlightenment, as explicated by Woodrow Wilson: Economic nationalism led to war; free access to markets and raw materials removed a major obstacle to peace. The beggar-thy-neighbor practices of the 1930s, the economic warfare practiced by the Nazis, had produced untold human misery, much evident even before the shooting started.

As early as 1936, Hull and Morgenthau had begun redirecting American foreign economic policy toward cooperation on currency exchange rates and nondiscriminatory trade patterns. They steered the United States into a tripartite agreement with Britain and France to stabilize currency values – a course Roosevelt had rejected in 1933. Hull's reciprocal trade agreements were designed similarly to open doors and expand international commerce.

In August 1941, as Roosevelt and Winston Churchill produced the Atlantic Charter, ostensibly an eloquent description of the aims of those who resisted Hitler, their aides fought below decks, where the Americans attempted to force their desperate British friends to surrender the system of imperial preferences that favored British trade, discriminating against all others, within the British Empire. Similarly, when the terms of the Anglo-American mutual aid pact, or "lend-lease" agreement, of 1942 were negotiated, American negotiators remorselessly pushed British supplicants a step further toward the multilateral, nondiscriminatory postwar economic order Hull and Morgenthau were determined to create.[1]

The apotheosis of the American vision emerged from the Bretton Woods (New Hampshire) Conference of 1944. In July of that year the representatives of forty-four nations agreed to the outline of a postwar monetary system. American officials, specifically Roosevelt, Morgenthau, and his principal deputy at the Treasury Department, Harry Dexter White, perceived the conference and the agreements they sought as the economic basis for the postwar operation of the Grand Alliance. Economic interdependence, a shared stake in a postwar

---

[1] Roy F. Harrod, *The Life of John Maynard Keynes* (New York, 1951), 510–14; Richard N. Gardner, *Sterling-Dollar Diplomacy*, expanded edition (New York, 1969), 40–53, 56–68; Gabriel Kolko, *Politics of War* (New York, 1968), 248–50.

economic order, would bind Great Britain, the Soviet Union, and the United States in peace, as fear of Hitler had brought them together in war. The cooperation of the British, the world's leading traders, whose pound sterling, like the dollar, constituted a basic currency of international trade, was perceived by American leaders to be essential. The Bretton Woods Conference quickly became a negotiation between White for the Americans and John Maynard Keynes, representing Great Britain. Officials of the Soviet Union participated, but, as a nation committed to state-controlled trade, the Soviets were less interested in the details of the agreement than in demonstrating their great-power status and their willingness to work with their allies to eliminate trade and currency issues as causes of international tension. Eager to keep them on board, White indulged them from time to time, but the Soviets were peripheral to what was primarily an Anglo-American show.[2]

The principal goal at Bretton Woods was the creation of mechanisms for assuring stable exchange rates to facilitate the expansion of international trade. The participants created an International Monetary Fund (IMF), designed to provide member nations with assistance whenever their balance of payments (the balance between funds coming in through exports, services, tourism, remissions, etc., and funds expended for imports of goods or services, overseas travel, investments by one's own nationals, etc.) was in deficit. A second institution, a bank for reconstruction and development, which came to be known as the World Bank, was intended to provide or guarantee loans in situations private bankers might find unattractive. In addition, beyond the scope of the conference, the planners envisioned an international trade organization that would gradually eliminate restrictive trade practices. The United States, as the wealthiest nation in the world, with an economy that had rebounded from the Depression and manifested extraordinary productivity during the war, would provide much of the funding required by these institutions – and maintain a proportionate share of control over their activities. There was never any doubt, in Washington or abroad, that the Bretton Woods system was designed to serve the long-term interests of the United States, at least as perceived by the New Deal

---

[2] Gardner, *Sterling-Dollar Diplomacy*, 11–12; Alfred E. Eckes, Jr., *A Search for Solvency: Bretton Woods and the International Monetary System 1947–1971* (Austin, Tex., 1975), 139–64; Harrod, *Keynes*, 525–85.

coalition, the combination of economic forces prevailing in Washington at that time. In general, however, in a willing suspension of disbelief, the leaders of other nations accepted the idea that the system that was good for America would be good for the world; that the world would benefit from the responsible and generous position to which the United States had committed itself. Lord Keynes would have done things rather differently, but he was not distressed by the outcome.

On the other hand, Keynes and White, the other participating planners, and knowledgeable bankers and economists who had not been invited to Bretton Woods, understood that the new liberal international trading order would not materialize the day after the war ended. They were committing their countries to a goal whose realization would have to be postponed until the exigencies of reconstruction had been met. In retrospect it seems clear that the Americans, at least, had underestimated the damage war had inflicted on the British economy, the general problems and costs of postwar reconstruction, the needs of developing countries, and the opposition to an international trade organization designed to dismantle protectionist structures. Certainly few if any among them imagined that it would be 1958 before anything approximating full currency convertibility could be instituted – and even then for only that part of the world that looked to the United States for protection.

Roosevelt, Hull, and Morgenthau were very much aware that their plans for multilateral free trade would face opposition at home; that free enterprise ideologues would resent this further intrusion of the government into economic affairs; that bankers would be apprehensive about government competition for overseas loans; that protected industries and especially those that had long since lost hope of comparative advantage would oppose trade liberalization and might well be supported by some labor organizations; that men and women uneasy about American involvement in world affairs would be unwilling to accept the leadership role projected. In fact, the Bretton Woods agreements constituted a classic case of preemption, of an attempt to commit the nation to the desired role, to a particular international economic regime, before the opposition had the opportunity to act. For all its power internationally, the American government could be thwarted relatively easily by domestic special-interest groups, each with its own conception of what was best for the nation. Indeed, however successful

Roosevelt and his colleagues were in committing the United States to their vision of an international economic order, they failed to persuade Congress to create an international trade organization, and settled for less funding and less altruism than they had hoped.[3]

Although their success was incomplete, their timetable askew, with the general ratification of the Bretton Woods agreements by December 1945, American leaders had succeeded in launching the world on a new order of their design, based on what the historian Michael J. Hogan has called the "New Deal synthesis."[4] The stalwart forces of economic nationalism had been driven back, and much of the trading world committed to the liberal program. The emphasis would be on increasing trade, increasing productivity, on a larger share for everyone rather than a struggle to redistribute existing wealth. Government, business, and labor would work in tandem to realize the new order. When the deadline for ratification was reached, the Soviet Union held back, but its trading role was minor, its interest in the Bretton Woods regime never more than marginal, its absence regretted, but not enough to spoil the party.

If Roosevelt left much of the economic planning to lesser figures in his administration, he was deeply engaged in the political and strategic planning for the postwar world – although attention to detail was not his forte here either. Central to his thoughts was the conviction that a condominium of the great powers – the United States, Great Britain, and the Soviet Union – was essential to keep the peace, to prevent future acts of aggression. He committed himself to the United Nations Organization, to an international organization, primarily to soothe public opinion and the Wilsonians around him – to demonstrate American willingness to accept participation in and leadership of the postwar world – but he had few illusions about a future in which the Big Three did not cooperate. He knew the British could be difficult: Keynes had been tenacious in protecting the pound and British markets, Churchill no less so when prodded on freedom for the colonies. But Churchill and Roosevelt had developed a personal friendship, and their countrymen drew deeply from a well of shared values. Stalin and the Soviet Union

---

[3] Eckes, *A Search for Solvency*, 165–202; John H. Williams, *Postwar Monetary Plans and Other Essays* (New York, 1947); Gardner, *Sterling-Dollar Diplomacy*, 129–44.
[4] Michael J. Hogan, *The Marshall Plan* (Cambridge, 1990), 12–18.

were more of an enigma. Soviet and American statesmen were still circling each other warily, mistrustful after a generation of enmity, which Hitler had forced them to shelve. But the Soviet Union and the United States had no vital interests in conflict, cooperation would be nearly as urgent after victory, and Roosevelt was confident that he and Stalin could find a way to sustain it.[5]

When the Big Three met at Tehran in November 1943, and throughout 1944, Stalin's anxieties had been evident, his fear of a resurgent Germany palpable. Roosevelt shared Stalin's apprehensions and unhesitatingly offered his assurances that the steps necessary to prevent a postwar resurrection of German power would be taken: Germany would be subdued, pacified, and perhaps even dismembered. Stalin's security concerns in Eastern Europe were marginally more troublesome. Certainly he was entitled to a buffer of not unfriendly nations on Soviet borders, to what some would call a "sphere of influence." The Soviet desire to rearrange Poland's geographic position, to move the country some distance to the west – at Germany's expense, and to the advantage of the Soviets who would annex a slice of eastern Poland – would surely upset the Poles. It would likely upset Cordell Hull and a host of other Americans religiously committed to the principle of self-determination. But if some modest rearranging of the map was all that was necessary to bind the Big Three in peace, it was hardly too high a price to pay. Certainly Roosevelt would not scruple to barter German for Polish real estate, though he had title to neither, in the name of world peace. The Poles, to be sure, had the right to self-determination, which was still possible, albeit with minor territorial adjustments. On the other hand, the Soviet Union had won the right to secure borders. Rather than a case of right versus wrong, Roosevelt saw a matter of conflicting rights, in which the Soviet need took precedence, especially while the Red army bore the burden of the battle against Hitler's Wehrmacht.[6]

The Polish question posed a domestic political problem for Roosevelt, which he assumed he could finesse. If Polish Americans concluded he was betraying Poland, they might well desert the Democratic party,

---

[5] Robert Dallek, *Franklin D. Roosevelt and American Foreign Policy, 1932–1945* (New York, 1979), 282–4, 317ff.; Herbert Feis, *Churchill, Roosevelt, and Stalin* (Princeton, 1957), 121–4, 269–79, 596–9.

[6] John L. Gaddis, *The United States and the Origins of the Cold War* (New York, 1972), is most persuasive on this issue.

hurt his reelection prospects in 1944 and the prospects for his party for a generation after. Ideologues might harass him and hamper his efforts toward a just peace, as they had used territorial concessions to Japan made at Versailles in 1919 to savage Woodrow Wilson and his peace treaty. Opponents of Roosevelt's conception of America's role in the postwar world order or of cooperation with the Soviet Union might distort the issue to their advantage. He conveyed his concerns to Stalin at Tehran and in the months that followed – and he depended on Stalin to arrange affairs in Poland in a manner that would be acceptable to the American people. It was important that Stalin understand that even a strong president in the most powerful nation the world had ever known faced restraints and could use a little help from his friends.

Roosevelt had been in politics too long to believe in sure things, but he was reasonably confident of realizing his vision of the great powers working together after victory to maintain a just peace. He was reasonably confident that he could manage both Churchill and Stalin. But he was also a prudent man who hedged his bets. By fiat Roosevelt declared his Asian ally, China, to be a great power, to share in the condominium that would rule the postwar world, to sit in the Security Council of the United Nations and, as Churchill complained, be a "faggot vote" at America's side. China's hostility to British imperialism in Asia might be useful if the British became unruly. Should the Soviets prove less cooperative than he hoped, Roosevelt had another, more awesome weapon up his sleeve, the atom bomb. Urged by one of his scientific advisers to deny critical data about the bomb to the British and on another occasion by a group of atomic scientists to share its secret with the Soviets, Roosevelt chose to share the information with his British allies and to withhold it from the Soviets. The United States would not be without resources should the Soviets revert to being as disagreeable as they had been prior to being invaded by the German army in 1941.[7]

We are far less certain even today – and likely will never be certain – about Stalin's vision of the postwar world. There seems no reason to doubt his indifference toward the liberal international economic order the United States wanted. He saw no place in that system for the Soviet

---

[7] Kolko, *Politics of War*, 218–21; Dallek, *FDR and American Foreign Policy*, 389–91; Martin J. Sherwin, *A World Destroyed* (New York, 1975), 90ff.

Union, with its command economy and state trading organizations. It might have been vaguely threatening, but Stalin gave no indication that he was much troubled by it before 1947. The lessons he drew from the 1930s – every man his own historian – had little to do with exchange rates and tariff barriers. The Soviet Union strove toward autarky and would risk economic dependence on no foreign power. No, the Soviet Union had suffered because the capitalist world, led by Great Britain, had been implacably hostile, and, having failed to prevent the success of the Bolshevik Revolution, had encircled and attempted to destroy its heirs. Ultimately, the enemies of the Soviet Union had unleashed Hitler. Shrewdly, Stalin had bought nearly two years with the Nazi-Soviet pact, but Hitler had attacked nonetheless – and come dangerously close to toppling the Soviet regime. More than twenty million Soviet citizens had lost their lives. The country had been devastated by the Nazi invaders. Grudgingly, the British and the Americans had joined forces with the Russians against Hitler, providing modest but essential material support. For two and a half years, however, Roosevelt and Churchill had rejected Stalin's pleas for a second front in France, leaving Soviet troops to engage 80 percent of the German army. Like Roosevelt, Stalin saw no harm in the United Nations Organization, provided the Soviet Union had multiple votes in the General Assembly (he thought sixteen would be adequate) and a veto in the Security Council to protect its interests. But he was no fool: He would rely neither on the goodwill of his newfound friends nor the efficacy of the United Nations to provide for Soviet security. German power would have to be broken, its wealth used to repair the damage the German military had inflicted on the Soviet Union. Germany would have to be occupied. The so-called Baltic republics would have to be restored to the Russian empire, as would territory the Poles, Finns, and Romanians had taken. No Eastern European country could be allowed to become a springboard for a new aggression against the Soviet Union: All would have "friendly" governments, responsive to Soviet requirements. Optimally, there would be adjustments to the south, at the expense of Iran, Afghanistan, and pro-German Turkey. And when the time came for Soviet forces to participate in the defeat of Japan, Stalin had ideas for buffers and bases in East Asia, not only in what was now the Japanese empire, but in China, where both Nationalist and Communist contenders for power had displeased him, as well. Stalin even had occasional dreams of extending his reach into Africa, of being awarded some of Italy's former colonies on that continent by his grateful allies.[8]

Curiously, Churchill had proved relatively easy to deal with. He sat at the table with Stalin one night in the autumn of 1944 and in a matter of minutes the two men had achieved an equitable division of influence in Eastern Europe. Roosevelt was more elusive, apparently more sympathetic to Soviet aspirations, even suggesting the possibility of Soviet-American collusion against British imperialism, but unwilling to make firm commitments about giving the Soviet Union a free hand in Eastern Europe, forever blathering about the need to appease public opinion in the United States, dallying with anti-Soviet Poles. And then there was the evidence Soviet intelligence had brought Stalin that the United States was working with the British on a secret weapon, an atom bomb, about which Roosevelt had said nothing to his loyal Soviet ally. Clearly, satisfactory postwar relations among the victors were by no means assured. It was a time for caution – and however ruthless he was, Stalin had not survived in the Soviet system of his day without being a very cautious man.

In East Asia, a very different set of circumstances prevailed in the closing months of the war. Chiang Kai-shek, the tenacious Chinese leader, sat in Chongqing (Chungking), husbanding his forces, waiting for his American allies to rid his country of the Japanese invaders. His concerns were, conceivably, even graver than those of Roosevelt and Stalin: The survival of his regime was still very much in question. In 1944 the Japanese were still capable of – and did in fact launch – another offensive. Within Chiang's government, there were several prominent figures, mostly military men, ready and eager to succeed him if he faltered. Off in Yan'an, in the northwest of his country, Communist forces hostile to his regime controlled an extensive area and were primed to expand as soon as the Japanese retreated. Indeed, Chiang, to the irritation of the Americans, had posted half a million of his best-equipped forces as a barrier to Communist expansion rather than risk those assets against the Japanese. Increasingly, the Americans were pressing him to engage the Japanese more, threatening to align themselves with other forces

---

[8] Feis, *Churchill, Roosevelt, and Stalin*, 26, 510–11, 550–5; Dallek, *FDR and American Foreign Policy*, 389–91; William Taubman, *Stalin's American Policy* (New York, 1982), 75–82.

in the country more willing to fight. Inevitably, the Americans would expel the Japanese, but then what? Resumption of civil war with the Communists was inescapable. An increased Soviet presence on China's borders was certain – and a victorious Stalin, unchecked by Japan, would be a demanding neighbor. And the British imperialists would return to Hong Kong. With limited control over his own country, with China no match for the allegedly friendly great powers moving in on it, Chiang had to count on his own demonstrated ability to manipulate Roosevelt and Stalin. He had to rely on the traditional Chinese practice of playing barbarians off against each other, to China's advantage.

Chiang had not been allowed to confer with the Big Three at Tehran in 1943, but Roosevelt had agreed to enhance China's great-power status by meeting him in Cairo before and after the conference. Part of the time, the two men met alone, with Chiang's American-educated wife serving as translator. Chiang, as always, wanted more aid from the United States, wanted more action by American forces in China. Roosevelt, as always, made vague promises, and asked for more action from the Chinese. Promises of postwar assistance to China may have been offered, but there were no witnesses to support some of the later claims by Madame Chiang and her husband.

In 1944, Roosevelt lost patience with Chiang's inaction and demanded that he send his troops into battle under the leadership of the American general, Joseph Stilwell, an abrasive infantryman with whom Chiang had fenced unhappily for two years. Chiang refused, demanded Stilwell's recall, and forfeited a major role in the liberation of China. Roosevelt turned to the Soviet Union to help do the job the Chinese were not going to do themselves. At the Yalta Conference, in February 1945, Roosevelt bought Soviet participation in the war against Japan by agreeing to support Soviet imperial claims in China.[9]

Stalin had feared – and much of the world had expected – a Japanese attack on Soviet East Asian territory, but the Japanese had turned south instead, after crippling the U.S. fleet at Pearl Harbor. So long as Hitler's army battered the gates of Moscow and Leningrad, Stalin's attention

---

[9] Herbert Feis, *The China Tangle* (Princeton, 1953), 166–201; Barbara Tuchman, *Stilwell and the American Experience in China, 1911–1945* (New York, 1970); Charles Romanus and Riley Sunderland, *Stilwell's Command Problems* (Washington, D.C., 1956). For a view from a perspective close to Chiang's, see Liang Chin-tung, *General Stilwell in China, 1942–1944* (New York, 1972).

was riveted on his European front. Stalin nonetheless had claims on Chinese territory and, when the Germans had been turned back in 1943, and Soviet forces took the offensive, he remembered Chinese intrusions into the sphere of influence he had fashioned in Xinjiang (Sinkiang) in Central Asia. No longer needing Chinese forces to engage the Japanese, confident the Americans could manage that, Stalin attempted in 1944 to drive the Chinese from territory he considered his domain, reminding Chiang that the Soviet Union was not to be taken lightly.[10] And, as the months passed, Stalin perceived new opportunities for the Soviet state to rival the achievements of tsarist imperialism, regaining not only territory from the Japanese, whom he would attack in due course, but a sphere of influence from the Chinese, whom he would soon help liberate. At Yalta, Roosevelt was not troubled by Stalin's aspirations. No price was too high to save American lives – when it was paid in other people's currencies.

In Yan'an, Mao Zedong, the Chinese Communist leader, struggled to maneuver against the Japanese and Chiang, uncertain of what to expect from the Americans or the Soviets. The Japanese had interrupted Chiang's efforts to exterminate the Communists during the 1930s; Chiang would certainly resume his effort at war's end. The Americans, however, had been friendly throughout the war, and Mao's trusted emissary, Zhou Enlai, had spent much of the war years in Chongqing successfully wooing the Americans and alerting them to the seamier side of Chiang's activities. Concerned primarily with defeating the Japanese, the Americans had enlisted Communist support and appeared determined to prevent Chiang from precipitating a civil war. Progressive forces seemed to be in control in the United States, cooperating with the Soviet Union. Mao and Zhou wondered whether the Americans would remain friendly after the war and what role the United States might play in China.

Mao could not count on a benign Stalin. Stalin had betrayed the Chinese Communists to serve his own ends in the past. He had tried

---

[10] John W. Garver, *Chinese-Soviet Relations, 1937–1945* (New York, 1988), 153–81, 196–230; Allen S. Whiting and Sheng Shih-ts'ai, *Sinkiang: Pawn or Pivot?* (East Lansing, Mich., 1958), remains useful. See also U.S. Department of State, *Foreign Relations of the United States, 1944, China* (Washington, D.C., 1967), 758–823 and Vladislav M. Zubock, *A Failed Empire: The Soviet Union in the Cold War from Stalin to Gorbachev* (Chapel Hill, 2007), 25.

to impose upon them leaders amenable to his control. He had tried unsuccessfully to use, perhaps even sacrifice, the Chinese Communists, in suicidal attacks on the Japanese, to protect the Soviet Union in the late 1930s. He had chased Chinese Communist forces out of territories Mao considered Chinese. And the intensely nationalistic Mao was aware of Stalin's plans for Mongolia and perhaps suspected other Soviet claims on Chinese soil—as in Xinjiang, where Stalin was financing and arming Uighur separatists. It had taken a great deal of ingenuity and good fortune for Mao to rise to the top of the Communist party and for the party to survive the misfortunes of the 1920s and 1930s. Mao and his colleagues would need all of that – and perhaps more – to prevail after the war.[11]

Elsewhere in East Asia, war had brought the usual unpredictable turmoil. Throughout 1944 and on into 1945, as the Japanese fought ferociously to stave off defeat, the peoples they had oppressed and the peoples who perceived them as liberators – Koreans, Malays, Burmese, Filipinos, Vietnamese, Javanese, Sumatrans, subjects of the Japanese, British, American, French, and Dutch empires – waited, some passively, some armed and ready, to learn what peace would bring them.

Franklin D. Roosevelt, four-time president of the United States, died in April 1945, on the eve of victory in Europe. Before his death, at Yalta in February 1945 and in the weeks that followed, he tried desperately to secure the enduring peace toward which he had labored so valiantly. At Yalta, discussions with Churchill and Stalin had gone well. Roosevelt found the other allied leaders frank but reasonable in their demands. Toward his own requirements, they were remarkably responsive. Roosevelt's primary objective was to get Stalin to agree to abrogate his nonaggression pact with Japan, due to expire in 1946, and attack Japan's Kwantung army in Manchuria. The Chinese had demonstrated their inability to do the job, and Roosevelt did not want American lives lost on the mainland. He would call in the Red army and let the Chinese pay the piper. Stalin agreed, with the understanding that the Soviet Union would be allowed a sphere of influence in Manchuria. Next, Roosevelt sought assurances that the Soviet Union would join the United Nations,

[11] Garver, *Chinese-Soviet Relations*, 58–80; Benjamin I. Schwartz, *Chinese Communism and the Rise of Mao* (Cambridge, Mass., 1958), 172–88; Charles B. McLane, *Soviet Policy and the Chinese Communists, 1931–1946* (New York, 1958), 29–34.

without sixteen votes. Stalin settled for three. Finally, Roosevelt wanted Stalin to set aside the puppet government he had established for Poland and respect the principle of self-determination. Stalin would not dismiss the "Lublin" government, composed primarily of Communists long absent from Poland and Communist sympathizers, but he offered to prettify it by giving more posts to non-Communists, and he presented vague assurances about democracy and free elections in Eastern Europe generally. Roosevelt accepted. No agreement was reached on Germany, although the United States and Great Britain accepted the Soviet demand for extracting $10 billion in reparations as a basis for negotiations. Afterward, Churchill praised Stalin's loyalty and cooperativeness effusively before the British Parliament. There seemed to be no issues to divide the Big Three. The war was going well, thanks to Stalin's agreement to launch his spring offensive in February, rescuing British and American soldiers savaged by Hitler's Ardennes offensive, and peace seemed well in hand. But Roosevelt lived long enough to see his hopes for Big Three postwar cooperation begin to unravel.

Perhaps because of fatigue or the imminence of death, Roosevelt blundered seriously in March 1945. Uncharacteristically insensitive to Soviet anxieties, he authorized American intelligence operatives to meet secretly in Switzerland with senior German officers to discuss the German surrender in Italy. Stalin immediately suspected the worst: a deal between the Germans and his Anglo-American allies, a deal that would allow the Germans to concentrate their resistance against the advance of the Red army. At Munich in 1938, the British and French had tried to redirect Hitler's demonic energies against the Soviet Union, but Stalin had outsmarted them. Very likely they were trying again, this time under the leadership of his self-proclaimed American friend. Outraged, Stalin protested without pretense of diplomatic niceties. Roosevelt in turn was offended by Stalin's accusation, conceivably unable to imagine himself capable of such a betrayal. Stalin, clearly, was more imaginative. The incident passed, but not without abrading the thin veneer of trust that might have existed between the two men. Unquestionably, the atmosphere was less conducive to an amicable resolution of the differences that resurfaced over Poland.[12]

[12] Feis, *Churchill, Roosevelt, and Stalin*, 583–96; Kolko, *Politics of War*, 375–9; Taubman, *Stalin's American Policy*, 95–6.

Reports from Poland, underscored by a cable from Churchill, indicated that Soviet control was being inflicted on that country with less subtlety than that of the American machine politicians whom Roosevelt had expected Stalin to emulate. Opposition to the Soviet-imposed Communist-dominated regime was being suppressed ruthlessly and blatantly. Roosevelt probably had less sympathy for the Poles, who had behaved badly in the 1930s, than did Churchill, whose nation had gone to war to defend their country. Roosevelt was reluctant to allow the intransigence of non-Communist Polish leaders to jeopardize his hopes of Soviet-American cooperation. Nonetheless, he could not acquiesce in the Soviet denial of any semblance of self-determination to the Poles. It would be wrong, opponents of his conception of America's role in the new world order would exploit the issue against him, and the American people would be angered. Roosevelt's last days were roiled by the disagreeable task of trying to redefine the concessions he had offered Stalin at Yalta – a redefinition that Stalin could hardly see as less than a reversal of American willingness to grant the Soviet Union a sphere of influence in Eastern Europe and the assurance of a friendly government in Poland.

Roosevelt died and Harry S. Truman became the thirty-third president of the United States. Truman had few illusions about his knowledge of world affairs and understood full well how poorly Roosevelt had prepared him for the position. As the Third Reich crumbled before the combined forces of the United States, Great Britain, and the Soviet Union, and as American forces in the Pacific positioned themselves to strike the fatal blow at the Japanese homeland, Truman, the onetime Kansas City haberdasher, would have to preside over victory; he would have to make the decisions necessary to gather the fruits of that victory and to preserve the peace that followed. He was appropriately awed and, quite reasonably, looked to the men who had advised Roosevelt for guidance.

Truman was untroubled by any of Roosevelt's goals or commitments, as he understood them. The Hull-Morgenthau plan for a liberal international economic order was consistent with Democratic party programs he had supported as a senator. Doubtless there would be trouble with Congress after the war – time enough for that. The German surrender came only a few weeks after Truman took office, without much need for presidential direction. Accelerated planning for the defeat of Japan required more of his attention, including consideration of the range of options to minimize American casualties. The most immediate problem, according to his advisers, was smoothing out the kinks that seemed to be developing in Soviet-American relations.[13]

In a typical off-the-cuff remark years before, Truman had expressed satisfaction at the Nazi invasion of the Soviet Union, suggesting that the weakening of both regimes was equally desirable. He had no sympathy whatever for communism. But in 1945, Truman evidenced no hostility to the Soviet Union, perceived that nation as a loyal ally, and accepted, without apparent reservation, Roosevelt's conviction that Soviet-American cooperation was essential to the vision of a just and peaceful postwar world. Like most Americans, however, Truman was inclined to measure Soviet cooperativeness by the degree of deference the Soviets accorded the United States.

Immediately after he became president, Truman was apprised of the disagreement that had arisen between Roosevelt and Stalin over Soviet behavior in Eastern Europe. The issue was not whether to continue cooperation, but how best to achieve it without sacrificing American ideals or interests. Several of Roosevelt's advisers, most notably his White House chief of staff, Admiral William Leahy, and W. Averell Harriman, ambassador to the Soviet Union, argued that difficulties had emerged because Roosevelt had been too generous with the Soviets, that he had encouraged them to be demanding, to take American support for granted while offering little or nothing in return. They argued that the Soviets rather than the Americans were reneging on the Yalta agreement regarding Poland. And Harriman, in particular, pressed for a policy shift, for tougher bargaining by the American side, for a carrot-and-stick approach, a quid-pro-quo approach. If the Soviets wanted something, economic aid for example, require them to yield something to the United States in return. If the United States was to help finance Soviet postwar reconstruction, the Soviets in return could ease their control over Eastern Europe, allow free elections, and refrain from incorporating Poland, Hungary, Romania, and Bulgaria into a

---

[13] Gaddis, *U.S. and Origins of the Cold War*, 198–206; Deborah Welch Larson, *Origins of Containment* (Princeton, 1985), 150–8.

Soviet-controlled political and economic bloc. Again, the idea was not to give up on collaboration, not to be unfriendly, but to find a course more likely to lead to a mutually satisfying Soviet-American relationship, one consistent with the preeminent position of the United States.[14]

Truman accepted the advice to be less gentle with the Soviets and gave Soviet foreign minister Vyacheslav Molotov an undiplomatic dressing-down at their first meeting. Not normally a sensitive man, Molotov protested against Truman's tone, but he had little difficulty understanding the message: American policy had changed. What he could not discern was whether American objectives had changed. Molotov and his aides readily assumed that Roosevelt's death had resulted in a seizure of power by recently dormant anti-Soviet forces in the United States. Truman's language showed little respect for Molotov and the country he represented. With victory in reach, the Americans had apparently concluded they had no further need to cooperate with the Soviet Union. Were the Americans unwilling to concede that the Soviet Union had contributed mightily to the allied cause, that it was now the second-greatest power in the world, entitled to the perquisites of that status? Truman probably raised more questions in the minds of Soviet leaders than he had intended. They would be increasingly wary in the months ahead.[15]

In July 1945, Truman went to Potsdam where, amid the ruins of Hitler's Reich, he met with Churchill (and Clement Atlee, who succeeded him as prime minister) and Stalin in the last major conference of the war. Initially uneasy given the importance of the issues to be resolved and the stature of the other two men, Truman had his confidence greatly bolstered by word that America's secret weapon, the atom bomb, had been tested successfully and would soon be available for use against Japan. He had never doubted that the United States would emerge from the war as the world's leading power. Now that power would be enough to finish the war alone, if necessary, and to maintain the peace alone, should that prove necessary. The atom bomb ensured imminent victory in East Asia and seemed likely to gain the United

[14] Kolko, *Politics of War*, 390–403; Gaddis, *U.S. and Origins of the Cold War*, 200–5; Larson, *Origins of Containment*, 66–125.

[15] See, for example, *Andrei Gromyko, Memoirs* (New York, 1989), and the "Novikov Telegram," in Kenneth M. Jensen, ed., *Origins of the Cold War* (Washington, D.C., 1991), 3–16.

States additional leverage in postwar international politics. Casually, he mentioned the new weapon to Stalin, who seemed uninterested.[16]

In general, Truman responded favorably to what he saw of Stalin at Potsdam and came away from the meeting persuaded that like his early Missouri political mentor, Boss Pendergast, Stalin was a man with whom one could do business.[17] Indeed, neither Roosevelt nor Churchill – or even Harriman – doubted that a reasonable agreement could be reached with Stalin if the right man (e.g., Roosevelt, Churchill, or Harriman) conducted the negotiation. For all his brutality, Stalin was not to be equated with the maniacal Hitler. Moreover, ideological differences seemed irrelevant. Fundamental security issues between the United States and the Soviet Union did not appear to exist. Disagreement over Poland persisted, but Truman recognized that Poland constituted a vital Soviet interest and was, at most, a secondary concern of the United States. The minor adjustments the United States required would be granted ultimately to the world's only atomic power, to the nation on which the Soviet Union would have to depend for reconstruction financing. Truman and his advisers were confident he and Stalin could work things out. Truman set sail for home, ordered atom bombs dropped on Hiroshima and Nagasaki, and World War II was over.

---

[16] Herbert Feis, *Between War and Peace: The Potsdam Conference* (Princeton, 1960), 172–9; Gar Alperovitz, *Atomic Diplomacy: Hiroshima and Potsdam*, expanded and updated edition (New York, 1985), 198–204; for a superb historiographic essay, see J. Samuel Walker, "The Decision to Use the Bomb: An Historiographical Update," *Diplomatic History* 14 (1990): 97–114.

[17] Larson, *Origins of Containment*, 132–6, 178, 197.

2

ORIGINS OF THE
COLD WAR

The end of the killing brought enormous relief to peoples all over the world – and a new set of problems. For the Germans and the Japanese, the years ahead promised to be grim, their well-being, their very survival, dependent on the whims of the victors, including those who not long before had suffered, sometimes terribly, at the hands of German and Japanese troops. For most of the allies, a daunting task of reconstruction awaited. The Soviet Union had lost at least twenty million, perhaps as many as forty million of its citizens before the Nazi onslaught. France, Belgium, the Netherlands, Denmark, Norway, and Great Britain had to rebuild severely damaged industrial infrastructures and recover the means to feed and clothe their people. In China, civil war loomed and the task of regaining even the marginal living standards of the prewar era was gravely threatened. And in the colonial world, millions stood poised to end the age of imperialism, violently if necessary.

By comparison, conditions in the United States were glorious. Relatively few Americans had died in the fighting. Only an occasional shell from a submarine or hostile balloon had reached the shores of the continental United States. American industry was intact, prosperous on war contracts. American agriculture was ready to feed the world's starving masses. Across the country, the call was to "bring the boys home" and return to what an earlier president, Warren Harding, had called "normalcy."

But nothing is ever so simple. Much as the United States might have been the envy of the rest of the world, it was a nation riddled with grave problems that would have to be faced when the euphoria of victory passed. In the early 1930s, Americans, too, had endured the misery of the Great Depression. Millions of able-bodied men, skilled as well as unskilled workers, had been unemployed. Millions of Americans had lost their homes, watched their children go hungry. Yes, Franklin Roosevelt's New Deal welfare programs, resisted bitterly by most wealthy Americans, had alleviated the suffering, but it was the war that revitalized the economy and brought full employment. Now the war was over, and the millions of men and women who had fought for their country would come back – and would be looking for work. Would they be forced to the streets to sell apples, as had the veterans of World War I? What would happen to the factories that produced tanks, ships, planes, munitions? What would they produce now? Who would work in them? Who would buy their products? And what would happen to the millions of black Americans who had been drawn to the factories of northern cities during the war – and whose presence had created explosive racial tensions in the midst of the war? And to "Rosie the Riveter" and other women who had taken jobs traditionally held by men? In short, the richest and most powerful nation in the world would be forced to confront profound structural problems in its economy and economic and social issues likely to prove deeply divisive. With Roosevelt gone, in what direction would Harry Truman lead the country? Could Harry Truman lead the country?

To most Americans, in and out of Washington, the creation of a sound peacetime economy was the highest priority. With Hitler gone, the attack on Pearl Harbor avenged, external affairs were of marginal importance to them. The professional diplomats and military officers, and others in and out of the bureaucracy who earned their living worrying about the rest of the world, could not ignore the public and congressional clamor to bring the troops back, to release millions of young men from military service, and to leave the world's problems to the United Nations.

Those responsible for American foreign policy scoured the horizon, calculating overseas interests and requirements, ever vigilant against potential threats. Most immediate was the need for troops to occupy Germany and Japan and funds to maintain them and the civilian-military administrations that would oversee the pacification and rectification of the people of those countries. Contingency plans for the next war had to be developed and steps taken while American power was supreme to secure the bases and other assets that would make America invincible. The newly empowered military establishment wanted funds to preserve the massive forces the United States had assembled in the course of the war, forces that could now be used to deter would-be aggressors. Civilians involved in implementing the Bretton Woods agreements and working toward the international trade organization and other instruments of the new liberal international economic order could see that reconstruction aid was not going to be sufficient. But at war's end, requests for money for the military or for erstwhile allies – let alone those nations that had started the war – were not welcome. If there was ever a time to put America first, this was it. The message from the people was clear enough, and, in a democratic society, government ignores the people at its peril. In 1945, the foreign affairs specialists, the nascent national security bureaucracy, had to step aside.

The troops came home from war in one of the most extraordinary demobilizations the world had ever seen. Discharge from the military was granted democratically, on an individual basis, depending on time in service, wounds, and medals – rather than unit by unit. A ship might be left without a navigator, a tank crew without a gunner – the combat efficiency of units decimated by the loss of key personnel. What was left was far less than the sum of its parts. A mighty military force became a shambles. But who needed it?

When the men came back, the women who had been mobilized to work during the war returned to the home, and many black workers were shunted aside. This time veterans would be cared for, given priority for jobs, for homes. The GI bill enabled millions of them to learn new skills, to obtain educations they might never have been able to afford; it enabled them to buy houses for themselves and the women who had waited for them – and together they produced the "baby boom" that shaped American demography for the rest of the century. Issues of race and gender seemed peripheral in the closing months of 1945 – at least to the society's dominant white males.

The struggle over the parameters of the welfare state, over how America's wealth would be distributed, reemerged at war's end. Labor unions, their activities protected by the Roosevelt administration in the 1930s, generally had accepted his demand for restraint during the war. Some, like the Congress of Industrial Organizations (CIO), were more eager to take on corporate America than ever. All were determined to improve the lot of workers, to obtain a fair share of the profits. The country was hit hard by strikes in the last months of 1945, and labor tensions continued to run high. Many employers, eager to exploit a presumed surplus of workers, were determined to reverse some of Roosevelt's prolabor reforms, to break the new power of the unions. Political analysts wondered whether Truman could hold the New Deal coalition together, whether the United States could escape intensification of class conflict.

Much of the outcome of the economic and social tensions in American society would be determined by how the economy performed as it shifted from war to peace industry. The auspices were splendid. With little available for them to purchase during the war, American consumers were eager to spend their savings. It was quickly evident that for the immediate future, before European and Japanese industry was rebuilt, there would be no shortage of overseas markets for American goods, few nations that could compete with the United States for the control of needed raw materials. As in the 1920s, the domestic market flourished and American exports flooded out of the country. Trade and currency agreements engineered by Cordell Hull and Henry Morgenthau facilitated the efforts of American business executives to seize the unusual opportunities of the first months after the war. Increased production and increased profits allowed for more jobs at increased wages, without class warfare. The pattern could not last forever: Sooner or later, without anything to sell to the United States, foreign buyers would run out of dollars with which to buy American goods. If and when that problem was solved, the industries of prewar competitors would eventually be restored and the struggle for markets, even the domestic American market, would resume. But in 1945, that all seemed very far away.

The handful of Americans still focusing attention on world affairs would have noted a number of trouble spots in the Soviet-American relationship during the months immediately following the war. The Soviets, like the British, needed reconstruction funds and wanted low-interest loans from the United States – which neither Congress nor the public was eager to provide. There were disagreements about the amount and disposition of German reparations. America's allies, especially the Soviets, were displeased with the imperious manner in which the United States monopolized the administration of the occupation of Japan. American journalists and diplomats reported comparably arbitrary behavior by Soviet authorities in Eastern Europe. In Poland, in particular, Soviet actions were brutal. In New York, where diplomats and technical specialists of the Preparatory Commission worked to create the operative arms of the United Nations, Soviet and American negotiators found each other difficult, sometimes unpleasant, especially those assigned to develop the UN's military peacekeeping apparatus and those working for international control of atomic energy.[1]

Soviet suspicions angered Americans. American arrogance, bordering on contempt, infuriated the Soviets. Americans could not understand why the Soviets did not accept the benign preeminence of the United States. The Soviets, accustomed to being treated as equals by Roosevelt, were troubled by Truman's apparent disdain. Cultural differences aggravated the mutual irritation. The loss of the common enemy left both sides free to remember past differences and allowed the luxury of recalling earlier, ideologically tainted perceptions. A deep undercurrent of anti-communism in the United States survived wartime cooperation, as did Soviet apprehension about British and American intentions. Certainly the Soviets could never feel secure so long as the United States retained its monopoly of nuclear weapons. After the success of the July 1945 American atomic bomb test, Soviet elites feared the balance of power had been altered to their detriment, threatening loss of the security gained by victory over Germany. In the absence of a common enemy, of shared values, peacetime cooperation would not be easy. With perhaps declining enthusiasm, Soviet and American diplomatists kept at it.

Across the Pacific, there were other problems tugging at American leaders. For a brief moment, it looked as if the situation in China might get out of hand. American forces had been providing transportation to facilitate the movement of Chiang Kai-shek's government troops into regions threatened by the Chinese Communists. U.S. Marines denied the Communists access to urban areas liberated from the Japanese, holding the cities until Chiang's forces could reach them – while Washington rejected charges it was interfering in China's internal affairs.

In November 1945, Patrick J. Hurley, American ambassador to China, resigned in frustration over his inability to mediate successfully between Chiang's government and the rebellious Communist forces of Mao Zedong. Hurley publicly spread blame for his failure among imperialists,

---

[1] Thomas G. Paterson, "The Abortive Loan to Russia and the Origins of the Cold War, 1943–1946," *Journal of American History* 56 (1969): 70–92; interview with Dean Rusk, April 1977; Warren I. Cohen, *Dean Rusk* (Totowa, N.J., 1980), 9–14.

Communists, and foreign service officers. For domestic political reasons, Truman's aides deemed it essential that the president respond. The nature of the response was shaped by their interest in determining the Soviet role in China. There had been ambiguous indications of Soviet assistance to Chinese Communist forces in Manchuria, and there was some fear that the Soviet presence in Manchuria might extend beyond the spheres agreed to at Yalta, to which Chiang had acceded in exchange for Soviet professions of support in the Sino-Soviet Treaty of August 1945. On the other hand, the looting of Manchuria by Soviet forces suggested they were on their way home. Truman decided to send America's most prestigious military man, General George C. Marshall, architect of victory in the war against Germany and Japan, to China to try to avert civil war there and, more important, to determine Soviet intentions.[2]

When Stalin learned of Marshall's assignment, he expressed pleasure. Soviet interests in China had been served by the Yalta agreements and the treaty with China. Stalin and Chiang had worked together before and understood although they did not trust each other. Stalin urged caution on the Chinese Communists. Their presence in China gave him valuable leverage in dealing with Chiang. A civil war, which they were not likely to win, could complicate relations with the United States. There was no point to tension between the Soviet Union and the United States in a peripheral area, vital to the interests of neither. Moreover, Mao could be difficult, unresponsive to control from Moscow. From Stalin's perspective, a divided China, with the Chinese Communists dependent on Moscow, was most desirable. A Communist China, led by an assertive Mao, might not be an asset. Stalin was probably sincere in hoping Marshall would succeed in averting civil war, thus keeping China from becoming an issue in Soviet-American relations. He demonstrated his goodwill by adjusting the scheduled withdrawal of his forces from Manchuria at Chiang's request to assist Chiang's effort to move his forces there before Communist-led troops could seize control.

There was no question but that the United States and the Soviet Union had emerged from the war as the world's two dominant powers.

---

[2] Herbert Feis, *The China Tangle* (Princeton, 1953), 406–24; Russell D. Buhite, *Patrick J. Hurley and American Foreign Policy* (Ithaca, 1973), 253–78; Steven I. Levine, "A New Look at American Mediation in the Chinese Civil War: The Marshall Mission and Manchuria," *Diplomatic History* 3 (1979): 349–75.

Sometimes unilaterally, sometimes together, they groped toward some means of creating order and providing for their security and that of their friends in an anarchic world. Peoples over whom neither had much if any control struggled in pursuit of their own interests all over the globe. In Washington and in Moscow, men with little comprehension of other people's cultures and history tried to make decisions for the world. The Soviet experience provided that nation with no basis for trust in the outside forces that had tried to isolate and destroy the regime throughout its history. American repugnance toward the terror Stalin had inflicted on his own people, toward the totalitarian dictatorship he had consolidated at home and now extended into Eastern Europe, hampered cooperation after Hitler's defeat. What was extraordinary was the effort of each side, however warily, to ease the apprehensions of the other, to overcome the legacy of mistrust, to combine forces to keep the Germans and the Japanese down, and to create a peace that would endure. And they kept at it to the end of 1945 and on into 1946, with Stalin recognizing the absurdity of a gratuitous affront to the overwhelming power of the United States, and Truman still persuaded he and Stalin could resolve any differences that emerged. A poll taken in December 1945 showed that an overwhelming majority of Americans were pleased with Truman's handling of foreign relations.[3]

In 1945, Soviet leaders seemed more suspicious, more apprehensive of the United States than American leaders were of the Soviet Union. In 1946, however, attitudes in Washington shifted significantly. Soviet actions throughout 1946 forced Truman and his advisers to reevaluate Soviet intentions, to reconsider their assumptions about the possibility of Soviet-American cooperation. Some of these Soviet actions and the American perceptions of them were classic demonstrations of what political scientists call the "security dilemma," where an increase in one state's security will automatically and inadvertently decrease that of another. Stalin was determined to demonstrate that he would not be intimidated by American nuclear weapons. On the basis of their historic experience of Western hostility and confronted by superior American power, the benign use of which could not be assured, Stalin

---

[3] Hadley Cantril and Mildred Strunk, eds., *Public Opinion, 1935–1946* (Princeton, 1951), 889–901.

and other Soviet leaders took a series of actions designed to enhance their national security. But each step they took to add to their security was viewed by American leaders as detracting from the security of the United States. Eventually, the United States responded with policies to enhance its security – which the Soviets saw imperiling their own. Each nation defined its own policies as defensive but saw the other's as threatening.[4]

A number of American officials had begun thinking of the Soviet Union as the next enemy well before the end of the war. A poll in December 1945 indicated that although hardly more than a third of Americans expected another major war in the next quarter of a century, those that did were most likely to name the Soviet Union as the nation that would start it.[5] In February 1946, Stalin, speaking in the context of elections to the Supreme Soviet, stressed the need for ideological purity, a new five-year plan, and new sacrifices in a world in which communism struggled for survival while the contradictions among capitalists threatened the peace. Those Americans who feared the Soviet Union and the ideology for which it stood deemed Stalin's speech hostile, a declaration of war.

Most Americans, however, and their president, were still not ready to surrender hope of Soviet-American cooperation. In March, Churchill, now out of office, visited the United States and, in Fulton, Missouri, with Truman at his side, denounced the "Iron Curtain" he alleged the Soviets had drawn across Europe, separating the areas they controlled from the rest of the continent. His clarion call, warning America against the Soviet threat, resonated with those already of his persuasion but attracted few converts. Cynics suspected a connection between the dangers he evoked and the British loan bill, which was endangered in Congress. Many journalists and some in Congress feared Churchill was stirring fears in the United States designed to stimulate Americans to save the British Empire yet again. Cautiously, Truman disassociated himself from the speech. Although there was growing unhappiness with Truman's management of foreign affairs and increasing irritation with

---

[4] See Melvyn P. Leffler, *A Preponderance of Power: National Security, the Truman Administration, and the Cold War* (Stanford, 1992), for a similar and more detailed presentation of the security dilemma argument in this context.

[5] Cantril and Strunk, *Public Opinion*, 783–4.

Soviet behavior, as late as September 1946 only 8 percent of Americans polled were willing to give up on accommodation with Moscow and 74 percent thought both countries were responsible for the misunderstandings that seemed to have developed between the United States and the Soviet Union.[6]

The serious differences developing between Moscow and Washington were inescapable. American behavior in Germany troubled, perhaps even frightened, the Soviets. In January 1946, Christian Democrats, unfriendly to the Soviet Union, unhappy with Soviet compensation of Polish losses with German territory, won elections in the American zone of Germany – and subsequently in the British and French zones. A few months later, the American proconsul in Germany, Lucius Clay, decided to withhold further reparations from the American zone. In July, the Americans began a program of amnesty for ex-Nazis. Soviet informants had long been aware that American agents were protecting Nazi civilians and military personnel who were considered to be scientific or intelligence assets – as were the Soviets. In September, James Byrnes, the American secretary of state, announced in Stuttgart a new, more lenient American policy toward Germany, an action that suggested that Washington was more concerned about the well-being of its erstwhile German enemies than about Soviet needs. Finally, in December, the Americans and their British friends merged their occupation zones, with offers to the French and Soviets to join them. In due course the French did. The Soviets could hardly be expected to surrender that fragment of Germany they could still exploit, any more than they could consider as serious Byrnes's April offer to demilitarize Germany. Twice in Stalin's lifetime the Germans had wrought enormous suffering on Mother Russia. Preventing a resurgence of German power was the highest priority of Soviet policy. American moves to rebuild Germany, to exonerate fascists, to encourage German revanchism were not to be taken lightly.

Truman and his advisers seemed oblivious to Soviet concerns and worried instead about Stalin's intentions in the Middle East – in Iran, Turkey, and Greece. In none of these countries could American leaders conceive of a threat to Soviet security, of any justifiable reason for

[6] Deborah Welch Larson, *Origins of Containment* (Princeton, 1985), 263–7, 288; Cantril and Strunk, *Public Opinion*, 964.

Soviet behavior. The United States, Great Britain, and the Soviet Union had joined in a preemptive occupation of Iran, to deny its oil to the Germans and to preserve a route for lend-lease aid from the Americans to their Soviet allies. They had agreed to withdraw their forces after the war. The Americans and the British had withdrawn. The Soviets had stayed and were clearly scheming to separate an oil-rich province from the rest of Iran and to join it and its residents to their ethnic compatriots in the Soviet Socialist Republic of Azerbaijan. When the Security Council of the United Nations met in its inaugural session in January 1946, the United States denounced the continued Soviet presence in Iran. When Soviet tanks menaced Tehran in March, the United States sent a sharp warning – and the Soviets pulled back.

At war's end Moscow began to press Turkey for minor territorial adjustments and for a share in the control of the Dardanelles, the Soviets' only access to the Mediterranean. Truman, initially sympathetic to a Soviet role in the administration of the straits, reversed course as disagreeable Soviet behavior elsewhere raised doubts in his mind about Soviet intentions. When Soviet pressure came to a head in August 1946, Truman ordered the *U.S.S. Franklin D. Roosevelt,* the world's mightiest warship, to the eastern Mediterranean to strengthen Turkish resolve. Again Stalin backed off.

In Greece, a country Stalin had conceded to Britain's sphere of interest, a nasty civil war was under way between a corrupt, repressive regime, members of which had collaborated with the Germans, and Communist-led guerrillas, many of whom had been active in the resistance. The British were supporting the Greek government. Communist regimes in Yugoslavia, Bulgaria, and Albania were aiding the rebels. There was scant evidence of Soviet involvement, but Soviet press attacks on the British left no doubt where Stalin's sympathies lay. His influence with, if not control of, the Balkan Communists was assumed.

No American leader accepted the idea of a major role in the Middle East for the Soviet Union. The region was considered a British sphere. If the British faltered, historic Russian ambitions there would have to be thwarted by someone else. To a Soviet sphere of interest in Eastern Europe, to Soviet dominance in Eastern Europe, Roosevelt, Truman, and most of their principal advisers were prepared to accede, but not in Iran, nor Greece, nor Turkey, not in the Middle East. Even as they contemplated projecting American power more than five thousand miles from their shores, substituting it for declining British power in the proximity of Soviet borders, they perceived Soviet behavior in the area as threatening, American actions as defensive.

The matter of international control of atomic energy, of nuclear weapons, also served to undermine the ability of the two nations to cooperate. Truman and his aides knew that the Soviet Union would eventually develop nuclear power. Some thought it wisest to share the secret of the bomb as a demonstration of goodwill, to win Soviet confidence in American intentions. Others, less inclined to the grand gesture, nonetheless thought international control of weapons, international oversight of the uses of nuclear power, was feasible and could be managed without risk to the security of the United States. A number of proposals surfaced within the administration, most notably one with the imprimatur of Dean Acheson of the U.S. Department of State and David Lilienthal, chairman of the Tennessee Valley Authority, who worked with a group of scientific consultants, led by J. Robert Oppenheimer, who had directed the effort to build the bomb. The Acheson-Lilienthal report provided for the destruction of existing nuclear weapons once UN control had been established. UN control, and the inspection that entailed, would preclude research on weapon development, conceivably leaving the United States as the only nation with that capability. Before the United Nations had an opportunity to consider the plan, it was modified by presidential adviser Bernard Baruch to include sanctions *not subject to the veto*, leaving the security of the Soviet Union at the mercy of a United Nations easily dominated by the United States and its friends. Not surprisingly, the Soviets rejected the "Baruch Plan" when it was introduced in June 1946.

George Kennan, the foreign service officer who emerged as the leading American specialist on the Soviet Union, found his government depressingly slow to understand Soviet objectives and the need to be firm in resisting Stalin. In February 1946, from Moscow, he sent a long reflective cable, which made the rounds of Washington. He described the Soviet leaders as driven by the needs of the political system they had created and their own insecurities to expand their influence and power as far as other nations would permit. He warned that Stalin and his associates would interpret generosity and bluster as weakness and responded only to firmness, to clear signs that their actions would not be tolerated. The United States had to draw the line, stand firmly and patiently behind it, and wait until the Soviet system collapsed of its own weight and its inability to expand. His "long telegram" was welcomed by a number of American leaders who were in the process of formulating similar analyses of Soviet behavior and the appropriate American response. In March they persuaded Truman to obtain a one-year extension of the draft, to delay completion of the demobilization of American armed forces.[7]

Secretary of State Byrnes resisted the Kennan-Harriman analysis, but his confidence in his own negotiating skills wore thin before the year was over. In the spring the Soviets rejected American terms for a loan they were not likely to get and dismissed the opportunity to join the International Monetary Fund (IMF) or the World Bank. In August, the Soviet diplomat Andrei Vishinsky denounced American "dollar diplomacy," and Byrnes was enraged to observe Czech diplomats applauding. It was time for adjustments in American foreign economic policy. Perhaps having a liberal international economic order was less important than rewarding friends and punishing antagonists. In April the Soviets rejected Byrnes's proposals regarding Germany; in September he announced what he would do with or without them. Similarly, Acheson, who had not allowed his contempt for communism to cloud his vision, who had persistently been able to understand how the Soviets might view things from their presumably warped perspective, and who had been willing always to concede Soviet security requirements, concluded that Soviet demands in the Middle East were unreasonable – and they would have to be resisted.[8]

The last major American figure to hold out hope of continued cooperation with the Soviets was Henry Wallace, onetime vice-president, serving as Truman's secretary of commerce. In September, with Truman's acquiescence, casually granted, Wallace publicly criticized the direction in which he believed American policy to be drifting and insisted the United States was needlessly alienating the Soviets. Before the month was out, Truman felt constrained to fire Wallace, lest the Soviets – and the American people – receive the wrong message. And a few weeks later, Marshal Georgii Zhukov, the great Soviet war hero, viewed in

---

[7] See Kennan's long telegram and comparable cables sent by the British and Soviet ambassadors to the United States to their respective governments at approximately the same time in Kenneth M. Jensen, ed., *Origins of the Cold War: The Novikov, Kennan, and Roberts "Long Telegrams" of 1946* (Washington, D.C., 1991), and a symposium focused on the Novikov cable in *Diplomatic History* 15 (1991): 523–63.

[8] Robert L. Messer, *The End of an Alliance* (Chapel Hill, 1982), 181–94; Larson, *Origins of Containment*, 256–7, 283–8.

some quarters as friendly to the United States, was replaced as commander in chief of Soviet armed forces.

Few of the year's events augured well for the Soviet-American relationship, but Truman had other problems that seemed hardly less pressing. He did not need and did not want an adversarial relationship with the Soviets. Mostly, he wanted them to behave civilly, carry out their obligations, defer to American plans for a peaceful and prosperous world, and leave him alone to cope with labor unrest, inflation, and the threatened resurgence of the Republican party – for all of which he was being held responsible by various sectors of American society. And the election results of November 1946, sweeping the Republicans back into control of Congress for the first time since 1930, suggested he was losing control of that small part of the world that had been his. It promised to be a lousy Christmas.

The Republicans returned to Washington determined to savage Roosevelt's legacy and Truman's efforts to maintain New Deal programs. Some of them were determined to carry out a rectification campaign, to purge the society, beginning with the federal government, of ideas about government responsibility for the welfare of the people, those "cryptocommunist" ideas of the New Dealers. They would stop the use of tax policy for social purposes, for the redistribution of wealth. They would end the government's protection of labor unions and the radicals who threatened the free-enterprise system. They would prevent the government from wasting American money subsidizing the British Empire. Hating "creeping socialism" at home, they would force Truman to stand up to Soviet Communists, to reverse Roosevelt's "treason" at Yalta. If Truman had any leadership ability, the Eightieth Congress would give him a chance to demonstrate it.

When they could obtain the president's attention, his foreign affairs advisers hammered home two grave and immediate concerns: first, the unexpected difficulty Western Europe was having with postwar recovery, the enormous suffering that had resulted, and the threat to civil society that now existed there; second, the collapse of European power, especially British power, around the world, and the importance of the United States acting promptly and convincingly to fill the vacuum. The 1946 loan to the British had proved inadequate, in part because of inflated U.S. prices for the goods they needed. The British were rationing bread at home, giving up India and Burma, unable to maintain their support to the government of Greece, and reeling under the attacks of Zionist terrorists in Palestine.[9]

In France, Charles de Gaulle, the imperious leader of the Free French during the war, had resigned as president in the face of strong opposition from both Communists and Socialists in January 1946. In the November elections, the Communists won a plurality of seats in the French parliament. As the Republican-led conservative coalition seized power on Capitol Hill in Washington in January 1947, the Communists seemed on the verge of winning control of the government in France. In Italy, too, a weak government was perceived in Washington as threatened by a strong Communist minority. Perhaps worst of all was the uncertainty about the direction in which the Germans would move, whether they might ultimately choose to align themselves with the Soviet Union.

None of Truman's advisers imagined a Soviet attack on the United States *or* Western Europe. Kennan, despite rhetorical flourishes that obscured his intent, was arguing that a political threat existed. Most of the others were contemptuous of existing Soviet power, secure in America's nuclear monopoly. But all of them recognized the importance of Western Europe to the United States. Western Europe was the heart of the civilization with which Americans identified. Its participation was critical to the liberal economic order Americans believed essential to the world's peace and prosperity. American leaders considered friendly control of Western Europe vital to the security of the United States. Any student of geopolitics knew that control of the Eurasian landmass by one state would give that state the power to dominate the world. Conceivably, the Soviet Union could achieve that control – not with the bayonets of the Red army but by the collapse of existing Western European societies unable to recover from war damage unaided, and subverted by the activities of local Communists. The danger was not "clear and present," as Justice Oliver Wendell Holmes would have demanded, but no country with a choice could risk inaction.[10]

If one assumed Truman understood the danger and was willing to act, the scale of aid required by the Europeans was enormous, the range

---

[9] Joyce Kolko and Gabriel Kolko, *The Limits of Power* (New York, 1972), 365–7; Anton W. dePorte, *Europe Between the Superpowers*, 2d ed. (New Haven, 1986), 131–2; Walter Isaacson and Evan Thomas, *The Wise Men* (New York, 1986), 386–9; Leffler, *Preponderance of Power*, 188–92.

[10] Leffler, *Preponderance of Power*, 162–3.

of activities required of the United States beyond anything it had ever attempted in peacetime. And the cost would be astronomical. How could a Congress, hostile to the administration, committed to cutting its budget, be persuaded to appropriate great sums of money to reconstruct the economies of America's competitors in order to oppose an imperceptible threat? How could a people who had been promised that the United Nations would spare them further concern with world affairs be persuaded to make the sacrifices necessary for the United States to exercise leadership in once remote corners of the globe?

An otherwise Herculean task was brought to manageable proportions as a result of an exceptionally wise appointment by Truman. In January 1947, George Marshall, denied the opportunity to retire after a frustrating year in China, replaced Byrnes as secretary of state. Marshall brought Kennan back from Moscow to head a newly created policy planning staff. He had Acheson in the first months and then Robert Lovett as undersecretary. It was, arguably, the strongest leadership the department had ever had, and it used its resources well. Quickly, it fashioned a coherent set of policies and persuaded first the president, then the Congress, and finally the public to support those policies. As implemented, the policies developed by the Truman administration from 1947 to 1949 were hardly without flaws, but they constituted a sound, measured, manageable set of steps toward preserving the interests of the United States and those who shared its economic and political values. They provided the foundation for an extraordinary level of material prosperity for all who accepted American hegemony for the next two decades. These policies were unquestionably designed first and foremost to serve American interests, but they were designed by men and women who understood that those interests would not be well served by efforts to maximize economic or political advantage. Initially, it was America's friends abroad that were the greatest beneficiaries.[11]

Almost immediately, Marshall, Acheson, and Kennan accepted the notion that the United States had to assume Britain's historic role of

---

[11] Isaacson and Thomas, *Wise Men*, 386–418; Charles S. Maier, "Politics of Productivity: Foundations of American International Economic Policy," in Peter Katzenstein, ed., *Between Power and Plenty* (Madison, 1978), 23–49; Robert O. Keohane and Joseph S. Nye, *Power and Interdependence* (Boston, 1977), 135–6; Michael J. Hogan, *The Marshall Plan* (Cambridge, 1990), 443.

containing the expansion of Russian power and influence in the eastern Mediterranean. Kennan had been eager to contain the Soviets every-where in Europe and Acheson had been particularly troubled by Soviet pressures on Turkey. A crisis in Greece, which the British had lost the will and lacked the resources to manage, provided the opportunity to apply and explain what came to be known as the "containment" policy. The techniques devised to win support for the policy were successful, but created unexpected and ultimately uncontrollable problems.

Marshall, Acheson, and Kennan knew that the Greek government they intended to support was unworthy: corrupt, repressive, inept. They knew also that there was little indication of direct Soviet involve-ment in the Greek civil war, although they assumed the Soviets would benefit from and Stalin would be pleased by a Communist victory in Greece. Their ultimate concern was not Greece, but rather the assertion of American power in the Middle East. The region was of enormous strategic importance in the event of war with the Soviet Union, and its oil reserves could not be allowed to fall into unfriendly hands. The three strategists intended to signal the succession of the United States to Britain's role as the dominant power in the area.[12]

Stalin found himself in an awkward situation. He had been willing to concede Greece to the West, as he had indicated to Churchill. Turkey and Iran interested him more, as evidenced by direct Soviet pressures on those countries. He did not want to provoke a confrontation with the United States over Greece. But Tito, the Yugoslav Communist leader, was eagerly supporting the Greek Communists. Stalin suggested restraint, but the Yugoslav dictator was not dependent on Soviet bayonets to maintain his power. He had seized control of Yugoslavia in the course of leading the resistance against the Germans. He would determine his country's goals and policies with minimal deference to Moscow. Stalin was caught between his fear of provoking the United States and his unwillingness to alienate an independent ally. Not until the Americans acted was Tito persuaded to lessen his role in Greece.[13]

---

[12] Joseph M. Jones, *The Fifteen Weeks* (New York, 1955), 73; Kolko and Kolko, *Limits of Power*, 232–42; Larson, *Origins of Containment*, 302–23; Leffler, *Preponderance of Power*, 237–46, 286–91.

[13] Milovan Djilas, *Conversations with Stalin* (New York, 1962), 81–2; William O. McCagg, Jr., *Stalin Embattled, 1943–1948* (Detroit, 1978), 242, 297, 300; William Taubman, *Stalin's American Policy* (New York, 1982), 150–1.

In February 1947, when the British officially informed the United States that they could no longer support the Greek government, Marshall's team was ready, as was Truman. Congressional leaders were called to the White House, where Marshall explained the situation in Greece and Turkey, described the inability of the British to play their historic role, and asked for appropriation of the funds necessary for the United States to take over. The administration's worst fears were immediately realized. The leaders of the Eightieth Congress were unwilling to spend taxpayers' dollars to feed hungry Greeks or to solve Great Britain's problems. A more generous, Democratic party–controlled Congress had barely agreed to the British loan of 1946. This Congress had already rejected requests for increases in foreign aid and defense spending. It was not interested in rescuing British interests at American expense.

Acheson, however, knew which chords to sound. These lawmakers were outspoken opponents of Soviet expansion, of communism. He warned them that the Soviets were on the march; they were engaged in a bold maneuver to gain access to three continents. If Greece fell into their hands, Turkey and Iran, Asia Minor, would follow. Nothing would stand in the way of the Russians moving on into Africa through Egypt, penetrating Europe through Italy and France. The stakes were high, the danger was imminent, and, with the collapse of British power, only the United States could stop the Soviets. Senator Arthur Vandenberg (R.-Mich.), who spoke for his party on foreign policy matters, assured Truman that if he addressed Congress as Acheson had, the Congress would respond favorably.

Truman's message to Congress, in March 1947, requesting $400 million in aid for Greece and Turkey, included the statements that became known as the Truman Doctrine:

> We shall not achieve our objectives [of freedom and independence for all members of the United Nations] unless we are willing to help free peoples to maintain their free institutions and their national integrity against aggressive movements that seek to impose upon them totalitarian regimes.... I believe that it must be the policy of the United States to support free peoples who are resisting attempted subjugation by armed minorities or by outside pressures.

Grudgingly, Congress appropriated the funds.

At the time and for many years afterward, critics questioned the wisdom of describing the Soviet threat in such apocalyptic terms. As the historian Melvyn Leffler subsequently argued, Soviet actions "hardly justified the inflammatory rhetoric Acheson and Truman used."[14] Clearly, American leaders did not consider a Soviet attack anywhere to be imminent. American forces were not being readied for war. On the other hand, Marshall, Acheson, and Kennan were convinced that the Soviet Union was expansionist, that it would extend its influence beyond its security needs into any unguarded area in the world, and that both the Middle East (via Greece) and Western Europe were in imminent danger of being subverted by indigenous Communist forces. Only the United States had the power to stop them: Did it also have the will?

The overblown rhetoric Kennan used in his dispatches and his famous "X" article in *Foreign Affairs* (July 1947) were designed to gain attention, to shock readers into recognition of the existence of a serious problem. Acheson and others of Truman's aides shared a similar belief in the need to shock Congress and the American public into recognition of an external threat worthy of their attention and their money. In the American political system, presidential mastery over Congress is often limited, especially when it is controlled by the opposition. Legislators have their own agendas and are generally more responsive, certainly in peacetime, to the demands of domestic special-interest groups than to the foreign-affairs concerns of the executive. In wartime it is relatively easy to focus congressional attention on foreign policy, relatively easy for the executive to get what it wants. The tactics applied by the Truman administration in 1947 were designed to create an atmosphere, in Washington at least, in the country as a whole if necessary, that would enable the executive to dominate the legislative agenda much as it would in time of war. If misleading Congress and the people about the nature and immediacy of the Soviet threat to American interests was necessary to gain congressional and public support, it seemed a small price to pay. Conceivably, there was no alternative means of obtaining funds from the Eightieth Congress.[15]

---

[14] Melvyn P. Leffler, "The American Conception of National Security and the Beginnings of the Cold War, 1945–1948," *American Historical Review* 89 (1984): 368.

[15] Kolko and Kolko, *Limits of Power*, 329–58, 374–6. See Dean Acheson, *Present at the Creation* (New York, 1970), 489, for his explanation of the need (in the context of

Kennan quickly perceived that the approach taken with the Truman Doctrine posed serious problems. So did Walter Lippmann. Although Truman's words were designed primarily for domestic consumption, they could be read by everyone in Moscow. The words, the contemplated military aid mission to Turkey, could be viewed by Stalin as provocation, as a threat to the Soviet Union. Moreover, Truman's words implied the United States was prepared to aid any country anywhere in the world that was threatened by Communist subversion, without calculation of American interests in the area. He had implied a universal crusade, which the United States could not afford and which, in any event, made little sense. Acheson had little patience with such subtleties. His was an exercise in politics, designed for minds more responsive to blunt instruments.

Kennan and Lippmann proved to be right in ways Acheson had not anticipated. What about China, asked Representative Walter Judd (R.-Minn.), and other friends of Chiang Kai-shek? China, all of George Marshall's efforts notwithstanding, had embarked upon a civil war in which Communist forces linked to the Soviet Union threatened to overthrow Chiang's regime. Certainly China was at least as worthy of being rescued as Greece. Weakly, Acheson insisted that the Truman Doctrine did not apply everywhere, that each situation would be judged on its merits, and that China was different. Yet more insidious was the question of why the Truman administration was so eager to stop communism abroad when it was doing so little to check its advance at home. Unwittingly, Acheson and his colleagues had armed those elements in the society determined to roll back the New Deal, to equate democracy with capitalism, the welfare state with communism, as well as Chiang's supporters. But for the moment he was successful. The funds had been appropriated; Greece and Turkey would be "saved."

The more critical problem was Western Europe. The economic situation in Britain, France, Italy, and Germany was desperate. Productivity had barely reached prewar levels, dollars to purchase essential goods

NSC-68) to mislead the American people: "If we made our points clearer than truth, we did not differ from most other educators." See also Stephen O. Krasner, "United States Commercial and Monetary Policy: Unravelling the Paradox of External Strength and Internal Weakness," in Katzenstein, *Between Power and Plenty*, 51–87, for a persuasive argument on the weakness of the American political system.

from the United States were in short supply, inflation was dangerously high, internal distribution systems had collapsed, and there was mounting unrest. Accounts of terrible suffering filled the press and cables to the Department of State. These reports evoked humanitarian concerns in Washington, but the decision to act was driven by self-interest, by fear of chaos and subversion. It was essential to keep Western Europe out of Stalin's orbit, partly because of the area's enormous importance to America's trade and defense, but also because it was the repository of the shared values of Western civilization. It was essential to keep Western Europe free for twentieth-century Americans to feel free, to have any sense of security. European leaders, well aware of American anxieties, played upon them, exaggerated the Communist threat in hope of obtaining urgently needed aid.[16]

With help from Lippmann, Acheson, Kennan, and their colleagues devised a brilliant approach for providing economic aid to Europe. The United States would invite European governments to take the lead in developing an integrated plan for the recovery of Europe. American leaders had recognized the importance of the German economy to the economic well-being of Europe and were groping for a politically acceptable way to rebuild Germany. The integration of western Germany into a revitalized European economy might be less threatening to France and tolerable to Congress and the American people. As the historian Wolfram Hanrieder has argued, American policy was one of "double-containment," serving to contain Germany as well as the Soviet Union.[17] But of greater importance was the central idea of allowing Europeans to design their recovery program rather than imposing one made in Washington.

To be sure, the Americans who worked on what Truman called the "Marshall Plan" developed a clear conception of what they wanted to see emerge. Again, they were intent on creating the liberal international economic order envisaged at Bretton Woods, stressing free trade and currency convertibility, exporting the social ideals of Roosevelt's New Deal program, emphasizing increased production, more for everyone, rather than class conflict and the redistribution of wealth. Postwar chaos had delayed implementation of the Bretton Woods system. The

[16] Jones, *Fifteen Weeks*, 239–54; Hogan, *Marshall Plan*, 445–7.
[17] Wolfram F. Hanrieder, *Germany, America, Europe: Forty Years of German Foreign Policy* (New Haven, 1989).

Marshall Plan would provide the funds to realize it. The system would serve the economic needs of the United States. It would be good for Europe. It would be good for the world. The European planners had ideas of their own, some less generous toward the working class, some less responsive to American economic needs, and they shaped the plan to suit themselves. The result was a tribute to farsighted men and women on both sides of the Atlantic.[18]

Although American officials and business executives primarily worried about the economy were gratified by the promise of the Marshall Plan, the impetus for a European recovery plan was political as well. Truman and Marshall saw the plan as a means of defending American interests in Europe against Soviet encroachment, shoring up Western European economies so that the region would not be susceptible to Moscow-directed subversion. Their advisers, however, argued against presenting the program to the world as anti-Soviet. Indeed, they insisted that the Europeans be free to invite Soviet and Eastern European participation. They assumed no Communist country would accept such an invitation and were unnerved when the Soviet Union and the Polish regime chose to attend the first planning meeting in Paris. But the Soviets quickly withdrew, dragging after them the reluctant Poles and Czechs. Stalin was not interested in integrating his economy or that of any country he controlled in an American-dominated economic order. As Kennan anticipated, the Soviets took upon themselves the onus for dividing Europe into those who accepted Marshall Plan aid and those who did not.

Had the Soviet Union chosen to participate one might imagine a new world order in which the Soviet Union and its satellites opened their borders and their books to Marshall Plan auditors, surrendered communism and its command economy for a chance to compete in world markets, and allowed all the tension building between Moscow and Washington to drain away. On the other hand, given the resistance the Truman administration had encountered obtaining $400 million for aid to Greece and Turkey, it is difficult to conceive of the Eightieth Congress appropriating billions of dollars for foreign aid without some sense of the need to head off impending doom. In fact, even after the Soviets withdrew and denounced the plan, Congress appeared recalcitrant.

[18] Hogan, *Marshall Plan*, 427–45.

Conservatives like Senator Robert Taft (R.-Ohio), hostile to the New Deal at home, were not eager to subsidize efforts to extend it abroad. Others had never liked the commitment to tariff reduction implicit in this new economic order. Still others, liberals as well as conservatives, were reluctant to send American tax dollars overseas. Liberals could find needy Americans; conservatives preferred to spend the money on defense – or to deny the government the tax revenues. Funding of the Marshall Plan was in doubt until February 1948, when Stalin inadvertently gave the Truman administration a little help.

Throughout the fall of 1947, on into the winter, into 1948, the Communist parties of Western Europe, under orders from Moscow, fought hard to prevent implementation of the Marshall Plan. The local economies were shaken, as were the governments the Communists attempted to bring down with general strikes. There were many indications that Stalin's strategy had changed, and there was less ambiguity in Soviet actions. Moscow created the Cominform, an organization designed to coordinate Communist activities around the world, an attempt to give substance to the myth of a monolithic international Communist movement. Soviet control over Eastern Europe increased. Stalin had not seemed markedly disturbed by earlier evidence of American displeasure. His most interesting reaction to the Truman Doctrine, which some scholars have seen as a declaration of cold war against the Soviet Union, was to assure Marshall only a few days later that all differences could still be compromised. But the Marshall Plan, especially the indications of American intent to rebuild Germany and incorporate it into an anti-Soviet bloc, set off alarms in Moscow. It was another classic illustration of the security dilemma at work. The Americans and their Western European friends were preparing what they perceived as defensive action to preserve their security against a potential threat from the Soviet Union. That action diminished what little sense of security the Soviets enjoyed. The Soviets responded quickly to the threat from the West, tightening their grip on what they had, but every step they took was perceived by the United States as threatening its security and that of its friends. As the United States and the Soviet Union moved along the spectrum from allies to adversaries, each lessened the security of the other by seeking to enhance its own.

On February 25, 1948, the Czech Communists, already dominant, staged a coup, punctuated by the unexplained death of the pro-Western foreign minister, Jan Masaryk, on March 10, assuring the Soviets of complete control over the country. In Washington, American leaders wondered if a major Soviet move was in the offing, if war might be imminent. The recently formed Central Intelligence Agency would only assure the president that war would not come in the next sixty days. The American military deliberately heightened anxieties in an effort to extort an increase in congressional appropriations. At the request of the Pentagon, General Clay reported from Germany that war could come with "dramatic suddenness." Ignoring Marshall's advice to the contrary, on March 17, Truman shrewdly used the war scare to ask Congress to fund the Marshall Plan. In the same message he asked for restoration of the draft and additional funds for defense spending, and for universal military training, stressing the threat posed by Soviet ruthlessness in Czechoslovakia. Congress gave him much of what he wanted. Stalin's "defensive" actions had facilitated passage of the program he dreaded. American economic power would unite the West against him – and this time the West included most of Germany.[19]

Tension increased significantly in June 1948. The Russians were unquestionably troubled by conditions in Germany – unification of the western zones, the end of denazification, and the decisions to rebuild German industrial power, create a strong West German state, and integrate it with Western Europe. Although the Soviets had provoked some of these developments, they had every reason to fear them and to attempt to reverse the process whereby a powerful Germany might rise to threaten them again. Stalin moved cautiously, harassing traffic between the western occupation zones and Berlin, part of which, although in the Soviet zone, was nonetheless under British, French, and American jurisdiction. On June 24, however, the Soviets stopped all traffic to West Berlin. General Clay called for action to force the blockade, for an ultimatum and an armed convoy to call the Soviet bluff. War seemed possible.

In Washington, Truman and his advisers, including the Joint Chiefs of Staff, rejected Clay's recommendation. They did not want to start a war. The military was not ready to fight one. But they could not acquiesce in the Soviet effort to deny access to Berlin, to cut off the millions

[19] Daniel Yergin, *Shattered Peace* (Boston, 1978), 343–53; Jean Edward Smith, *Lucius D. Clay* (New York, 1990), 466–8; Tony Judt, *Post War: A History of Europe Since 1945* (London, 2005), 100–28.

44

of Berliners from the West. Politically, the president could not appear weak. Public opinion polls already indicated that the American people thought his policies toward the Soviet Union "soft," and 1948 was an election year. Equally important was the need to demonstrate American resolve to the Soviets and the people of Western Europe. Eventually, the United States responded with an airlift, carrying food and coal in extraordinary quantities to the people of Berlin. Day after day, week after week, month after month, another huge cargo plane landed every few minutes. The operation was a costly but impressive success. Soviet planes occasionally harried the transport planes, but never threatened. Stalin was no more ready for war than Truman.

In May 1949, the Soviets admitted defeat and the blockade was lifted. With relative caution, Stalin had tried to prevent the creation of a potentially powerful and threatening German state – the most threatening step the United States had taken since the end of the war. He failed, but the confrontation over Berlin changed the nature of the relationship between the United States and the Soviet Union. American reproaches over Eastern European, especially Polish, affairs, had been irritating, but Stalin had brushed the Americans aside, thrown them an occasional bone, surrendered nothing of substance. Truman's prattle over Greece was also bothersome. Control of Greece would have been welcome, but the Soviet Union had long since conceded Greece to the West. It was Tito, not Stalin, who was engaged there. Unfriendly American gestures regarding Soviet interests in Iran and Turkey rankled more, but in due course, as Soviet power relative to the United States increased, there would be opportunity to bring about more satisfactory results. The rebuilding of Germany, however, the integrating of a German state in an American-led coalition against the Soviet Union, was frightening. The Germans had defeated Russia in World War I. They had wreaked enormous havoc on the Soviet nation, coming within a hair of defeating it in World War II. With the Americans behind them, vengeful Germans could erase all of Stalin's gains since 1945 and once again bring misery to the Soviet people. American actions had to be perceived as hostile, and the Soviet Union responded accordingly, using all means short of war to persuade the Americans to back off – and failed. Unable to contest American power, the Soviet Union was forced to accept the division of Germany and of Europe on American terms.

The perception from Washington was quite different. The United States had no hostile intent toward the Soviet Union. It had indicated its willingness to recognize the requirements of Soviet security, to accept a Soviet sphere of influence in Eastern Europe and in northeastern China (Manchuria). It had offered the Soviets a role in the international economic order planned at Bretton Woods. The Soviets had behaved abusively, at times brutally, in Eastern Europe and rejected the Bretton Woods agreements. They had threatened Iran, Turkey, and Greece. Moscow was using Communist parties in Western Europe to disrupt efforts toward reconstruction and recovery. It had destroyed all semblance of independence in once democratic Czechoslovakia. Finally, it had challenged Western rights in Berlin. Truman's advisers suspected the Soviet Union of seeking to dominate the Eurasian landmass. Some thought that Stalin, like Hitler, sought to conquer the world. The Soviet Union threatened America's friends and America's interests abroad. Unless it was stopped, it would soon threaten the security of the United States. Years later, Andrei Kozryev, a senior Soviet diplomat, blamed Stalinism for the tensions that developed between his country and its wartime allies, arguing that there could be no trust in a "dictatorial, anti-popular regime" that "all but inevitably" spread violence beyond its borders. "Our partners [were] frightened by Stalinism [because] it is difficult to have confidence in a society which is mired in all-out suspicion, it is hard to trust a regime that has no faith in its own people."[20]

By the end of 1948, the United States and the Soviet Union were obviously no longer allies or friends. Certainly they were adversaries, but perhaps they were not quite enemies. Lippmann's term, "Cold War," seemed apt. Both nations had ended their processes of demobilization and had begun military preparedness programs, including planning for war against each other. Yet even the Berlin blockade, unsettling as it was, had been handled cautiously by both nations. They left each other room to retreat and they managed the crisis without bloodshed. The division of Germany, which both Moscow and Washington considered essential, had been achieved. There were no remaining issues. The world reflected an uneasy balance, superficially bipolar, in which preponderant American power, including sole possession of nuclear weapons, assured

---

[20] Quoted in Bruce Russett, *Controlling the Sword: The Democratic Governance of National Security* (Cambridge, Mass., 1990), 144.

the security of the United States and its friends. The United States might have used its power to roll back Soviet gains; it might have been able to topple the Communist regime in Moscow. Clearly it was unwilling to pay the price, and there is little to indicate that Stalin apprehended an American attack. With Europe divided tolerably, without any vital interests in conflict, the two greatest powers might have focused their energies on their considerable internal problems. They did not.

The successful airlift to Berlin saved Harry Truman's political career. Given an opportunity to demonstrate that he could wield America's might, force a feared adversary to bend to his will, Truman won another chance to lead his people. In one of the great upsets in American electoral history, he defeated the highly favored Republican candidate, Thomas E. Dewey of New York – despite losing votes on the left to Henry Wallace running as a Progressive and to Strom Thurmond on the right, running as a Dixiecrat, drawing away the votes of Southern Democrats who thought Truman too sympathetic to black Americans. A seriously ailing George Marshall was allowed to retire. Dean Acheson was elevated to secretary of state, and most of the rest of Truman's team stayed with him.

The next step was the creation of the North Atlantic Treaty Organization (NATO), derived from European initiatives early in 1948. The recipients of Marshall Plan aid were delighted by American generosity but feared economic assistance would not be enough to contain what they perceived as a political threat from the Soviet Union and the Cominform. Far across the Atlantic, thousands of miles from the nearest Soviet tank, hardly aware of their infinitesimally tiny, pathetically powerless Communist party, Americans in Washington might feel secure. Europeans did not. In March 1948, Great Britain, France, Belgium, the Netherlands, and Luxembourg joined forces in the Brussels Pact, aimed at protecting themselves from the Soviets and, if necessary, from a resurgent Germany as well. They hoped the United States would join their alliance, knowing full well that American power was essential to their security.

A peacetime military alliance with European states was unprecedented and not very appealing to American leaders (although they had signed a mutual defense pact with Latin American countries in 1947). Obviously, the Americans were displeased by Soviet behavior on the Soviet periphery, irritated by Soviet-style diplomacy, and disappointed by the lack of Soviet deference toward the world's greatest power, but through 1947, on into early 1948, they perceived no military threat from the Soviet Union, little likelihood of war in Europe or elsewhere. They saw no problems that economic assistance, American dollars, could not alleviate; nothing that required so radical a step as a peacetime alliance – a step that might outrage many members of the Eightieth Congress.

The coup in Czechoslovakia, followed by fears of a similar coup in Italy and Norwegian complaints of Soviet pressures, carried the day for those Americans who advocated a mutual security arrangement with European friends. Reluctantly, the U.S. military, ever fearful of overcommitment, of having to share supplies and secrets with Europeans, allowed itself to be dragged along. The Berlin blockade provided another needed stimulus, although the U.S. government held out for provisions that would reshape the ultimate organization more to its liking. Washington insisted, for example, on membership for Denmark, Iceland, Italy, Norway, and Portugal, diluting the influence of the original signatories. The politics of the 1948 American election campaign precluded consummation of an agreement before 1949. The treaty establishing NATO was finally signed in Washington in April 1949. At least on paper, Western European leaders had the assurance they desired of American political and military support.[21]

The diminished sense of urgency in Washington in the closing months of 1948 and early 1949, during the NATO negotiations, is striking. The American campaign to block a Communist victory in the April 1948 Italian elections had succeeded. The airlift had succeeded. The Norwegians were less apprehensive. Tito had split with Stalin and survived. If there had been a Soviet offensive, it appeared to have subsided. Moscow was clearly on the defensive. Stalin and his diplomatists were telling everyone who would listen of their urgent desire for peace. Conceivably, NATO would prove to be unnecessary, a response to a danger that had evaporated. Confronted with evidence of American resolve, comfortable with what they had already gained in Eastern and Central Europe, unwilling to pay the price of further expansion, the Soviets were ready to accept the status quo and exist in peaceful competition with the West, ending the tension before it brought the world any closer to the brink of war.

[21] Lawrence Kaplan, *NATO and the United States* (Boston, 1988), 16–30.

Of course, even peaceful competition meant the Soviet Union would strive for equality with the United States. Whether under Stalin's leadership or that of any subsequent, less villainous leader, the Soviet Union would demand respect as a superpower and exert every effort to develop the economic, political, and military power that required. Given ideological differences, Soviet leaders would likely remain mistrustful of their Western counterparts. They would not assume that every expansion of American influence was benign; they would not concede control of the periphery, of newly independent nations to the United States.

Again in 1949, as in 1946, the structure of the international system dictated Soviet-American competition. But in 1949, the United States and the Soviet Union had gained four years of experience in coping with each other, had managed their differences without bloodshed. Stalin clearly recognized the preponderance of American power, had a sense of its utility, and apprehended the circumstances in which it was likely to be used. Truman and his aides had drawn the line and forced Stalin to toe it. Again, there was a promise of respite, of time for each state to serve its people. But Soviet efforts to compete, and the decline in America's relative power, proved unacceptable to American leaders. They were appalled by evidence that areas on the periphery were slipping out of control. They continued to prepare for the worst.

The election of 1948 did not relieve the tensions in American society. Truman's surprise victory meant that at least four more years, a total of twenty years, would pass without a Republican in the White House – and he brought a Democratic majority in the Congress back to Washington with him. Rank-and-file Republican politicians were angered by the absence of power and patronage for which American political parties exist. They pressed their leaders for radical changes in strategy, for an end to bipartisanship in foreign policy, for an end to what they considered "me-tooism." They demanded and orchestrated a savage attack on the policies of the Truman administration. Criticism of Truman for being "soft on communism" was difficult to substantiate in face of the Truman Doctrine, the Marshall Plan, the Berlin airlift, and the NATO alliance, but the collapse of Chiang Kai-shek's regime in China provided an opportunity antiadministration forces did not waste.

Despite Marshall's mediation efforts in 1946, civil war broke out in China. Chiang dissipated the material assistance with which the United States provided him, the enormous manpower and firepower advantages with which he had begun the war, and was on the verge of total defeat at the hands of the Chinese Communists as Acheson took office as secretary of state in January 1949. Desperately, Chiang and his American friends begged the United States to redress the balance in China, to rescue Chiang's regime. Had Marshall or Acheson been able to conceive of a way to prevent the Communist victory in China, they doubtless would have done so, but their advisers warned that the task was impossible, the cost in lives and treasure more than the United States could bear. American strategists had a low regard for China's importance relative to Europe, the Middle East, and Japan. Marshall, the architect of America's Europe-first strategy in World War II, and Acheson, the consummate Atlanticist, saw no reason to question their advisers. The fall of China to the Chinese Communists was undesirable and unfortunate, but it was not catastrophic. China was a weak country, likely to remain so for the foreseeable future, and more likely a burden than an asset to the Soviet Union. In due course the Chinese Communists, like Tito and Yugoslavia, would assert their independence of Moscow. The United States would do what it could to hasten that process.[22]

Neither Marshall nor Acheson, despite previous experience with lobbyists and lawmakers supportive of Chiang, had anticipated the domestic political uses to which Chiang's defeat would be put. The Democratic administrations of Roosevelt and Truman were accused of betraying their loyal Chinese ally to the Soviets, of denying Chiang the material assistance with which he could have won. Government officials who had been critical of Chiang's corrupt, repressive, and inefficient regime were accused of being Communist agents. The Democrats were charged with responsibility for the "loss" of China, harassed mercilessly by their political opponents, many of whom in fact cared little about China's fate. One prominent antiadministration journalist, George Sokolsky, wrote signed columns attacking the administration for its failure to aid Chiang – and unsigned editorials attacking the administration for wasting the taxpayers' money aiding Chiang. All that mattered was to pillory the Democrats in quest of political advantage.[23]

---

[22] Dorothy Borg and Waldo Heinrichs, *Uncertain Years: Chinese-American Relations, 1947–1950* (New York, 1980), is the standard work on the subject.

[23] Nancy Bernkopf Tucker, *Patterns in the Dust* (New York, 1983); Warren I. Cohen, *The Chinese Connection: Roger S. Greene, Thomas W. Lamont, George E. Sokolsky and American–East Asian Relations* (New York, 1982), 260–72.

The attack on the Truman administration was also ideological, how-ever, transcending party politics. Anti–New Deal forces had won an important victory over organized labor in 1947 with passage of the Taft-Hartley Act, significantly weakening unions, over Truman's veto. The Senate consistently blocked Truman's modest efforts to prevent dis-crimination against blacks in the job market. Self-styled conservatives identified the New Deal – one of those occasional efforts in American history to provide a minimal level of decency for less fortunate citizens, to protect them from the miseries that accompany the business cycle in a market economy – with communism. Support for workers, for minorities, for health insurance, even for Social Security, was labeled Communist agitation. In the 1930s, capitalism had been a dirty word in the United States, as Americans held capitalists responsible for the Great Depression. Now some of those elements in the society who had lost status in the 1930s were on the offensive. Tension with the Soviet Union and the widespread perception of communism as an alien and hostile force served their purposes well.

The Alger Hiss case, which created a sensation in 1948 and 1949, provided the perfect link for those who wanted to identify pro–New Deal Democrats with communism and treason. Hiss was a Harvard Law School graduate, a protégé of Felix Frankfurter, law clerk to Oliver Wendell Holmes, who had served in Roosevelt's Agricultural Adjustment Administration and Solicitor General's Office and held several midlevel positions in the Department of State, before accepting appointment as president of the Carnegie Endowment for International Peace. He could be associated with the New Deal social and economic reforms and the liberal internationalism that was also anathema to conservatives. Hiss seemed typical of the eastern establishment WASPs whose rule was so bitterly resented in much of the country. In 1948, Hiss was accused of having passed classified information to the Soviet Union in the late 1930s and indicted for perjury (for having denied espionage charges under oath). After a first trial ended with a hung jury in July 1949, he was convicted in January 1950, in part due to the successful efforts of Representative Richard Nixon (R.-Calif.) to turn up evidence against him. Here was proof – or so it was alleged – that New Deal Democrats had betrayed the country. Their programs at home and abroad had violated the principles for which America stood and would have to be reversed. Acheson, sometime law partner of Hiss's brother, played into the hands of the administration's enemies by declaring that he would not turn his back on Alger Hiss.

Acheson and Truman, contemptuous of their tormenters, convinced they were on the right course, held steady. Chiang's China would be abandoned, the modest reforms of Roosevelt's welfare state preserved, and the nation's public servants protected against vilification by the House Un-American Activities Committee and other bastions of the men Acheson dismissed as the "primitives." But Truman and Acheson yielded a little here and there to lubricate the political process, to appease their more reasonable critics, to arm their defenders in the Congress and the press. They refrained from recognizing the Communist regime in China and continued their ties to Chiang's government, the remnants of which had fled to Taiwan, waiting for the Communists to apply the coup de grace. Truman instituted a loyalty program to search for Communists in the government. The administration had to combat congressional obstruction, but the restraints were not severe.

Unlike the hapless Chiang, West European leaders were successful in their efforts to reconstruct their societies and protect them against the threat of communism. The French economist Jean Monnet, a man with a vision of a united Europe, was the principal architect of a structure, the European Coal and Steel Community, designed to alleviate fears of a resurrected Germany and integrate that country into the Western alliance. The primary supporting role was played by Konrad Adenauer, elected first chancellor of the Federal Republic of Germany in 1949.

Monnet worked through Robert Schuman, the French foreign minister, to produce the Schuman Plan, a scheme that the historian Tony Judt called "a genuine diplomatic revolution."[24] The goal for France was to draw Germany into a European framework in which its economic power would accelerate the reconstruction of the rest of Europe. The plan, if implemented, would place vital German resources, especially those of the Ruhr valley, under the shared control of participating states, reducing, even eliminating, the threat to France.

Adenauer's response was critical, and he saw the plan as an opportunity to achieve his aim of gaining recognition of West Germany as an equal independent state bound to the West. Although an ardent nationalist, he

---

[24] Judt, *Post War*, 153.

was not troubled by indications that his prospective allies were determined to prevent Germany from becoming a military threat to them. He and other German leaders of his generation blamed the military for the nation's travails in the age of Hitler and had no intention of allowing it a major role in the foreseeable future. Germany was the first of six West European states to ratify the Paris Treaty of April 1951. Throughout his career – and he remained chancellor until 1963 – Adenauer was committed to the integration of Europe and the alliance with the United States, which he saw as crucial to a democratic and prosperous Germany, an end for which he was willing to postpone reunification with East Germany. Confidence in his leadership eventually won the Federal German Republic a restoration of full sovereignty and membership in NATO.

Perhaps the major foreign policy issue the second Truman administration had to resolve in its first year was defense spending, the military posture the United States would take in its confrontation with the Soviet Union. Truman had resisted strenuously efforts by the military to obtain significant budget increases. He was satisfied that American economic assistance to its friends abroad, backed by a nuclear arsenal that had been increased substantially, would suffice to protect the security and interests of the United States. Truman had presided over a reorganization of the American military establishment, now headed by a secretary of defense, and, in 1949, appointed to that post Louis Johnson, a man committed to holding down military spending. Acheson was less certain. Some of his advisers were troubled by the size of Soviet conventional forces, troubled by what they argued was the ability of the Soviets to march through Western Europe at will. Acheson believed in operating from a position of strength. He had little patience with men like Kennan who argued that the Soviets had no intention of marching through Europe. Acheson doubted whether anyone could determine the intent of the closed, secretive Stalinist state. The United States had to respond to the capabilities of the Soviet military. It had to prepare for the worst, to be able to overwhelm the Soviets at every point of interest. But an extensive program of military preparedness was unlikely, given the opposition of the president, the secretary of defense, the Congress, and the American people.[25]

[25] Leffler, *Preponderance of Power*, 304–11.

The Soviets eased the burden of those who argued for an American military buildup by exploding a nuclear device in August 1949. Scientists had warned Roosevelt in 1944 that the Soviets likely would develop their own bomb in five years, but when the day came, Truman was shaken and there was evidence of enormous anxiety among the American people. Now Americans, too, would have to live in the shadow of Hiroshima and Nagasaki. Now the American nuclear arsenal might not suffice to deter Stalin from war. The United States had to build a bigger and better bomb. The United States had to reconsider the size and deployment of its conventional forces. In January 1950, Truman approved development of the hydrogen bomb and authorized a reappraisal of American security policy.

The Communist conquest of China, the Alger Hiss case, and the Soviet nuclear explosion fed disparate but overlapping forces in the United States.[26] Men and women displeased with the Truman administration – for political and ideological reasons or because of genuine concerns about the adequacy of the American strategic posture – pressed for changes, all of which might be satisfied with a more aggressive anti-Soviet policy. The Soviet Union had done little to create the climate. It had contributed little to Mao's victory in China, a fact of which the Chinese would remind Soviet leaders often. Spying was a nasty business, in which both sides unquestionably were engaged in 1949, but Hiss was charged with acts of treachery in the late 1930s. And surely the Soviets had not been expected to allow the United States the luxury of a nuclear monopoly forever. In short, the Soviets had provoked without being provocative, almost by existing. Truman and Acheson took steps designed to maintain American military superiority, but in the same month, January 1950, they rejected demands from prominent Republican leaders that they intervene in the Chinese civil war. In an important speech, Acheson declared that the Asian mainland and the island of Taiwan lay outside the defensive perimeter of the United States.

In March, the new study of security policy was ready, labeled NSC-68. It was intended to justify, in no uncertain terms, a major expansion of American military forces, sufficient to ensure the continued ability

---

[26] Eric F. Goldman, *The Crucial Decade – and After, 1945–1960* (New York, 1960), captures the mood in America in 1949.

of the United States to meet any threat with overwhelming force. An aggressively expansionist Soviet Union was postulated, its capabilities exaggerated, the danger estimated on a worst-case basis: If every variable were evaluated as being as favorable as possible to the Soviet Union, what would the United States need to counter the threat? The answer was a tripling of the military budget. Again, the security dilemma was obvious. The Soviets had no choice but to acquire nuclear weapons. They might reasonably perceive a threat in the Marshall Plan and the creation of NATO and arm against it. But any increment to Soviet power, any effort by the Soviets to enhance their security, was perceived by Washington to be a threat to the security of the United States. And yet Acheson was preparing to stimulate the next cycle, projecting a major "defensive" buildup by the United States, unable to imagine how his adversary might perceive such action as threatening. Perhaps fortunately, although Truman shared his premises, Acheson was unable to persuade the president to commit the required resources. The program languished, the Cold War stabilized, Stalin called for peace – and, in the early months of 1950, there seemed a chance he might get it.

The structure of the international system that emerged after the defeat of Germany and Japan contained two major powers – the United States and the Soviet Union – each with the opportunity to expand its influence. Historically, when such opportunities have existed, nations have seized them. The United States and the Soviet Union acted predictably. Equally predictable was the likelihood of friction between them as they competed for dominance over some of the areas between them. Soviet determination to control Eastern Europe had been apparent throughout the war. The reemergence of the traditional Russian goal of dominating northeast Asia, Iran, and Turkey should not have been surprising. That the United States, long abstaining from influence in the Eastern Hemisphere, content to dominate much of the Western Hemisphere, should assert itself not only in East Asia but in the Middle East, Western and Central Europe as well, would probably have surprised Roosevelt as much as it apparently did Stalin. In the ensuing struggle for influence, wealth, and power, the economic and technological strength of the United States provided it with a huge advantage, if it did not overreach itself.

The competition that began after World War II would have existed no matter which two countries had emerged triumphant. The nature of the competition that occurred, the hostility, the Cold War, derived from the fact that one of the competing states was a brutal dictatorship that brought intolerable misery to the peoples who came under its control, a totalitarian state whose methods engendered fear everywhere, a closed society whose secretiveness allowed no means for verifying agreements. Moreover, the Soviet state had rejected customary diplomatic practice in the two decades following the Russian revolutions and had had little time to develop new habits on the eve of World War II. Communication between Moscow and Washington was always difficult, suspicion quick to bubble up from beneath the surface, mutual understanding and trust perhaps decades away.

The attributes of the American political system exacerbated the problem. The political scientist Stephen Krasner has referred to the "paradox of external strength and internal weakness."[27] The leaders of the world's most powerful nation were constantly constrained by domestic interest groups and the reins given to Congress by the Constitution. Roosevelt and Truman evaded those constraints in pursuit of their conceptions of the national interest. Truman and his advisers concluded that overcoming public and congressional lassitude required magnification of the Soviet threat, the Soviet role in undesirable outcomes. That exaggerated view of the Soviet threat took root, to the advantage of anti-Communist ideologues who ultimately dominated American political discourse after 1950.

The United States perceived itself – and was perceived by much of the world – as the great liberator. Its leaders were prepared to be generous, but they expected deference and acceptance of American principles for the reorganization of the world. They were angered by Soviet mistrust of the United States, by Soviet unwillingness to accept a subordinate role in the Pax Americana. They had little respect for the Soviet Union, were appalled by its political culture and the ruthlessness with which it was extended to other peoples. Having learned from Hitler of the unspeakable atrocities of which totalitarian dictators were capable, they expected comparable horrors from Stalin. They equated the two men

---

[27] Krasner, "United States Commercial and Monetary Policy: Unravelling the Paradox of External Strength and Internal Weakness," in Katzenstein, *Between Power and Plenty*, 51–87.

and the systems by which they ruled. But, arguably, the most important point was that despite Stalin's malevolence, despite American arrogance, despite the systemic rivalry, the United States and the Soviet Union had not gone to war. Glower at each other they did indeed, bristle with weapons they would when they could, but neither side had incentive to fight. In time they might learn how to talk to each other.

3

THE KOREAN WAR AND ITS CONSEQUENCES

The principal focus of Soviet-American tensions was Europe. The Soviets considered control of Eastern Europe vital to their security. The Americans considered a non-Communist Western Europe vital to theirs. Neither was ready to risk a united Germany that might align itself with the other. The only serious crisis of the postwar era had come when the United States, Britain, and France confronted the Soviet Union with their plans to create a strong German state out of their occupation zones and to integrate that state politically and economically with the West. Stalin had responded with the blockade of Berlin.

Both the United States and the Soviet Union had important interests in Asia. Indeed, the Soviet Union dominated the northern part of the Asian landscape, shared borders with Korea, China, Mongolia, and Afghanistan. The United States had long vied for and had finally achieved dominance in the Pacific. Asia had not been excluded from great power rivalries in the past. It would not be excluded from the competition between the Soviet Union and the United States. But for both, Asia was less important than Europe.

And yet, East Asia was destined to be the region in which a war would be fought, a war that would alter the nature of the Soviet-American confrontation, change it from a systemic political competition into an ideologically driven, militarized contest that threatened the very survival of the globe. Local actors played an enormous role in shaping that conflict and others in Asia, as elsewhere in what came to be known as the Third World. Over time, and especially after Stalin's death, the Soviet Union developed a policy of assisting all movements hostile to imperialism, all movements with "socialist orientations." American leaders, once eager for the United States to be seen as the leading opponent of imperialism, quickly concluded that all leftist movements were either instruments of Moscow or likely to become adjuncts of Soviet power, that "wars of national liberation" were Communist plots that had to be crushed. Generally too cautious to risk direct confrontation, the superpowers shed the blood of their surrogates. But more than 100,000 American servicemen and -women lost their lives fighting communism in East Asia.

World War II had set the stage for decolonization, probably the most important series of events in the last half of the twentieth century. The great colonial powers – Britain, France, and the Netherlands – had been weakened seriously by the war. Throughout Asia, the Japanese had stirred nationalist sentiment, promising an Asia for Asians and succeeding in driving the Westerners out of East Asia, out of French Indochina, out of British Malaya and Burma, out of the Dutch East Indies, out of the American Philippines. When the war ended, the peoples of those colonies did not welcome back their imperial masters, nor were the people of the Indian subcontinent, however less responsive to Japanese promises, content to remain British subjects. With the defeat of Japan, the peoples over whom they had held dominion, not least the Chinese and Koreans, sought to establish their freedom and independence from all would-be overlords. And, in time, they all did, a few with Soviet help, a few with American support, some with minimal suffering, some with terribly destructive wars. These wars were fought not only for independence but to determine who would rule whom after independence. It was a scene that would have been chaotic, even deadly, under any circumstances. The success of local leaders in drawing in the superpowers intensified and enlarged the dangers, with renewed world war a conceivable outcome.

Japan itself was shielded from much of the unrest that swept Asia. Devastated by the war, by merciless American bombing, including the firebombing of Tokyo and the atomic attacks on Hiroshima and Nagasaki, their armed forces decimated by fierce battles such as had occurred on Iwo Jima and Okinawa, the Japanese were relatively docile. They accepted the benign rule of the American proconsul, General Douglas MacArthur, manipulating him as best they could. The Soviets had obtained control of Sakhalin and a small group of islands to the north of the Japanese main islands, the so-called Northern Islands that had troubled Japanese-Soviet relations for generations. They were otherwise excluded from any substantive role in the occupation of Japan.

The American occupiers proceeded to demilitarize and democratize Japan with considerable success, largely as the result of Japanese receptivity. Great concentrations of industrial power, the *zaibatsu,* were broken up, land redistributed, and organized labor empowered. Visions of a New Deal for Japan emanated from MacArthur's civilian planners in Tokyo. In due course, however, American leaders in Washington, increasingly more fearful of the Soviet Union than of a resurgent Japan, "reversed course," choosing to rebuild Japanese economic power and integrate Japan with the emerging anti-Soviet bloc, much as they were doing with Germany. As in Germany, the United States had little trouble finding an anti-Soviet leadership among traditional Japanese elites. Led by the indomitable Yoshida Shigeru, as hostile to his nation's military as Adenauer was to his, these conservative officials skilfully maneuvered between the reforms imposed by the occupiers and their own determination to serve Japan's national interests and regain its sovereign independence. And as with the reconstruction of Germany, the reconstruction of Japan was at least as frightening to America's friends in the western Pacific as to its rivals.[1]

At the end of the war, Roosevelt's reflexive interest in eliminating French imperial rule over Indochina was forgotten, liberation of the territory left to the British and Chinese. The Chinese effort to impede the return of the French was not equal to the British effort to facilitate it. Vietnamese nationalists, the Communist-led Vietminh, were unable to attain independence peacefully and, by 1946, were engaged in a revolutionary war. Vietnamese appeals to the memory of Jefferson and Lincoln notwithstanding, the United States showed little interest in their cause and became increasingly unfriendly as Communists everywhere came to be viewed with suspicion.[2]

---

[1] Michael Schaller, *The American Occupation of Japan* (New York, 1985). For a discussion of the issues and the literature, see Carol Gluck, "Entangling Illusions – Japanese and American Views of the Occupation," in Warren I. Cohen, ed., *New Frontiers in American–East Asian Relations* (New York, 1983), 169–236. For Yoshida, John W. Dower, *Empire and Aftermath: Yoshida Shigeru and the Japanese Experience, 1878–1954* (Cambridge, Mass, 1988), is essential.

[2] Bernard Fall, *Street Without Joy* (New York, 1972); Ellen J. Hammer, *The Struggle for Indochina, 1940–1955* (Stanford, 1956); Gary Hess, *The United States' Emergence as a Southeast Asian Power, 1940–1950* (New York, 1987), 159–214, 311–32.

In contrast, the United States gradually became more supportive of the men and women fighting for their freedom against the Dutch in the Indies, providing the pressure that ultimately assured Indonesian independence. In this instance, however, the Americans intervened largely because of fears that a non-Communist independence movement would succumb to the Communists if it could not rid the islands of the Dutch. As in Indochina, the long-standing American commitment to the principle of self-determination, historic American opposition to imperialism, was subordinated first to the determination not to undermine an important European friend – and then to anticommunism.[3]

The pattern could be seen with situational variations in two countries with which the United States was more deeply involved: the Philippines and China. In 1946 the United States, demonstrating its antiimperialism in the most substantial way, granted independence to its own subjects, the Filipinos. The imperial power did not leave cleanly, however. The United States retained control of major bases in the islands and continued to manipulate local politics so that traditional elites, who had often collaborated with the Japanese as they had with the Americans before and after the war, retained control. The disintegration of the islands' economy, suddenly bereft of colonial connections, troubled few in Washington until a leftist-led peasant revolution, the Hukbalahap, gathered force. Thereafter, the United States government was quick to provide the advice and assistance necessary to suppress it.[4]

China was a more complicated and much more important case. At war's end, Washington was unsympathetic to Chiang's regime, which had proved to be a difficult ally. But wartime camaraderie with Mao's Communist rebels quickly gave way to concern for their connection to Moscow. As everywhere else, Americans would have liked to re-create China in their own image, serving their sense of mission by creating a coalition of Kuomintang and Communist "moderates" – a New Deal for China. Clearly, the United States anticipated a patron–client relationship with China, not easily achieved in dealing with obstreperous patriots like Chiang and Mao. When Marshall failed, in 1946, to prevent civil war, American leaders surrendered their hope of a China that would advance

---

[3] Robert J. McMahon, *Colonialism and the Cold War: The United States and the Struggle for Indonesian Independence, 1945–1949* (Ithaca, 1981).

[4] James C. Thomson, Jr., Peter W. Stanley, and John Curtis Perry, *Sentimental Imperialist* (New York, 1981), 268–75; Hess, *U.S. Emergence as Southeast Asian Power*, 217–50.

American ends. A victory for Chiang became their clear preference and they continued to provide his forces with aid, not as much as he would have liked, but more than they thought his regime was worth. His collapse in 1948 and the subsequent establishment by the Communists of the People's Republic of China was perceived by men like Marshall, Acheson, and Kennan as unfortunate, contrary to American interests, but not a disaster. They knew Mao would be more responsive to Moscow than to Washington, but they also knew that he and those closest to him were intensely nationalistic. They assumed, as they devised policy toward China in November 1948, that Communist China could be prevented from becoming an "adjunct of Soviet power."[5]

In the course of 1949, Acheson determined to abandon Chiang, who had fled to Taiwan, and to seek accommodation with the People's Republic. The domestic political context hampered his efforts, and the activities and pronouncements of the Chinese Communists did little to facilitate his task. Most of his advisers in the Department of State, the secretary of defense and his aides, and key lawmakers of both parties opposed and sometimes obstructed Acheson's policies. He held course, supported by a wavering president. Time, he assumed, was on his side. In due course the Communists would eliminate Chiang, and Americans would learn to live with the reality of a Communist China. Mao's trip to Moscow in December 1949 and the resultant Sino-Soviet alliance were a clear setback, but Acheson persisted in believing that China and the Soviet Union were not natural allies. Chinese nationalism would prevent the Soviets from controlling China, and the day would come when the issues between the two countries would divide them. In January 1950, Acheson had spoken publicly of an American defensive perimeter that excluded Taiwan and had hinted that the United States would recognize Mao's Peking government when the dust of the civil war had settled. His aides were struggling desperately to come up with a plan to save Taiwan as spring passed and summer came to Washington. And then war broke out in Korea.[6]

---

[5] Warren I. Cohen, "Acheson, His Advisers, and China, 1949–1950," in Dorothy Borg and Waldo Heinrichs, eds., *Uncertain Years: Chinese-American Relations, 1947–1950* (New York, 1980), 13–52.

[6] Cohen, "Acheson, His Advisers, and China," and Nancy B. Tucker, *Patterns in the Dust* (New York, 1983). For views contrary to the "Cohen-Tucker thesis," see Robert Blum, *Drawing the Line* (New York, 1982), and William W. Stueck, Jr., *The Road to Confrontation* (Chapel Hill, 1981).

That a civil war in Korea would provide the critical turning point in the postwar Soviet-American relationship, and raise the possibility of world war, seems, in retrospect, nothing short of bizarre. Quite likely, an explosion elsewhere would have done as well, sooner or later, but perhaps not. In the tense days of 1949 and 1950, American analysts waiting for the Soviets to strike looked toward Europe. Yugoslavia was the most plausible target. The Soviet Red army did not move, however, even to punish a deviant Communist leader who had challenged Stalin's claim to speak for all Communists. But on June 25, troops and tanks of the Soviet-trained and -equipped forces of the Democratic People's Republic of Korea launched a major offensive across the thirty-eighth parallel, against the American-trained and -equipped forces of the Republic of Korea to the south.

American missionaries, businessmen, and naval officers had established contacts with Korea in the nineteenth century, but the United States had little contact with that country after the Japanese established their hegemony there in 1905, at the conclusion of the Russo-Japanese War. In the closing days of World War II, the United States and its Soviet allies agreed to liberate Korea jointly, dividing the areas of their responsibilities at the thirty-eighth parallel, the very point at which Japan and tsarist Russia had once divided their spheres of influence. Soviet forces reached Korea first, drove past the thirty-eighth parallel, but unhesitatingly moved north of it when American forces arrived, several weeks after the war was over. Neither the Soviets nor the Americans knew a great deal about Korea, but the Americans, thousands of miles away, doubtless knew less than the Russians, who shared a tiny border with the Koreans and had a historic interest in controlling the country.

Korea was liberated. The Koreans demanded their independence. Neither the Americans nor the Soviets were quite sure what to do with them beyond the vague idea of establishing some kind of trusteeship until unspecified conditions for independence were met. Koreans, regardless of their politics, were outraged by the concept of trusteeship, intent upon achieving freedom immediately. As the liberating forces set about the temporary business of administering their respective sectors, the Soviets turned to local Communists and Koreans who had fought alongside Soviet forces against the Japanese. The Americans were attracted to those most familiar with the vocabulary of liberal democracy, many of whom had collaborated with the Japanese. When Soviet-American tensions developed, the thirty-eighth parallel ceased to be a temporary line dividing the operational theaters of two allied forces and hardened into something more akin to an international border in the eyes of Russians and Americans, if not Koreans. Each side trained and armed Koreans under its jurisdiction. Several years passed without agreement on reunification. Separate governments were established in 1948. Koreans on both sides refused to accept the division of their country, fought constant skirmishes at the border, and did what they could to infiltrate territory controlled by the other. Politics in the American sector were incomprehensible and unpleasant, with Syngman Rhee, a ruthless Princeton-educated autocrat – anti-Communist to be sure, but unamenable to American advice – emerging as the dominant figure. The American military wanted to go home.[7]

By 1949, the Joint Chiefs were able to persuade the National Security Council to order the withdrawal of American troops from Korea. The Department of State was opposed, leery of what intelligence estimates indicated were superior Korean Communist forces, of estimates that indicated that perhaps as many as one-third of Rhee's citizens were sympathetic to the Communists and probably many more simply hostile to Rhee. Without the presence of American forces, southern Korea likely would be overrun by the Communists and a united Communist Korea would result. The threat caused minimal concern in Washington in 1949. The president and the secretary of defense were committed to limiting the defense budget. Korea was low on nearly everyone's list of priorities. The Asian mainland was determined to lie beyond the defensive perimeter of the United States. Troops in Korea would be useless in a war with the Soviet Union. They were needed elsewhere. Economic assistance, military advice, and supplies would have to suffice to keep the Rhee regime afloat. In Acheson's speech in January 1950, in statements by other military and political leaders that spring, and most obviously by the earlier withdrawal of American troops, the United States had signaled its low estimate of Korea's strategic importance in a global confrontation with the Soviets.[8]

---

[7] Bruce Cumings, *Origins of the Korean War*, 2 vols. (Princeton, 1981, 1990); Burton I. Kaufman, *The Korean War* (New York, 1986), 7–22.

[8] Kaufman, *Korean War*, 22–5; James I. Matray, *The Reluctant Crusade* (Honolulu, 1985), 175–225.

We do not know much about thinking in Moscow at this time. Stalin clearly did not want war with the United States. He was fully aware of American strategic superiority. He still needed several years before his forces would have credible nuclear weapons. He probably assumed the United States would not hesitate to use its growing nuclear arsenal if he were to unleash the Red army against Western Europe. To everyone who would listen – and to many who would not – he and his agents, covert as well as overt, spoke of the need for peace, of their belief that communists and capitalists could coexist on this planet. Stalin's peace offensive was doubtless tactical, designed to buy time until the Soviet Union could match or surpass American power. He was not ready in 1950; a united Communist Korea was not worth the risk.[9]

On the other hand, his Korean protégés, like Rhee's regime to the south, were determined to fight, to unite Korea by force. For some long time, Stalin's policy had mirrored American policy. He tried to keep Korean Communist forces on a tight rein and supplied primarily with defensive weapons. But when American troops left the Korean penin-sula, Stalin and his advisers might have concluded, quite reasonably, that the United States was indifferent to the outcome of the Korean civil war. Stalin had urged prudence on the Chinese Communists, appre-hensive of American intervention in the Chinese civil war. The Chinese had ignored him – and his fears had not been realized. Korea was far less important to the Americans, and the threat of intervention had all but vanished. Stalin decided to provide the Korean Communists with the equipment they needed to carry out an offensive. The operation promised to be brief and carried little risk. Stalin's successor, Nikita Khrushchev, subsequently contended that "no real Communist would have tried to dissuade Kim Il-sung [the North Korean Communist leader] from his compelling desire to liberate South Korea from Syngman Rhee and from reactionary American influence."[10]

Stalin and his advisers, little understanding the United States, misjudged the American response. Arming the North Koreans and

---

[9] Marshall D. Shulman, *Stalin's Foreign Policy Reappraised* (New York, 1966), 80–138.
[10] Okonogi Masao, "The Domestic Roots of the Korean War," in Akira Iriye and Nagai Yonosuke, eds., *The Origins of the Cold War in Asia* (New York, 1977), 299–320; Edward Crankshaw and Strobe Talbott, *Khrushchev Remembers* (Boston, 1970), 368; Katherine Weathersby, "New Findings on the Korean War," *Cold War International History Project, Bulletin* 3 (1993).

acquiescing in their invasion of the South proved to be Stalin's most disastrous Cold War gamble. It postponed détente with the United States for twenty years. It intensified a confrontation that continued for forty years at enormous cost to the major antagonists and to much of the rest of the world. The war shifted the balance of forces within the United States to the advantage of the most militant opponents of social justice, racist politicians like Eugene Talmadge of Georgia and John Rankin of Mississippi; opponents of organized labor like the journalist George Sokolsky, the National Association of Manufacturers, and the R. J. Reynolds Tobacco Company; opportunists like Joe McCarthy and Richard Nixon, and powerful bureaucrats like J. Edgar Hoover of the FBI, allowing them to divert the attention and energies of the American people from needed reform to the hunt for Communists at home and abroad. It allowed people and organizations like these, working with the aviation industry in particular, to create a military-industrial complex that consumed the productive power of the American economy and fueled conflict all over the world. These elements existed in American society independently of any Soviet threat. They might well have dominated the society in any event. They might have succeeded in conjuring up a threat from Mars. But it was Stalin's opportunism in Korea that opened the door for them.

The initial response of American leaders to news of the outbreak of war in Korea was relief that Rhee had not started it. Given the opportunity he no doubt would have – but he had not. The Communists had invaded the South and Truman would have to decide whether to respond and, if so, how. If Korea was outside the defensive perimeter of the United States, if the National Security Council had reached consensus on its relative lack of importance, why respond at all? Surprisingly, all of Truman's advisers reversed themselves and argued that the invasion had to be repelled, that the United States could not stand by and allow what was perceived as an act of aggression to go unchallenged. Some contended that the credibility of the United Nations was at stake if aggressors were allowed to go unpunished; some feared the credibility of the United States as guardian of the non-Communist world was at risk. All of Truman's advisers saw the events in Korea as a test of American will to resist Soviet attempts to expand their power, and their system. If Stalin were allowed to succeed in Korea, he would probe somewhere else – and keep probing until he had either conquered the Eurasian landmass or started World War III. Now was the time to stop him.[11]

Unspoken was another grave concern – for the political future of Harry Truman, for his ability to govern for the remainder of his term as president. His administration had been accused of betraying China, of allowing the Soviet Union to expand its influence into Asia. Acheson's relative indifference to Asia was notorious and troubled many of his most loyal aides, several of whom had been working on elaborate plans to provide at least the appearance of administration action in East Asia. Failure to respond in Korea could be politically catastrophic. Successful action could silence the administration's critics and perhaps even provide a third term in the White House for Truman.

The combination of reasons for action – stopping an aggressor, containing Soviet expansion, demonstrating American resolve to Stalin, to America's European allies, and to nervous Asians, preserving the credibility of the United Nations, protecting Truman at home – was overwhelming. To Stalin's dismay, the United States intervened in the Korean civil war. Mobilizing the United Nations, which it still dominated, assisted by units as disparate as British, Turk, and Ethiopian, the United States sent its military forces to fight alongside those of Syngman Rhee. He was an unworthy ally, but the United States could not risk the consequences of inaction.

Initially, UN forces under the command of American general Douglas MacArthur, fared poorly. Rhee's troops were not as well equipped as their northern counterparts, the American troops included few with combat experience, and they were chewed up by the invading forces. American airpower functioned ineffectively. Eventually, however, MacArthur's troops held a line outside of the southeastern port city of Pusan from which they counterattacked simultaneously with a brilliantly conceived and extraordinarily risky landing he ordered at Inchon on the northwest coast of southern Korea. By late September, they had trapped the troops from northern Korea in a classic pincer movement and had routed them. In less than three months, UN forces under American leadership had defeated the aggressor, were on the verge of liberating the south, and had

---

[11] Glen D. Paige, *The Korean Decision, June 24–30, 1950* (New York, 1968); Dean Acheson, *Present at the Creation* (New York, 1969), 524–37; Warren I. Cohen, *Dean Rusk* (Totowa, N.J., 1980), 51–2. See also the fascinating analysis of the policy reversal in Jack Snyder, *Myths of Empire* (Ithaca, 1991), 289–96.

demonstrated both the viability of the United Nations and the resolve of the United States to the entire world.

Unfortunately, in its moment of triumph, the Truman administration succumbed to one of the most treacherous temptations confronting any victor, the temptation to expand war aims. Repelling aggression, liberating southern Korea would not be enough. Truman and his advisers concluded that Stalin would not come to the aid of his Korean surrogates, that they could send UN forces across the thirty-eighth parallel dividing non-Communist South from Communist North, purge the North of Communists, and unite all of Korea, presumably under a government more democratic than that of Rhee. There were risks to be sure – and the Chinese were threatening to intervene if UN forces crossed the thirty-eighth parallel – but Acheson, no less than MacArthur, was contemptuous of the Chinese, inclined to discount their threats as bluff, confident that they would not dare risk confrontation with overwhelming American firepower. And, judging by American experience with Chinese troops during World War II, American leaders assumed that if the Chinese dared to intervene, they would be disposed of quickly. The Communists were in retreat, the United States resurgent.[12]

There were voices in Washington favoring a halt in the vicinity of the thirty-eighth parallel. George Kennan argued that there was an opportunity to divide the Chinese from the Soviet Communists, that they had responded differently to an Indian proposal for a cease-fire agreement that would have included seating the Chinese Communists in the United Nations. Paul Nitze, architect of NSC-68, the plan for the massive military buildup to contain the growing Soviet threat, argued that the time was not propitious for risking a larger war, that until his plan was implemented, military advantage in what would likely become World War III rested with the Soviets. Military leaders who saw the Soviets as the enemy were disinclined to commit their forces in a peripheral area. And there were some who thought the Chinese might well intervene, forcing a larger war.

The opportunity to roll back the Communists in Korea, the vision of creating a united Korea as a showcase for democracy and an answer

---

[12] Kaufman, *Korean War*, 84–7; James I. Matray, "Truman's Plan for Victory: National Self-Determination and the Thirty-eighth Parallel Decision in Korea," *Journal of American History* 66 (1979): 314–33; Rosemary Foot, *The Wrong War* (Ithaca, 1985), 66–74.

to critics who claimed Truman was soft on communism, proved irresistible. MacArthur sent his men racing up the coastal plains on both sides of the Korean peninsula, on both sides of the mountain spine that ran up the center. The only restraint placed on him was to send Korean troops ahead into those provinces bordering on China and the Soviet Union and to halt his advance if he ran into significant Chinese or Soviet forces. Truman, uneasy about the Chinese, flew to Wake Island in the Pacific to meet his field commander. An exuberant MacArthur assured the president of a quick victory even if the Chinese were so foolish as to intervene.

In Beijing, Mao and his advisers were terribly apprehensive about American intentions. Communications between China and the United States had broken down early in 1950 after the Chinese had seized U.S. government property in Beijing despite a warning that seizure would result in the recall of all American diplomats. The alliance Mao and Stalin signed in February 1950 forced Acheson to surrender hope of a rift between the two Communist states in the immediate future. Ever the realist, Acheson still looked toward eventual recognition of the People's Republic of China, but he was in no hurry to reward the friend of his enemy. Mao, on the other hand, was convinced that the United States was implacably hostile, that sooner or later it would attack the People's Republic of China and try to reverse his victory. American actions following the outbreak of the war in Korea intensified his anxiety. The United States ordered warships to the Taiwan Strait to prevent Mao's forces from invading Taiwan and mopping up the remnants of Chiang's army there. MacArthur flew to Taipei and stood shoulder to shoulder with Chiang, indicating his support for Chiang and his view of Taiwan as an unsinkable aircraft carrier that could not be allowed to fall to the Communists. Once again, the Americans were interfering in the Chinese civil war, supporting Chiang against the Communists.

Mao was troubled deeply by the dispatch of American troops to Korea and then by their success at Inchon. Relying on the *New York Times* for their information about the United States, his advisers reported growing sentiment in favor of uniting Korea and then continuing on into China to throw the Communists out.[13] China was weak. It

---

[13] Warren I. Cohen, "Conversations with Chinese Friends: Zhou Enlai's Associates Reflect on Chinese-American Relations in the 1940s and the Korean War," *Diplomatic History* 11 (1987): 283–9; see also Zhang Shuguang, *Deterrence and Strategic Culture* (Ithaca, 1993).

desperately needed time and all of its resources to reconstruct and then modernize the country, parts of which had been at war since 1931. It could hardly expect to win a war against the most powerful nation the world had ever known. Chinese leaders did not want to fight, but Mao, convinced the Americans would leave him no choice, chose to fight on Korean rather than Chinese soil. Even after Stalin reneged on his offer of air support and the Chinese politburo voted against intervention, Mao was undeterred. In October, as UN forces crossed the thirty-eighth parallel and marched toward the Yalu River, which separated Korea from China, Mao ordered Chinese troops into Korea. Again and again, the Chinese sent warnings that they would attack if UN troops continued to march north. Arrogantly, the Americans and their allies charged on, confident of a quick victory.[14]

Acheson tried to assure the Chinese that the United States did not intend to attack China, but American assurances lacked credibility in Beijing. The Americans had said Korea was beyond their defensive perimeter, but they sent their forces to defend it nonetheless. They said they wanted to repel aggression and drive the North Koreans back across the thirty-eighth parallel – and now they were headed for the Yalu. If unopposed, would they stop there? Acheson said they had no hostile designs on China, but various lawmakers were calling for restoring Chiang's government on the mainland. MacArthur and Chiang were conspiring. American planes were bombing Chinese airfields. Mao was not reassured. Given the absence of trust, of understanding, of unambiguous American signals, prudence required China to intervene in Korea.

In mid-October Chinese forces struck at American troops, bloodied them, and withdrew to observe the American response. MacArthur

[14] Chinese scholars have contributed mightily to our understanding of the Chinese decision to intervene. See Hao Yufan and Zhai Zhihai, "China's Decision to Enter the Korean War: History Revisited," *China Quarterly* 121 (1990): 94–115; Zhang Shuguang, "Preparedness Eliminates Mishaps: The CCP's Security Concerns in 1949–1950 and the Origins of Sino-American Confrontation," and Chen Jian, "China's Changing Aims During the Korean War," both in *Journal of American-East Asian Relations* 1 (1992): 42–72, 8–41; Chen Jian, *China's Road to the Korean War: The Making of the Sino-American Confrontation* (New York, 1994), 190–209; and Sergei N. Goncharov, John W. Lewis, and Xue Litai, *Uncertain Partners: Stalin, Mao, and the Korean War* (Stanford, 1993), 168–202. See also the classic by Allen S. Whiting, *China Crosses the Yalu* (Stanford, 1960). Alexandre Y. Mansourov, "Stalin, Mao, Kim, and China's Decision to Enter the Korean War, Sept. 16–Oct. 15, 1950," *Cold War International History Project Bulletin* 6 (1995/1996): 94–107, rejects the Chinese claim that Stalin reneged on the promise of air support.

was undeterred. Two weeks later, UN forces were attacked by 200,000 "volunteers" from the Chinese People's Liberation Army. The Chinese shattered discipline among the UN troops, who fled in disarray back across the thirty-eighth parallel, suffering severe casualties along the way. By the end of November, the American military was preparing to flee Korea, to accept defeat. Truman's opportunism had proved very costly.

In Washington, George Marshall had returned to take charge of the Department of Defense, and he, Kennan, and Dean Rusk, Acheson's assistant secretary for Far Eastern affairs, rallied the U.S. government. They rejected MacArthur's defeatism and vowed to go down fighting. American forces held again, north of the Pusan perimeter. Truman and his advisers, military and civilian, fearful of provoking Soviet intervention, rejected MacArthur's demand for permission to attack China. American forces were expanding rapidly, but they were not yet ready for World War III. Fierce aerial assaults against overextended Chinese lines began to take an enormous toll, and gradually the Chinese were driven back across the thirty-eighth parallel. Efforts to end the war largely on the basis of prewar conditions began in earnest in the spring of 1951. Instead of the popular victory Truman might have claimed in September 1950, the administration had continued fighting to the point where the war was intensely unpopular with the American people and enormously costly in blood and treasure. It had brought upon itself a war it could not win without risking a world war for which the American military was not ready. MacArthur, vacillating between manic euphoria and depression, at odds with both military and civilian leaders in Washington, had to be fired, a bitter end for a great American hero. Unfortunately, his firing brought added opprobrium on the administration.

It took two more years to end the war and by then Harry Truman and his aides had returned to private life. The scale of military spending Nitze had imagined in NSC-68 had begun. American military power, especially nuclear power, increased dramatically. An arms race, in which the Soviet Union could not easily compete, was under way. By the end of 1952, according to the historian Marc Trachtenberg, American military leaders thought they were ready to take on the Soviets.[15] Having perceived the outbreak of war in Korea and Chinese intervention as

---

[15] Marc Trachtenberg, *History and Strategy* (Princeton, 1991), 100–52.

Map 1. Conflict in Korea, 1950–53.

evidence that the Soviet Union did not fear the United States, American leaders interpreted Soviet willingness to allow their Korean and Chinese surrogates to be slaughtered as evidence that the balance had shifted in favor of the United States. Once again, America could act aggressively in support of its interests.

Throughout the Korean War, the Soviet Union gave diplomatic support to its Korean and Chinese allies, but reneged on the air cover Stalin had led Mao to expect.[16] The Soviets did provide the Chinese with military equipment, but at a cost the Chinese found outrageous. A few Soviet pilots flew missions in the North, but at no time did the Soviet Union ever threaten military action in Korea. At no time did it create a crisis

---

[16] Chen Jian, *China's Road to the Korean War*, 190–209.

in Europe, which might have distracted UN forces in Korea. At no time did it threaten to open up a "second front" in Europe. Moscow cheered on East Asian Communists confronting American military power, but it took no risks itself. However advantageous American analysts imagined the situation to be for the Soviets, Stalin would not countenance escalation. Caution was again the watchword in the Kremlin where Stalin had long proclaimed that interests of international communism were best served when Soviet interests and security were assured. However prudent he may have been with his own assets, he did not hesitate to urge his Chinese friends to sacrifice more of their own when he envisaged the possibility of their prevailing over the Americans. In a brief moment of euphoria as Chinese troops drove UN forces back down the Korean peninsula, he even considered the possibility that the time was ripe for World War III.

The Korean War ended in 1953, shortly after the death of Stalin. In the Kremlin the great succession crisis was being played out, and Soviet leaders were preoccupied with the power struggle at home, uninterested for the moment in foreign adventure. The Chinese had suffered huge casualties, including the loss of Mao's son. They had contained the American imperialists, preserved their regime, and won great prestige for it. They had preserved the North Korean Communist regime as a buffer between their border and the unfriendly forces to the south with minimal assistance from the Soviet Union. It was time to return to the task of building socialism at home.

The mood in the United States was ugly. The nation had been rent by wartime hysteria, stimulated by demagogues, some seeking personal power, some partisan advantage, some a return to the time when oppression of the poor, the blacks, the Jews, and anyone else outside the mainstream of middle-American culture, was condoned. There had long been a streak of nativism in American society that became explosive when combined with fear of radicalism. The Haymarket affair in 1886, the Red Scare of 1919–20, the Sacco-Vanzetti case in the 1920s were earlier indications of how the nation might respond. In the years immediately following the war, as conservatives attempted to roll back the New Deal, especially labor gains, they appealed to fear of radicalism, labeled everything they disliked communism, everyone who opposed them a Communist, and blurred the lines between democratic socialism and communism, even between liberalism and communism. Their cause was strengthened tremendously by the tensions that emerged between the United States and the Soviet Union.

One reason the Red Scare had evaporated so quickly in 1920 was the absurdity of suggesting that Soviet Russia posed a threat to the United States. In the late 1940s, that notion was no longer absurd. For reasons of its own, to gain popular acceptance of America's new hegemonic role and its costs, the Truman administration had exaggerated the Soviet threat. Stalin unquestionably attempted to use Communists and Communist sympathizers all over the world to serve the ends of Soviet policy. Though inconsequential in number and potential for damage, Communists serving as Soviet agents unquestionably existed in the United States. In the 1930s and 1940s they were more aggressive, more widespread than most Americans realized.[17] The Hiss case underscored the danger. As early as 1947, Truman had created a loyalty board to purify the bureaucracy and he indulged in Red-baiting to get himself elected in 1948. The House Un-American Activities Committee cast its net wide, and allegations spread alarmingly.

In February 1950, the obscure Republican senator from Wisconsin, Joseph R. McCarthy, bid for recognition with a speech claiming that he had a list of 205 card-carrying members of the Communist party who were employed by the Department of State to shape American foreign policy. The technique came to be known as the "big lie." McCarthy had a handful of names of men who had been accused several times in the 1940s, generally of being friendly to the Chinese Communists. Several proved guilty of indiscretion. None was a Communist; none was guilty of espionage; most were no longer in the government. But if a U.S. senator claimed there were 205 Communists in the State Department, surely there were some – maybe only 200, 100, 50 – but *some*. McCarthy had no evidence of any. His charges were investigated and rejected by a bipartisan committee headed by the conservative anti–New Dealer, Senator Millard Tydings (D.-Md.). McCarthy was undaunted. Moreover, he was encouraged by other Republican senators, eager to portray Democrats as the "party of treason," with an eye to achieving gains in the election of 1950 and regaining the White House at last in the election of 1952.

In coping with what he called the "attack of the primitives," Acheson's arrogance initially shielded him and American foreign policy.

---

[17] Mark Kramer, "Editor's Note," *Journal of Cold War Studies*, 11 (Summer, 2009), 1–5.

Disdainful of public opinion generally, and of Congress in particular, Acheson ignored the charges of McCarthy and others like him, and continued to do as he thought best. On occasion, he yielded to political expediency as directed by Truman, but only on matters he considered tactical. McCarthy and his colleagues were being fed information by the friends of Chiang Kai-shek, and Acheson was amenable to pressures to delay recognition of Mao's government until Chiang was eliminated. He would not countenance reversing his policy of seeking accommodation with Mao – until anti-Communist hysteria generated during the Korean War left him no choice.

The rantings of people like McCarthy seem to be a recurring thread in the fabric of a society that prides itself on free speech. The great American historian Richard Hofstadter wrote of the "paranoid style in American politics."[18] Occasionally, these men or women gain a small devoted following, flame incandescently for a moment, and are gone. A fraction of the American people believe in them and await the next prophet. Painful as their activities are for their victims, the impact of such demagogues on the larger society is usually minimal. McCarthy and other would-be leaders of the anti-Communist crusade would likely have disappeared from sight, an ephemeral blemish on the record of the American past, had it not been for the Korean War.

Once Americans were dying at the hands of Communists in Korea, the anxieties that had been generated by knowledge that the Soviets had the atom bomb, by the Hiss case, and by awareness that there were in fact Communist agents operating in the United States were channeled into an anti-Communist frenzy. Anyone who had ever been associated with a leftist organization, anyone committed to social justice for all Americans, anyone associated with unpopular views – such as support for labor or civil rights in the American South – anyone critical of Chiang Kai-shek or thought to be apologizing for Soviet behavior, anyone who had ever angered a neighbor, might be accused of being a Communist. The accusation, the investigation, often sufficed to destroy careers. Evidence was not necessary. Blacklists were created in the entertainment industry to keep suspect actors from getting parts in motion pictures or on television, to prevent suspect writers from having their work produced for the public. A great composer like Aaron

---

[18] Richard Hofstadter, *The Paranoid Style in American Politics* (New York, 1967), 3–40.

Copland could be harassed and ultimately spared only because George Sokolsky, at the heart of McCarthy's journalistic claque, was especially fond of his music. Many innocent government officials, university and public school teachers, civil rights leaders, and labor organizers were less fortunate, as they lost their jobs and sometimes the opportunity to find comparable work.

If the Korean War created a climate in which McCarthyism could flourish, the margin of difference between a minor footnote and a major disaster for the American people, McCarthyism created a climate in which reducing Soviet-American tensions became extraordinarily difficult. Most unfortunately, the success of McCarthy's supporters in exciting anti-Communist passions in the United States left little room for a nuanced foreign policy based on recognition of contradictions among Communist countries, on understanding of the difference between radical Third World nationalists who thought of themselves as socialists and Communists subject to the Kremlin's discipline. Red-baiting at home was unquestionably disagreeable. As the basis of a foreign policy, it resulted in the wasting of millions of lives and countless billions of dollars. The intersection of McCarthyism and the Korean War, of American paranoia and Soviet opportunism, brought recurring misery for the next four decades.

The first major victim of McCarthy and Korea was Acheson's policy toward China. Mao's Red hordes had killed thousands of Americans and maimed many more. Gone were the images of weak, docile Chinese, grateful for American largesse and hungering for Christianity, democracy, and the free-enterprise system. Now hundreds of millions of Chinese were perceived as being instruments of the international Communist conspiracy, attacking Americans at Stalin's orders. A Gallup poll indicated that only 5 percent of the American people believed the Chinese had intervened in Korea on their own initiative. Accusations that Truman and Acheson, advised by Communist sympathizers, had betrayed their loyal ally Chiang Kai-shek and "lost" China to the Communists took root, the best evidence of what McCarthy called "twenty years of treason" by the Democratic administrations of Roosevelt and Truman. Mao's China became America's most feared and hated enemy, the return of the yellow peril. Recognition of the Beijing regime was impossible, as was American acquiescence in seating it in the United Nations. Chiang's critics were purged from the

Department of State or assigned to obscure posts and those who tended to equate his interests with those of the United States came to dominate the Office of Chinese Affairs. In 1951, assistant secretary Dean Rusk signaled the shift in policy by denouncing Mao's China as a gigantic "Slavic Manchukuo," not to be recognized because it was a Soviet puppet rather than an independent Chinese state. That fiction poisoned Chinese-American relations for decades – even after China and the Soviet Union were at each other's throats.[19]

Direct confrontation led to intense hostility between the United States and China, but American leaders did not forget that their principal adversary was the Soviet Union. If, as General Omar Bradley, chairman of the Joint Chiefs of Staff, argued, in response to calls to attack China, it would be the wrong war in the wrong place at the wrong time, the right war would be against the Soviet Union when the American military buildup was completed. By the end of 1952, the American military was ready, eager to launch a preemptive strike against the Soviets.[20]

To meet the Soviet threat, European leaders wanted a stronger NATO. Consequently fearful that American dalliance on the Asian periphery would result in neglect of Europe, British, French, and German leaders anxiously sought a larger, permanent U.S. military force on the continent. The Soviet effort to create a united Communist Korea presaged an attempt to unite the two German states under the red banner. The American government shared some of Europe's apprehensions but wanted Europeans to contribute more to their own defense. Increasingly, the advisers in Washington thought in terms of the need to rearm Germany, of a German army that would provide critical manpower for NATO forces in Central Europe. In December 1950, formal discussions on a German contribution to the defense of Western Europe began. On the same day, as a symbol of American commitment, Dwight D. Eisenhower was named supreme commander of allied forces in Europe, with four additional American divisions to follow. There was considerable hesitation along the way, but the path to German remilitarization had been taken.

Perhaps the greatest beneficiaries of the Korean War were the Japanese. When the U.S. Navy had trouble clearing mines from Korean

---

[19] George H. Gallup, *The Gallup Poll: Public Opinion, 1935–1971* (New York, 1972), 2:955; Cohen, *Dean Rusk,* 62–7.
[20] Trachtenberg, *History and Strategy,* 100–52.

harbors, remnants of the former Imperial Japanese Navy were activated to do the job. Most of the goods and services required by American forces in Korea were procured in Japan, providing the economy with a $4 billion stimulus. And in San Francisco in September 1951, forty-eight nations, led by the United States, signed a peace treaty with Japan, leading to the end of the occupation in May 1952. On the same day the treaty was signed, Japan and the United States signed a mutual security treaty to provide a demilitarized Japan with protection in an uncertain world. The Americans, who retained bases in Japan, had simultaneously restored Japanese sovereignty and further integrated the country into the anti-Communist alliance.[21]

The Korean War was a momentous turning point in the Cold War. An almost inevitable civil war among a people, Communist and non-Communist, determined to unite their country, became an international war and a catalyst for a terrifying arms race. Whatever Stalin's responsibility, whatever his intentions, the results could hardly have been more disastrous for the Soviet Union or unfortunate for the rest of the world. His peace offensive was compromised, and American wealth rapidly extended American military superiority, especially nuclear, perceived as well as actual, over Soviet forces. The process of rearming Germany began. Turkey and Greece were brought into NATO. Japan and the Philippines, Australia, and New Zealand signed security treaties with the United States. American aid to the French in Indochina was increased. What little reluctance to replace British influence in the Middle East remained in Washington was overcome. For the people of the Soviet Union, the Korean War produced a nightmare, mitigated only by the coincidence of Stalin's death before it was over. In addition to Japan, the winners were the likes of Syngman Rhee, Chiang Kai-shek, and all the other merciless dictators who, professing anticommunism, could count on American support. In the United States the winners were the advocates of rollback, of rolling back the Communists abroad and programs of social justice at home.

---

[21] James E. Auer, *The Postwar Rearmament of Japanese Maritime Forces, 1945–1971* (New York, 1973); T. E. Vadney, *The World Since 1945* (New York, 1987), 363; Michael Yoshitsu, *Japan and the San Francisco Peace Settlement* (New York, 1983).

4

NEW LEADERS AND
NEW ARENAS IN THE
COLD WAR

Stalin died. Slowly the terror eased within the Soviet Union, especially after those competing for primacy within the leadership rid themselves of Lavrenti Beria, dreaded head of the secret police. Georgii Malenkov, who, in 1953, seemed to be Stalin's likely successor, sought to reduce international tensions as well. He called for peaceful coexistence with the capitalist world, held out his hand to Tito in Yugoslavia, and offered assurances of Soviet goodwill to Turkey, Iran, and Greece. Israel, India, and Japan similarly received indications that Stalin's death might mean improved relations with the Soviet Union. But Malenkov's hold on power was tenuous, and those who vied with him were critical of his efforts to redirect foreign policy. It was not until after he was shunted aside, and Nikita Khrushchev continued his initiatives while providing a few of his own, that the main outlines of post-Stalinist policy were manifest.[1]

The new Soviet leadership inherited a world in which the dominant power, the United States, had just undertaken a rapid military buildup and had demonstrated its ability to project its power many thousands of miles from its shores. Only weeks before Stalin's death, a new administration had arrived in Washington, led by men who called for a more aggressive anti-Soviet policy, for the liberation of Eastern Europe, and for the "unleashing" of Chiang Kai-shek. These were people who would deny the Soviet Union the fruits of victory in World War II, deny the Soviets the influence and respect to which the world's second most powerful nation was entitled. In addition, Stalin's death had prompted the Chinese government to become more independent,

---

[1] William Taubman, *Khrushchev: The Man and His Era* (New York, 2003), 236–69; Vladislav M. Zubock, *A Failed Empire: The Soviet Union in the Cold War from Stalin to Gorbachev* (Chapel Hill, 2007), 94–122.

a workers' revolt exploded in East Germany in June 1953, and unrest mounted elsewhere in Stalin's new empire. The outside world would not allow the men in the Kremlin the luxury of concentrating on the internal struggle for power.

The legacy of Stalinism handicapped the new Soviet leadership. Other than Molotov, the longtime foreign minister, its members had little experience with foreign affairs and knew little more of Soviet policies than Stalin had chosen to tell them. The study of international relations, or of the social sciences generally, hardly existed in the years of Stalin's rule. There were few academic specialists to come forward with fresh ideas, to scrape away the layers of ideological propaganda that passed for scholarship while Stalin lived. The analysis of the United States and its friends upon which Stalin had relied bore little relation to reality. Stalin had been confident that the capitalist world would be devastated by depression soon after the world war ended, that the capitalist countries would soon be at each other's throats. The leading scholar in the Institute of World Economy and World Politics, E. S. Varga, argued that the capitalist countries were likely to prosper after the war. Stalin was enraged, and Varga lost favor, his institute was disbanded, and the mere fact of his survival astonished his contemporaries. Varga's argument was not repeated in Stalin's lifetime as the dictator waited impatiently for catastrophe to strike the West.[2]

Similarly, Stalin had been traumatized by his experience of supporting Chiang Kai-shek's "bourgeois nationalist" revolution in the 1920s. Chiang had outmaneuvered him, massacred the Chinese Communists, and thrown out his Soviet advisers. Stalin was not going to repeat his mistake by supporting "bourgeois nationalist" leaders like Nehru of India, Sukarno of Indonesia, or Nasser of Egypt. The world, as Stalin saw it in the late 1940s, was divided into two camps: socialist and imperialist. Nehru, Sukarno, Nasser, and others of their ilk merely did the bidding of their former colonial masters, were still part of the imperialist camp. Stalin was contemptuous of the newly independent states and they found few defenders among Soviet scholars during his lifetime.[3]

Efforts to transcend Stalinist dogmatism began with the resurrection of the social sciences and the legitimate study of international

[2] William Zimmerman, *Soviet Perspectives on International Relations, 1956–1967* (Princeton, 1969), 26–32.
[3] Bruce D. Porter, *The USSR in Third World Conflicts* (Cambridge, 1984), 14–16.

relations. In 1956 an Institute of World Economics and International Relations was formed at the Soviet Academy of Sciences. Western sources of information became available. Cautiously at first and with increasing boldness after the Twentieth Party Congress in 1956, Soviet analysts discovered and described the achievements of the Marshall Plan, the successful integration of the American, Western European, and Japanese economies, and the absence of conflict among the capitalist countries relative to what dogmatic Marxists had predicted. They reported the rapid recovery of European economies and the impressive rates of growth they demonstrated. Neither war nor depression was imminent in the capitalist world. At the same time, they reevaluated the role played in world affairs by newly independent states and saw some of them as potential allies in the struggle against American imperialism. They recognized the need to study these countries more closely, to develop area specialists in the academy. In general, by the mid-1950s they were beginning to provide their leaders in the Kremlin with information and advice more closely related to reality, less circumscribed by ideology, than had been possible while Stalin lived.[4]

In February 1956, at the Twentieth Party Congress, Khrushchev roused the delegates with a stirring denunciation of Stalin and his crimes against his people. News of the speech quickly reached the West. But Stalin's successors had long since signaled their determination to change course. Their actions left no reason to doubt them. At home, Stalin's paranoid delusions, such as the alleged "doctors' plot," with its anti-Semitic implications and threat to all around him, were denounced. Men and women wrongly imprisoned or exiled, including Foreign Minister Molotov's wife and Politburo member Anastas Mikoyan's sons, returned to their families. Laws decreed in accordance with Stalin's whims were erased. In the satellite states of Eastern Europe, Soviet economic pressures were relieved, and, after the volatile summer of 1953, local regimes were allowed greater authority over the allocation of resources. In East Asia, Malenkov and his colleagues quickly indicated their willingness to bring the war in Korea to an end. A year later they surrendered to their Chinese comrades the imperial privileges Stalin had demanded at Yalta and obtained from China in 1945.

---

[4] Zimmerman, *Soviet Perspectives*, 32–62.

Further evidence of the relatively benign intentions of the new Soviet regime was apparent when Moscow dropped its territorial claims against Turkey and returned to Finland a naval base extorted by Stalin. Diplomatic relations were restored with Greece and Israel. The Red Army withdrew from eastern Austria, allowing the reunification and freedom of the Austrian people. The new Soviet leadership offered recognition to the West German state and accepted its rearmament with astonishing equanimity. It reached out to the United States in search of an agreement to limit the arms race. And, shortly after the Twentieth Congress, in April 1956, the Soviet Union formally abolished the Cominform, the instrument through which Stalin had attempted to control the international Communist movement.

Stalin was gone. First under Malenkov's leadership, then Khrushchev's, the apparatus of terror was being dismantled. The Soviet Union remained a Communist state. It continued to hold against their will most of the peoples of Eastern Europe. It had allies capable of menacing the interests and friends of the United States in East Asia. It had five million men and women under arms, and, in August 1953, it exploded a thermonuclear ("hydrogen") bomb. The Soviets would be dangerous rivals in the continuing competition for power and influence. But the post-Stalinist Soviet Union was a different country, led by relatively reasonable and responsible men, with whom agreement upon norms for peaceful competition might be attainable. Khrushchev quickly understood that the Leninist view that war between imperialism and socialism was inevitable was obsolete, that a major war had to be avoided in the nuclear age, when radiation and fallout respected no ideology. He remained ebulliently confident that socialism would prevail but without the cataclysm Lenin and Stalin foresaw. The superpowers would deter each other from using nuclear weapons, from a major confrontation, and the revolution would trickle in from the periphery, where the competition for wealth and power would continue. Soviet state interests would be protected and ideology adapted to reality. In Khrushchev, the United States encountered a bold and innovative leader, eager for good relations with the United States and yet unwilling to surrender the messianic vision of an ultimately socialist world. Much would depend on the response from Washington.

In Dwight David Eisenhower and John Foster Dulles, the Republican party and the American people had selected two men extraordinarily well qualified to manage world affairs. Dulles, grandson of one secretary of state, nephew of another, had been active in international politics since the Paris peace conference of 1919. He had been a prominent Republican spokesman on foreign policy issues throughout the years Roosevelt and Truman sat in the White House. Had Thomas Dewey been elected president in 1948, Dulles would have been his secretary of state. Seeking to stave off Republican attacks on policy toward East Asia, Truman had appointed Dulles to a post in the Department of State in 1950 and allowed him primary responsibility for negotiating the peace treaty with Japan. Dulles was intelligent, knowledgeable, experienced, and highly respected at home and abroad.

Eisenhower had been the prominent commander of the allied assault on Europe and the defeat of Hitler's legions. He subsequently served as Supreme Allied Commander, Europe, after the creation of a NATO military force. In both capacities, he had had extensive contact with European leaders and with the Soviets. A stint as president of Columbia University did little to diminish his stature, except among the faculty and students. He was a highly popular, avuncular figure, sought after as a candidate by both major parties. Affecting a posture of being above politics, he seemed the ideal man to put an end to McCarthyism, to calm the anxieties of the American people and reunite the country for the grave domestic and international tasks it confronted in 1953.

Both Eisenhower and Dulles, however, were viewed with suspicion by the right wing of their party. Their experience in world affairs, their service under Truman, their popularity with the eastern "international-ist" wing of the Republican party left them suspect. Would the "twenty years of treason" the Right attributed to the Roosevelt and Truman administrations become twenty-one under Eisenhower?

Throughout the campaign of 1952, Eisenhower and Dulles tailored their activities to appease the Right. Eisenhower accepted Richard M. Nixon, a young senator with a reputation for Red-baiting, as his running mate, and assigned Nixon the dirty work of discrediting the Democrats. Eisenhower allowed McCarthy to campaign for him, and stood by silently as McCarthy impugned the loyalty of George Marshall, to whom Eisenhower's career owed so much. Dulles condemned the containment policy of Truman and Acheson as immoral and promised the "liberation of captive nations," the rollback of Soviet influence in

·ope and East Asia. Aware of how anti-Communist hysteria
⅃ the Truman administration's ability to govern, Eisenhower
and Dulles hoped to deflect the Right with their rhetoric and by appointing a number of the darlings of the Right to nominally important posts.
For Eisenhower and Dulles, the dogmatism of the Right created shoals
only marginally easier to navigate than those Stalinist dogma left for
Khrushchev. The censure of McCarthy by the Senate in 1954 probably provided the administration with less additional leeway than
Khrushchev and his allies gained by denouncing Stalin in 1956.

The massive military buildup the United States carried out between
1951 and 1953 had eased fears in the American military and intelligence community of a Soviet nuclear attack in the mid-1950s. American
superiority became so obvious that even the normally cautious military leaders, heeding administration bluster, eager to strike at the heart
of Communist power, contemplated a preemptive attack against the
Soviets. It took Dulles two years to bury the idea. But the enormous
increase in military spending worried Eisenhower for other reasons. As
an experienced military planner, he considered military budgets to be
excessive, far higher than necessary to permit the armed services to perform their missions. As an economic thinker, Eisenhower ranked with
Truman – pre-Keynesian, determined to balance the budget, fearful
that deficits caused by the arms race would weaken the United States
dangerously and result in an economic collapse that would leave it vulnerable. As the only postwar president whose views on military budgets
were unimpeachable, Eisenhower was uniquely suited to depress the
appetite of the Pentagon.[5]

To cut military expenses, Eisenhower revised American Cold War
strategy. Whereas the Truman administration, when implementing
NSC-68, was attempting to expand both conventional and nuclear
forces to meet any Soviet action with overwhelming force of the same
kind, Eisenhower's New Look policy stressed air and nuclear power. The
historian John Lewis Gaddis has argued that Truman intended a "sym-
metrical" response, a policy of meeting Soviet probes with comparable
force. Eisenhower's strategy implied the possibility of a nuclear response
even if the offending Soviet act was carried out by conventional means,

5 Marc Trachtenberg, *History and Strategy* (Princeton, 1991), 100–52; Seyom Brown, *Faces of Power* (New York, 1968), 65–75.

of responding in an area other than that chosen by the Soviets – an "asymmetrical" response, designed to seize the initiative for the United States.[6] But at the time, with Gaddis unavailable, Eisenhower relied on Dulles to explain his strategy. Dulles put forward the doctrine of "massive retaliation," the notion that the United States might respond with overwhelming force to the slightest provocation. Others, aware of the president's fiscal conservatism, referred to the "New Look" as "more bang for the buck."

Eisenhower and Dulles were not insensitive to the changes taking place in the Soviet Union but responded cautiously. They were constrained by the intensity of anticommunism in the United States and persuaded that even after Stalin, the Soviet Union would be a dangerous adversary. Nonetheless, they were confident of American power, confident that the Soviets would not challenge NATO. Despite their rhetoric, they had no intention of mounting a military challenge to the Soviet sphere of influence in Eastern Europe. By the mid-1950s, with West Germany in NATO and Austria free, with impressive economic growth in those countries linked to the Marshall Plan, Eisenhower and Dulles perceived little reason for fear in Europe. With each superpower capable of launching a devastating nuclear strike against the other, they had achieved a stalemate in the central arena of their competition. And the United States still enjoyed an enormous advantage in ability to project power abroad.

The Soviet Union and the United States were preparing to arm themselves with thermonuclear weapons, capable of inflicting incredible damage on each other. With such weapons in place, the illusion of a winnable war faded. The cost of conflict became unacceptably high. Aware of the dangers, leaders in both countries began to develop proposals for arms limitation. They were hampered by mistrust of each other, by internal dissent as to the wisdom of specific proposals or agreement in general, or, on the American side, doubt about the wisdom of even negotiating. Dulles and others feared that sitting down with the Soviets, in addition to arousing the wrath of the domestic Right, might alleviate fear of the Soviet Union and thus weaken the resolve of the American people and their allies. The United States was further

---

[6] John L. Gaddis, *Strategies of Containment* (New York, 1982), 147–8.

handicapped by the inability to find a negotiating position satisfactory to its major allies and, not least, by Eisenhower's apparent ambivalence. And neither Soviets nor Americans seemed able to resist the temptation to seek propaganda advantages.

Despite too frequent suggestions that he viewed nuclear weapons like any others, devices to be used when appropriate – and the implications of his New Look emphasis on such weapons – Eisenhower was eager to find a way both to reduce the danger of nuclear war and to seize the opportunity to respond favorably to the overtures of the new Soviet leaders. After a speech he gave in March 1953 fell flat at home and abroad, he tried again with his Atoms for Peace plan, offered to the United Nations in December 1953. Eisenhower called for the nuclear powers to contribute fissionable material to an international agency that would oversee its use for peaceful purposes. Ultimately, his proposal led to creation of the International Atomic Energy Agency, but it had no impact on the arms race. The Soviets perceived the speech as a propaganda ploy, which they countered by repeating their call for a joint declaration banning the atom bomb. The United States did not follow up with any proposal to stop producing weapons or a diplomatic campaign to engage the Soviets in serious discussion of the issues. Eisenhower characteristically seemed satisfied with the applause his speech won, and Dulles had been dubious about the venture from the outset.[7]

A year and a half later, as Eisenhower prepared for his first meeting with the new Soviet leaders, one of his aides came forward with what came to be known as the "Open Skies" proposal. It gained support from men uninterested in arms control who saw an opportunity to gain an intelligence advantage or a propaganda victory over the Soviets. At the summit meeting in July 1955, Eisenhower proposed that each participant give the other a blueprint of its military establishments and permit aerial surveillance adequate to assure that no surprise attack was in preparation. Khrushchev, suspicious of American intentions, perhaps fearful that the United States would learn too much about relative Soviet weakness if granted broad access to Soviet airspace, was not interested. Two years later, however, when the Soviets agreed to a partial version of the aerial inspection proposal, the United States

[7] Herbert S. Parmet, *Eisenhower and the American Crusades* (New York, 1972), 385–90; McGeorge Bundy, *Danger and Survival* (New York, 1990), 287–95.

reversed itself. The best Eisenhower and Khrushchev could accomplish was a moratorium on nuclear testing, gingerly reached and unenforceable, but at least an indication that both men recognized the dangers of radioactive fallout and that the two nations, slowly and ineptly, were learning to work together.[8]

The major Soviet goal of the years immediately following the Korean War was a security agreement in Europe, preferably one that gained American recognition of the Soviet sphere of influence in Eastern Europe and protected the Soviet Union against a resurgent Germany. For a neutralized, unarmed Germany, committed to its existing boundaries, Moscow was prepared to offer important concessions, including reunification of both Germany and Austria. Harboring no ambitions in Western Europe, the new Soviet leadership was willing to reduce its armed forces and withdraw its troops from Central Europe, conceivably even much or all of Eastern Europe – provided American forces withdrew as well, presumably across the Atlantic.

American strategic thinking was moving in the opposite direction, however. American leaders were convinced that a rearmed Germany, integrated into the Western alliance, was essential to European and ultimately American security. The creation of a European Defense Community (EDC) had been proposed during the Truman administration, and the idea was pursued vigorously by Dulles. When the French balked, at least as fearful of potential German power as they were of Soviet, unwilling to have their forces submerged in a multinational force, Dulles threatened an "agonizing reappraisal" of the American role in Europe. Failure of France to ratify the EDC agreement did not deter the United States. In October 1954 the British brokered a new agreement, which narrowly won French approval. Critical among its provisions was a British commitment to send troops to the continent, an American pledge to retain forces in Europe, and German agreement not to challenge post–World War II boundaries or to acquire missiles or nuclear, biological, or chemical weapons without NATO approval. The occupation of the Federal Republic of Germany ended and Germany was invited to join NATO, which it did in May 1955.[9]

[8] Gregg Herken, *Counsels of War* (New York, 1987), 108–10, 122; Bundy, *Danger and Survival*, 295–305, 328–33.
[9] Lawrence Kaplan, *NATO and the United States* (Boston, 1988), 62–6; Frank Ninkovich, *Germany and the United States* (Boston, 1988), 90–106.

The Soviet response to the rearming of Germany and its membership in NATO was astonishingly benign. Initially, Moscow tried to purchase German neutrality with the promise of reunification and demonstrated its bona fides by withdrawing its forces from Austria and allowing a united, free nation to emerge. When that effort failed, the Soviets created an alliance designed to mirror NATO, the Warsaw Pact, to which the Democratic Republic of Germany (East Germany) adhered. Most striking was the Soviet invitation to the West German leader, Konrad Adenauer, to Moscow, where he won formal recognition for his country. The Soviet leadership had concluded that a rearmed Germany was tolerable and that accommodation with Adenauer's regime was its wisest course.

In July 1955, the United States, responding to pressures from its European allies and to the markedly less threatening Soviet posture, attended a summit meeting in Geneva, where Eisenhower met Khrushchev for the first time and recognized his power (although it was Premier Nikolai Bulganin who was the nominal head of the Soviet delegation). Little of substance was accomplished at the meeting, but the symbolic importance was enormous. Soviet and American leaders were talking for the first time since Potsdam in 1945 and attempting to persuade rather than bludgeon each other. The "spirit of Geneva," the reemergence of the idea that problems might be solved by diplomacy rather than force, was a source of hope to men and women of goodwill everywhere. Once again it was clear that the existing division of Europe was acceptable to both sides. War was unnecessary as well as unthinkable.

Despite the failure of a foreign ministers' conference that followed the summit, the year after the Eisenhower-Khrushchev encounter was marked by further indications that the Cold War might be winding down. In February 1956, Khrushchev delivered his famous speech to the Twentieth Party Congress, denouncing Stalin and endorsing peaceful coexistence. In April, Mikoyan announced dissolution of the Cominform, relinquishing Moscow's claim to control of all foreign Communist parties. In May, the Soviets reported major troop reductions, from 4 million to 2.8 million. Stalinist Russia was slowly being dismantled, and the Soviets were changing both their approach to world affairs and the nature of the regime. As fear drained out of Europe and the anti-Communist crusaders in the United States perceived a shrinking target, Dulles and other advisers to the president worried about the loss of American resolve.[10]

Events in Eastern Europe soon tested the limits of Soviet tolerance and rescued those Americans determined not to drop their guard. In Poland and in Hungary, demands for an end to Soviet domination erupted in riots in the summer of 1956. The Poles won the right to a Communist leader of their own choosing, but the Hungarians, encouraged by Voice of America and Radio Free Europe broadcasts, pushed harder, tried to withdraw from the Warsaw Pact, and were crushed by Soviet tanks. Much of the world was appalled by the uneven struggle of young Hungarians defending their government with rocks and broomsticks against tanks and machine guns, but no one came to their rescue. For all its prattle about "captive nations" and "liberation," the Eisenhower administration would not risk World War III by intervening in the Soviet sphere of influence, where Soviet interests were vital and the Soviets were certain to fight.

Soviet actions in Hungary, like Stalin's in Berlin and Korea, were a boon to those determined to maintain a high level of readiness to fight the Soviet Union. They were able to discount Soviet willingness to compromise in Poland and Soviet willingness to accept a considerable degree of diversity among Communist states. They were able to brush aside "de-Stalinization" and argue that all the perceived changes were cosmetic or tactical, that the United States still confronted a brutal, ruthless, totalitarian enemy, unyielding in its determination to dominate the world. And when the Soviets succeeded in winning the space race, sending Sputnik, the first space capsule, into orbit in 1957, Eisenhower was dismayed to find himself under attack for disregarding the security of the United States, for putting a price limit on American defense.

The Eisenhower-Dulles campaign promise to be more assertive in East Asia had pleased the American Right, especially the friends of Chiang Kai-shek. Visions of rolling back the Communists and restoring their idol to power on the Chinese mainland danced in their minds. But Eisenhower was eager to disengage American forces from the Asian mainland, determined to terminate the war in Korea and contain communism in the

[10] Walter LaFeber, *America, Russia, and the Cold War, 1945–2006*, 10th ed. (New York, 2008), 186–7; Taubman, *Khrushchev*, 282–3; Zubock, *A Failed Empire*, 112–3; Paul Y. Hammond, *Cold War and Détente* (New York, 1975), 97.

region with threatening gestures from offshore. Neither he nor Dulles trusted Chiang, and they were apprehensive of his schemes to return from his refuge on Taiwan to the mainland. They recognized his eagerness to use American troops to accomplish what his own could not and had no intention of indulging him. Had the domestic political climate been less inhibiting, Eisenhower would have sought accommodation with the People's Republic of China. He argued publicly against the trade embargo and ultimately forced the Washington bureaucracy and Congress to accept a relaxation of trade restrictions on Japanese and European trade with China. Qing Simei, a Chinese historian, has discovered that the Eisenhower administration secretly permitted American firms to trade with China through their Canadian subsidiaries.[11]

American policy toward East Asia in the Eisenhower administration was remarkably similar to that devised by the Truman administration, both in assumptions and goals. Both the president and his secretary of state considered East Asia less important than Europe. They were unwilling, nonetheless, to acquiesce in the expansion of communism, which they equated with Soviet influence, and were prepared to use American power and influence, short of a major troop involvement, to halt the Red tide. They were trapped moreover by their rhetoric, by their promises to be more aggressive than their predecessors.

In East Asia, the principal threat perceived by Washington emanated from Beijing. Eisenhower and Dulles knew China was not a Soviet puppet and were very much interested in the possibility of fomenting friction between the two Communist giants. After Chinese intervention in Korea, the intensity of public hostility to the Chinese Communists – whipped up by Chiang's supporters in Congress and the media, the so-called China Lobby – prevented the administration from attempting to woo the Chinese away from the Soviets by friendly gestures. Convinced that he had little choice but to exude belligerence toward Mao and his followers, Dulles worked out an elaborate justification for intensifying the pressure on the Chinese. He hoped that their demands

---

[11] Nancy B. Tucker, "John Foster Dulles and the Taiwan Roots of the Two Chinas Policy," in Richard H. Immerman, ed., *John Foster Dulles and the Diplomacy of the Cold War* (Princeton, 1990), 236–62; Qing Simei, "The Eisenhower Administration and Changes in Western Embargo Policy Against China," in Warren I. Cohen and Akira Iriye, eds., *The Great Powers in East Asia, 1953–1960* (New York, 1990), 121–42; Qing Simei, *From Allies to Enemies: Visions of Modernity, Identity and U.S. China Diplomacy, 1945–1960* (Cambridge, Mass, 2007), 169–204; Nancy B. Tucker, *The China Threat* (New York, 2012).

on the Soviets might be so great as to anger the Soviets, whose failure to respond adequately would alienate the Chinese. Increased pressure rather than American generosity would shatter the Sino-Soviet alliance. But when the Chinese, eager to lessen their dependence on the Soviets, reached out to the United States, Dulles was unwilling or unable to respond, revealing the sterility of his policy.[12]

The first post-Korean crisis in the region came in Indochina, where the Vietnamese were fighting for their independence from the French Empire. American anticommunism proved stronger than American antiimperialism. Eager for French support for the rearming of Germany and European integration against the Soviets generally, the United States had become, by 1953, an active supporter of France against the Vietnamese Communist–led revolutionaries. Proponents of American assistance to the French effort in Indochina also argued that the region's strategic resources had to be kept out of Communist hands, that its markets were essential to the viability of the Japanese economy. Aid to the French, begun before the Korean War, accelerated after it. American consciences were assuaged by giving much of the material support directly to Vietnamese who were collaborating with the French, an effort to distance the United States from French imperialism. But American money and equipment did not suffice. By March 1954, the French faced certain defeat and ultimate expulsion, unless American military forces came to their rescue.

As the French prepared to make their last stand at Dienbienphu, Eisenhower and Dulles contemplated intervention. General Nathan Twining, air force chief of staff, was persuaded that a few small nuclear bombs dropped on Vietnamese forces in the hills overlooking the French camp would turn the tide of battle. Admiral Arthur Radford, chairman of the Joint Chiefs of Staff, naval aviator, thought a carrier task force would be ideal for the assignment. General Matthew Ridgway, army chief of staff, the man who had cleaned up after MacArthur in Korea, argued that airpower would not suffice, that a half-million American troops would probably be necessary, and that it would be a mistake

[12] David Mayers, "Eisenhower and Communism: Later Findings," in Richard A. Melanson and David Mayers, eds., *Reevaluating Eisenhower* (Urbana, Ill., 1987), 88–120; John Lewis Gaddis, "The American 'Wedge' Strategy, 1949–55," in Harry Harding and Yuan Ming, eds., *Sino-American Relations, 1945–1955* (Wilmington, Del., 1989), 157–83.

to put them on the Asian mainland. Eisenhower was not eager to send troops, but he was unwilling to abandon Indochina to the Communists. Conceding that Indochina was itself of marginal importance to the United States, he outlined what came to be known as his "domino theory": If Indochina fell, the remaining states of Southeast Asia would fall one after another, like a row of dominoes. Wisely, however, the president insisted on prior congressional approval, a British agreement to join forces with the United States, and a French commitment to grant independence to Vietnam as preconditions for American intervention, none of which was forthcoming. The United States did not intervene militarily, and the French were defeated at Dienbienphu in May, on the eve of great power talks on Indochina at a conference in Geneva.[13]

Ho Chi Minh's forces had won a great victory in their long struggle for freedom from French imperialism, but the accords that emerged from the Geneva Conference in February did not reflect the triumph adequately. A truce was arranged between Vietnamese and French forces. Vietnam was partitioned *temporarily* to enable the combatants to disengage on either side of the seventeenth parallel. The temporary partition, to be followed by a nationwide election in 1956, was forced on Ho by his erstwhile Soviet and Chinese supporters, the former hoping to curry favor with France and the latter fearful that Vietnamese recalcitrance might bring American intervention and jeopardize their interests in the region. But Ho could count on an easy victory in the election and accepted the delay in the creation of a united, independent Vietnam.

The United States participated in the Geneva Conference but did not sign the accords, promising only that it would not upset them by force. Immediately, however, the American government set about subverting the agreement, substituting American influence for French and attempting to convert the truce line into a permanent boundary. The United States tried to create a separate Vietnamese state in the south, intended to be part of the anti-Communist bloc. There would be no election to unify Vietnam in 1956. Communism would be contained at the seventeenth parallel, with a southern Vietnamese regime, Cambodia, and

[13] Melanie Billings-Yun, *Decision Against War* (New York, 1988); George C. Herring and Richard H. Immerman, "Eisenhower, Dulles, and Dienbienphu: 'The Day We Didn't Go to War,' Revisited," *Journal of American History* 71 (1984): 343–63; Marilyn Young, *The Vietnam Wars, 1945–1990* (New York, 1991), 33–4.

Laos becoming American protectorates. None of these nations was of particular importance to the United States, but through use of the dom- ino analogy, the idea that the fall of any one of them would result in the "loss" of all of Southeast Asia, Eisenhower had invested each tiny state with the importance of the entire region. Declining to intervene militarily but refusing to accept Communist domination of Indochina, the Eisenhower administration directed the United States deeper into the quagmire.[14]

A few weeks after the Geneva Conference, in September 1954, the United States staged a fateful meeting in Manila. There, under Dulles's supervision, the Southeast Asia Treaty Organization (SEATO) was cre- ated to provide for the region's security. The United States joined Great Britain, France, Australia, New Zealand, Thailand, the Philippines, and Pakistan in an attempt to deter the further expansion of Communist influ- ence in the area, with specific reference to southern Vietnam, Cambodia, and Laos. India and Indonesia, the most important states of South and Southeast Asia, rejected membership, as did Burma. Obviously, SEATO was but a shadow analogue of NATO, but Washington now claimed a legal basis for intervention. Ho and Mao were forewarned.

One issue that plagued Eisenhower and Dulles was the shape of the security relationship with the Republic of China, Chiang's rump regime on Taiwan. Chiang's friends, including Walter Robertson, assistant sec- retary of state for Far Eastern affairs, had long urged including Taiwan in some kind of mutual defense pact. Most of the other SEATO partici- pants were adamantly opposed to so obvious a provocation to Beijing. A bilateral pact seemed to be the only option and Robertson pressed the idea on a reluctant Dulles. As the historian Nancy Bernkopf Tucker has demonstrated, Dulles mistrusted Chiang profoundly.[15] Dulles was convinced the Chinese Nationalist leader was searching for a way to entangle the United States in a war with the Chinese Communists, a war in which Americans would fight and die to facilitate Chiang's tri- umphant return to the mainland. Chiang was frustrated and angered by his failure to obtain the desired treaty. But a miscalculation by Mao forced Dulles into Chiang's embrace.

---

[14] Richard H. Immerman, "Between the Unattainable and the Unacceptable: Eisenhower and Dienbienphu," in Melanson and Mayers, *Reevaluating Eisenhower,* 120–54; George McT. Kahin, *Intervention* (New York, 1986), 66–92.

[15] Tucker, "John Foster Dulles and the Taiwan Roots of the Two Chinas Policy."

Uneasy about the creation of SEATO, fearful of an alliance between Chiang's government and the United States, Mao chose to precipitate a crisis in the Taiwan Strait, beginning with the bombardment of Nationalist-held islands a few miles from the mainland of China. The Chinese scholar He Di has argued that Mao and his colleagues were unaware of tensions between Taipei and Washington.[16] They perceived an American plot to separate Taiwan from the mainland permanently. Chinese leaders thought they could forestall the alliance by demonstrating its potential danger to the Americans: the danger of becoming embroiled in a war over tiny islands within reach of mainland batteries. Eisenhower and Dulles understood the message and took the necessary precautions when negotiating the alliance with Chiang, but they refused to be intimidated. Mao's display of power proved to be counterproductive.

Chiang won his treaty but at a very high price. He had to surrender the right to attack the mainland without the consent of the United States, and he could not commit the United States to the defense of any of the offshore islands still manned by his troops. Before the crisis ended, he was forced to evacuate the Dachen Islands. Jinmen and Mazu (Quemoy and Matsu) remained under Nationalist control, but the Americans would defend them only if Washington perceived a threat to Taiwan itself. Chiang was further angered in March 1955 when Dulles told him to stop telling his people that their return to the mainland was imminent. The mutual defense treaty to which the Americans agreed was designed not only to deter a Communist attack against Taiwan but also as a means of insuring Washington's control over Chiang.

Eisenhower and Dulles remained apprehensive of war with China, uncertain of Mao's intentions. An effort to obtain a UN-supervised cease-fire in the strait was rejected by Chinese on both sides. America's allies and much of the rest of the world appeared horrified by Dulles's willingness to risk war over Jinmen and Mazu. The administration had no illusions about the importance of the islands, but Eisenhower feared that if the Nationalists were forced to withdraw from them, their morale would drop precipitously and American credibility would suffer throughout Asia. Once again, Eisenhower, in a variation on his

---

[16] He Di, "The Evolution of the People's Republic of China's Policy Toward the Offshore Islands," in Cohen and Iriye, *Great Powers in East Asia*, 222–45.

domino theory, invested territory of little strategic import with enormous weight: If the United States let the Chinese Communists seize Jinmen and Mazu, the Taiwan regime might collapse, much of Asia might turn to the Communists, the Cold War might be lost. "For want of a nail ..." The solution Eisenhower and Dulles hit upon was atomic blackmail, indirect warnings to the Chinese that they would use nuclear weapons to defend the islands.

The Chinese, however, had already pushed as far as they had intended and were not prepared to invade Jinmen and Mazu. Their effort to prevent the mutual defense treaty between the United States and the Republic of China had failed, but they had succeeded in alarming many of America's allies, especially Europeans unwilling to participate in a third world war precipitated by a confrontation over the islands. Having gained Washington's attention, the Chinese offered to negotiate existing differences with the United States, including the release of Americans held in China and Chinese stranded in the United States when the two countries became enemies in 1950. When the United States agreed to ambassadorial-level talks in the summer of 1955, the crisis passed.

After a quick agreement on the exchange of each other's nationals, the talks degenerated into a stalemate on the Taiwan issue. The United States demanded that China renounce the right to use force to seize the island, and China refused. To Mao and his comrades in Beijing, the Taiwan issue was a domestic issue, unfinished business in a civil war. They hinted broadly that force would not be used, stressed the likelihood of peaceful liberation of the island, but would not give the explicit assurances the United States required. Hemmed in by Chiang's supporters in the United States, accepting as reality his own rationalization for a policy of maintaining pressure on the People's Republic, Dulles evidenced no flexibility. In the summer of 1957, despite Chinese efforts to continue the dialogue, the United States broke off the talks.

In Beijing the initiative passed to those Chinese leaders, Mao among them, who preferred a more aggressive approach. Buoyed by Soviet successes in the space race, Mao contended that the time had come for a bold Communist offensive against imperialism. He found Khrushchev unresponsive. Khrushchev, too, was confident that the tide was running his way, but he had no illusions about American power or Soviet vulnerability. He did not want a confrontation, certainly not one of China's choosing. Contemptuous of Khrushchev's prudence, Mao chose his own moment. In late August 1958, China initiated a campaign to seize Jinmen and Mazu, precipitating a second crisis in the Taiwan Strait.[17]

Chiang had used the intervening years to reinforce his garrisons on the offshore islands, deliberately raising the stakes to compel the United States to protect the islands. Eisenhower and Dulles tried unsuccessfully to get Chiang to withdraw his troops – and then decided they would be forced to come to the rescue. Once again, the Americans threatened to use nuclear weapons against China, and sent over a hundred warships, including seven carriers, to the strait. Khrushchev warned Washington that the Soviet Union would retaliate if the United States launched a nuclear strike. Fortunately, Chiang's air force was able to achieve supremacy over the islands, staving off the attack without an American offensive against the Chinese mainland.

Having gained the attention of the United States, Mao backed off. Quickly, he demonstrated his capacity for self-delusion by discovering that retreat was an act of genius: To have succeeded in capturing the islands would have eliminated Taiwan's last links to the mainland and contributed to the permanent division of China. By allowing Chiang to retain control of the islands, he had thwarted Washington's "two Chinas" plot.[18]

The Americans indicated their willingness to resume discussions. Responding to public outrage at home and abroad over the administration's willingness to risk world war over Jinmen and Mazu, Dulles openly criticized Chiang and began to explore the possibility of recognizing the Beijing government. Nothing substantial came of the renewed conversations between the two governments, but diplomacy had advantages over threats, especially if there was to be any hope of persuading China to abide by existing norms of international behavior. Dulles's policy of isolation and pressure increased the likelihood of China's behaving irresponsibly and dangerously. Regularly scheduled ambassadorial conversations provided a mechanism for venting rage, providing and obtaining explanations, exploring and even inching toward resolution of differences.

---

[17] He Di, "The Evolution of PRC Policy Toward the Offshore Islands"; Taubman, *Khrushchev*, 392, 402.

[18] He Di, "The Evolution of PRC Policy Toward the Offshore Islands"; Thomas E. Stolper, *China, Taiwan, and the Offshore Islands* (New York, 1985), 124–30; Zubock, *A Failed Empire*, 136–7.

Mao's tactics in the strait crises troubled Khrushchev perhaps as much as they did the Americans. Much like Eisenhower, the Soviet leader worried about his nation's credibility. He could not stand by idly while the United States pummeled his principal ally – not without sending the wrong message to uncommitted nations the Soviets were wooing. No Third World ruler could be expected to cast his lot with the Soviet Union if the Soviets could not be relied upon for protection. On the other hand, if the Soviet Union were to risk its own destruction in a nuclear confrontation with the United States, Khrushchev wanted to be sure that he was in control, that war would come over an issue he deemed worth fighting and dying for, and at a time and place of his choosing. But Mao – jealous of his prerogatives as leader of a great nation and capable of provoking war – was not amenable to Soviet advice. And perhaps worst of all, Soviet scientists and technicians were in China helping the Chinese to build an atom bomb!

Gradually the ties that bound the Communist giants began to fray. Soviet advice designed to moderate Chinese policy, to avoid provocation, irritated Mao. Soviet offers of military advisers and requests for submarine basing rights and a radio station on Chinese soil to broadcast to Soviet submarines aroused Mao's suspicions. The terms of Soviet economic and technical assistance did not satisfy Mao. In the late 1950s Soviet foreign policy generally evoked Mao's contempt, and Soviet domestic policies, specifically de-Stalinization, did little to warm his heart. Khrushchev's suggestion that Beijing accept the two Chinas policy toward which the United States had moved struck at the core of Mao's intense nationalism, confirmed Mao's sense of Soviet indifference to China's interests, and may have precipitated the break. Angry exchanges, focused primarily on differences over ideological matters, led to Khrushchev's recall of Soviet technicians in 1959 and his effort to scuttle China's atom bomb project.[19]

The Eisenhower administration, however, could not devise a policy to capitalize on the long-desired Sino-Soviet split when it finally occurred. Anticommunism, the containment of communism, did not provide a useful framework for exploiting a situation in which the two major Communist powers were at each other's throats. With Dulles's

[19] Edward Crankshaw and Strobe Talbott, *Khrushchev Remembers* (Boston, 1970), 463–71; John Wilson Lewis and Xue Litai, *China Builds the Bomb* (Stanford, 1988), 60–72.

death early in 1959 and Eisenhower's weariness of Asian affairs, there were no new initiatives coming out of Washington in 1959 or 1960. Only a growing involvement in Indochina and awareness of a falling domino in Laos marked Eisenhower's last days in office.

If Mao's assertiveness complicated life in the Kremlin, some American allies did what they could to prevent complacency in Washington. Foremost of these was Charles de Gaulle, the imperious French leader, who returned to power in 1958 and objected strenuously to what he perceived as Anglo-American control of NATO, and the relegation of France to an inferior role. He raised a question fundamental to the alliance in an era when the Soviets were preparing to deploy intercontinental ballistic missiles: Would the United States risk a nuclear attack on its own cities by responding to a Soviet attack on Western Europe? Unpersuaded by American assurances, de Gaulle developed an independent nuclear force for France. Dissatisfied by American unwillingness to share responsibility for directing the alliance, he began to withdraw French forces from NATO control. France remained a loyal ally but very much on de Gaulle's terms.

Less dramatically, the Japanese, too, became more assertive in the 1950s. Freed of the forces of occupation in 1952, secured from external threat by alliance with the United States, Japan concentrated on rapid economic growth, aided by profits from supply and support services it provided during the Korean War. The Japanese wanted access to American and Chinese markets and persuaded Eisenhower to support them. The president perceived Japan's economic stability as essential to American security interests. He argued frequently against protectionism in the United States and against posing obstacles to Japan's trade with Beijing. The bureaucracy procrastinated, and Eisenhower did little to prod it, but he opened whatever doors were under presidential control.[20]

The Japanese were also eager to regain territories lost to the Soviet Union at the close of World War II and toward that end responded to a Soviet initiative and reestablished diplomatic relations with Moscow

[20] Warren I. Cohen, "China in Japanese-American Relations," in Akira Iriye and Warren I. Cohen, eds., *The United States and Japan in the Postwar World* (Lexington, Ky., 1989), 36–60; Qing, "The Eisenhower Administration and Changes in Western Embargo Policy Against China, 1954–1958," and Burton I. Kaufman, "Eisenhower's Foreign Economic Policy with Respect to East Asia," both in Cohen and Iriye, *Great Powers in East Asia*, 121–42, 104–20.

in 1956. Dulles was apprehensive and did what he could to obstruct a Soviet-Japanese rapprochement, but it was the inability of the Soviet and Japanese negotiators to reach an acceptable compromise on the territorial question that kept the two nations apart for many years to follow.

Nonetheless, Japanese assertiveness worried American intelligence analysts, who warned that Japan might dissociate itself from the West unless the United States allowed for greater equality in bilateral relations. Japanese public anger over American nuclear testing in the Pacific was intense in the mid-1950s, especially after the crew of the Japanese fishing boat *Lucky Dragon* was irradiated by a thermonuclear test on Bikini atoll in March 1954. In 1960, anti-American riots in Japan, organized by opponents of the renewal of the Japanese-American security treaty, reflected pacifist and neutralist tendencies. There was cause for alarm in Washington.[21]

Much of the world, of course, went about its business with minimal regard for the antics of the United States, the Soviet Union, and their respective allies. The ethnic and religious strife, the class struggles and instability that have always been the stuff of human existence persisted, quite apart from the Cold War, quite apart from great-power politics. But as the United States and the Soviet Union acquired the ability to project their power all over the globe and as they achieved an uneasy balance in the areas of vital concern, such as Europe, the superpowers began to intervene in local struggles in Latin America, the Middle East, and Africa, as well as Asia. Some of the American and Soviet activity could be justified strategically, especially if one accepted variations on the domino theme or fretted about credibility. Some of it involved vital economic interests, such as American concern for the oil of the Middle East. Some of it was merely mechanical: The power to intervene existed; use it, demonstrate it, experiment with it.

The historian Odd Arne Westad has called attention to the competing ideologies used to justify or rationalize American and Soviet interventionism. Both countries were founded on universalist beliefs that prescribed a mission to better mankind. Each sought to demonstrate

---

[21] Cohen, "China in Japanese-American Relations," 47; Roger Dingman, "Alliance in Crisis: The Lucky Dragon Incident and Japanese-American Relations," in Cohen and Iriye, *Great Powers in East Asia*, 187–214; George R. Packard, III, *Protest in Tokyo* (Princeton, 1966).

that it offered a superior model for the modernization of developing states. And unless Third World leaders succeeded in manipulating both, their chosen model brought their countries into close ties with either the United States or the Soviet Union.[22]

Eisenhower was relatively relaxed about the struggle for control of the Third World. Concerned primarily with European affairs, he did not believe America's future rested upon the outcome of the struggle for dominance over distant, undeveloped, tribal societies. But there were those dominoes and the need to contain communism. Sometimes, Third World countries were important sources of raw materials, most obviously oil, or potential trading partners for the United States or Japan or Western Europe. Brandishing nuclear weapons might protect American interests when the Soviets or Chinese were involved, and demonstrations of power might suffice in other situations. And there was another, rather less well-defined tool at hand: covert operations, a less familiar device whose potential intrigued Eisenhower.

One of the administration's first major Third World interventions occurred in Guatemala, a Caribbean state assumed to be within the American sphere of influence, off limits to any other great power. Latin America was the lowest priority for American military leaders because Soviet intervention in the region was deemed highly unlikely. And, indeed, there was no evidence of Soviet involvement in Guatemala. There was, however, a nationalist, reformist government that had come to power by constitutional means and had dared to expropriate holdings of the United Fruit Company, an American-based firm that was a major force in Guatemalan politics as well as in the economy. The government unquestionably had the support of the handful of Communists in the country, but it was neither Communist-controlled nor Communist-led.[23]

The Guatemalan president, Colonel Jacobo Arbenz Guzman, rejected State Department demands for compensation deemed adequate by United Fruit and was generally unresponsive to American pressure. Prodded by United Fruit executives, the American government determined that Arbenz's recalcitrance and labor unrest in United Fruit

---

[22] Odd Arne Westad, *The Global Cold War* (New York, 2005), 1–7.
[23] My discussion of Guatemala derives largely from Richard Immerman's *The CIA in Guatemala* (Austin, Tex., 1982). See also Stephen Rabe, "Dulles, Latin America, and Cold War Anticommunism," in Immerman, ed., *John Foster Dulles and Diplomacy of the Cold War*, 159–87.

operations elsewhere in Central America were Communist-inspired. The cancer of communism had appeared in the American sphere, and it would have to be excised quickly. The Central Intelligence Agency (CIA) developed plans to remedy the situation.

As American pressure mounted and Arbenz learned of a scheme for an exile invasion of Guatemala, he searched desperately for arms, ultimately risking all by turning to the Soviet Union. The Soviets responded favorably to what was probably perceived as a low-cost, low-risk opportunity to worry the United States. In due course the CIA discovered that a shipment of Czech arms was en route to Guatemala, a public relations coup for those who saw international communism behind Guatemalan reforms. A CIA-organized raid (150 attackers and a handful of planes) followed, and the Arbenz government collapsed. An American-supported regime seized power in Guatemala and soon turned the country into one of the most repressive in the world. From Washington's perspective, it had won an important victory over communism, an important victory in the Cold War, at minimal cost and almost without showing its hand. The Guatemalan operation was impressive evidence of what could be accomplished by covert operations.

Judaism, Christianity, and Islam all had their roots in the Middle East. For centuries Christians and Muslims fought for control of the Holy Land. For centuries Jews in the diaspora called for a return to Jerusalem as part of their Passover celebration. Secular Jewish nationalism, Zionism, emerged in Europe late in the nineteenth century and a few thousand Jews trickled into Palestine in the years that followed. The British, who took control of Palestine from the Ottoman Empire during World War I, made conflicting promises to the Arab Muslims who lived there and to the European Jews who sought a homeland there. After the Holocaust, the German murder of six million Jews during World War II, American and British leaders saw Palestine as a convenient refuge for the Jewish survivors of the Nazi death camps. Palestinian Arabs and the Arabs of neighboring states forcibly opposed the UN decision to partition Palestine in order to create a Jewish homeland there. In April 1948, the Jews declared the existence of the state of Israel on that part of Palestine allotted to them by the United Nations. A major war followed, in which the Jews, thanks in part to arms provided by Soviet-dominated Czechoslovakia, prevailed over vastly larger Arab armies and created a state even larger than the United Nations had intended. The state of Israel had won the first round in an Arab-Israeli conflict that was to plague the region for decades to come.

Some American leaders, such as Harry Truman, seem to have been genuinely sympathetic to the living skeletons that emerged from Auschwitz and Buchenwald. They were responsive to the pleas of Zionists who argued that the Jewish people required their own state, to protect them from the persecution, the pogroms, and the massacres that had befallen them too often in Europe. American leaders were also conscious of the fact that in the aftermath of the Holocaust, there was enormous public support among American Christians as well as Jews for the creation of a Jewish homeland. Politicians were not unaware that there were votes to be gained from supporting creation of the state of Israel, from being quick to recognize it. And, in the election campaign of 1948, despite an effort to keep the issue out of partisan politics, Truman moved hastily to recognize Israel, undermining efforts by the American UN delegation to find a peaceful solution to the partition question.

Other American leaders, urging the president to put sentiment aside, argued that the national interest required the United States to align itself with the Arabs. The Middle East, loosely defined as Arab North Africa, the Arabian peninsula, and Southwest Asia, contained an enormous percentage of the world's estimated oil reserves. The area was almost entirely Muslim, largely Arab, and broadly hostile to the encroachment of Europeans. Support for a handful of Jews would alienate many millions of Muslims, who controlled the strategic crossroads connecting three continents – and those vast quantities of oil. George Kennan, who had shown himself strikingly insensitive to Jewish suffering, proved much more sensitive to the arguments of Arabists within the Department of State. Robert Lovett, undersecretary of state in 1948, worried about Soviet sympathizers among the Jewish refugees and ineptly warned Truman against "buying a pig in a poke" by accepting a Jewish state.

In brief, the Middle East, in the half-century following World War II, was an extraordinarily important repository of oil upon which the United States increasingly, and its European and Japanese friends to a much greater extent, were dependent. It was the site of the Arab-Israeli clash that rapidly became one of history's most intractable conflicts. And, with part of it constituting the rimland of the Soviet empire, it was, inevitably, a critical arena for the Soviet-American confrontation.

The Truman administration had responded sharply to Soviet pressures on Iran and Turkey and formulated the Truman Doctrine to prevent Communist guerrillas from overthrowing the Greek government. It had demonstrated the intent of the United States to succeed to the British role in the region and to deny the legitimacy of Soviet aspirations there. Stalin's blatant imperialism, his attempts to appropriate territory belonging to Iran and Turkey, were obviously objectionable, and relatively easy to counter. His meddling in the Arab-Israeli war of 1948, apparently intended to aggravate Britain's problems as regional hegemon, was more difficult to counter, more worrisome. It was Soviet economic and military support for Middle Eastern states that posed the threat to American interests in the area after Stalin's death.

The quest for freedom from the European imperialists who had dominated the region since the late nineteenth century united politically mobile Arabs. Iranians – Muslims but not Arabs – were equally restive. By 1947, Great Britain was drawing back; the French were more tenacious, but the process of decolonization ground on, slower in some places than others, but inexorably. The Soviets, forced to ease pressure on Turkey and Iran, displeased by the appeal to Soviet Jews of the Zionist state they had helped create, ignorant of and uninterested in the Arab world, were quiescent in the Middle East in the late 1940s and early 1950s. The United States, historically uninvolved, traditionally antiimperialist, perceived as nonthreatening by local nationalists, utilized its capabilities to project power by moving into the vacuum.

From the outset, the motives for American intervention in the Middle East were mixed, an extension of the nation's antiimperialist mission combined with determination to block Soviet expansion. American leaders were not willing to work toward the end of British and French imperialism to facilitate Soviet imperialism. Support for Israel was an irritating complication, driven by humanitarian and domestic political concerns – and a fervent prayer that somehow it could be reconciled with concrete interests. The leaders in Washington did what they thought they had to do for Israel and hoped for the best. The complexity of regional issues proved overwhelming, however. The Arab-Israeli conflict could not be isolated from the Soviet-American rivalry. Nor could a historic commitment to antiimperialism inoculate Americans against the virus of imperialism when the opportunity appeared.

American policy toward Iran in the early 1950s is highly illustrative of the corrupting influence of imperial responsibilities. The Soviet threat to Iran's territorial integrity and independence had been countered successfully in 1946. The British had withdrawn their forces from Iran almost immediately after the war. But British interest in Iranian oil remained intense, and the British continued to control Iran's oil long after the troops were gone. When tensions arose between an Iranian nationalist regime determined to command its own resources and the British, the United States tried to mediate. Efforts by the Truman administration to broker an Anglo-Iranian compromise failed, and the Iranian government continued to assert itself in a number of disturbing directions.

Washington came to fear that Communist influence was growing in Tehran, that Mohammed Mossadegh, the Iranian prime minister, might allow his country to slip under Soviet control. It was an unlikely scenario, but the Eisenhower administration was unwilling to allow Iran to alienate itself from the West. Like any nineteenth-century imperial power exercising suzerainty over a client state, the United States decided to replace the Iranian leadership. Covertly, with the assistance of British operatives, the American Central Intelligence Agency facilitated a military coup in August 1953, resulting in the arrest of Mossadegh and the shift of power in Iran to the Shah. For many years afterward, the Shah responded to American needs with appropriate gratitude, including a 40 percent share for American companies in a new international consortium to manage Iranian oil production. His own people fared less well.[24]

As Eisenhower, Dulles, and their advisers surveyed the world, they noted that the Middle East constituted a gap in the network of alliances with which they were determined to encircle the Communist bloc. Between Turkey and Pakistan sat the Arab world, Iran, and two-thirds of the oil reserves accessible to the West – all terribly vulnerable to a Soviet thrust. The Truman administration had recognized the danger but failed in its effort to enroll Egypt in a Middle East defense command. Egypt remained uninterested and opposed to any Arab nation aligning itself with the West. Nonetheless, it was time to complete the circle. Turkey was eager to strengthen its eastern flank against

[24] Barry Rubin, *Paved with Good Intentions* (New York, 1980), 54–90; George Lenczowski, *American Presidents and the Middle East* (Durham, N.C., 1990), 32–40.

the Soviets. Iraq saw an opportunity to protect itself against possible Soviet pressures while simultaneously alleviating its dependence on the British. Pakistan perceived an opportunity to obtain military aid more likely to be needed against India than the Soviet Union. As the Americans and British hovered in the background, desirous of proceeding, but still groping for a formula that would not enrage the Israelis and Egyptians, the Turks seized the initiative. In February 1956, Turkey and Iraq signed what came to be called the Baghdad Pact, to which the British, Pakistanis, and Iranians adhered in the course of the year. Unable to pacify Israelis or Egyptians, both resentful of Iraqi access to Western military aid, the United States never joined what became the Middle East Treaty Organization (METO), although it was the principal source of the groups support.[25]

With Turkey, Iran, and Iraq linked to each other and individually to the United States, the Soviet bloc was, nominally, ringed by hostile nations, all receiving military assistance from or protected by the Americans. But for most denizens of the Middle East, including Iraqis, the Soviet threat was imperceptible. Western, especially British, imperialism had blighted their lives for generations. They preferred to assert themselves against Western imperialism and Zionism, which they perceived as its most recent manifestation. Only the Turks and Iranians had experienced Soviet pressures, and many Iranians were at least as unhappy with the Americans, who had deposed Mossadegh. There was little popular support for the containment of the Soviet Union. On the other hand, there was a vast quantity of combustible material waiting to be ignited by a leader who would strike out against Israel and reverse the decades of humiliation by the West.

The man most likely to lead the Arab world to renewed glory and respect was Gamal Abdul Nasser of Egypt. Nasser emerged as master of Egypt after a group of young officers, appalled by defeat in the 1948 war with Israel and evidence of government corruption and incompetence, overthrew a decadent king in 1952. Nasser and his colleagues were quick to demand elimination of European restrictions on Egyptian sovereignty, and the British had neither the will nor the resources to resist. The United States, sympathetic to Egyptian aspirations, impressed favorably by Nasser and eager to win his friendship, favored the initial

[25] John C. Campbell, *Defense of the Middle East* (New York, 1960), 49–62.

British retreat. Nasser's satisfaction with the American position did not extend to the point of willingness to be enlisted in the containment of the Soviet Union; nor did he prove willing to moderate the anti-Israeli and antiimperialist rhetoric so popular in the Arab world.[26]

The Baghdad Pact angered the many Arabs who preached non-alignment in the Cold War, but Nasser especially. Iraq was undermining his vision of rejecting Western hegemony and uniting the Arab peoples under his leadership. The West was enhancing the power of his rival, maintaining Western influence in the region. Nasser was not unaware that the Soviet Union was equally unhappy about the pact and increasingly supportive of the Arabs against both Israel and the West in the United Nations and in its propaganda. When Israel launched a devastating and humiliating raid into Egyptian-controlled territory in February 1955, in retaliation for commando raids originating there, Nasser decided to turn to the Soviets for help.

Khrushchev, unlike Stalin, was definitely interested in competing with the United States for influence among the Arabs. Confident of the superiority of the Soviet system, unburdened by commitment to Israel, sharing Arab hostility to Western imperialism, Khrushchev and his colleagues accepted the challenge of the Baghdad Pact and the opportunity Nasser provided. The Soviets were prepared to supply economic and military assistance to nonaligned leaders who sought an alternative to dependence on the West or a more radical model for rapid development of their countries. In September 1955, arrangements were concluded for arms manufactured in Czechoslovakia to be shipped to Egypt. By inducing Iraq to join in the American-led effort to contain the Soviet Union, the United States had facilitated Soviet penetration of the region, giving the Soviets an opportunity to befriend Iraq's rival, Egypt.[27]

As Nasser's relations with the Communist bloc warmed, the United States continued to court him. For Nasser and leaders of other non-aligned states who mastered the art, it was a delightful situation. The competing superpowers were manipulated with varying degrees of artistry. American and Soviet leaders sang the virtues of a wide range of African and Asian rulers and contributed generously of their treasure, their technology, and their guns. With Czech arms on the way, Nasser

---

[26] Campbell, *Defense of the Middle East*, 63–72.
[27] Zubock, *A Failed Empire*, 109–10.

found the Americans (and the British) eager to build a dam for him, to help him subdue the Nile, and to use its power to irrigate and electrify the Nile Valley. He wanted the aid, but with Soviet assistance also available, he saw no need to trim his sails to comfort the Americans. The arms deal, perceived as a slap at the West, had enhanced Nasser's stature among the Arab masses. He promised them he would do something unpleasant to Israel. To demonstrate further his independence from the United States, he brushed aside American pleas to the contrary and recognized the People's Republic of China in May 1956.[28]

There were many in the U.S. Congress who did not like giving money to foreigners. There were Southern lawmakers unwilling to subsidize cotton-growing nations such as Egypt. There were a substantial number of congressmen and women who did not like giving aid to countries that threatened Israel. And there was also a congressional bloc sympathetic to Chiang Kai-shek and utterly opposed to assisting any country that recognized the People's Republic of China. Giving foreign aid to countries that demonstrated no gratitude, that performed in a manner contrary to American wishes, was not politically popular or sensible. Eisenhower and Dulles, skeptical of Soviet willingness to commit the necessary funds, decided to back away from Nasser's dam project, did so publicly and in a manner designed to embarrass the Egyptian leader.[29]

Enraged, lacking assurance of Soviet funding for his dam, Nasser nationalized the Suez Canal, which was owned by a British-controlled corporation. Once again, he stuck his finger in the eye of the Western imperialists, to the delight of many Arabs. Perhaps he would be able to finance his dam project with the canal's revenues. Eisenhower and Dulles responded cautiously; British prime minister Anthony Eden did not. To the Americans, Suez was far away, a convenience rather than a vital interest. Who controlled the canal was less important than keeping the Arabs friendly, friendly enough to keep oil flowing to the West and Soviet influence out of the region. The use of force to keep the canal under European or international management was not an acceptable

---

[28] Campbell, *Defense of the Middle East*, 72–6; Kennett Love, *Suez* (New York, 1969), 297–327.

[29] W. Roger Louis, "Dulles, Suez, and the British," in Immerman, *Dulles and Diplomacy of the Cold War*, 133–58, notes reporting by the British Embassy in Washington on lobbying activities against the Aswan loan.

option. To Eden, however, the canal was a critical artery linking British and Western European industry to Persian Gulf oil. Nasser had committed an act of wanton aggression. As he had opposed the appeasement of Hitler in the 1930s, Eden was determined not to appease Nasser. He was convinced that Nasser, like Hitler, could be stopped only with force.[30]

In deference to American insistence on a negotiated resolution of the canal issue, the British restrained themselves through the late summer and early autumn of 1956. They talked, they listened, and they prepared for the military action they believed necessary. In the French and the Israelis they found willing accomplices. The French shared British concerns about the canal and were angered by Nasser's support for Algerian efforts to achieve independence from French rule. The Israelis were profoundly troubled by the shipment of Soviet arms to Egypt and the refusal of the United States to provide Israel with either additional arms or assurances. Israeli leaders perceived the United States as having abandoned the Jews as the Arabs prepared to destroy them. They would not watch passively: After the Holocaust, never again! British and French assistance provided an opportunity that could not be wasted. American intelligence analysts underestimated the likelihood that Nasser's enemies would strike.

On October 29, 1956, while much of the world focused on the Soviet response to the Hungarian Revolution, Israeli tanks raced across the Sinai and, in a matter of hours, destroyed much of the Egyptian army. The following day, in a move coordinated with Israel, the British and French warned Israeli and Egyptian forces to stay away from the canal and, ostensibly to protect the canal, attacked nearby Egyptian forces. Before the military activity ended, British and French troops headed for Suez. America's allies had resorted to a classic nineteenth-century means of coping with unruly natives.

Eisenhower and Dulles were in an extraordinarily difficult situation. To support the British, French, and Israelis would mean alienating the Arab world and almost certainly much of the rest of the Third World. It would mean abandoning traditional opposition to imperialism and

---

[30] Lenczowski, *American Presidents and the Middle East,* 40–52, is a succinct overview of the Suez Crisis. See also Love, *Suez,* for an account highly sympathetic to Nasser, and Herman Finer, *Dulles over Suez* (Chicago, 1964), for a diatribe against American policy during the crisis. Peter L. Hahn, *The United States, Great Britain, and Egypt* (Chapel Hill, 1991) 211–39 is a balanced corrective to both.

aggression, exposing the nation to charges of hypocrisy. It would mean allowing the Soviets to claim the high ground in the Middle East, allowing them to pose as the sole supporters of the Arabs against Western and Zionist imperialism. It would give Khrushchev, who was threatening the British and French with nuclear weapons, an enormous propaganda victory at a time when the world should have been railing against Soviet brutality in Hungary. The price was too high, and the United States chose to lead the attack on the British and French in the United Nations. For once the United States and the Soviet Union were on the same side of an issue, denouncing imperialism as they vied for influence in the Arab world. The British, French, and ultimately the Israelis were forced by American pressure to withdraw, although the Israelis were able to exact from Eisenhower assurances of access to the Gulf of Aqaba. Relations with its NATO allies might never be the same, but the United States had preserved its influence in the Middle East. Unfortunately from Washington's perspective, so had the Soviet Union, and it seemed poised to improve its position in the region.

It was evident from Nasser's actions that he was competing with the United States and the Soviet Union for power and influence. Like a number of other Third World leaders, he was at least as shrewd as his American and Soviet counterparts in using them for his ends as they attempted to use him for theirs. Neither Washington nor Moscow could ever hope to control him or the Middle East. Throughout the 1950s and 1960s, however, Nasser threatened American rather than Soviet interests. It was the United States and its allies that had a growing dependence on Middle Eastern oil and feared that Nasser's Pan-Arab movement would one day control the spigot, would one day interrupt the flow so essential to Western and Japanese industry. It was the United States that could not abandon Israel and dreaded the moment when Nasser or another Arab leader would attempt to reclaim Palestine for the Palestinians. And Khrushchev, unlike Stalin, was willing to aid Nasser, confident that a stronger Egypt would be an asset to the Soviet Union, that disruption of the flow of oil and conflict between Arabs and Israelis would weaken the United States.

In the aftermath of the Suez crisis, Eisenhower, signaling the gravity of American concern, asked for and received from Congress a resolution that declared the Middle East to be a vital national interest. It gave the president discretion to aid countries there, with American forces if necessary, when a country asked for help to repel "overt armed aggression from any nation controlled by international communism." The resolution was soon known as the Eisenhower Doctrine. Designed to check Nasser's influence as well as Soviet, it was applicable to no known situation in the region. The doctrine was used in 1957 when the king of Jordan, threatened by pro-Nasser forces within his country and without, appealed for help, claiming, not surprisingly, that the danger came from "international communism." The U.S. Sixth Fleet showed the flag in the eastern Mediterranean, and the king received $10 million in American aid.

A more dangerous situation shocked Washington in the summer of 1958. The Christian president of Lebanon had been appealing for help against pro-Nasser forces to anyone with an available ear. There was no evidence that international communism was involved, although both Egypt and Syria, with links to the Soviets, were. Washington was unresponsive until a coup in Iraq substituted a pro-Nasser, pro-Soviet regime for the one that had signed the Baghdad Pact. Confronted with a situation in which Nasser's power seemed to have united the Arab world, eliminated the West's principal ally, and become an increment to Soviet influence in the area, the United States sent marines to Lebanon. Khrushchev, fearing American intervention in Iraq, threatened war. Quickly, the United States determined that the Soviets were not involved in the coup in Iraq; that the new Iraqi leadership was intensely nationalistic, anti-Western to be sure, but unlikely to submit to their country's becoming a Soviet satellite. Recognition of the Baghdad regime by Washington defused the crisis. Nasser, undesirous of a permanent American military presence in the region, used his influence to calm his friends in Lebanon and Syria, facilitating the withdrawal of the marines. The United States made few friends among the Arabs, but no shots were fired in anger.[31]

The American position in the Middle East, as it developed in the 1950s, was that of a traditional great power. The United States was interested primarily in the resources of the area, in an uninterrupted flow of oil at a reasonable price. Toward this end it desired order and stability – exotic commodities in the Middle East, as in most of the developing world. The problems for American policymakers would have been

---

[31] Lenczowski, *American Presidents and the Middle East,* 57–64; William Stivers, "Eisenhower and the Middle East," in Melanson and Mayers, *Reevaluating Eisenhower,* 206–9.

similar and difficult had the Soviet Union not existed. Intra-Arab rivalries – especially those involving Egypt, Iraq, and Syria, states seeking to lead pan-Arab movements, but also between secular and religious nations – would have created turbulence. Similarly tensions within countries – religious, ethnic, and socioeconomic – promised strife in the absence of established patterns for the peaceful resolution of differences, assuming such differences were resolvable. All of these issues bubbled in a cauldron to which the addition of Israel's presence guaranteed an explosive mixture. American ties to Israel constituted a further, inescapable vexation.

The Soviets played the classic role of the competing but weaker great power. Although it bordered the Middle East, the Soviet Union was unable to dislodge the United States from the region. It could, and in the 1950s did, stir the pot at times and in places of its own choosing, facilitating local resistance to American visions, raising the cost of the Pax Americana. To Arabs dissatisfied with their relations with the United States, for whatever reason, the Soviet Union provided an alternative. None of this had much to do with international communism, which had little appeal in the Arab world and gained a foothold nowhere within it during this period.

The American effort to contain the Soviet Union by enlisting the so-called northern tier states (Turkey, Iraq, and Iran) in the Baghdad Pact does not explain the Soviet role in the area. The Soviets did not jump in because they were provoked. The Baghdad Pact gave the Soviets an opportunity to establish ties with Egypt at a particular moment, but as the world's second greatest power, with a historic interest in the region, they could not have been kept out. After Stalin's death, the Soviet leadership actively pursued links in the Arab world. Sooner or later an Arab leader would have found it in his interest to accept their overtures.

Two other examples are perhaps more useful in illustrating Khrushchev's confidence that the Soviet Union could compete successfully on the periphery. Indonesia and the Congo were places where the Soviets had no historic concerns and were far removed from any vital interests. To establish footholds in Southeast Asia and Africa, but perhaps primarily to demonstrate that the Soviet Union was worthy of respect as a world power, Khrushchev committed Soviet resources at critical moments in the development of both countries.

Sukarno of Indonesia had hosted the Bandung Conference of non-aligned states in 1955 and developed the delusions of grandeur that so often accompany power. He perceived himself to be a world leader, sought to arrogate additional power to himself at home and to expand the territory under Indonesian rule. Dissatisfied with the extent and conditions of American aid, he flew to Moscow, where Khrushchev offered a $100 million credit. Returning to Indonesia, Sukarno attempted to use the Soviet offer to encourage greater generosity in Washington. At the same time, with the support of the Indonesian Communist party, he changed the existing Indonesian parliamentary system into something he called "guided democracy." It was by no means a Leninist system that he had created, but he had increased his personal power and reduced the chances for genuine democratic government.

Washington found Sukarno's egomania distasteful, but it was much more troubled by his flirtation with the Soviets, by evidence that local Communists had lined up behind him, and by his claims to territory on New Guinea still held by America's Dutch allies. The United States increased its aid to Indonesia and Southeast Asia generally in 1957, trying to protect the region against a possible threat from Mao's China, but it was unwilling to provide the Indonesian army with weapons it might use against the Dutch and unhappy about competing with the Soviets. Khrushchev, on the other hand, was delighted to have the opportunity to provide the Indonesian military with arms. The Soviet Union became its principal supplier in the late 1950s, a role the Soviets played for almost a decade.

Never very influential in Indonesia, having supported independence there primarily as a means of preempting Communist control of the country, the United States could view the breakup of the nation with notable ease. Eisenhower and Dulles had each indicated his preference for several smaller island states to a unified Indonesia aligned with the Communists. In 1958, the CIA, Eisenhower's weapon of choice, was instructed to support Sumatran secession. The Sumatran rebels received equipment and training from CIA agents, and CIA-operated planes flew bombing missions in their support. The effort failed and was exposed when one of the bombers was shot down and its pilot captured. Washington's efforts to deny culpability were unsuccessful.[32]

---

[32] Howard Palfrey Jones, *Indonesia: The Possible Dream* (New York, 1971), 129–46.

Indonesia's resources and strategic location were beyond American control. Soviet aid sustained an unpredictable friend in Indonesia, and the United States continued its own modest aid program, fearful of driving Sukarno into dependence on the Soviets. Neither superpower gained much of substance from wooing Sukarno, but Khrushchev had more to be happy about.

In the Congo, Khrushchev's gambit was less successful and the Soviets were no match for the CIA. The Republic of the Congo was granted independence by Belgium in June 1960, and its first premier was Patrice Lumumba, a man American Africanists regarded highly. Lumumba was perceived as the only national leader in a country in which tribalism posed a serious threat to internal unity. Although the mineral resources of the area were valued, neither Eisenhower nor Dulles conceived of strategic interests in Central Africa. No one in the Eisenhower administration thought American economic interests in the Congo were endangered. Here was one part of the world that might be spared the taint of superpower rivalry.[33]

A few days after the Congo became independent, Lumumba had reason to suspect that the Belgians were not quite ready to leave their holdings in his hands. A mutiny in the Congolese army was followed first by the rapid reinforcement of the forces the Belgians had retained in the Congo and then by the secession of Katanga province, the center of European investment. Belgian paratroopers prevented Lumumba from landing at Katanga's principal airport. Shaken by these events, Lumumba appealed successively to the United States, the United Nations, and the Soviet Union.

Initially, both the Americans and the Soviets deferred to the United Nations. A resolution calling for the withdrawal of Belgian troops and military assistance to Lumumba's government passed the Security Council. Several weeks passed without progress toward reunification. Lumumba appealed again to the Soviet Union. This time Khrushchev could not resist. Stretching the limits of Soviet airlift capabilities, he sent large quantities of equipment and a number of Soviet and Czech technicians to the Congo.

Soviet involvement changed the American perception of Lumumba and of the strategic importance of the Congo. Despite the fact that

[33] Stephan R. Weissman, *American Foreign Policy in the Congo, 1960–1964* (Ithaca, 1974), is my principal source on the Congo. See also Brian Urquhart, *A Life in Peace and War* (New York, 1987), 145–73.

Lumumba had appealed first to the United States, the Eisenhower administration came to see him as an unstable and dangerous radical likely to facilitate Communist inroads into Central Africa. The Congo, once Soviet interest had been manifested, became the keystone of sub-Saharan Africa. If Communists seized control of the Congo, they would be in position to dominate black Africa. Once again, the value of a peripheral area was enhanced by imbuing it with the weight of a dozen or more countries in its vicinity. Its loss became tantamount to the loss of the region, perhaps of a continent. Ultimately the world balance of power was at stake. The Soviets had to be stopped. The United States had to intervene.

The Eisenhower administration hoped to thwart Soviet designs without a direct confrontation. It rested its hopes on the United Nations, supplemented by a CIA operation to assassinate Lumumba. In September 1960 the president of the Congo, acting upon the advice of the American ambassador and the UN representative in the Congo, dismissed Lumumba. Lumumba attempted to seize power, but UN forces closed the airports, preventing Soviet planes from moving pro-Lumumba forces to the capital. Lumumba was placed under house arrest, and Joseph Mobutu, supported by the CIA, emerged as the strong man in the new regime.

The activities of the UN force in the Congo in opposition to Lumumba infuriated Khrushchev. For the next few months the battlefield shifted to New York, where the Soviet delegation, led by Khrushchev personally, attacked Secretary General Dag Hammarskjold. It was in the midst of this verbal abuse that Khrushchev performed his long-remembered shoe-pounding scene, expressing his displeasure at the remarks of another speaker. But the Soviets had been outmaneuvered in the Congo. They could not match American ability to project power into the region. The internal strife in the Congo continued for several years, through the Kennedy and Johnson administrations, through the end of Khrushchev's tenure, until Mobutu consolidated his power. Lumumba was murdered in 1961, and the Soviets and several African states supported his political allies, but ultimately a regime satisfactory to the United States prevailed. In the 1960s, the Soviets were a distant second in the competition with the United States for establishing influence in Africa.

After Stalin's death, after the Korean War, the Soviets and the Americans again began to grope toward some means of regulating their rivalry, of confronting each other without threatening the survival of the world. Khrushchev and his colleagues began the dismantling of the Stalinist state. They were dedicated Communists and, in Khrushchev's case, more committed to a messianic vision than Stalin had been. But they wanted to spare their people the terror and brutality of Stalinism, and they were willing to allow greater freedom to the peoples of nations within their sphere of influence. Haltingly, clumsily, they tried to create a more open, humane society in the Soviet Union. They tried to be less terrifying to their neighbors than Stalin had been. But the Soviet Union under Khrushchev's leadership became more of a threat to world peace. Stalin was malevolent, but a prudent man. Khrushchev was a decent man, but at times an impulsive, high-stakes gambler. Khrushchev was convinced that communism would prevail and that the days of American hegemony were numbered. He craved respect for his country and worked assiduously to plant the Hammer and Sickle around the world. The desire to make the Soviet Union a world power, at least equal to the United States, drove him to invest Soviet resources in remote regions of dubious importance. He would not concede the periphery to the Americans.

Soviet activity in the Third World raised the stakes in American eyes. Wherever a Soviet threat was alleged, the American national security apparatus was eager to counter it and Congress was likely to provide the necessary funds. Because Soviet capabilities were limited in the 1950s, the American response was usually a CIA operation. Some were arguably successful, as in Iran, Guatemala, and the Congo; others, as in Indonesia, were not.

In the 1950s, Europe, the central arena for both the United States and the Soviet Union, was relatively stable, the great-power contest stalemated. In Moscow, as in Washington, advisers to the leaders looked to the Third World for areas in which their nations might compete, might test the allure of their ideas and the skill of their operatives. The involvement of one superpower invariably changed a peripheral affair into an important one. Each had to demonstrate its resolve, lest its image as would-be hegemon be questioned, its ability to lead its bloc become suspect, as indeed occurred when Mao challenged Soviet leadership and de Gaulle refused to defer to the Americans.

5

CRISIS RESOLUTION

The tension of the years 1958–62 was without parallel in the four decades following World War II. Concerns over Berlin and Cuba led American forces to confront Soviet forces in situations in which a misstep, a rash action by an aggressive or nervous officer, might have led to war, might have led to the incineration and irradiation of much of the world. Nikita Khrushchev provoked each of these crises. The Soviet triumph in the space race – the launching of Sputnik in 1957 – confirmed his faith in the ultimate triumph of communism, and he hoped to accelerate the process in the era of his leadership. He found American arrogance intolerable and was intensely eager to terminate it by reversing the strategic balance. Berlin he delighted in calling the "testicles" of the West: "Every time I give them a yank they holler."[1] Cuba, ninety miles from the coast of Florida, provided a convenient platform for placing the nuclear missiles that would teach Americans what it felt like to live under the shadow of the bomb and would put an end to the American penchant for nuclear blackmail.

Although provoked or precipitated by Soviet behavior, the crises of this era cannot be understood without recognizing the interactive quality of Soviet actions and statements, the extent to which they were responses to the policies of the United States and its allies. The Soviets had reacted with notable calm to West German integration into NATO,

---

[1] Quoted in Cyrus Sulzberger, *Last of the Giants* (New York, 1970), 860. Much of Khrushchev's personality and style is apparent in Edward Crankshaw and Strobe Talbott, *Khrushchev Remembers* (Boston, 1970) and William Taubman, *Khrushchev: The Man and His Era* (New York, 2003). For a more pragmatic, "realist" Khrushchev, see Aleksander Fursenko and Timothy Naftali, *Khrushchev's Cold War: The Inside Story of an American Adversary* (New York, 2006).

presumably recognizing that NATO contained the Germans as well as the Soviet bloc. Soviet apprehensions about a resurgent Germany did not disappear, however. Germany's economic revival probably worried all non-Germans, but it was fear that the West Germans would gain access to nuclear weapons that most troubled Khrushchev and his colleagues. The United States was stockpiling "tactical" nuclear weapons and ballistic missiles capable of reaching the Soviet Union on German soil. The Germans had demanded and had been given nuclear-capable artillery and fighter-bombers. The Soviets were anxious to negotiate a settlement of European political issues that would recognize the status quo, including a divided Germany. They were equally interested in arms talks that would lead to a demilitarized or at least nuclear-free Central Europe. But Soviet overtures were unwelcome in Washington, where domestic and alliance politics precluded serious consideration of any plan approximating the neutralization of Central Europe, even when it came from George Kennan in his "disengagement" lectures of 1957. Provoking a crisis was a crude and dangerous means of winning Eisenhower's attention, but Khrushchev was not known for his finesse – and there may well have been no other means.

Similarly, widespread evidence of intensive American efforts to overthrow the Castro regime in Cuba led Soviet and Cuban leaders to anticipate an American attack in 1962. CIA and U.S.-based emigre operations against Cuba were frequent, the development of contingency plans for an invasion of Cuba by American forces was known to Soviet and Cuban intelligence, and plans for major U.S. military exercises in the Caribbean in the fall were no secret. The desire to protect his new-found friend in Cuba may not have been Khrushchev's primary reason for installing nuclear missiles on the island, but it unquestionably entered into his thinking and was later used by the Soviets to justify their actions.

The point is a simple one: Each step by one of the superpowers was taken in accord with its assessment of the other's intentions. Soviet activity in Berlin and Cuba was prompted by Soviet perceptions of German and American aggressiveness. Perceiving themselves as defenders of the status quo in Europe and Cuba and as victims of American intimidation, Soviet leaders sought to forestall change in both while simultaneously using missiles in Cuba to deter the American nuclear threat, to redress the strategic balance. American leaders who sent missiles to Germany out of fear of superior Soviet conventional capabilities could not conceive of Khrushchev's pressure on Berlin as defensive. When they determined to destroy Castro, they were eager to prevent Cuba from becoming a Soviet bastion in the Western Hemisphere. They were defending vital American interests. As usual, each saw the other's actions as threatening, its own as defensive. Neither acted in a vacuum: Each responded to its sense of the adversary's machinations.

Khrushchev's foreign policy seemed to be driven by three emotions, ultimately constrained by a pragmatic concern for the well-being of the Soviet state. He wanted the Soviet Union to achieve a status of at least equality with the United States and be accorded the respect due a superpower. He wanted to see communism prevail in the competition with capitalism. And he feared German power. The Berlin crisis he created in 1958 provides a useful example of how he functioned.

The revival of German power in the late 1950s, and evidence of growing German influence within the Western alliance, worried Soviet analysts. The ability of the West German government to frustrate American demands that it enlarge its conventional forces, and to obtain nuclear-capable weapons instead, demonstrated the lengths to which Washington would go to court the Bonn regime. It was obvious that the West German army wanted at least tactical nuclear weapons and was interested in strategic missiles – and that the United States was leaning toward acquiescence. In February 1958, the American commander of NATO declared that "defensive atomic weapons are absolutely indispensable for the strengthening of the defensive power of the Bundeswehr."[2] A project to train a German air force unit for atomic attack and the installation of a storage facility near where it was stationed were completed late in 1958. These were not the kinds of operations that could be hidden from Soviet and East German intelligence.

Similarly, Bonn's refusal to countenance the permanent division of Germany was troublesome. For the Soviet Union, a divided Germany was a relatively safe Germany. Unable to achieve an unarmed or neutral Germany in the mid-1950s, the Soviets were prepared to accept the status quo. They wanted to gain American assent to an independent East

---

[2] Quoted in Catherine Kelleher, *Germany and the Politics of Nuclear Weapons* (New York, 1975), 94.

Germany, and they wanted assurances that the West Germans would never obtain control of nuclear weapons. The United States remained committed to German reunification and increasingly looked to nuclear arms as essential to NATO forces outnumbered by the Red army.

For the Eisenhower administration, always skeptical of Soviet intentions, unwilling to concede legitimacy to Soviet striving for strategic parity, negotiations with Moscow were not an easy option. To the Republican Right any arrangement with the Soviets short of Soviet capitulation was likely to evoke cries of appeasement, of "Munich" or "Yalta." Any concessions to the Soviets over Germany would be labeled a betrayal. Similarly, the Bonn government was apprehensive of any Soviet-American talks that might compromise its stated goal of a unified Germany or its sovereignty. The NATO allies were not of one mind about negotiations with the Soviets over Germany. Only the British were enthusiastic supporters of the idea. Rather than risk antagonizing Bonn and roiling the political waters at home, the Eisenhower administration ignored Soviet signals.

Late in 1957, after the launching of Sputnik, Khrushchev began to campaign for a summit meeting with Eisenhower. Mao, in Beijing, certainly thought the time had come for the international Communist movement to take the initiative, as did several of Khrushchev's more belligerent colleagues in the Kremlin. Auspicious as the moment may have been from the Soviet perspective, it was hardly an opportune time for the Americans, who were left sputtering like their fizzled Vanguard rockets. Khrushchev waited a year, until after the Taiwan Strait crisis had passed, until after the midterm congressional elections of 1958, and then announced that the Western powers had six months in which to negotiate the status of West Berlin with East German authorities. When the deadline passed, the Soviets would sign a separate peace treaty with the East Germans, leaving them responsible for Western access to Berlin. To Dulles's warning that the West would use force if necessary to ensure its access to Berlin, Khrushchev replied that World War III would follow. Later in the Berlin crisis Khrushchev told Averell Harriman, "If you send in tanks, they will burn and make no mistake about it. If you want war, you can have it, and remember it will be your war. Our rockets will fly automatically."[3]

---

[3] Quoted in David Holloway, *The Soviet Union and the Arms Race* (New Haven, 1983), 84; Taubman, *Khrushchev*, 396–412.

Eisenhower was not stampeded by Khrushchev's rhetoric and refused to negotiate under ultimatum. He and Dulles, before the latter's death in 1959, both recognized the need to treat the Soviets with more civility, however – a relatively easy matter at the end of their days in office, when there was no political capital left to squander. Khrushchev was invited to the United States, spent a weekend at Camp David with Eisenhower, toured Hollywood, and went home unfulfilled when security precautions cheated him out of an opportunity to visit Disneyland. The deadline on Berlin was lifted, nonetheless. Khrushchev continued to raise the issue and apparently expected to resolve it at the summit meeting scheduled for May 1960. West German opposition, however, probably precluded any compromise over Berlin. By the spring of 1960, the American government knew unequivocally, from intelligence gathered by U-2 overflights of the Soviet Union, that Khrushchev's claims of missile superiority were unwarranted. Khrushchev knew, from the downing of a U-2 on the eve of the conference, that the Americans were aware that he was bluffing, were aware of the relative weakness of the Soviet Union. Khrushchev walked out of the summit, ostensibly over the U-2 issue; the Berlin issue smoldered, and flared dangerously again in June of 1961, to be confronted by the administration of John F. Kennedy.

Closer to home, the Eisenhower administration became intensely irritated with Fidel Castro, the Cuban leader who had been transmogrified from a Robin Hood–like figure, liberating his people from the evil ruler, Fulgencio Batista, into a possible Marxist-Leninist, an instrument of the international Communist movement suddenly rooted in America's sphere of influence. Batista had lost the confidence of Cuban elites and ultimately any hope of support from Washington, despite rumors of Communist influence in the revolutionary forces that sought to depose him. In due course he left for Miami, and early in January 1959, Castro led his guerrillas, the major fighting force of the revolution, into Havana and quickly organized a government.

The new Cuban government was passionately nationalistic and moderately leftist. In Latin American terms, that meant suspicion of the United States, longtime regional hegemon, and especially of American economic power. But initially, the regime in Havana was non-Communist, even anti-Communist, and included many men considered proponents of democratic capitalism, of programs no more radical than Roosevelt's New Deal. Quickly, however, moderate leaders gave way to radicals, the pace of reforms, including the expropriation of property owned by Americans, accelerated, the prospects for liberal democracy dimmed, and Castro gave a series of speeches critical of the United States. The Cuban Communist party was legalized and its members began to play a role, although relatively minor, in the implementation of Castro's programs. Indications of increased Communist influence worried Eisenhower, but the CIA detected no evidence of a Soviet role, no evidence that Castro might himself be a Communist. In February 1960, however, responding to Castro's overtures, Khrushchev sent his deputy premier, Anastas Mikoyan, to Cuba, ostensibly to visit a trade fair. A Cuban-Soviet trade agreement followed. That was enough to galvanize Eisenhower. An alternative to Castro, a Cuban government composed of the kind of democratic reformers who had worked with Castro to overthrow Batista, was clearly necessary. Eisenhower would not countenance sending in the marines, as Teddy Roosevelt or Woodrow Wilson might well have done. On the other hand, he hardly needed the marines: He had the CIA.[4]

Eisenhower's preference for dealing with unruly Third World leaders was to minimize overt American involvement. As with Iran and Guatemala, he wanted the CIA to find local forces more receptive to American political and economic values and to support such forces in a coup. Soon the CIA was training Cuban exiles for the invasion of their homeland, but the CIA could never pull together the Cuban "government-in-exile" that was the prerequisite for Eisenhower's order to send the men ashore. In the interim, the American government initiated a process of economic pressures, beginning with reduction of the quota of Cuban sugar the United States was committed to buy. Ultimately, the CIA developed a series of bizarre plots to assassinate Castro, including subcontracting the assignment to the Mafia in the early 1960s.[5]

American hostility served Castro well, both in rallying the Cuban people behind his increasingly radical domestic program and in gaining

[4] Taubman, *Khrushchev*, 532–3. See Leycester Coltman, *The Real Fidel Castro* (New Haven, 2003), for a balanced analysis of Castro's rise and ideological transitions; and Richard E. Welch, Jr., *The Response to Revolution: The United States and the Cuban Revolution, 1959–1961* (Chapel Hill, 1985), 3–63.

[5] Thomas Powers, *The Man Who Kept the Secrets: Richard Helms and the CIA* (New York, 1979).

the support of a wary Khrushchev. In May 1960, diplomatic relations were established between Cuba and the Soviet Union, and Khrushchev once again rattled his rockets, warning the United States not to attack Cuba. Soviet leaders were still skeptical about Castro's intentions and uneasy about challenging the United States in its sphere of interest, but the opportunity to twit the Americans proved irresistible. A pattern that men like Nasser and Sukarno had previously exploited quickly developed. As the United States intensified its pressures on Castro, he turned more and more to the Soviet bloc for support. Unlike Nasser and Sukarno, somewhere along the line, in late 1960 or 1961, Castro decided to become a Marxist-Leninist.

In December 1960, Moscow and Havana issued a joint communique in which the Cubans declared their support for Soviet foreign policy. In January 1961, Castro ordered the drastic reduction of American embassy personnel in Cuba. Eisenhower angrily withdrew American recognition of the Castro regime. Plans for the CIA-sponsored Cuban-exile invasion of the island gathered momentum. As he prepared to leave office, Eisenhower was warned that the operation might soon be irreversible. But in a few days, Castro would become John F. Kennedy's problem.

Clearly, the key player in the interaction between Cuba, the United States, and the Soviet Union was Fidel Castro. Castro dominated the Cuban revolution and determined its pace and direction. Castro decided correctly that the United States would be an obstacle to his objectives and that the Soviet Union might prove a useful counterweight. Castro needled the Americans and reeled in Khrushchev. It was not a matter of great powers exploiting an underdeveloped country, manipulating its unsophisticated leaders. Castro played the great powers like a virtuoso, and once he declared himself a Communist, in December 1961, he made it extraordinarily difficult for the Soviets to abandon him.

American policy might have been wiser. On the other hand, American political culture precluded support for the radical revolution Castro wanted. Friendly relations are not readily imaginable between Cuban revolutionaries weaned on tales of American imperialism, and American leaders convinced of the benign role their country had always played since it liberated Cuba from Spanish brutality in 1898. A less hostile policy, an acceptance of the Cuban revolution, however grudging, without assassination and invasion plots, might have lessened Castro's need for Soviet assistance and might have left Khrushchev less of an opportunity for mischief. But the odds were not good: The Soviet-American competition was simply too rich a field for a clever leader like Castro to exploit, and American responses to a whiff of communism too reflexive.

The election returns were hardly in before Khrushchev began overtures to President-elect Kennedy. The Soviets had given up hope of progress on any of the issues dividing the superpowers in the waning months of the Eisenhower administration. They were eager to signal their desire to work with the new administration, to give and gain assurances on the status quo in Europe, to establish mutually acceptable guidelines for the peaceful competition in the Third World that Khrushchev was confident would result in the triumph of communism. They hoped the new administration would be less prone to using nuclear blackmail, more respectful of Soviet interests, more accepting of the Soviet right to compete for influence around the world, more tolerant of Soviet support for radical regimes in the Third World, of "socialist internationalism."[6]

Soviet hopes for accommodation were matched in Washington, but Khrushchev's terms were not acceptable. No less than its predecessors, the Kennedy administration was committed to containing communism, to preventing the spread of Soviet influence, and to maintaining and capitalizing on American strategic superiority. Kennedy and his advisers were profoundly troubled by Khrushchev's threats regarding Berlin as well as Soviet activities in the Congo, Laos, and Cuba. Moreover, Khrushchev's signals were often confusing, an unfortunate mixture of appeals for peaceful coexistence and attempts to intimidate. On January 6, 1961, addressing a Communist party rally in Moscow, Khrushchev stressed Soviet commitment to "wars of national liberation," just wars that would ensure communism's ultimate victory in the struggle with the West. Kennedy's Soviet specialists interpreted the speech as an intensely hostile warning of increased guerrilla activity and subversion in the Third World.[7] On February 17, the Soviets resumed

---

[6] John Lewis Gaddis, *The Soviet Union and the United States* (New York, 1978), 233; William Zimmerman, *Soviet Perspectives on International Relations, 1956–1967* (Princeton, 1969), 133–35, 179–82, 213–25; Marc Trachtenberg, *History and Strategy* (Princeton, 1991), 215–16.

[7] Llewellyn Thompson, American ambassador to Moscow, cable, January 19, 1961, John F. Kennedy Papers, President's Office File, Box 127, John F. Kennedy Library. See also Charles Bohlen, draft of approach to Khrushchev, June 1, 1961, and George Kennan, cable, June 2, 1961, Box 126.

pressure on Berlin. However peaceful Khrushchev's intentions may have been, American analysts perceived him as a volatile and dangerous adversary.

Kennedy, in his first days in office, found crises in Laos, where the Western position was deteriorating rapidly, the Congo, where the new nation's disintegration appeared to allow the Soviets a foothold in Central Africa, and Cuba, which seemed to move closer to the Soviets daily. CIA support of the Laotian Right had destabilized a neutralist regime but had proved inadequate to combat the Soviet and Vietnamese support of the Laotian Left it had stimulated. The agency was faring better in the Congo, where efforts to eliminate Lumumba were on track. Implementation of the plan for an exile invasion of Cuba required the new president's prompt attention. The exiles trained and equipped by the CIA had to be sent in or there would be a "disposal problem." One could not simply send hundreds of armed Cubans back to Miami.[8]

Kennedy and his advisers considered themselves to be supportive of social revolution in the underdeveloped world. They could not conceive, however, of the legitimacy of Communist involvement or Soviet assistance to such a movement. Castro was reputedly a Communist. He had unquestionably allowed known Communists to play an increasingly important role in his government. He had opened the door to Soviet influence in the Caribbean. He had betrayed the dream of freedom that drove the Cuban people when they rose against Batista. The CIA reported that more Soviet-bloc military equipment was headed for Cuba. Castro was unacceptable: His regime had to be destroyed.

In meetings among Kennedy's advisers, the CIA and the Department of Defense pressed for orders to implement the exile invasion plan. Dean Rusk, the secretary of state, skeptical of CIA estimates of a popular uprising in support of the invaders, fearful that American involvement would be exposed, preferred economic sanctions. But in addition to the exile disposal problem, there was the likelihood that rejection of the CIA plan would be leaked to the public. Kennedy, who had been critical of Eisenhower's "loss" of Cuba, could ill afford the domestic political ramifications of appearing weaker than Eisenhower, of having canceled a plan the Eisenhower administration had devised for overthrowing Castro. To meet Rusk's concerns, the operation was

[8] Warren I. Cohen, *Dean Rusk* (Totowa, N.J., 1980), 112–32.

whittled back, the invaders denied air cover the CIA deemed essential. On April 17, 1961, the CIA-trained Cuban exiles were sent ashore at the Bay of Pigs.

Air raids by CIA-operated bombers two days earlier had failed to eliminate the tiny Cuban air force but had prompted a Cuban military alert and protest to the United Nations. A second raid, scheduled for the morning of the invasion, was canceled to avoid further implicating the United States. The exile force landed on inhospitable terrain without air cover and without critical ammunition and communication equipment, lost in the course of the operation. An attempt to blow up the causeways leading to the beach failed, the Cuban air force pinned down the invaders, and the Cuban army poured into the area to mop them up. The uprising of the Cuban people predicted by the CIA and essential to the success of the plan never occurred. The CIA scheme proved to have been poorly conceived. Implementation, undermined by administration modifications, proved to be a disaster. Only a major assault by the armed forces of the United States could succeed – and Kennedy was not ready for that.[9]

The Bay of Pigs invasion was a humiliating defeat for the United States, equal to that of the British and French at Suez. Having castigated its allies for resorting to atavistic imperialism, for failing to appreciate Egyptian nationalism, American leaders had violated their much beloved principle of nonintervention, to which they were bound by treaty. They attempted to overthrow the Cuban government and they had failed miserably. Adlai Stevenson, the American ambassador to the United Nations, having denied vehemently that his government would ever commit such an act, was greatly embarrassed to discover that the president he served had deceived him. Castro's popularity with his people increased, as did his appeal to Nikita Khrushchev. In July 1961 a Soviet-Cuban alliance was announced, and in December Castro declared himself a Marxist-Leninist. With Washington's assistance, Castro transformed revolutionary Cuba from an irritant to a powder keg.

A month after accepting responsibility for the Cuban debacle, Kennedy decided the time had come for a summit meeting with Khrushchev. The two men met in Vienna on June 3 and 4, where whatever good

[9] Tim Weiner, *Legacy of Ashes: The History of the CIA* (New York, 2007), 173–9.

intentions either may have had evaporated in an atmosphere of confrontation. The desire both leaders had to prevent conflict in areas remote from their nations' vital interests and the hope that they could reduce tensions between the two countries were forgotten as each took a rigid ideological position. Khrushchev, insisting that socialism was on the rise, accused Kennedy of trying to deny the Soviet Union the fruits of impending victory. Kennedy fell back on containment, denying the Soviet Union a right to support any new radical movements that might emerge. Perhaps surprisingly in that context, the two men were able to agree to try to neutralize Laos.

The most troublesome issue to arise at Vienna was Berlin. Khrushchev was convinced Kennedy could be pushed around, that he was inexperienced and immature, less intelligent than Eisenhower. He presented the young American president with an ultimatum, threatening to sign a peace treaty with the East Germans that would terminate Western access to Berlin. Kennedy replied that the United States would stand by its commitment. Each man warned that war would follow if the other did not back down. Each went home to take steps to increase the credibility of his threat.

Kennedy's advisers had been preparing for a crisis over Berlin since entering office. Dean Acheson, Truman's secretary of state, had been consulted and his advice was harsh: The Western position on Germany and West Berlin was nonnegotiable; American forces should be mobilized to demonstrate the willingness to fight. Kennedy was dissatisfied with so rigid a posture. He thought de facto acceptance of the division of Germany was sensible, that agreement to negotiate was superior to brinkmanship. Neither Kennedy nor any of his colleagues were willing to surrender anything of substance, but before the Vienna meeting, most were willing to negotiate as a means of easing tensions. Khrushchev's attempt to intimidate Kennedy at Vienna and afterward, however, provoked a more Achesonian, macho response.

On July 25, 1961, Kennedy spoke to the American people on national television, explaining the importance of Berlin and declaring that the American military position there and Western access to Berlin were not negotiable. He then announced a large, 25 percent increase in American conventional military forces, expanding the draft and ordering a partial mobilization of the reserves. Lest the point be missed, he warned the

Soviet Union against miscalculating the determination of the United States to preserve its position in Germany. Khrushchev had created the crisis, but the United States would not back off. The decision for war or peace would have to be made in Moscow.

Khrushchev retreated immediately. On July 27, he sent assurances through an American visitor that he did not want war. In a speech on August 7, he called for an easing of tension, an end to the war psychosis. He promised to take no military action and softened his position on Berlin markedly: The Soviets would not "infringe upon any lawful interests of the Western powers. Any barring of access to West Berlin, any blockade of West Berlin, is entirely out of the question."[10] In another speech a few days later, he pleaded for negotiation.

The crisis took a new direction as Khrushchev spoke. West Berlin had long been the principal escape route for East Germans fleeing to the West. In July, fearful that the West would surrender to Khrushchev's threats, thirty thousand East German refugees slipped into West Berlin. On August 12, four thousand crossed into West Berlin. The East German regime, faced with imminent collapse, begged Khrushchev for permission to staunch the flow.

Soviet analysts examining Kennedy's July 25 speech noted that he had said nothing of guaranteeing continued access between East and West Berlin. They decided to gamble. They would block access between the Western and Soviet sectors of Berlin, preventing escape from the East – and hope the American response would not be violent. On August 13 barriers started going up. The United States did not respond: The barriers did not infringe on interests Kennedy deemed vital. The Soviet gambit worked, and what began as barbed wire obstacles became the Berlin Wall. Quickly the crisis receded. The United States would not attack the barriers, would not take the offensive in a situation in which the stakes were very high for Khrushchev. He had achieved his minimal goal, an end to the bleeding of the East German regime.[11]

[10] *New York Times*, August 8, 1961.

[11] Paul Y. Hammond, *Cold War and Détente* (New York, 1975), 169–70; Robert M. Slusser, *The Berlin Crisis of 1961* (Baltimore, 1973), 93–5; Alexander L. George and Richard Smoke, *Deterrence in American Foreign Policy* (New York, 1974), 436–40; James L. Richardson, *Germany and the Atlantic Alliance* (Cambridge, Mass., 1966), 286; Jean E. Smith, *The Defense of Berlin* (Baltimore, 1963), 258–78.

In a variety of ways, including the use of a "back channel" line to Kennedy established at the Soviet leader's request, Khrushchev again signaled his desire to reduce tensions between the superpowers. In September, Secretary of State Dean Rusk met with Soviet Foreign Minister Andrei Gromyko three times, and in mid-October, Khrushchev withdrew his deadline for settling the Berlin issue. The Soviet Union had not achieved its goals in Central Europe, but it had dragged the United States into a dialogue over its concerns. Kennedy had shown his administration to be firm on essentials, willing to give a little at the edges.

American strategic supremacy left Khrushchev little room to maneuver. On October 21, Deputy Secretary of Defense Roswell Gilpatric underscored the point in a public address, declaring that the United States could absorb a Soviet first strike and devastate the Soviet Union in retaliation. The United States was not negotiating from weakness. Any Soviet pretense to superiority was brushed aside, and Khrushchev's bluster proved unproductive. Indeed, his oscillation between threats and peaceful gestures served to discredit Soviet diplomacy, to serve best those ideologues who argued that changes in Soviet tactics should not obscure the inexorable Communist drive toward world domination.

The failure of Khrushchev's efforts to advance Soviet ends in Germany appears to have weakened him at home. Some of his critics were troubled by his crude threats and embarrassing retreats. Others, echoing Mao's fulminations from Beijing, charged Khrushchev with excessive caution. The historian Robert Slusser has suggested that a Soviet-American tank confrontation on October 26 that came close to starting World War III might have occurred in a moment when Khrushchev's opponents in the Kremlin temporarily controlled the apparatus of government. To prevent further encroachment by East German police, the American military commander in Berlin had ordered tanks into position at a checkpoint between East and West. The East German government called for help and the local Soviet commander sent his armor rumbling forward. The tanks faced each other, with an officer in any one of them capable of starting a war. Suddenly, the next day, Soviet tanks withdrew. Slusser contends that the tank movement had been arranged by Khrushchev's opponents at the Communist Party Congress then in session and that their removal was a partial victory for Khrushchev and his attempt at peaceful accommodation with the West. Recent accounts by William

Taubman and Vladislav Zubock do not support Slusser's hypothesis and downplay the incident.[12]

The Soviets increased the pressure again in February 1962, harassing Western flights into Berlin, but once more Rusk and Gromyko talked the tension away. The issue did not disappear: It could not until both sides committed themselves to the status quo in Germany, or the two German states had worked things out satisfactorily between them. But the aura of crisis faded once the Soviets concluded the United States could not be persuaded under any circumstances to remove its forces from West Berlin. As Rusk remarked to the Senate Foreign Relations Committee, the Soviets might have postponed the attempt to resolve the issue until they achieved strategic parity, a day toward which they were working frenetically.

In preparation for a meeting between President Kennedy and Soviet Foreign Minister Gromyko on October 18, 1962, the head of the Department of State's Berlin Task Force prepared a memorandum and "talking points on Berlin" for the president. The talking points contained a succinct summary of seventeen months of confrontation and negotiation, describing the talks as useful to both sides, especially as a means of clarifying their respective positions. But "no one could realistically claim ... that much progress has been made toward an understanding on Berlin which would remove this problem as a point of possible confrontation in which a grave danger of war inheres."[13]

The author of the memorandum and the expert on Soviet affairs who advised Kennedy wanted the president to leave no doubt in Soviet minds that the West was united and would fight, if necessary, over Berlin. What they did not mention – because they did not know – was that the United States and the Soviet Union were on the verge of nuclear war over Cuba. On October 14, an American U-2 flight had obtained unmistakable evidence that the Soviets were building missile sites in Cuba. For Kennedy and other American leaders, Berlin had become a secondary issue.

The Kennedy administration had not been inactive toward Cuba since recovering from the failure of the Bay of Pigs operation. Diplomatically,

---

[12] Slusser, *Berlin Crisis of 1961*, 430, 440–1. Taubman, *Khrushchev*, 773–4, footnote 29; Vladislav M. Zubock, *A Failed Empire: The Soviet Union in the Cold War from Stalin to Gorbachev* (Chapel Hill, 2007), 142.

[13] Rusk for Kennedy, undated [October 17, 1962], drafted by Martin Hillenbrand, obtained from Department of State through the Freedom of Information Act.

it had won modest support for its efforts to isolate the Castro regime within the hemisphere and nominal support from its NATO allies for its economic warfare against Cuba. Although Kennedy had declared publicly that a Communist regime in Cuba was intolerable, no further thought was being given to using Cuban exile forces to overthrow Castro. On the other hand, the American government was doing little to suppress piratical acts by exiles against Cuban vessels; and far worse, it was experimenting with a variety of covert operations, some of which were designed to humiliate Castro – and others, to murder him. Perhaps most threatening were contingency plans for American forces to invade the island and the major exercises conducted in the spring of 1962 to test these plans. Soviet and Cuban intelligence services were aware of some of the plots and of the existence of contingency plans for an invasion, which they may have believed imminent. The Cuban government unquestionably had reason to be anxious, to lean more heavily on the Soviet Union, to allow the Soviets to build missile sites directed against the United States.[14]

Although eager to have Soviet protection against the mounting danger to his regime, Castro preferred to perceive his acceptance of the missiles as a Cuban contribution to the Communist cause. He was allowing the Soviets to station missiles on his territory, with the consequent risk of American reprisals, in order to allow the Soviets and the international Communist movement they served to gain a strategic advantage. In short, he was doing Khrushchev a favor. Khrushchev and the generation of Soviet analysts that survived him have insisted, on the other hand, that they had acted to defend the Cubans, that the missiles, the planes, and the Soviet combat troops they sent to Cuba were intended to stave off the American invasion.[15]

Men and women usually see their self-serving acts as altruistic, their aggressive acts as defensive. The study of motivation is no easier when one examines foreign policy decisions than other human endeavors. Khrushchev may well have contrived an explanation for his decision after he decided impulsively to send the missiles. Without doubt he chafed at the fact of Soviet strategic inferiority and its implications for

---

[14] Raymond L. Garthoff, *Reflections on the Cuban Missile Crisis*, rev. ed. (Washington, D.C., 1989), 6–8.
[15] Crankshaw and Talbott, *Khrushchev Remembers*, 493–500; Garthoff, *Reflections*, 11–24.

Map 2. The Caribbean, 1954–91.

Countries in which U.S. perceived Communist threat

ATLANTIC OCEAN

LEEWARD
ISLANDS

GRENADA

VIRGIN
ISLANDS

WINDWARD
ISLANDS

PUERTO
RICO

DOMINICAN
REPUBLIC

CARIBBEAN SEA

VENEZUELA

BAHAMA
ISLANDS

HAITI

Nassau

Guantánamo

COLOMBIA

CUBA

JAMAICA

FLORIDA

Key West

PANAMA

COSTA
RICA

GULF OF MEXICO

NICARAGUA

HONDURAS

MEXICO

BELIZE

EL SALVADOR

GUATEMALA

PACIFIC OCEAN

the German question and every other matter at issue with the United States. The Gilpatric speech of October 1961 had revealed to the world the lack of substance behind Khrushchev's claims of Soviet superiority. Something had to be done to redress the strategic balance. In April 1962, Khrushchev was troubled at the news that American intermediate-range ballistic missiles (IRBMs) in Turkey, on the very border of the Soviet Union, had become operational. It was at that moment that he apparently conceived of the idea of placing Soviet IRBMs in the shadow of the United States, in Cuba. As Raymond Garthoff, a participant in the events and later scholarly analyst of them, has argued, the most likely reason for Soviet leaders' risking the Cuban missile venture "was almost certainly a perceived need to prevent the United States from using its growing strategic superiority to compel Soviet concessions … a shared judgment of the leadership that world political perceptions of the strategic balance mattered, and that the Soviet Union's position in 1962 needed shoring up."[16] The fact that Cuba would simultaneously be protected was a likely collateral virtue of the action but, as students of causality might argue, not a "sufficient cause." It is quite clear that the Soviets did not anticipate a crisis: They expected to be able to install the missiles secretly and to present the United States with a fait accompli, to which Washington would acquiesce reluctantly.

In late August 1962, the director of the CIA informed Kennedy and his senior foreign policy advisers that he suspected the Soviets of placing offensive missiles in Cuba. A review of the evidence led Rusk and the others to reject the idea. There was no doubt that the Soviets were providing the Cubans with military equipment, but the secretaries of state and defense and their analysts concluded that the buildup was defensive. The Soviets had been warned categorically that offensive weapons would not be tolerated in Cuba, and there was no inclination to believe they would take the risk.

As the midterm election of 1962 approached, the Republican opposition was increasingly critical of the administration's failure to eliminate the Communist regime in Cuba. Kennedy's aides argued that Cuba was not an offensive threat, that the military buildup was defensive,

---

[16] Garthoff, *Reflections*, 21; see also Jack Snyder, *Myths of Empire* (Ithaca, 1991), 246–7; Zubock stresses the defense of Cuba in analyzing Soviet motivation. See *Failed Empire*, 143–5.

and that allegations of Soviet missiles were without foundation. Quick to discredit their domestic political opponents, administration leaders discounted the mounting evidence of Khrushchev's gamble. They were further misled by a deliberate Soviet program of deception, of Soviet assurances it would not put offensive weapons into Cuba, a tactic that continued even after the Americans had discovered the missiles. As late as October 14, McGeorge Bundy, Kennedy's national security adviser, assured a television audience that there was no evidence the Soviets were preparing an offensive capability in Cuba. That very day the U-2 returned with unmistakable evidence of a missile complex under construction at San Cristobal. The films were processed on October 15, and by midnight all of the top policymakers except the president were aware that the United States, and especially the Kennedy administration, faced catastrophe.

Briefed as he awoke the next morning, the president called together a group of advisers called the Executive Committee of the National Security Council, or Ex Comm. What were the Soviets up to? How should the United States respond? Contingency plans anticipated an invasion or an air strike, and the U.S. military commenced preparations for both. There was considerable support for an air strike but the opposition prevailed. Secretary of Defense Robert McNamara argued that Soviet missiles in Cuba meant little more than Soviet missiles in Russia. Should the Soviets launch an attack, the United States would destroy the Soviet Union no matter where the attack originated. He was unmoved by the contention that Soviet missiles in Cuba might eliminate the strategic advantage the United States enjoyed. He contended that parity was inevitable and it might be advantageous to American security if the Soviets achieved it sooner rather than later.[17]

After two days of discussion, even McNamara was persuaded that a strong response was required. For domestic political reasons as well as for his image abroad, the president had to demonstrate that the United States could not be deceived and challenged with impunity. The choices of action narrowed to an air strike against the missile sites or a blockade, to be followed by an air strike or an invasion if the Soviets did not respond adequately. Tense debate ensued among the president's

---

[17] Graham Allison, *Essence of Decision* (Boston, 1971), 195–6; James G. Blight and David A. Welch, *On the Brink* (New York, 1989), 23–4.

advisers, with Dean Acheson, supported by the military leaders, calling for military action. Ultimately, agreement on a blockade was reached, at least in part because Kennedy was not convinced that the air strike would suffice. He very likely suspected the military, dismayed by his equivocation at the Bay of Pigs, of attempting to draw him into the invasion of Cuba. His principal Soviet analyst, Llewellyn Thompson, warned against the possibility of Khrushchev responding irrationally if Soviet troops were killed in an air strike. Kennedy would start with a blockade. American forces began to move into position October 20. On October 22, the Soviets, the American people, and the rest of the world would be informed.[18]

An hour before Kennedy addressed a national television audience, the Soviet ambassador was apprised. He claimed then, and forever after, that he knew nothing of the missiles until Rusk told him. At 7:00 P.M. Eastern Standard Time, Kennedy told Americans of the discovery of the missile sites, spelled out their meaning for the United States, and explained the response he was making. To Americans – to knowledgeable people everywhere – there came an awareness that they hovered on the edge of extinction. The danger of nuclear incineration hung over Rusk's briefing of the ambassadors of nonaligned nations. With a sense that they might never see each other again, each ambassador shook Rusk's hand, perhaps murmuring a word of hope on the way out. The initiative had returned to Nikita Khrushchev. His choice was war or surrender and his response might come as swiftly as an intercontinental ballistic missile.

Khrushchev and his advisers were taken completely by surprise and badly shaken by the president's address. Soviet intelligence had failed to pick up any indication that the United States had discovered the missiles or that the president and his most senior advisers had spent the week in emergency meetings. Firing the missiles and provoking certain retaliation against the Soviet Union was inconceivable. The central question was what could be salvaged. Might the United States accept the weapons already in Cuba in exchange for an agreement not to send more? How serious was the United States about the blockade? Would the Americans use the opportunity to invade Cuba, and, if so, how would the Soviet Union respond?[19]

---

[18] Elie Abel, *The Missile Crisis* (Philadelphia, 1966), 80–93.
[19] Garthoff, *Reflections*, 56–9.

Initially, the Soviets denied the American charges, condemned the blockade as piracy, sent in submarines to probe the blockade ahead of their surface ships, and ordered Soviet forces in Cuba readied for combat. They were 42,000 strong, far in excess of the numbers estimated by American intelligence, and armed with tactical nuclear weapons, to be used at the discretion of the local commander.[20] The Cubans mobilized their reserves, tripling their forces under arms to a total of 270,000 men. Construction at the missile sites accelerated. World War III was approaching rapidly.

Directed by the president to track Soviet submarines in the area and protect American vessels, the U.S. Navy used low-explosive depth charges to force the Soviet submarines to the surface. On October 24, the Strategic Air Command (SAC) was put on full alert, with the order given "in the clear," leaving nothing to Soviet imagination. Khrushchev could have no illusions about the seriousness of American intent. He chose not to challenge the blockade. On October 25 the last Soviet ships heading for Cuba stopped and turned back. "Eyeball to eyeball," the Soviets had blinked.[21]

Kennedy and his advisers were enormously relieved by the reports of Soviet ship movements, but they were also aware that Soviet forces in Cuba were still working around the clock to get their missiles operational. One member of Ex Comm noted that the difference between war before the missiles could be used and war afterward would be millions of American lives. The United States would have to attack before any of them were ready, an eventuality estimated to be only two or three days away. The Soviets were informed of the American intent. Castro was so certain the attack was coming that he spent the night of October 26 at a bomb shelter in the Soviet Embassy from whence he urged Khrushchev to stand firm.[22]

On October 26, Aleksander Fomin, the senior KGB officer in the Soviet Embassy in Washington, suddenly contacted John Scali, ABC's State Department reporter, to ask if his friends in the department would be willing to offer a public pledge not to invade Cuba if the

[20] Raymond L. Garthoff, "The Havana Conference on the Cuban Missile Crisis," in Woodrow Wilson International Center for Scholars, *Cold War International History Project Bulletin* 1 (Spring 1992): 2–4.

[21] Garthoff, *Reflections*, 61–2, 67–9.

[22] Garthoff, *Reflections*, 91.

Soviets removed the missiles, promised not to reintroduce them, and allowed UN verification. Scali went immediately to a contact in the State Department, who passed the message to the secretary of state and the president. Rusk remembered that an unofficial exchange of views had led to the cease-fire in Korea in 1951 and thought a breakthrough possible. Scali was instructed to inform Fomin that time was short, no more than two days, and given a piece of paper with a message from the "highest levels" in the U.S. government indicating that the Americans saw "real possibilities" in the proposal. It was later alleged by Soviet authorities that Fomin was exploring on his own, but in October 1962, the president and his advisers assumed the terms he proposed came from Moscow. Later that day, Kennedy received a long cable from Khrushchev indicating that he understood the danger of the situation, wanted to avoid conflict, and was prepared to negotiate. He implied that if the United States agreed not to invade Cuba, the missiles could be removed, but he did not specify his terms. Rusk and Llewellyn Thompson concluded that the settlement outlined by Fomin represented Khrushchev's thoughts, that the Soviets were prepared to back off, that the crisis was over. They guessed that Khrushchev had been struggling with other Soviet leaders eager to challenge the United States and had used Fomin to circumvent them.[23]

That night Robert Kennedy, the president's brother, met secretly with the Soviet ambassador, who indicated that removal of the American missiles in Turkey might help to resolve the affair. Bobby called the president, who authorized him to tell the Soviets that he had long considered removing the missiles and that he expected to do so shortly after the crisis was over. Kennedy's message was passed to Khrushchev.[24]

On the morning of October 27, a second cable was received from Khrushchev, this time demanding that the missiles in Turkey be removed as a condition for removal of the missiles in Cuba. Unaware of the meeting between Bobby Kennedy and the Soviet ambassador the night before, most members of Ex Comm argued for rejecting what they perceived as Khrushchev's additional demand. They feared a trade could

---

[23] Cohen, *Dean Rusk*, 156–7; Garthoff, *Reflections*, 80–1, is inclined to accept Fomin's claim he was acting on his own. No evidence indicating that Fomin was serving as Khrushchev's back-channel contact has emerged.

[24] Blight and Welch, *On the Brink*, 337–8.

damage relations with Turkey and other American allies, who might fear that the United States would sacrifice the protection it offered its allies whenever it was threatened.

Shortly after Khrushchev's second cable was received, Ex Comm was informed that a U-2 had been shot down over Cuba. Later that morning, for the first time, low-level reconnaissance flights were fired upon. A sudden sense that the Soviet position might be stiffening, that military action might still be necessary, swept through the group. Acheson and American military leaders suspected the Soviets were hiding something, that they were stalling until some of the missiles were operational. They still favored air strikes and an invasion. In fact, local Soviet air defense commanders, uninformed of the delicate negotiation under way, had heightened the tension.[25]

That afternoon, Ex Comm agreed to a proposal put forward by Robert Kennedy. Khrushchev's second cable was ignored and the president agreed to the terms implied in the first cable, presumably spelled out by Fomin. Robert Kennedy personally took the president's message to the Soviet Embassy and informed the Soviet ambassador that his brother was prepared to give the required assurances that the United States would not invade Cuba. The United States, however, could not unilaterally remove the missiles from Turkey. Nonetheless, the president was confident that NATO would withdraw them shortly. If, on the other hand, the Soviets did not agree promptly to remove their missiles from Cuba, the United States would remove them. Although Khrushchev was not told, plans for an air strike on October 29 or 30 had been developed. Again, the decision for war or peace rested with the Soviet leader – unless one of his officers or an American naval or SAC commander acted precipitately.

On Sunday morning, October 28, it was all over. Khrushchev announced that he had ordered the weapons Americans described as offensive to be dismantled and returned to the Soviet Union. The joy in Washington was not matched in Cuba, where Soviet officers wept at the news and Castro was enraged. Castro never permitted UN supervision or verification of the removal of the missiles, and there were disagreements about Soviet bombers and troops stationed in Cuba, disagreements that took weeks to resolve. The United States never gave formal

---

[25] Garthoff, *Reflections*, 82–85.

assurances that it would not invade Cuba and remained hostile to the Castro regime long after relations with the major Communist powers improved. But the gravest crisis of the Cold War had ended with a victory for the forces of peace.[26]

In 1962, Nikita Khrushchev brought the world close to nuclear war. It is not necessary to ignore American provocations against Cuba or nuclear blackmail of the Soviet Union to charge that Khrushchev gambled impulsively, putting at risk the lives of hundreds of millions of people. He acted deceitfully, putting the missiles in Cuba while sending Kennedy assurances that he would do nothing of the sort. There can be no doubt that he hoped to score a diplomatic and military coup against the United States.

John F. Kennedy's response to the missiles discovered in October 1962 brought the world a step closer to disaster, perhaps unnecessarily. McNamara was probably right – that strategic parity between the United States and the Soviet Union was inevitable and that the gap was merely being closed sooner rather than later; that Soviet missiles in Cuba were strategically tolerable. By treating the discovery of the missiles as an event of no great import, by accepting Soviet claims that they were defensive, by stressing the enormous retaliatory power of the United States, as Gilpatric had the previous year, the Kennedy administration might have found the rest of the world impressed again by American confidence. It might be argued that the only grave threat posed by the discovery of the missiles was to the political future of the Kennedy administration; that Kennedy's greatest fear was that the Republican opposition would use the missiles, the existence of which the administration had consistently denied, to ride the Cuban issue to victory in the congressional elections of 1962 and, yet more troubling, in the presidential election of 1964.

Once the administration decided on a strong response, its plans were conceived carefully and executed with an appropriate balance of courage and flexibility. Perhaps most interesting is the fact that Kennedy chose to keep his flexibility secret from the American people. It was six years before they knew that he had agreed that American missiles would come out of Turkey, and more than a quarter of a century before

[26] Melvyn Leffler, *For the Soul of Mankind* (New York, 2007), 151–8.

Americans, including Ex Comm members, discovered that the president's brother had discussed the trade in one of a series of secret meetings with the Soviet ambassador before Khrushchev raised it. Apparently obsessed with a need to present a public image of toughness, convinced that it was essential to his political success, Kennedy chose to have the American people believe he had won in a man-to-man showdown with the Soviet premier.

In the months that followed, the missile crisis came to be seen by many analysts as a watershed in Soviet-American relations. Both American and Soviet leaders generally acted with greater prudence and sought détente. Much of the tension drained out of the confrontation in the last year of Kennedy's life. A Moscow-Washington "hot line" was set up, permitting direct and immediate communication between the leaders. Agreement was reached on a treaty banning atmospheric nuclear testing by the superpowers. These arguably were not major steps, but they reversed the direction of the previous two years, suggesting that the future might well be one of peaceful coexistence instead of inevitable conflict, that the bomb shelters being built across the United States might not be necessary. They were steps toward building the mutual trust that had never been possible in Stalin's day and that Khrushchev had precluded by his bluster and deceit. Further improvement of relations would depend on the performance of each country, on the respect and confidence that might develop between its leaders. Unanticipated in 1963 was the rapid disappearance of both Kennedy and Khrushchev, the one murdered and the other forcibly retired by his colleagues in the Kremlin.

To be sure, there were fleeting moments of crisis between the superpowers in the years that followed, but they deterred each other from threatening acts by spending enormous sums on nuclear warheads and delivery systems sufficient to destroy each other's people several times over. Out of this emerged the strategic doctrine of Mutual Assured Destruction (MAD), based on the fact that each side would be vulnerable to destruction by the other side, no matter which one started a war.[27] Given such incentive to avoid direct confrontation, the United States and the Soviet Union indulged in costly games on the periphery,

---

[27] See Robert Jervis, *The Meaning of the Nuclear Revolution* (Ithaca, 1989), esp. 74–106.

primarily, although not exclusively, in areas where neither had vital interests at stake. There, in countries like Vietnam, Afghanistan, and Ethiopia, they brought misery to the local peoples, squandered the lives of their own young, and expended resources desperately needed for the shoring up of their own societies.

6

AMERICA'S
LONGEST WAR

America's war in Vietnam is the textbook example of great-power arrogance and self-deception, of the abuse and dissipation of wealth and power. Neither American leaders nor American scholars knew or cared much about the people of Vietnam, their history, their culture, their aspirations. Not until the historian Mark Bradley wrote in the late 1990s was the early fascination of Vietnamese intellectuals with American history apparent.[1] Vietnam was of no intrinsic importance to the United States. In the years when the French controlled Indochina, they pursued a mercantilist policy, allowing minimal foreign involvement in the region's economy. American business developed no stake there, and although the area was potentially rich in natural resources, there was nothing there that could not be obtained elsewhere or that the locals could afford to deny to the world market. Similarly, the region was of minimal strategic importance. A case could certainly be made for keeping Cambodia, Laos, and Vietnam from being controlled by a presumed adversary, whether Japan in 1941 or China or the Soviet Union in the context of the Cold War. But, of course, a case for containing the influence of an antagonist could be made for every corner of the earth – and outer space as well. Friendly control of what had once been French Indochina was unquestionably desirable. But if Cambodia, Laos, and Vietnam were all hostile to the United States, the shift in the world balance of power would be imperceptible. No vital American interest would be threatened. Nonetheless, more than fifty thousand

[1] Mark Philip Bradley, *Imagining Vietnam and America: The Making of Postcolonial Vietnam, 1919–1950* (Chapel Hill, 2000).

Regrettably, the war in Vietnam is no longer America's "longest" war.

Americans gave their lives in a war in Indochina, as did hundreds of thousands of Cambodians, Laotians, and Vietnamese.

Once a nation develops the ability to project its power to distant regions of the globe, to intervene in the affairs of other peoples, the temptation to do so seems very nearly irresistible – at least until its leaders are sobered by disaster or its ability diminishes. American power in the first two decades after World War II, both relative and absolute, was extraordinary. No place in the world was beyond the reach of the United States. And equally important was the sense Americans had of themselves as "winners," as a people who had never lost a war (most Americans seem to think the United States won the War of 1812), a people who could accomplish anything to which they set their minds. They were an ahistorical people, unable, perhaps unwilling, to learn from the failures of others.

The lessons of the past, insofar as American leaders drew on them, taught that aggressors could not be appeased, that the United States had a responsibility to use its power to thwart those who would extend totalitarian systems, that when the will was there, Americans had found ways to stop Hitler and Stalin and would-be perpetrators of evil in Greece, Iran, Guatemala. Contrary examples, such as Indonesia and Cuba, were either forgotten or perceived as negative examples, as occasions when only the will had been lacking. The fact that American "successes" against leftist movements usually resulted in vicious military dictatorships was rationalized by the conviction that military dictatorships were anachronisms, had no external source of support, and might evolve into democracies, whereas Communist regimes, supported by the Soviet bloc, were forever.

American leaders discovered Indochina early in World War II, when the Japanese intruded on the French empire. Japanese pressures on Southeast Asia and the southwestern Pacific worried Franklin Roosevelt and his associates, who were fearful the Japanese maneuvers would distract the British and their allies from the task of containing Nazi Germany in Europe, North Africa, and the Middle East. Toward the end of the war, as victory for the Grand Alliance loomed and the retreat of Japanese forces from Indochina was imminent, Roosevelt, contemptuous of the French generally, suggested that the people of Indochina be put under a UN trusteeship rather than subjected anew to French imperialism. The handful of Americans who reached the area before the end of the war discovered a well-organized resistance movement, which had harassed the Japanese and had no intention of submitting to the French. In Vietnam in particular, the will to independence was strong and deemed worthy of American support. Indeed, the leader of the Vietnamese resistance, Ho Chi Minh, was enlisted as an American agent on the eve of Japan's surrender.[2]

When the war ended, the French returned to Indochina in force, determined to reassert their control. French leaders warned Washington that American opposition to French suppression of the Vietnamese independence movement would alienate the French people, strengthen the French Communist party and, conceivably, drive France into the arms of the Soviets. Ho invoked Thomas Jefferson and the Declaration of Independence, but to no avail. He was, after all, a Communist. More to the point, Vietnam was distant and unimportant. France, on the other hand, might well be a major partner in the new world order American leaders envisaged in the late 1940s; French leaders angered by American opposition to the grandiosity of their imperial vision certainly could undermine American plans for Europe. The United States chose to facilitate the return of French power to Southeast Asia, subordinating traditional American antiimperialism to the exigencies of great-power politics. The responsibility of world leadership took precedence over the principles upon which America's claim to moral superiority had rested.

When the French failed and were forced to come to terms with Ho's Vietminh in 1954, the United States determined to do the job right itself. (See Chapter 3.) Eisenhower and Dulles imagined that the Vietnamese still perceived the United States as the beacon of democratic revolution, that the United States could intervene in Vietnam untainted by colonialism and provide a rallying point for Vietnamese nationalism, an umbrella under which Vietnamese who wanted independence not only from France but from international communism would flourish. For the moment, the president and the secretary of state were prepared to concede Vietnam above the seventeenth parallel, where the Vietminh had regrouped, to Ho Chi Minh's Communist regime. They

---

[2] For quick sketches of the initial American encounter with Indochina, see Gary R. Hess, *The United States' Emergence as a Southeast Asian Power, 1940–1950* (New York, 1987); George Herring, *America's Longest War*, 4th ed. (New York, 2002); and George M. Kahin, *Intervention* (New York, 1986).

Red R.

Mekong R.

NORTH
VIETNAM

BURMA

Dien Bien
Phu

Red R.

Hanoi

Haiphong

GULF OF
TONKIN

HAINAN
(CHINA)

Mekong R.

L
A
O
S

Vientiane

17°
(Partition line)
(1954–1975)

Rangoon

THAILAND

Hue

Da Nang

Bangkok

Pleiku

CAMBODIA
(KAMPUCHEA)

Mekong R.

SOUTH
VIETNAM

Cam Ranh

Phnom
Penh

Saigon
(after 1975;
Ho Chi Minh City)

ANDAMAN
SEA

GULF OF
THAILAND

MEKONG
DELTA

SOUTH CHINA SEA

MALAYSIA

SUMATRA
(INDONESIA)

Map 3. Vietnam and Southeast Asian Mainland, 1954–75.

intended, however, to build a separate, non-Communist nation to the south, where the French, whom they quickly pushed aside, and their collaborators had regrouped. The Americans hoped to use the southern state they would create as a magnet to draw the North out of the Communist orbit.

Indochina became enormously important to the Eisenhower administration primarily because it was perceived in 1954 as the site of the next round in the battle with the Sino-Soviet bloc. The Communists were seeking to extend their influence everywhere. For the moment they were quiescent in Europe. They lacked a toehold in Africa or the Middle East. They had been checked in Korea, but retained an enormous potential for mischief in East Asia. Chinese support for the Vietminh against the French in 1954, as well as Chinese and Soviet recognition of Ho's regime in 1950, helped shape the expectations of Eisenhower and his colleagues. They appear to have overlooked Soviet and Chinese indifference to Vietnamese goals at Geneva, Soviet and Chinese pressures on Ho that forced him to concede to the French far more than they had salvaged on the battlefield. Domestic political pressures, from the Republican Right, also informed Eisenhower and Dulles's conception of the need to draw the line at the seventeenth parallel in Vietnam. Those who had found the Truman administration guilty of losing China did not wish to be charged with losing Indochina.

Once Eisenhower had concluded that he had to act in Indochina, he applied his domino theory. Indochina alone may have lacked strategic and economic importance, but if Indochina fell to the Communists, then all of Southeast Asia would follow. Certainly no one would deny the economic and strategic import of all of Southeast Asia, gateway to South Asia and the southwestern Pacific. Laos or Vietnam could each be invested with the value of all of Indochina, Indochina with the value of all of Southeast Asia, Southeast Asia with the value of a large chunk of the globe. Like Truman, Eisenhower seems to have developed his rationale for intervention after he decided to intervene and to have strained to offer something plausible to the American public. In 1956 and 1958 the National Security Council restated the proposition that "the national security of the United States would be endangered by Communist domination of mainland Southeast Asia"; that "the loss to Communist control of any single free country would encourage tendencies toward accommodation by the rest"; that "the loss of the entire area would have a serious adverse impact on the U.S. position elsewhere in the Far East, have severe economic consequences for many nations of the free world … and could result in severe economic and political pressures on Japan and India for accommodation to the Communist bloc."[3]

The Ngo Dinh Diem regime, created by the Eisenhower administration, proved to be an imperfect instrument for achieving American ends. Diem, the prime minister, was suitably anti-Communist but failed to become the popular leader who would draw the Vietnamese people away from Ho Chi Minh. The elections mandated by the Geneva accords for 1956 had to be avoided because of American intelligence estimates that Ho would win 80 percent of the votes. The principle of support for free elections lost its attractiveness in Washington when the victor was likely to be a Communist.

Diem had some initial success in suppressing potential rivals and consolidating his control in the South. His methods, however, alienated much of rural Vietnam and antagonized Buddhist activists, intellectuals, and politicians who might have constituted the loyal opposition. In the countryside, land reform promoted by his American advisers was less attractive to the peasants than the more radical programs that had been instituted by the Vietminh. Provincial and county leaders sent to the countryside from Saigon generally proved more sympathetic to landlords than to peasants and less popular than the local authorities they replaced. Diem's efforts to root out the Vietminh infrastructure in the South included the dislocation of peasants. His "strategic hamlet" program required villagers to leave their homes and burial grounds to take refuge in fortified encampments. Buddhists were troubled by the preference enjoyed by Catholics, often refugees from the North, both in obtaining government positions and in the freedom to practice their religion. Intellectuals and much of the rest of the politically mobile elite, repressed by Diem's secret police, turned against him. Even before Eisenhower left office, an insurrection was under way in the countryside and there was minimal support for Diem outside of the Catholic minority in the cities. The American nation-building experiment in Vietnam was in trouble.

John F. Kennedy had visited Vietnam in 1954 and come away with views not significantly different from those of Eisenhower and

---

[3] U.S. Congress, House, Committee on Armed Services, *United States-Vietnam Relations, 1945–1967* (hereafter *Pentagon Papers*), Book 9, V.B.3, 1083, 1088.

Dulles: Indochina had to be denied to the Communists; American antiimperialists could succeed where French imperialists had failed; a viable non-Communist nationalist regime could be created with support from the United States. Warned by Eisenhower of the crisis in Indochina, Kennedy, as president, was determined to stop the erosion of the American position there.

Kennedy's first emergency in Indochina came in Laos, where Eisenhower's attempts to create a pro-Western, anti-Communist regime had proven counterproductive. American subversion of the Geneva agreements in support of a right-wing general had triggered an increase in aid to the Communist Pathet Lao from Ho's regime in Hanoi and a deeper Soviet involvement in Laos. In January 1961, Washington's man in Laos was on the ropes. Kennedy's advisers concluded that victory for pro-Western forces was improbable, and that the United States would be fortunate if it could induce the other side to accept a return to a neutral Laos. A major military intervention by the United States was rejected by the president when the Joint Chiefs, disinclined to fight another limited war, demanded freedom to use nuclear weapons and to attack China. Instead, Kennedy ordered the carrier U.S.S. *Midway* to the Gulf of Siam, sent a Marine detachment to Thailand, put forces on Okinawa on alert, signaling to the Soviets the apparent willingness of the United States to fight rather than allow the Communists to take over Laos.[4]

American actions may have frightened their allies as much as they did the Soviets. British prime minister Harold Macmillan thought the issue could be resolved without war "if the Americans do not suddenly run amok."[5] Khrushchev recognized the risk, did not consider total control of Laos worth what it might cost to overcome a major American escalation, and indicated a willingness to negotiate. A cease-fire was arranged in May 1962 and negotiations began shortly thereafter. A Soviet-American agreement on a neutral Laos was reached fourteen months later.

Kennedy's willingness to compromise over Laos did not extend to Vietnam. Throughout the early discussions within the administration of appropriate responses to the crisis in Indochina, the president and

[4] Warren I. Cohen, *Dean Rusk* (Totowa, N.J., 1980), 125–28.
[5] Harold Macmillan, *Pointing the Way* (New York, 1972), 344–5.

his advisers indicated a determination to take their stand in Vietnam. The situation there was retrievable; the Vietnamese protégés of the United States would fight. Initially, Kennedy's principal concerns were standing up to Khrushchev and preventing a domestic political disaster. He had been deeply troubled by Khrushchev's strident advocacy of wars of national liberation before and during their meeting in Vienna in June 1961. Subsequently, as the reality of the Sino-Soviet split penetrated their consciousness, he and his advisers were more likely to see the Chinese, working through the Vietnamese Communists, as the evil demons responsible for their distress in Southeast Asia. But no matter whether the initiative came from Moscow, Beijing, or Hanoi, Kennedy was profoundly fearful of being labeled "soft on communism" if he could not prevent a Communist sweep through Indochina. The Republicans had capitalized on the "loss" of China in 1949, and McCarthyism remained a force in the society. Should the Communists prevail in Vietnam, Kennedy's chances of reelection in 1964 would be slight, the Democratic party would be devastated again, and the forces of reaction would erase the gains of Roosevelt's New Deal, Truman's Fair Deal, and whatever he hoped to achieve with his own New Frontier program. Success in Vietnam would teach Khrushchev that the indirect aggression constituted by wars of national liberation did not pay, might erase the embarrassment of failure at the Bay of Pigs, and provide the margin necessary to assure Kennedy of a second term.

For Kennedy and his colleagues, Vietnam became a convenient ground for demonstrating America's will and power and credibility to friends and enemies alike. To those around the world who feared that the United States was intimidated by Soviet missiles and nuclear capabilities, there would be proof that the Americans would still ride to the rescue, even in places as distant and inhospitable as the jungles of Vietnam. To those at home who worried that a Democratic president would not stand up to the Communists, there would be evidence to the contrary. To the men in Moscow and Beijing who thought they could accomplish through subversion the conquest they dared not seek through direct, overt acts of aggression, there would be a warning that this, too, would fail. In Vietnam, Kennedy could test the counterinsurgency techniques to which he had become attracted; his Green Berets could be sent into action. There the Pentagon could test a myriad of technological innovations, products of countless billions spent on weapons development. Throughout the Kennedy administration there were brilliant men, the "best and the brightest," as the journalist David Halberstam named them – McGeorge Bundy, Robert McNamara, Maxwell Taylor, and Walt Rostow most prominent among them – who were confident that they had the ideas necessary for nation-building and that under their leadership the United States had the will and power to succeed in the great-power contest in Vietnam – and ultimately all over the globe.[6]

As they juggled the initial crises inherited from Eisenhower in the Congo, Cuba, and Laos, Kennedy and his advisers found time to focus on the situation in Vietnam. It was deteriorating quickly as the Diem government's influence and support eroded, as the Vietminh became increasingly active in the South and succeeded in obtaining support from Hanoi. American intelligence concluded that the insurgency in the South was indigenous, that the cadres dribbling in from the North were primarily Southerners returning to their homes, and that Ho Chi Minh, while hardly uninterested, was still husbanding his resources to strengthen that part of Vietnam under his control. There was no evidence of Chinese or Soviet involvement. Kennedy's colleagues concluded that the insurgency could be crushed at minimal cost to the United States; that an increase in military supplies and advisers to Diem's forces would be sufficient to compensate for the increase in opposition forces, the men and women Diem called the Viet Cong. The object was to enhance the performance of Diem's troops. Rostow, who had become the president's principal adviser on Vietnam, argued for using "un-exploited counter-guerrilla assets ... armed helicopters; other Research and Development possibilities; our Special Forces units." He contended that it was "somehow wrong to be developing these capabilities but not applying them.... In Knute Rockne's old phrase, we are not saving them for the Junior Prom."[7]

The president began by increasing the number of American military "advisers" in Vietnam, including four hundred members of the Special Forces, in direct violation of the limits placed by the Geneva agreements. He demanded more aggressive tactics and did not flinch when these required Americans to engage in combat, a further violation of the

---

[6] David Halberstam, *The Best and the Brightest* (New York, 1972).
[7] Memorandum to the president from Rostow, March 29, 1961. Quoted in Kahin, *Intervention*, 131.

Geneva agreements. In due course Kennedy authorized the dropping of napalm and herbicidal defoliants, the former a jellied petroleum product that clung to the skin while it burned, and the latter chemicals that would denude the forest, destroy the productivity of the soil, and have unpredictable effects on humans who came in contact with it.

The Joint Chiefs were less enamored of counterinsurgency operations than were Kennedy, Taylor, and Rostow. The military leaders pressed for sending regular U.S. army combat forces to Vietnam to warn off Hanoi and Beijing. Diem, fearful of losing control of his country to the Americans, apprehensive about being perceived by his people as an American puppet, indicated that American combat troops were not needed. In October 1961, as insurgent successes became more threatening, Kennedy sent Taylor and Rostow to Vietnam to determine whether American troops were necessary. The Taylor-Rostow report, which might have been expected to call for intensifying the counterinsurgency effort, called instead for the introduction of combat forces in the guise of a flood relief team. Kennedy continued to temporize: He did not want to send American troops to take over the war in Vietnam, he did not want to negotiate with the insurgents – and he did not want to risk a Communist victory over Diem.

In response to his perception of the irreducible needs of the Diem regime, Kennedy decided to send American "support" units to Vietnam. These forces dribbled over by the hundreds and then by the thousands. By the end of 1961 there were more than 2,000 American soldiers in Vietnam, roughly three times the number allowed by the Geneva agreements. There were more than 11,000 by the end of 1962, more than 16,000 when Kennedy died in 1963. These support units quickly engaged in combat operations, accompanying Vietnamese pilots on missions, flying the helicopters that carried Diem's troops into battle, killing insurgents as necessary in "self-defense." Despite Diem's opposition and Kennedy's reluctance, the United States had taken an important step toward Americanization of the war.

Kennedy and his advisers had engaged in a sophisticated exercise in self-deception. They considered the alternative of abandoning an unpopular and sometimes difficult ally, but allowing southern Vietnam to fall to the Communists by default was inconceivable. During Kennedy's years in the White House, victory seemed possible if Diem instituted some modest political, economic, and social reforms and if his military was strengthened and provided with more aggressive leadership. And the domestic costs of the "loss" of Vietnam might well be devastating. If sending a few thousand troops to buoy the morale of Vietnamese forces would suffice to turn things around, it seemed a safe, sensible move, less provocative, less dangerous than a major military escalation, politically wiser than withdrawal. Kennedy and his aides deluded themselves into believing that they were still in control, that they had retained their freedom of action. A little military intervention, however, turned out to be like "a little pregnant." There was no painless way to reverse the process. Kennedy was only a few steps behind the Joint Chiefs.

Throughout 1962, Kennedy was told by his aides that American policy was working, that the insurgents had lost their momentum, that the strategic-hamlet program was succeeding. The American military advisory group in Vietnam began drafting plans to reduce American forces present. The president, pleased with the results of the Cuban missile crisis, pleased with the official reports from Vietnam, reached a new peak of self-satisfaction. He was irritated increasingly, however, by press accounts that suggested the battle in Vietnam was going less well, that the Diem regime was repressive and corrupt, that reports of its strategic successes were exaggerated. Imperiously, the president demanded that the *New York Times* recall its correspondent. He failed in that endeavor but more easily intimidated the television networks.[8]

By January 1963, Kennedy was receiving other indications that all was not well in Vietnam. His friend Senator Mike Mansfield (D.-Mont.) went out to the field at the president's request and confirmed the negative reports of the journalists. Mansfield warned that the Diem regime was less stable and less popular in 1962 than it had been in 1955. The battle against the insurgents was in the process of becoming an American war likely to cost the United States far more in lives and dollars than control of Vietnam was worth to the United States. In mid-January, Diem's troops, supported by U.S. planes and helicopters, were battered by a numerically inferior Viet Cong force they had surrounded in the Mekong Delta near Saigon. The Viet Cong, learning to cope with modern military technology, shot down five American

---

[8] Kahin, *Intervention*, 142.

helicopters and damaged nine others. But the American military advisory group in Vietnam remained optimistic, and the president clearly preferred to hear that his policy was working.

A CIA estimate of mid-April 1963 offered fewer grounds for confidence in the administration's course. Although the analysts argued that the Viet Cong drive had been blunted, the enemy had not been crushed by American "involvement." If aid from Hanoi remained minimal, the Viet Cong could probably be contained, but the situation remained "fragile." The CIA was skeptical about the likelihood of Diem's carrying out the reforms necessary to convert the military successes of the moment to "lasting political stability."[9]

The fragile situation shattered in June 1963. In the years that followed, not even hundreds of thousands of American troops could put the Saigon regime back together again. Largely owing to the activities of his brother, Ngo Dinh Nhu, Diem's administration had become increasingly repressive in the early 1960s. In May there had been trouble with Buddhists in the city of Hue. Government forces fired on a demonstration, killing several participants. Protests spread through the coastal cities, and Americans in Vietnam feared the impact on the struggle against the Viet Cong. They urged Diem to be conciliatory. Nhu urged him to crush the Buddhists. On June 11, a Buddhist priest seated himself crosslegged in a major Saigon intersection, other priests poured gasoline over him, and he set himself afire – an incredible scene that horrified Americans and people all over the world who watched it soon afterward on television.

Under U.S. pressure, Diem and Nhu agreed to end both the special privileges of the Catholic church and the harassment of Buddhists, but the agreement collapsed within weeks. By August the protest movement was out of control, and Diem seemed immobilized by an inability to choose between the advice of his brother and the demands of the American Embassy. On August 21, Nhu sent his security forces into the pagodas. Wielding billy clubs and truncheons, they suppressed the Buddhist movement. Kennedy and his advisers were appalled and embarrassed by the brutality of Nhu's men. They preferred that the United States not be associated with a tin-pot dictatorship that survived by Gestapo methods. They concluded that, at the very least, Nhu

[9] *Pentagon Papers*, Book 12, V.B.4, 524.

should be sent out of the country and that it was time to consider alternatives to Diem's regime.

On August 24, Henry Cabot Lodge, Jr., the American ambassador to Saigon, received a cable from Washington that contained a thinly veiled instruction to encourage a coup against the Diem regime. Lodge was to inform interested Vietnamese military leaders that the United States could not long support a government that included Nhu or suppressed Buddhists. Should the central government collapse, the Vietnamese generals were to be assured of a continued flow of supplies. With the arrogance in which only great powers can indulge, the Kennedy administration had decided to invite a coup against a regime that had been created and sustained by the United States. Heaven, now located on Pennsylvania Avenue, had withdrawn its Mandate from the Diem dynasty.[10]

There was very nearly a coup before the end of August, but the generals proved timid and Kennedy's advisers had second thoughts. Kennedy decided to muddle on until the war was won, gradually increasing efforts to force Diem to liberalize his administration, to rein in his brother. But reports that Nhu was dallying with the National Liberation Front (NLF), the political arm of the insurgents, generated unease in Washington. Kennedy's men feared that Nhu and Diem might respond to American pressure by coming to terms with the NLF and Hanoi and demanding that the Americans leave. Once more advocates of a military coup against Diem prevailed on the president. Finally, on November 1, the generals launched their operation. Regrettably, in the course of the coup, Diem and Nhu were murdered. With their liquidation, however, the American-supported cause in Vietnam had been purged of the stigma of repression. Now the people of Vietnam would be mobilized to use American assistance to defend their freedom against Communist-controlled insurgents.

The United States, a nation whose people had long prided themselves on their adherence to the principles of nonintervention and anti-imperialism, had arrogated to itself the archetypal privileges of imperial power. Out of the southern portion of Vietnam it attempted to build a nation: Southern Vietnam became "South Vietnam." It designated the

---

[10] Roger Hilsman, *To Move a Nation* (Garden City, N.Y., 1967), 488.

leaders of that "nation," funded their programs, armed their troops, and had them removed when they did not meet American standards of performance. All this was done in accordance with what was perceived to be in the national interest of the United States. The best interests of the people of Vietnam were determined by men in Washington. By preventing the elections scheduled for 1956, the American government consciously denied the Vietnamese their only chance to express their preferences peacefully. By introducing American military power into Vietnam, the United States attempted to deny the Vietnamese the right to overthrow a government they had come to despise. The result was to bring extraordinary misery to the Vietnamese, to come close to destroying their country in order to save it from communism.

Dwight Eisenhower eagerly seized imperial responsibility in 1955 and warned John Kennedy against "losing" Southeast Asia. Kennedy's narrow margin of victory in the election of 1960, his fear of appearing weak, and his own intense anticommunism precluded the alternative of leaving the future of Vietnam to be determined by the Vietnamese. It was Kennedy who began the Americanization of the war, who increased the 600 American military advisers Eisenhower had sent to more than 16,000 – and Kennedy's men in Vietnam were not merely advising. His death, only a few weeks after that of Diem, left a perilous situation in the hands of Lyndon Johnson.

A relatively popular general, Duong Van Minh, headed the junta that replaced Diem's regime. In the closing weeks of 1963, the level of violence in Vietnam declined. The NLF and its allies in Hanoi were eager to explore the possibility of a negotiated peace with Minh, who had a brother active in the NLF. Minh and several of his colleagues were interested, desirous of ending the suffering of their people. They were not willing to turn southern Vietnam over to the North, where Ho and his comrades had demonstrated their ruthlessness, or to accept Communist control, but they were less anti-Communist than Diem and Nhu had been. They could conceive of sharing power with the NLF, of a neutral southern Vietnam free of foreign soldiers, troops from the North, and of the war that had racked their country since 1946. The twin desires for peace and freedom from foreign domination ran fast and deep through Vietnamese society.[11]

[11] Kahin, *Intervention*, 182–6.

Relative quiet in Vietnam suited Lyndon Johnson just fine. Asked by the advisers he inherited from Kennedy what he wanted to do about Vietnam, he told them he wanted it put aside for the moment. He did not want an escalation of the American role; he did not want a wider war. His principal concern in late 1963, early 1964 was the presidential election scheduled for 1964. Nothing would be allowed to interfere with his campaign to be elected in his own right. Toward that end, he wanted to concentrate on his domestic programs, on building the Great Society in America. That was where his vision lay; that was where the votes could be found.

Neither the Vietnamese nor the American military accepted Johnson's timetable. American military men responsible for overseeing the Saigon regime's war effort were disappointed by Minh's lack of aggressiveness. They were deeply troubled by reports of his interest in a negotiated settlement, of his willingness to ask the Americans to go home, and by his resistance to greater American control over the operations of his forces. Moreover, Minh and his colleagues were opposed to the Pentagon's recommendation that the war be taken to the North, fearful of provoking a major attack across the seventeenth parallel by Hanoi's regular army. Before long, American military advisers in Vietnam were shopping for a new Vietnamese leader, encouraging creation of a government more responsive to their guidance.

Three months after Minh's group seized power, General Nguyen Khanh mounted a successful coup against it with the knowledge and assistance of American military advisers in Vietnam.[12] As the reins slipped out of Minh's hands, the last chance for avoiding catastrophe slipped away as well. But the United States was delighted with Khanh, particularly with his eagerness to receive American political advice, to increase the number of American military advisers in the country, and to participate in covert operations against Hanoi. American aid increased rapidly. Unfortunately for Khanh and his American sponsors, his popularity among the Vietnamese never matched that which he enjoyed in Washington. His government had little support among his own people at the outset and that little eroded quickly.

[12] See Kahin, *Intervention*, 182–202, for a fascinating investigation of the role of the U.S. government in Khanh's coup.

Johnson did not want any major initiatives in Vietnam before November 1964, but he could hardly accept the loss of Vietnam during the campaign. It became increasingly clear that the major danger to his election came from the Right, from people such as Senator Barry Goldwater (R.-Ariz.), who were demanding more vigorous prosecution of the war, who were probably aware of the Pentagon's desire to bomb northern Vietnam. Johnson chose to pose as the peace candidate, the man who would prevent extremists like Goldwater from widening the war and costing the United States tens of thousands, perhaps millions of casualties. But as the collapse of the Saigon regime loomed, the need for American boys to go over there and do the job right, for the full force of American power to be brought to bear on the North, became harder to deny.

Johnson and his advisers, an eye constantly on the American electorate, tried covertly to halt the deterioration of the situation. Rather than bomb the North, Khanh was encouraged to run small-scale guerrilla operations against the Hanoi regime without overt American assistance. Evidence of large numbers of northern Vietnamese regulars in Laos led to secret American bombing runs against suspected Communist positions. Of course, these covert operations were less a secret from their targets than from the American people and Congress. The executive was running its own war in Vietnam.

Pressure to attack the North mounted through early 1964. Some of the president's aides thought an attack on the North would demonstrate American resolve; others thought it would bolster Khanh; the Joint Chiefs wanted to provoke Hanoi into acts that would justify systematic bombing; Ambassador Lodge thought nuclear weapons might be necessary. In May, Johnson's advisers agreed to an *eventual* program of using selected and gradual force against the North. The principal barrier to an immediate attack was the president's perception of his domestic political needs. When that perception changed briefly in August and disappeared in November, no one could restrain the application of America's great power against the Hanoi regime.

On August 2, 1964, an American destroyer was attacked by North Vietnamese torpedo boats while patrolling in the Gulf of Tonkin, off the coast of North Vietnam. American analysts suggested the assault was the result of an assumption by North Vietnamese leaders that the ship was involved in clandestine operations such as the South Vietnamese had just completed in the area. The ship was ordered to return to the same area, accompanied by a second U.S. warship, to demonstrate American resolve. On August 4, the North Vietnamese allegedly launched a second attack. The incident came at night, and there was uncertainty about whether it had occurred, but naval authorities assured the president that it had. Almost reflexively, Johnson ordered reprisals against what he called aggression on the high seas. It was an extraordinary opportunity to demonstrate American power and determination, to demonstrate North Vietnamese vulnerability, and to undercut Goldwater's criticism. The peace candidate would leave no doubt that he would respond fiercely to provocation.

The incident in the Gulf of Tonkin not only gave the Johnson administration the desired excuse to attack North Vietnam but also provided the occasion for the president to ask Congress for authority to take whatever steps he deemed necessary, including the use of force, to protect any endangered state in Southeast Asia. His advisers had long agreed that a congressional resolution was an essential part of the preparations for carrying the war to Hanoi. In August, the House voted 416–0 and the Senate 88–2 to give Johnson a blank check. Preparations were completed to cash it after the election.

Although Hanoi's role in the insurrection in southern Vietnam had been marginal – and American intelligence analysts knew that – the United States was preparing to go to war against Ho Chi Minh's regime. The war in the South was going badly. The Khanh government was faring worse than its predecessors. Johnson's advisers, excepting only George Ball, undersecretary of state, could not accept defeat, would not countenance American withdrawal. They could not tolerate the "loss" of southern Vietnam to the Communists, its domestic consequences, its impact on the credibility of the American imperium. They could not believe that the greatest power the world had ever known lacked the means to crush a peasant rebellion in what the president would call some "pissant" country. An attack on the North would probably reduce the rate of infiltration and cut the Viet Cong off from supplies and reinforcements. It would warn the Vietnamese, the Chinese, and the Soviets that the United States was determined to hold the line. It would raise morale in the South. The decision to attack North Vietnam was born of frustration and arrogance, taken by men who were losing a relatively minor skirmish and could not bear it. The historian Frederik Logevall has argued persuasively that they had other choices and gives credence to the possibility that had Kennedy lived, he might have given diplomacy another chance. Logevall notes that opposition to escalation was broad, including Vice President Hubert Humphrey, Senate Democratic leaders, the mainstream press – and the country's allies.[13] But Johnson and his advisers chose to invest the revolutionary struggle in Vietnam with weight in the world balance of power, with the potential of tipping the scales in favor of international communism. They chose to widen the war, to increase the stakes, to use America's vast power to intimidate the Vietnamese, to impose an American vision of their future on an unwilling and uncomprehending people.

On November 3, 1964, the Americans gave Lyndon Johnson an enormous victory over Barry Goldwater. In much of the world, those men and women who concerned themselves with issues of war and peace rejoiced at what they perceived as a victory for peace. In Washington, preparations for war were complete. In Saigon, the generals were playing at musical chairs again, thwarting American efforts to operate from a stable base in the South. The president resisted a powerful argument for commencing systematic bombing of the North presented by McGeorge Bundy and Secretary of Defense Robert McNamara. The dogs of war strained at their leashes.

Suddenly, on February 7, 1965, the Viet Cong attacked an American installation at Pleiku, killing seven Americans and wounding more than one hundred others. Johnson immediately ordered attacks on barracks and staging areas in North Vietnam. A few days later he gave the order to implement the full-scale bombing plan, put into effect February 28. Less than a week later, two battalions of U.S. Marines went ashore at Danang to protect the airfields from which the bombing attacks were being launched. Johnson and his advisers hoped that Hanoi and the Viet Cong could be brought to heel without a major combat role for American ground forces. Rusk and Taylor worried that "white-faced" troops would be counterproductive; that they would be viewed with hostility by the local people, discredit the side on which they fought, and have trouble distinguishing between friendly and unfriendly villagers.

[13] Frederik Logevall, *Choosing War: The Lost Chance for Peace in Vietnam* (Berkeley, 1999).

But intelligence reports soon indicated that the bombing had not affected Hanoi's will, that North Vietnamese regular army troops were beginning to cross into the South. On April 1, the president approved the use of American troops for offensive operations. On election day, in November 1964, there had been 25,000 American military men and women in Vietnam. In July 1965 there were 75,000. In November, a year after the election, there were 165,000 and reports that more were on the way. American boys were trying to do what candidate Lyndon Johnson had promised Asian boys would be allowed to do for themselves. Gradually Americans realized they were at war.

Unhappiness with the American role in Vietnam manifested itself as early as March 1965 as student activists, religious pacifists, and academics specializing in Southeast Asian affairs began to challenge the administration. The first of the antiwar demonstrations was mounted in Washington in April. In May there was a national teach-in involving over a hundred campuses across the country. Opposition to the war grew in intensity as the Americanization of the struggle continued, slowly drawing more and more ordinary middle-class Americans into the antiwar coalition. Attempts by Johnson and his advisers to counter criticism were often disingenuous, increasing rather than allaying doubts. The president's gift for hyperbole served him poorly.

One critical step toward the undermining of Johnson's credibility was his handling of an unrelated crisis in the Dominican Republic in April and May of 1965. The deviousness with which he justified sending in the Marines cost him the trust of a valued and powerful ally, Senator J. William Fulbright (D.-Ark.), chairman of the Committee on Foreign Relations, and much of the foreign policy establishment. Fearing that Communists might be on the verge of turning the Dominican Republic into another Cuba, Johnson responded with characteristic vigor, sending first a small detachment of Marines and then more than 20,000 soldiers to suppress a mutiny by democratically inclined officers against a conservative military junta. The United States intervened in the internal affairs of the small Caribbean country, and the president greatly exaggerated both the danger to Americans resident there and of Communist involvement. Skepticism about Johnson's shifting explanations and distaste for his eagerness to assume imperial responsibilities stimulated Fulbright and others to reexamine policy toward Vietnam. They were dismayed by what they found.

Between January 28 and February 18, 1966, Fulbright held six televised hearings on the war. Reflecting the hardening of the administration's commitment to a non-Communist South Vietnam, Rusk insisted that the war was an act of outside aggression by the Hanoi regime, that the United States had commitments to repel that aggression. He argued that what was at stake was not merely Vietnam, but the credibility of American commitments all over the world: "We must make clear that the United States keeps its word wherever it is pledged."[14] Presumably, if the United States did not fight in Vietnam, the whole postwar edifice of collective security would collapse. Others spoke in support of the administration's policy, but of greatest consequence was the appearance of George Kennan in opposition. Consistent with his low regard for the importance of developing countries, Kennan argued that the war was foolish and might well lead to a disastrous encounter with China. He insisted that withdrawal – and, by implication, Communist control of the South – would not hurt any major American interest. The televised hearings, highlighting the doubts of prominent and highly respected observers, assured millions of Americans of the respectability of dissent. Even Robert Kennedy and other intimates of the late president openly criticized the administration.

Johnson and his advisers were unmoved by their critics. The war went on. Every week scores, sometimes hundreds, of Americans and thousands of Vietnamese died. Billions of dollars that might have been spent on Lyndon Johnson's vision of a Great Society were drained away for war-related expenses. Slowly the fabric of American society strained, threatened to unravel, and finally was rent apart as the president and his aides concentrated their time, energy, and the nation's resources on the war. Around the world men and women of goodwill viewed the United States with a contempt hitherto reserved for Chiang Kai-shek, Franco, and Stalin. America the liberator, the protector was gone, replaced by the brutal oppressor of tiny Vietnam.

Johnson's advisers saw the criticism as a public relations issue. Without changing course, the administration might have to steer a more sinuous line. The American public and critics all over the world would have to be pacified with evidence that Lyndon Johnson was a reasonable man second to none in his desire for peace. The administration agreed to several bombing halts and accepted or sponsored a series

---

[14] *Department of State Bulletin* 54 (March 7, 1966): 346–56.

of missions – Canadian, Russian, Hungarian, Polish, and British, as well as American – in search of peace. The president offered Vietnam a rural electrification program for the Mekong Valley to rival the Tennessee Valley Authority at home. But it was all a charade. The United States was not interested in negotiations for peace while the momentum in Vietnam was with the insurgents. American terms for peace required the surrender of Hanoi's dream of unifying Vietnam, of the NLF's demand for a share of the government of the South, of everything for which the opposition had been fighting and had every expectation of winning.

The massive use of American airpower failed. Johnson lifted a variety of restrictions on targeting, to no avail. Estimates by the CIA and the Defense Intelligence Agency indicated that the bombing had not significantly affected North Vietnamese morale or ability to send men and materials south. Equipment destroyed by the bombing raids was being replaced by the Soviets and Chinese, who vied with each other to win Ho's fealty. The Soviet Union had remained virtually uninvolved until 1965, until the massive attacks on the North began. Accused by the Chinese of abandoning the cause of international socialism, the Soviets demonstrated their commitment by sending Hanoi large quantities of modern military equipment, including surface-to-air missiles (SAMs) and jet interceptors.

To all indications that the military effort of the United States was ineffective, the Joint Chiefs replied with demands for more men, more bombs, and more freedom to choose targets. In June 1966, the president authorized a troop buildup to 431,000. By fall, McNamara began to despair. He, too, came to question the value of the escalation of the war. But he could think of no way to end it.[15]

Johnson was determined to win, was irritated by McNamara's doubts, and turned increasingly to those of his advisers who continued to be optimistic. Friends like Clark Clifford and Abe Fortas urged him on. General Earle Wheeler, chairman of the Joint Chiefs of Staff, assured him that the war was going well. Walt Rostow, surpassed by none in his confidence that the United States could win in Vietnam, succeeded Bundy as the president's national security adviser. Doubters lost their influence with the president, and the inner circle became one of "yea-sayers," of "can-doers."

---

[15] Cohen, *Dean Rusk*, 273–4.

In May 1967, with 436,000 American troops in Vietnam, the military was talking of needing 565,000 to win in three years, 665,000 to win in two. The CIA reported, however, that "short of a major invasion or nuclear attack, there is probably no level of air or naval actions against North Vietnam which Hanoi has determined in advance would be so intolerable that the war had to be stopped."[16] The Communist regime was confident of victory, and the Pentagon's own analysts contended that more American troops would do little good and probably great harm, especially to the economy of South Vietnam.

The United States could not win and could not seem to end the war. Popular dissatisfaction grew. As American casualties multiplied, demonstrations, draft resistance, and desertions from the military increased. In the field the phenomenon of "fragging," of the murder of American officers by men resisting being led into battle, spread ominously. In July 1967, riots exploded in Newark and Detroit. Scores were killed, thousands arrested, millions of dollars in property damage sustained. The anger of the black ghettos was not related directly to the war in Vietnam, but the riots added to the sense of a society breaking apart. There were demands that funds being used to kill in Vietnam be used for saving lives at home, for a War on Poverty. The war was now costing the American people $20 billion per year. It was becoming clear that the government lacked the resources for both the Great Society and Vietnam. In August, Johnson averted financial disaster by agreeing to a 10 percent surcharge on income taxes. The response in the public opinion polls was immediate: For the first time a plurality of Americans, most of those with an opinion, thought the war in Vietnam was a mistake. Pressure on the United States to end the war intensified. Even the pope called for suspension of the bombing. Senator Eugene McCarthy (D.-Minn.) stepped forward as a peace candidate to challenge Johnson for the Democratic party presidential nomination.

Johnson's reaction was to start 1968 with a new team, on which there were no doubters in evidence. The military braced for a major North Vietnamese attack on a U.S. Marine garrison near the Laotian border, at Khesanh, perceived as a replay of the 1954 battle of Dienbienphu. There the Americans intended to demonstrate to the Vietnamese the difference between the United States and France. American military

---

[16] Cited in Cohen, *Dean Rusk*, 277.

leaders were convinced they were on the verge of victory: All they needed was another 100,000, perhaps 200,000 men and a little more freedom to attack the North. They assured the president that the Viet Cong had been weakened to the point where they lacked offensive capability without support from the North.

The president and his aides received a rude shock on the morning of January 30, while most Vietnamese relaxed during the Tet or lunar new year holiday. As Americans focused on the base at Khesanh, the Viet Cong penetrated the American Embassy compound in Saigon, besieging it for six hours before they were overcome. But the attack on the embassy was only a symbol of what was happening across the length and breadth of South Vietnam. In Saigon the airport, the presidential palace, the headquarters of the general staff all came under attack. Simultaneously, the Viet Cong attacked four of the other five major cities, capturing the ancient Citadel in Hue, and scores of provincial and district capitals. An insurgent force alleged to be on the verge of liquidation launched a brilliantly conceived attack that demonstrated, most obviously at the American Embassy, that no one was beyond its reach.[17]

The Viet Cong and North Vietnamese took very heavy losses in their Tet offensive, suffering as many as forty thousand deaths. Viet Cong main force units did most of the fighting, suffered most of the casualties, and never recovered. All the territory they held during the attack was regained by South Vietnamese and American troops, although it took three weeks to recapture Hue. The people in the cities did not rise to welcome their Communist liberators. The American military command expressed pride in the performance of the Vietnamese troops it had trained and claimed victory. In terms of kill ratios and territory controlled, the Americans were unquestionably correct.

The primary target of the North Vietnamese planners, however, was American public opinion, and with that audience they were strikingly successful. The optimism expressed by the president and military leaders just weeks before seemed absurd. The war would be endless, a bottomless pit. Every week in February at least four hundred Americans were killed in Vietnam, with no indication of what had been accomplished,

---

[17] See the book-length study by Don Oberdorfer, *Tet!: The Turning Point in the Vietnam War* (Garden City, N.Y., 1971).

of when it would all be over. Walter Cronkite, the most respected of American television news commentators, declared the war a hopeless stalemate: "To say that we are closer to victory today is to believe, in the face of the evidence, the optimists who have been wrong in the past."[18]

In the United States, not only the public but the government evidenced profound shock at the demonstration of Viet Cong capability and the failure of American and South Vietnamese intelligence to anticipate the attacks. The ability of the Saigon regime to recover from the onslaught, to capitalize on its military victory, was widely doubted. Support for the war eroded not only among the unwashed masses, but within the establishment, among the "in and outers," to whom presidents and cabinet officers were most responsive. The Communists won the psychological victory they sought. Johnson could not hold course. The military would not get the additional 206,000 troops requested. There would have to be changes in American policy.

On March 12 the domestic political context in which Johnson acted began to change radically. On that day, Eugene McCarthy, the quixotic peace candidate for the Democratic nomination, received a stunning 40 percent of the votes in the New Hampshire primary, very nearly defeating an incumbent president. Four days after McCarthy demonstrated Johnson's vulnerability, Robert Kennedy reassessed his chances and declared his candidacy. Massive "Dump Johnson" rallies were organized by antiwar activists. The president was in political trouble. Peace in Vietnam was likely to provide his best chance of recovering.

Moreover, the economy was verging on disaster. To mobilize the reserves and deploy 200,000 additional troops overseas would exacerbate long-standing balance-of-payments difficulties. Gold was flowing out of the country at an alarming rate, largely to finance the war in Vietnam. Unless there was a tax increase, difficult to obtain in an election year, there would be serious inflation in the United States, panic in Europe, and possibly a collapse of the international monetary system. The president's advisers groped for a way out.

On March 25, a group of leading establishment figures, the so-called Wise Men – highly prominent former government officials including Dean Acheson, McGeorge Bundy, Douglas Dillon, John McCloy, and Matthew Ridgway – assembled in Washington to be briefed on Vietnam

---

[18] Quoted in Marilyn B. Young, *The Vietnam Wars, 1945–1990* (New York, 1991), 226.

and to advise the president. With few exceptions, they concluded that the war was absorbing too much of the nation's energy, too much of its resources. They urged a scaling down of American objectives and of the American effort. Two, George Ball and Arthur Goldberg, insisted on a bombing halt. A few months earlier, most of these men had supported the war. No one had anticipated so radical a change of attitude. The Wise Men were deeply troubled by the divisions in American society, by the decline of American standing in the world, by the gold drain, and most concluded it was time to find a way out. Johnson was shaken by their response.[19]

On March 31, the president addressed the American people. He spoke of his efforts to achieve peace in the past, and he announced the cessation of attacks on North Vietnam except for staging areas just north of the demilitarized zone – and those attacks would cease if Hanoi showed restraint. Then he shifted suddenly to a discussion of the accomplishments of his presidency and to his concern for national unity. Contending that the stakes were too high to allow the presidency to become involved in election-year partisanship, he announced dramatically, "I shall not seek, and I will not accept, the nomination of my party for another term as your president." It was a striking bid for national unity and a signal to the North Vietnamese of the seriousness of his peace initiative. Three days later Hanoi agreed to negotiate, but Lyndon Johnson had not run up the white flag, was still unwilling to accept defeat, and peace in Vietnam remained many years away. Indeed the air war in the South soon intensified, almost mechanically. The air force had the planes, the pilots, and the bombs. Deprived of targets in the North they simply concentrated on the South.

On April 4, Martin Luther King was murdered in Memphis, Tennessee. Hours later Washington was in flames. Riots followed across the nation. In June, Robert Kennedy was murdered in Los Angeles. In August, anti-war demonstrators outside the Democratic National Convention in Chicago were attacked viciously by the police, in what a subsequent investigation labeled a "police riot." When Governor Abraham Ribicoff of Connecticut protested on the convention floor against police action, Mayor Richard Daley led his claque in chanting "kike, kike." This was

---

[19] Herbert Y. Schandler, *Unmaking of a President* (Princeton, 1977), 262–4; Gabriel Kolko, *Anatomy of a War* (New York, 1985), 316–20.

not the America God had blessed, liberator of oppressed people. The war had changed all that, and another side of American life surfaced, ugly, brutal, reminding some of the rise of fascism. In Vietnam, American boys were destroying villages "to save them," committing unspeakable atrocities against an alien people whose savage struggle for independence frightened and confused them. At home, Americans were turning on each other, divided by the war, by race, by class. The Great Society had become a sick society. The tension caused by the war in Vietnam and racism at home had infected almost every aspect of American life. Nerves were taut and international affairs had to be conducted in this atmosphere. Johnson and his advisers were pitted against the sweep of the hour hand. Could they find an acceptable peace in Vietnam before the bell tolled for America?

It was May before Washington and Hanoi agreed on a site for the talks, May 13 before the first formal session was held. That week 562 Americans were killed in Vietnam, the highest weekly total of the war. It was July before the American negotiators perceived a breakthrough and a chance for peace. Johnson was not convinced by their reports and continued the military pressure. By late August, supporters of Richard M. Nixon, Republican presidential candidate, had persuaded the South Vietnamese to reject any peace terms the Johnson administration might be prepared to accept. They assured the Saigon regime they would obtain better terms after the election, after Richard Nixon became president. Saigon became increasingly recalcitrant, especially on the place of the NLF at the talks.[20]

In October, Johnson's negotiators finally convinced him that an agreement was in reach. He authorized them to try, and they succeeded with astonishing speed – and the help of the Soviet Union. Rusk worked with the Soviet ambassador in Washington, and the American negotiators in Paris worked with the Soviet embassy there. The Soviets took it upon themselves to make sure that the Vietnamese knew what was expected of them and pressed them to agree to the American terms. Issue after issue was ironed out and on October 31, Johnson ordered the cessation of all attacks on North Vietnam. But that was only a part of the war. The struggle for the control of the South continued. Johnson was

---

[20] Lyndon B. Johnson, *The Vantage Point* (New York, 1971), 517–18; see also William P. Bundy, Lyndon B. Johnson Oral History Collection, Lyndon B. Johnson Library.

still determined to deny it to the Communists. The Saigon regime, convinced Nixon would gain more for it, charged Johnson with betrayal and refused to participate in the talks if the NLF was present as a separate delegation. Nixon's victory had the opposite effect on Hanoi: The North Vietnamese were eager to reach a settlement before facing the Nixon administration. Concessions by Hanoi produced a formula that won Saigon's consent to sending a representative to Paris, but nothing came of the expanded talks. The war went on – and on.

Nixon had indicated that he had a plan for ending the war in Vietnam, but once elected he was no more willing than Johnson to be "the first American president to lose a war" – and victory was nowhere to be found. "Peace with honor" became the administration slogan. Nixon was alleged to have interpreted that to mean leaving the Saigon regime strong enough to survive his tenure in office, so that its inevitable collapse would be blamed on Teddy Kennedy, by whom he expected to be succeeded.

The new president and his principal foreign policy adviser, Henry Kissinger, had no illusions about the importance of Vietnam to the security of the United States. Both were ruthless practitioners of great-power politics, eager to be relieved of the burden of an unpopular war, eager to concentrate their intellectual energy on relations with the Soviet Union and China. But the president had to be perceived as strong at home and abroad. His dilemma was to find a way to get out of Vietnam short of surrender, yet quickly enough to stay ahead of antiwar sentiment at home. The basic formula was a reversion to elements of the Eisenhower administration's New Look, reliance upon American airpower and local forces, in this instance called "Vietnamization." Gradually, on a fixed schedule, American troops were pulled back from combat and out of the country. In support of South Vietnamese troops, the air war was stepped up and extended to infiltration routes in neutral Cambodia and to staging areas in Laos. The killing went on, but fewer of the corpses were American. With declining American casualties, Nixon and Kissinger assumed the American people would give them more leeway to negotiate an acceptable settlement. Successful manipulation of domestic opinion was essential. Kissinger's staff at the National Security Council referred to the efforts to end the war as "political theater."

Hopes for a quick decisive end to the American military presence faded as the North Vietnamese stubbornly held their ground, confident that one day the American people would tire of the war and bring their children home, leaving the future of Vietnam to be determined by the Vietnamese. But there was reason for satisfaction with the Vietnamization policy. The performance of Saigon's forces improved markedly, largely because the Viet Cong had suffered enormous casualties during their Tet offensive, and by 1970, the countryside was securer than at any time since the insurgency began. The balance of forces in the South had shifted in favor of the government. More and more the burden of fighting Saigon and its American supporters fell to North Vietnamese regulars. Supplied with Soviet SAM ground-to-air missiles that took a heavy toll of American bombers, the Northerners resisted American pressures. Shipments of the latest Soviet tanks gave Ho Chi Minh and his colleagues confidence that they could counter any invasion. Infiltration rates increased. It was clear to Nixon and his advisers that infiltration routes had to be blocked.

Cambodia was a tiny, weak country, whose volatile leader, Prince Norodom Sihanouk, had been remarkably adept at protecting his people from the war in neighboring Vietnam. To accomplish this, he was forced to tolerate the presence of North Vietnamese bases on his territory. The United States frequently urged him to drive the Vietnamese out of his country, but he lacked the means. An assault on the Vietnamese by the weaker Cambodians would be suicidal. The Vietnamese affront to Cambodian sovereignty seemed a small price to pay for peace and survival.

The American military had long advocated a strike at Vietnamese sanctuaries in Cambodia, including what they believed to be the headquarters for the Communist insurgency in the South. Johnson had refused, but Nixon immediately authorized secret bombing raids in 1969. The secret, of course, was to be kept from the American people, not from the recipients of the bombs. Early in 1970, to the delight of the American government, Sihanouk was overthrown by a military coup led by officers friendly to the United States. In May, American troops invaded neutral Cambodia, determined to destroy the Vietnamese sanctuaries. The results were unbelievably disastrous for Cambodians, led to anti-American demonstrations around the world, and death on American college campuses.

Caught between the Americans and the Vietnamese, hundreds of thousands of Cambodians died. Their country was devastated, and control gradually passed to a murderous group of Communist insurgents known as the Khmer Rouge, who subsequently, in an act of extraordinary depravity, slaughtered hundreds of thousands more, perhaps as many as two million of their countrymen. Whatever joy Americans may have felt at Sihanouk's departure was short-lived. The May 1970 invasion also resurrected the antiwar movement in the United States. Protesters at Jackson State and Kent State were shot and killed by police and National Guardsmen. The president was besieged in the White House, with troops posted on the premises in case of an attack.

The Nixon administration withstood the aftermath of the invasion of Cambodia, but the situation in the field and on the home front deteriorated. In February 1971, South Vietnamese forces supported by American planes and helicopters struck at North Vietnamese sanctuaries in Laos, another major expansion of the war – and another disaster. Apparently Hanoi's intelligence operatives had advance notice of the operation and hit the South Vietnamese hard, using some of their new Soviet tanks. Saigon's troops suffered a casualty rate of 50 percent and fled ignominiously from the battlefield, in some instances clinging to the skids of helicopters. At home, Lieutenant William Calley was convicted for his role in the massacre of women and children at the village of My Lai, and other veterans came forward to reveal that such atrocities were not isolated incidents. Then, in June 1971, the *New York Times* began publishing a secret Defense Department documentary history of American decision making in Vietnam, revealing many of the ways the Kennedy and Johnson administrations had deceived the American people. Polls taken soon afterward indicated that 71 percent of the American people thought it had been a mistake to go to war in Vietnam. Even more striking was the fact that 58 percent thought the war was immoral. Nixon knew he had to find a way out before he ran for reelection in 1972 – and so did his adversaries in Hanoi.[21]

Intensive efforts to reach an agreement in late 1971 failed, largely because of the inability to agree on the disposition of the Saigon government. But Nixon and Kissinger succeeded in their efforts to move closer to the Soviet Union and the People's Republic of China, ultimately gaining the support of Moscow and Beijing for the peace process. They assumed that they could isolate North Vietnam and force it to come to

---

[21] Herring, *America's Longest War*, 243.

terms. The initial response from Hanoi, in March 1972, was a conventional attack across the demilitarized zone that caught the Americans and their Vietnamese protégés by complete surprise. The United States responded with yet more massive air attacks on the North and ultimately the mining of Haiphong harbor. The North Vietnamese were stopped well short of the collapse of the Saigon government.

Renewed military stalemate, additional American concessions, pressure from its Soviet and Chinese allies, both now eager to improve relations with the United States (see Chapter 7), and the realization that Nixon was likely to be reelected finally led Hanoi to accept a diplomatic arrangement short of victory in the fall of 1972. The Saigon regime rejected the agreement, but the exigencies of the election campaign led Kissinger, a few days before the voters decided, to announce, "Peace is at hand." His aides readily admitted that they could have achieved the same agreement at any time in the previous year: The announcement was designed to help bury George McGovern, the Democrats' peace candidate.

After the election, Nixon proved more responsive to Saigon's cries of betrayal and demanded changes in the agreement. The North Vietnamese balked. Nixon ordered the most devastating bombing of the war, the "carpet bombing" of parts of the North, a series of raids in which more bombs were dropped in twelve days than had been dropped in the two years between 1969 and 1971. At the same time massive supplies of military equipment were delivered to the Saigon regime, with Nixon's personal assurance that the United States would return if the North violated the agreement. Finally, in February 1973, the war ended for the Americans.

Nixon continued efforts to sustain Saigon after the peace agreement led to the withdrawal of American forces, but the Watergate scandal soon crippled him and ended, at least temporarily, the "imperial presidency." Congress reasserted itself in foreign affairs and restricted the president's power to reinvolve the United States in the war in Vietnam. American support for the Saigon regime declined and with it so did one of the regime's principal reasons for existing. Although the military initiative appeared to rest with the South Vietnamese army throughout 1973, by mid-1974 operations had to be curtailed for lack of adequate supplies. The departure of the Americans and the reduction of American aid affected morale in Saigon adversely, and the will to fight had ebbed palpably by early 1975. Enormous numbers of government troops deserted. When the North Vietnamese struck in March 1975 with the first in what was supposed to be a two-year series of major attacks, the South Vietnamese army panicked and then disintegrated. Calls for help from the United States were to no avail. Richard Nixon was gone in disgrace, and his secret promises to the authorities in Saigon could not be honored by President Gerald Ford. A few weeks later the fighting stopped. The Communists controlled all of Vietnam, and Saigon became Ho Chi Minh City. After a war of roughly thirty years, the Vietnamese revolution had triumphed over the French, the Americans, and all internal opposition. Unhappily for Washington, the revolution was dominated by Communists, by men and women with ties to America's adversaries in Moscow and Beijing, by men and women who had watched their countrymen suffer terribly because of American intervention in their affairs. But it was over.

Fifty-five thousand Americans and millions of Vietnamese died in the American phase of the Vietnamese revolution. It was a struggle in which the United States should never have intervened, in which a weaker power could not have intervened so massively and for so long. No vital American interest was threatened by events in Indochina. Defeat in Vietnam was of little consequence, without impact on the strategic balance between the United States and its adversaries. Indeed, before the war ended, the United States had taken major strides toward reconciliation with the Soviet Union and the People's Republic of China, the very nations Americans had sought to contain by killing and dying in Vietnam. The dominoes of Southeast Asia did not fall. To be sure, the Khmer Rouge triumphed in Cambodia shortly before the fall of Saigon, and the Pathet Lao seized control of Laos not long afterward, but the remaining nations of the region remained independent and non-Communist, friendly to the United States, ultimately creating in the Association of Southeast Asian Nations (ASEAN) an important force in world affairs.

But if losing the war had little impact on the strategic position of the United States, the cost of fighting the war hurt the nation badly, accelerating its decline as a hegemonic power. The achievement of strategic parity by the Soviet Union and the regaining of their economic edge by Japan and Western Europe were all but inevitable, but the disastrous economic policies of the 1960s and early 1970s, including the means of financing the war in Vietnam, contributed mightily to the timing and depth of the slide.

The dollar had been weak since the late 1950s and balance-of-payments deficits had troubled Kennedy, but the deficit did not get out of control until 1964. After Eisenhower, no president gave adequate consideration to the cost of American security. Kennedy, Johnson, and Nixon proudly refused to put a price tag on the foreign policy goals they chose to pursue. Balance-of-payments concerns were consistently subordinated to security concerns. There was a sharp increase in the rate of inflation in the 1960s as the government printed more and more dollars to pay for its imperial activities. Both the Johnson administration and the Nixon administration tried to export the cost of the war, export inflation, to their trading partners. The French rebelled in 1965, demanding gold for the dollars they held, and the British and Germans objected to American international monetary policy in 1971. The world had grown tired of collecting inflated American dollars in return for protection against a Soviet threat they perceived as much diminished or to support an American war in Vietnam of which most Europeans disapproved. Tensions grew as currency issues began to compete with security concerns in the minds of allied leaders. The political scientist Robert Gilpin explains that "for both foreign policy and domestic reasons, successive American administrations pursued expansionary and inflationary monetary policies that eventually undermined the dollar and destabilized the monetary system. [The United States had become] the rogue elephant of the global economy."[22]

The inflated dollar priced U.S. goods out of overseas markets, and, in 1971, the United States ran its first trade balance deficit of the century. In the course of the year, to staunch the outflow of gold, the Nixon administration refused to redeem dollars for gold. Nixon's advisers chose to end the dollar's status as a reserve currency and to destroy the Bretton Woods system Harry Dexter White and John Maynard Keynes had designed in the 1940s, which had brought striking prosperity to those who participated in it. Many of the economic problems facing the United States in the late 1960s and 1970s would have existed without the war, the result of inflationary domestic programs to provide

---

[22] Robert Gilpin, *The Political Economy of International Relations* (Princeton, 1987), 149, 153.

jobs and services to the American people, but they were exacerbated by the billions spent in Vietnam. Stagflation, a stagnant economy with rapidly rising prices, hit the United States in the 1970s. Germany and Japan, denied the opportunity to play the great-power game by defeat in World War II, became the principal beneficiaries of American decline. The Japanese, who spent 99 percent of their research-and-development budget on civilian production, easily captured markets from the United States, which devoted 50 percent of its research-and-development expenditures to armaments. Richard Rosecrance, another political scientist, points to the rise of the "trading state," of nations like Germany and Japan that have chosen, however involuntarily, trade over military means to acquire wealth and power.[23] Without denigrating the brilliance of the Japanese industrial planning, we cannot ignore the fact that by its senseless struggle in Vietnam the United States at the very least hastened the day when the world had to confront the idea of "Japan as number one." The opportunity for the United States to fashion a new, posthegemonic style of leadership, along with American wealth and power, had been squandered.

[23] See Richard Rosecrance, *The Rise of the Trading State* (New York, 1986).

7

THE RISE AND FALL OF DÉTENTE

In 1969, when Richard Nixon, Cold Warrior personified, entered the White House, it was clear that most Americans had had their fill of war and confrontation. The country was eager to end the wasting of American lives abroad, no longer persuaded that a hostile world would deny Americans their freedom if they stopped spending billions to support the appetite of the military-industrial complex. The endless war in Vietnam had changed American attitudes, led the people to question the wisdom of their leaders, eroded support for overseas military adventure. The United States had to disengage from the Vietnamese conflict. Perhaps the time to end the Cold War had arrived as well. No one was quicker to perceive the new public mood than Richard Nixon. No one was better able to free the country from the tyranny of hysterical anticommunism than the man who had contributed so much to fanning that hysteria. As one Washington wit remarked, he was the first president since the end of World War II who did not have to guard his flanks against attack by Richard Nixon.

Nixon and his national security adviser, Henry Kissinger, like all postwar American leaders, sought a stable world order in which American interests would be preserved. Like their predecessors, they considered the containment of Soviet influence central to that end. But they confronted a Soviet Union that had gained strategic parity with the United States and whose leaders believed their country to be on the verge of becoming the world's preeminent power. Moreover, as Soviet strength and assertiveness grew, Nixon and Kissinger found themselves constrained by public and congressional weariness with the battle, and by a fragile economy seriously weakened by Lyndon Johnson's attempt to provide guns *and* butter. Their strategy had to overcome these domestic handicaps in order to cope with increased Soviet capabilities.

Central to the Nixon-Kissinger approach was their determination to control foreign policy from the White House, to prevent opposition in the bureaucracies, the press, Congress, or the streets from interfering. Rather than attempt to educate the public, they chose to circumvent the weaknesses of the American political system by finessing constitutional restraints on the president. They wanted to end the asymmetry between Washington and Moscow, to be free to act as quickly and ruthlessly in pursuit of American interests as they imagined the Soviet Politburo acted. Neither man had great respect for traditional American political culture. At home and abroad they were practitioners of power politics. When the interests of the United States or their personal interests were at stake, no holds were barred.

To contain the Soviet Union at a time when the relative wealth and power of the United States were in decline and public support at low ebb was the task that confronted them – and Nixon and Kissinger were almost equal to it. Their negotiating strategy was often labeled "linkage." They offered the Soviets recognition of their strategic parity, tolerance of the aberrant political philosophies and human rights abuses of which the Soviets and their satellites were guilty, and a promise of access to Western capital and technology. In exchange they asked Moscow to recognize the mutuality of superpower interest in stability, especially in maintaining order in the Third World. They wanted Soviet assistance in extricating the United States from Vietnam. Nixon and Kissinger were telling Leonid Brezhnev and his colleagues that the Soviet Union would benefit more from cooperation with the United States than from attempting to capitalize on unrest on the periphery. They were asking the Soviets to contain themselves at a time when America's will to hold the line was in doubt.

Simultaneously, Nixon and Kissinger were striving to restore the public consensus in support of the leadership role the United States had played in world affairs throughout the postwar era. Ending the war in Vietnam would contribute mightily toward that goal. Easing tensions with the Soviet Union could help, although there was always a risk that if the public concluded that the Cold War was over, willingness to make the sacrifices necessary to lead abroad would decline further. But the risk had to be taken in the hope that the demonstration of the administration's new approach to Soviet communism, its acceptance of peaceful coexistence, would regain supporters alienated by the war in Vietnam. Finally, there was the tactic the president liked to have called the "Nixon Doctrine," a devolution of American responsibilities in the Third World upon regional powers like Brazil, Iran, Indonesia, and Zaire. Rather than use American troops to intervene, the United States would arm surrogate forces to do the fighting and dying for it. Presumably, the reduction in American casualties and the "lower profile" of the United States would be more acceptable to the American people: They would rather pay taxes to arm and train friendly foreign troops than send their own children into combat abroad.

From the Kremlin, Brezhnev and his colleagues looked at the United States with growing disdain. Racial unrest, antiwar demonstrations, chaos in the streets – all confirmed their estimate of the weakness of democratic society. Americans were tearing their society apart, and the government lacked the power or the will to impose order. Clearly, the United States was in decline. Soon, in their lifetime, Soviet leaders anticipated supplanting the Americans as the world's hegemonic power.[1]

In the years since they had deposed Nikita Khrushchev, the members of the Brezhnev Politburo had not waited passively for the Americans to self-destruct. They did what they could to hasten the process with large-scale aid to Ho Chi Minh's regime, by seeking to undermine the American position in the Middle East, and by expanding their own military power enormously. They had continued the rapid buildup of their strategic nuclear forces to the point where they could claim parity with the United States. They had also expanded their conventional forces and capabilities to the point where they could contest American power in most parts of the Third World. Not even the Western Hemisphere would be left as an American preserve. These were not impulsive men like Nikita Khrushchev. They were cautious and they were conservative, but they were also convinced that the "correlation of forces" in the world had shifted in their favor and they were prepared to act aggressively to achieve a position of dominance.

Requests from the United States for Soviet pressure on Hanoi to allow the Americans to extricate themselves from Vietnam through "peace with honor" could hardly be taken seriously in Moscow. Except for 1968, when the Soviets aided the peace process in an apparent

---

[1] Harry Gelman, *The Brezhnev Politburo and the Decline of Détente* (Ithaca, 1984), 135–7.

attempt to preclude the election of Nixon, there was little incentive for the Soviet leadership to betray its commitment to support "wars of national liberation." America's war in Vietnam could not have been more advantageous for the Soviets had it been planned in the Kremlin. The war drained American resources, exacerbated tensions within American society, alienated NATO allies as well as Third World countries, and heightened Vietnamese dependence on the Soviet Union. In blood, in treasure, in the sullying of America's image in the world, the war in Vietnam was enormously costly to the United States and a great boon to the Soviet Union. The Soviets increased their aid to Vietnam and ultimately facilitated Hanoi's victory.

At no time were Brezhnev and his colleagues willing to end their efforts to expand Soviet influence in the world, preferably at the expense of the United States. Like Khrushchev before them, they saw American efforts to place the Third World outside the arena of superpower competition as an effort by the United States to maintain its advantage, to deny the Soviets their coming victory. Similarly, Soviet leaders were skeptical of Nixon's interest in arms control, suspecting the Americans of attempting to halt the arms race before the Soviets overtook them. They had the power to deter a nuclear attack by the United States, and they perceived the momentum to be on their side. This was no time to commit themselves to the existing world order. Certainly the Soviet military saw little to be gained by an easing of superpower tensions, by the détente for which the Americans were striving.

The Soviet Union did have a few problems that might be alleviated through better relations with the United States. Although excellent weather in the late 1960s had meant good crops, there were bound to be lean years ahead. The leadership had maximized its commitment to agriculture, was subsidizing food prices in the cities, and could spare no more without reducing military spending. Industrial growth was slowing, and capital for new investment in industrial infrastructure was not available. The Soviet standard of living had risen in the late 1960s, and consumer expectations had grown, but the prospects for the 1970s were less reassuring. Like Lyndon Johnson, Brezhnev was trying to provide both guns and butter, trying to project Soviet power abroad while improving the lot of Soviet citizens, and the economy was beginning to strain. The Soviet Union could benefit from an infusion of capital and technology from West Germany, Japan, even the United States. The

Germans and the Japanese seemed interested but were too timid to act without American approval. A reduction of tension between the United States and the Soviet Union seemed to be a prerequisite.[2]

Similarly, Soviet efforts to drive a wedge between the United States and its European allies on political issues had fallen short. The Soviets were eager for formal European acceptance of their World War II gains and of the status quo in Europe, especially the borders of the two Germanies. Again, the West Germans were very interested, but some resolution of the Berlin issue would be necessary. That, too, involved the United States. Détente with Western Europe, desired primarily as a means of separating the United States from its allies, was unlikely without an improvement in Soviet-American relations.

Once the massive military buildup of 1965–1968 had pacified a Soviet military-industrial complex disdainful of Khrushchev's budgetary priorities, Brezhnev was free to pursue his dream of becoming the great peacemaker, of reaching an accommodation with the United States and its allies in Western Europe. His action to crush the "Prague Spring" in the summer of 1968 had assured his more aggressive colleagues in the Politburo that he would act as necessary to protect Soviet interests. Both Melvyn Leffler and Vladislav Zubock perceive Breshnev as a man convinced that nuclear war had to be avoided and the pursuit of détente was the surest route to peace and security for the Soviet Union – and international acclaim for its leader.[3]

And, of course, off to the east, there was Mao Zedong, forever sticking his finger in Brezhnev's eye. A series of efforts to conciliate the Chinese had proved unsuccessful. Soviet military intervention to crush an heretical reform movement in the Communist party of Czechoslovakia in 1968, followed by the Brezhnev Doctrine claiming the right to use force in defense of "socialism," failed to intimidate the Chinese. Incidents along the Sino-Soviet borders increased in number and intensity. As Soviet leaders considered their options for punishing the Chinese, it seemed advisable to neutralize the United States. A Chinese-American connection might not be in the interest of the Soviet Union.

[2] Gelman, *Brezhnev Politburo*, 85–6; Raymond L. Garthoff, *Détente and Confrontation* (Washington, D.C., 1985), 87–90.
[3] Melvyn Leffler, *For the Soul of Mankind* (New York, 2007), 238–42; Vladislav M. Zubock, *A Failed Empire: The Soviet Union in the Cold War from Stalin to Gorbachev* (Chapel Hill, 2007), 210–22.

From the perspective of the men in the Kremlin in 1969, an improvement in bilateral relations with the United States might have value after all, provided the Soviet Union remained free to outmaneuver the Americans throughout the Third World. The Soviets were satisfied with the situation in Europe and sought only to ratify it. They were interested in Western trade and investment. Arms control appealed to them less, but there were areas in which they might reap advantage, or be spared disadvantage through an agreement. And perhaps through bilateral ties to the United States some new leverage could be obtained. American capitalists profiting from business in the Soviet Union might prove useful in mitigating anti-Soviet sentiment in the United States. Washington might acquiesce in whatever sanctions the Soviets applied against the Chinese. But for none of these possible gains were the Soviet leaders prepared to cease their efforts to extend Soviet influence around the world. Now, with Soviet power ascendant, was not the time to accept restraints.

Meanwhile, in Beijing, the turmoil of the Great Proletarian Cultural Revolution did not blind Chinese leaders to the danger from the Soviet Union. In November 1968, Zhou Enlai called for talks with the newly elected Nixon administration, but more radical leaders, determined to struggle against both superpowers simultaneously, forced cancellation of a scheduled meeting. In the months that followed, Sino-Soviet tensions erupted in serious border incidents, provoked by the Chinese, over Chenbao Island in the Ussuri River, followed by a sharp retaliatory strike by the Soviets in Xinjiang. Fearful of a preemptive attack on their nuclear installations in the region, the Chinese backed off. Their hostility toward the Soviets greater than ever, they proved receptive to overtures from the Nixon administration. Ambassadorial-level talks began anew early in 1970, but the year was almost over before Zhou persuaded the aging Mao that the United States was no longer a threat to China and might prove a valuable counter to Soviet pressure.

Nixon and Kissinger were eager to engage China diplomatically, primarily to seek help ending the war in Vietnam but also to use China as a possible lever against the Soviet Union. Further, rapprochement with the Chinese would facilitate the withdrawal of American forces from East Asia. American troops would no longer be required to prepare to fight major wars in Europe and Asia simultaneously, reducing force requirements. The Chinese could contain the Soviets and Vietnamese in East

Asia, and American resources could all be focused on the Soviet Union. In sum, détente with China fit magnificently with the Nixon-Kissinger approach to the Soviet Union and with the Nixon Doctrine.[4]

Secret cables flew back and forth between Beijing and Washington through a variety of sources, friendly signals were raised, and one day the world discovered that Kissinger had just returned from Beijing. On July 15, 1971, without warning to friend or foe, Nixon announced that Kissinger had met with Zhou and that he, the president of the United States, had accepted an invitation to visit China. Brezhnev and his fellow Soviet leaders were not amused.

In August and September the United States accepted the seating of Beijing's representative in the United Nations while giving nominal support to the effort by the Kuomintang regime in Taipei to retain a seat for itself. An American motion to seat both delegations failed to obtain a majority. An Albanian motion to substitute Beijing's representative for Taipei's won easily. It was one of the least painful diplomatic defeats the United States had ever suffered. In February 1972, Nixon flew to China, where the old Red-baiter enjoyed a personal audience with Mao. An astounded worldwide television audience watched the American president sit through and then warmly applaud a dreary ballet heavily laden with Communist propaganda. A new era in Chinese-American relations had begun.

As the two sides talked during that memorable week, it was clear that the principal obstacle to regular diplomatic relations, to "normalization," was American policy toward Taiwan. The Chinese stressed their opposition to all variations on the idea of two Chinas and insisted that all American forces be withdrawn from Taiwan. The Americans conceded that Chinese on both sides of the Taiwan Strait insisted that Taiwan was part of China, that there was but one China. The United States would not challenge that position. Washington had moved to a "one China, but not now" policy: It would accept the idea of one China, with a tacit understanding that the future of Taiwan would be determined later, by the Chinese themselves, in their own peaceful way. The Americans agreed to the ultimate withdrawal of their forces and installations from Taiwan, promising to do so progressively as tension in the area subsided. Fearing a reaction from Chiang's friends in the

[4] Henry Kissinger, *The White House Years* (Boston, 1979), 163–82, 191–4.

United States, Kissinger and Nixon prudently concealed the full extent of their concessions. In fact, Kissinger conceded more on the issue than the Chinese anticipated, leaving no doubt of American willingness to abandon Taiwan as soon as feasible. In short, if Beijing helped the United States out of Vietnam and refrained from threatening action in the strait, it could speed the attainment of its objective.[5]

In Moscow, Brezhnev and his advisers watched uneasily. Their worst fears had not been realized: There was no indication of any military understanding between the United States and China. The United States had not wiggled out of its commitment to Taiwan, and the Kremlin's specialists on China were certain that Sino-American relations would not advance appreciably until the Americans abandoned Chiang's regime. To the Soviet leaders, it was apparent, however, that they would have to include the Sino-American relationship in their calculation; they would have to try to control the strategic triangle that had emerged. The Soviet Union could not appear so indifferent to American overtures for détente as to drive Washington and Beijing closer together. Nixon's trip to China enhanced the possibility of success in Moscow significantly.[6]

The Soviets correctly estimated that an arms control agreement would be the most effective instrument for demonstrating their surpassing importance to the United States. Once such an agreement was reached, the Americans were unlikely to jeopardize it by entering into a military alliance with the Chinese. Moreover, the Soviets were troubled by the Nixon administration's effort to obtain funding for deployment of an anti-ballistic missile (ABM) system. This was not only an area in which Soviet technology was inferior; at least as worrisome was the potential cost of an extensive ABM system. Military expenditures already stretched the Soviet budget to the limit. Further cuts in expenditures for consumer goods might be dangerous. Military leaders were not eager to reallocate resources committed to existing programs, especially in areas where the Soviet technology was equal to or superior to that of the United States. Despite Nixon's decision to bomb Hanoi and mine Haiphong harbor a few days before his scheduled visit to

---

[5] Harry Harding, *A Fragile Relationship: The United States and China Since 1972* (Washington, D.C., 1992), 40–7; Nancy Bernkopf Tucker, *Strait Talk: United States-Taiwan Relations and the Crisis with China* (Cambridge, Mass., 2009).

[6] Garthoff, *Détente and Confrontation*, 240–3.

Moscow, Brezhnev persuaded his colleagues to let the invitation stand. They were ready to deal on strategic arms limitations.[7]

Soviet and American arms control negotiators had been talking to each other since 1969, but Nixon and Kissinger were not much interested in an arms control agreement for the sake of limiting the development and deployment of weapons systems. The particulars of an agreement concerned them less than the fact of accord. They wanted to signal a change in the superpower relationship from one in which differences prompted confrontations to one in which resolution was achieved through negotiation. Secretly, Kissinger and the Soviet ambassador bypassed the official negotiators, spared themselves mastery of the technical details, and helped their respective principals come up with a document they could both sign, achieving their political goals. Efforts to reach a comprehensive settlement, limiting all strategic weapons, were put aside by a skeptical and impatient Kissinger.[8]

The first Strategic Arms Limitation Talks (SALT) agreement, signed by Brezhnev and Nixon in Moscow in May 1972, contained an important provision for limiting the deployment of ABM complexes, saving both sides enormous sums for systems deemed of marginal utility. Arrangements for offensive weapons were less satisfying, reflecting pressures on the Soviet and American leaders from their respective military-industrial elites. At home and abroad, Brezhnev and Nixon reaped the political capital they sought. The Soviet ruling class was pleased by the indication that the United States had conceded strategic parity and was satisfied that little had been sacrificed. A few months later, a Soviet-American trade agreement brought closer the economic gains the Soviets expected. The American people warmed to the prospect of ending the Cold War, and the "new" Nixon glowed with the aura of a man who had achieved rapprochement with his nation's two principal adversaries. Around the world there was a perception of a new and less dangerous era dawning.

One likely glimpse of the future emerged when tensions developed between the United States and Japan over issues of trade. Sato Eisaku, Japan's foreign minister, failed to respond promptly to Nixon's 1969

---

[7] David Holloway, *The Soviet Union and the Arms Race*, 2d ed. (New Haven, 1984), 44–6; Gelman, *Brezhnev Politburo*, 131–3; Leffler, *For the Soul of Mankind*, 218.

[8] Garthoff, *Détente and Confrontation*, 148–50.

request for restraints on textile exports. Washington retaliated in 1971 with the "Nixon shocks," acts designed in part to undermine Sato. First, the president announced his opening to China without consulting the Japanese, who, out of loyalty to their American allies, had long resisted internal pressures to recognize the Beijing government. Second, Nixon unilaterally declared that dollars could no longer be converted into gold and that a 10 percent surcharge would be levied on all imports. Japan was forced to revalue the yen and to limit exports to the United States. Economic issues, long subordinated to security concerns, were becoming paramount in Japanese-American affairs. The tacit arrangement whereby the Japanese accepted American political and strategic dictates in exchange for a privileged position in their bilateral trade relationship was unraveling. The success of Nixon's overtures to the Chinese and Soviets had reduced the urgency of security matters and increased the relative importance of domestic economic issues.

There was, of course, that dirty little war in Vietnam in which the United States was still engaged. If it had ever made sense for American resources to be so deeply committed to Indochina, Nixon's maneuvers in Beijing and Moscow obviated two imperatives. And, of course, it was 1972. Richard Nixon, who in 1968 had argued that anyone who could not end the war in four years did not deserve to be president, was up for reelection. On the eve of the election, Kissinger announced that peace was at hand. It took an incredibly ruthless bombing campaign in December to wrap up the agreement with Hanoi, but the last American troops left in February 1973. For Americans, the ordeal was over. For the Vietnamese there were two more years of fighting and dying. For the Cambodians the worst was yet to come.

For a few months, Nixon basked in the glory of his landslide victory over George McGovern. Americans, with the atrocities of Southeast Asia relegated to the back pages of their newspapers and disappearing from their television screens, might well have imagined a world at peace. In June 1973, Leonid Brezhnev traveled to the United States, where he and Nixon signed the Agreement on the Prevention of Nuclear War. But the Watergate scandal that was to destroy Nixon had already surfaced to distract him, and trouble was just over the horizon, as usual, in the Middle East.

The Middle East has long been – and perhaps always will be – an area of exceptional volatility. Communal strife, primarily religious, plagues the region. The great-power decision to grant the Jews a homeland in Palestine and the creation in 1948 of the state of Israel overshadowed all prior grievances, especially among Arab Muslims. And Israel survived the first onslaught against it, in 1948, in large part thanks to Stalin's facilitating of Czech arms shipments to the embattled Jews. As the Soviet leader anticipated, the Jewish nation was perpetually at odds with its Arab neighbors, creating difficulties first for the British and then for the Americans, who succeeded the British as the principal Western influence in the area.

Stalin had paid little further attention to the Arab Middle East, but his successors extended Soviet influence to those states confronting Israel, most importantly Egypt from 1955 to 1974. Soviet bloc arms had buoyed Nasser en route to the Suez crisis in 1956, and the closing scenes of that engagement included Khrushchev's rattling of rockets at the already humbled British and French imperialists. The historic Russian claim to influence in a region that it bordered was reasserted by Moscow in the 1950s and remained a major irritant in Soviet-American relations throughout the Cold War.

In 1967, under Brezhnev's leadership, the Soviet Union threw a match into the powder keg. Soviet agents in Syria spread false allegations of an impending Israeli attack. The Syrians appealed to Nasser for support. Shortly afterward, the president of the Soviet Union repeated the allegations to the Egyptians, who regarded Soviet information as independent confirmation of Syrian fears. Nasser, attempting to intimidate the Israelis with the threat of a two-front war, demanded the withdrawal of UN peacekeeping forces, which separated his troops from the Israelis, and sent his forces toward the Gulf of Aqaba, where they could harass the vital port of Elat. Thus provoked, the Israelis attacked preemptively and, in what came to be known as the Six-Day War, routed Egyptian, Jordanian, and Syrian troops, seizing control of the Sinai Peninsula, the west bank of the Jordan River and Jerusalem, and the Golan Heights. At that point, when the Israelis seemed likely to continue on to Damascus, the Soviets threatened to intervene, a hardly credible threat given the limits of Soviet ability to project its power into the Mediterranean and the presence of the American Sixth Fleet. But Moscow's capacity for mischief had been demonstrated anew, and the Soviets quickly resupplied their Syrian and Egyptian friends and sent thousands of military advisers. In return, the Soviets obtained naval rights in Arab ports and air bases from which they could counter the operations of the Sixth Fleet in the future.[9]

In 1969, Nasser began a "war of attrition" against Israel, to which the Israelis responded after nine months of restraint with air attacks that penetrated deeply into the Egyptian heartland. The Israeli air force demonstrated anew that it could fly where it pleased against its Arab enemies. Humiliated again, Nasser asked the Soviets for air-defense support. This time, in 1970, the Soviets were ready and sent missiles, planes, and thousands of air-defense personnel, including fighter pilots. Soon Soviet warplanes, flown by Soviet pilots, changed the nature of the war – although in one engagement the Israelis shot down five Soviet interceptors. As the war escalated and the Israelis threatened to invade Egypt to knock out the Soviet missile sites, the Soviets proved more amenable to American calls for a cease-fire, achieved in August 1970. But now the Soviets had approximately 20,000 military "advisers" in Egypt and more credibility with the Arab states.[10]

A month after the cease-fire went into effect, Nasser died of a heart attack. His successor, Anwar Sadat, called upon the Soviets for the support he considered necessary to regain the territory lost to Israel. Although the Soviets were generous with their supplies, Sadat did not get everything he wanted as quickly as he wanted it. He resented Soviet skepticism about his plans. He suspected Brezhnev of betraying Egyptian interests as he moved toward détente with the United States. Abruptly, in July 1972, two months after Nixon and Brezhnev met in Moscow, he expelled his Soviet advisers. The American leaders viewed Sadat's actions as evidence of the wisdom of their policy. Staunch support of Israel had demonstrated that the Arabs could achieve their goals only through the United States. The spread of Soviet influence had been checked, and there would be peace in the Middle East.

The Soviet government knew the extent to which Sadat and his Syrian counterpart, Hafez Assad, had armed for war and were aware, by 1973, that the Egyptians and Syrians were serious about taking action to force the Israelis to disgorge the spoils of the Six-Day War. In July, Brezhnev

---

[9] William B. Quandt, *Decade of Decisions: American Policy Toward the Arab-Israeli Conflict, 1967–1976* (Berkeley, 1977), 37–71, is a useful introduction to the Six-Day War. See also Gelman, *Brezhnev Politburo*, 111; and Zubock, *Failed Empire*, 200.

[10] Quandt, *Decade of Decisions*, 94–102; Gelman, *Brezhnev Politburo*, 112.

failed to get Nixon to force the Israelis to be more forthcoming and felt no obligation to warn the Americans of the likely result of continued Israeli intransigence. The U.S. government had similar information available to it, including Egyptian war plans. It had been warned by the State Department's intelligence analysts. But Kissinger underestimated Sadat's determination and Soviet willingness to see the United States embarrassed once more by its ties to Israel.[11]

The Israelis, too, were surprised by the attack, which caught them as they observed the holiest of the Jewish holidays, Yom Kippur. Initially, the Egyptians punched through Israeli defenses in the Sinai and the Syrians scaled the approaches to the Golan Heights. A few days into the war, the Soviet Union, attempting to retain influence in the region, launched a massive airlift to resupply its Arab clients. At the same time, the Soviets appealed to other Arab states to join in the fray. For a week, the United States left the Israelis to their own devices, until Golda Meir, the Israeli premier, threatened to use nuclear weapons to save her country. Then the American airlift to Israel began, followed immediately by the Israeli counteroffensive. Quickly the Israelis drove back the attackers on both fronts and in a few days were in position to annihilate the Egyptian army. Sadat, who thought his forces were still winning, resisted suggestions of a cease-fire until the Soviets provided him with satellite photographs to demonstrate the precariousness of his position. At the initiative of the Soviets, Brezhnev and Kissinger worked out the terms of a cease-fire acceptable both to the Israelis and their Arab adversaries.

The Israelis, however, took advantage of relatively minor Egyptian provocations to justify further advances. Sadat appealed to both Washington and Moscow to send troops to enforce the cease-fire. An angry Brezhnev called upon the United States to join the Soviets in sending troops to stop the Israeli violations. Ominously, he warned that Soviet troops would be sent in alone if necessary, and he mobilized airborne troops to demonstrate the seriousness of his intent. Nixon and Kissinger responded by putting American forces on strategic alert to hold the Soviets in place and compelling the Israelis to comply. Brezhnev chose not to respond to the alert, "perhaps one of the finest moments" of his statesmanship. A Soviet-American

[11] Garthoff, *Détente and Confrontation*, 360–8; Quandt, *Decade of Decisions*, 165–70.

confrontation was averted, but neither side was satisfied with the actions of the other.[12]

The October 1973 war in the Middle East dispelled some of the illusions both American and Soviet leaders may have had about the meaning of détente. In Washington, there was disappointment in the obvious Soviet effort to undermine the American position in the Middle East. The Soviets did not warn the United States that war was imminent. They worked assiduously to incite the Arab world against the United States, disseminating lies about the American role in the conflict and applauding the oil embargo when it finally came. In Moscow, the outcome of the war was probably the major source of frustration, but the American strategic alert and the implication that the United States had forced the Soviets to back down rankled Brezhnev and his colleagues. Subsequent attempts by Kissinger, largely successful, to exclude the Soviets from efforts to resolve Middle East problems, and Sadat's decision for rapprochement with the United States could be interpreted only as a serious setback. The United States might have conceded strategic parity to the Soviet Union, but it clearly had no intention of allowing the Soviets to play a major role in the Middle East. The great-power rivalry seemed little changed.[13]

The most stunning event of the mid-1970s was, of course, the forced resignation of Richard Nixon from the presidency in August 1974. It was the culmination of years of illegal activities directed from the White House designed to destroy political opponents, uncover possible acts of disloyalty to the president among his supporters, and, in particular, to preserve the secrecy with which he and Kissinger conducted foreign policy. Hearings on the Watergate scandal, the incident in which the White House "Plumbers" unit broke into and searched the headquarters of the chairman of the Democratic party, began in mid-1973. As the weight of the evidence of wrongdoing grew heavier against the president, his power ebbed and Congress reasserted itself in the realm of foreign policy. The once troubling "imperial presidency" faltered, and the system of checks and balances created by the Founding Fathers came back into play.

[12] Henry Kissinger, *Years of Upheaval* (Boston, 1982), 569–99; Garthoff, *Détente and Confrontation*, 374–85; Zubock, *Failed Empire*, 240.
[13] Gelman, *Brezhnev Politburo*, 151–6.

In 1973, Congress passed the War Powers Act, designed to restrain the president's use of military force without a declaration of war – and demonstrated its determination by overriding a presidential veto. Before the year was out Congress ordered an end to the merciless bombing of Cambodia, passed a law preventing American troops from returning to Vietnam, and signaled its intent to hold trade relations with the Soviet Union hostage to Soviet performance on human rights issues, specifically the freedom of Soviet Jews to emigrate. These limits on the ability of Nixon and Kissinger to manage foreign affairs brought about the collapse of the intricate schema they had contrived. Their game plan for Indochina and détente could not be executed. They could not deliver on promises to their allies in Indochina or their adversaries in Moscow. Once again, the United States served as an illustration of the strong-state, weak-government paradigm. The Nixon administration and its replacement, the administration of Gerald Ford, successive governments of the most powerful state in the world, were not strong enough to act as they wished in world affairs. In Nixon's mind, the United States was in danger of becoming "a pitiful, helpless giant."

Whether the weakened presidency was a boon or tragedy will depend on the perspective of the beholder. When the North Vietnamese launched their final assault on the Saigon regime and the United States did not ride to the rescue, a war of thirty years' duration came to an end. The suffering of the Vietnamese people did not end, as thousands of refugees demonstrated in the years that followed, but peace was a blessing for most and the country could begin the arduous task of reconstruction. Cambodians, relieved of the terror of American B-52s, enjoyed little respite before facing horrors of far greater magnitude at the hands of their new Communist leaders, the Khmer Rouge. The Jackson-Vanik amendment to the Soviet-American trade agreement and the Stevenson amendment to the Export-Import Bank authorization indicated that Congress would not provide the economic rewards Brezhnev had anticipated and reduced the likelihood of moderating Soviet behavior. The unraveling of the fabric of détente Nixon and Kissinger had woven seems more likely, however, to have been an inevitable outcome of the many deceptions they practiced, their general contempt for democratic practices, and the mistrust their high-handedness provoked in the bureaucracy, in Congress, and ultimately among the American people.

Chinese-American relations also fell victim to Nixon's disgrace. Liaison offices had been opened in Beijing and Washington with the expectation that they quickly would be elevated to embassies, that the United States would abandon the pretense that Taiwan was China, disengage from Chiang's regime, and establish normal diplomatic relations with the People's Republic. Fighting to stave off impeachment, the president became increasingly dependent on the support of conservative lawmakers, many of whom were longtime supporters of Chiang's "Free China," implacable enemies of "Red China." Unable to risk alienating them, Nixon chose not to abrogate the defense treaty with Taiwan. Recognition of Mao's China was not quite equal in importance to the preservation of Richard Nixon's presidency. His successor, Gerald Ford, likewise needed the support of the Republican right wing, especially after he was challenged for party leadership by Ronald Reagan, long the first choice of the Right. Recognition of the People's Republic would have to wait. And in China, American delays undermined advocates of rapprochement with the United States and a dying Zhou Enlai lost control of policy. Succession crises in both countries precluded decisive action in the mid-1970s.

Perhaps the most serious problem the United States faced in the 1970s was posed by the decline in its economic power, especially as aggravated by the policies of the Johnson and Nixon administrations. It is important to stress that the decline was relative, that although the United States ceased to dominate the international economic order as it had in the first two decades after World War II, it remained an enormously wealthy and powerful country. The American economy was troubled and mismanaged but never in danger of collapse.

The American economy had been the engine that drove the nations linked to it to extraordinary prosperity in the 1950s and 1960s. The United States had accepted the imperial burden of protecting its friends and allies while they reconstructed or developed their economies. The patchwork system that evolved out of Bretton Woods (see Chapter 1) had worked. Real wealth had increased among the countries participating in the American-led liberal order. But, by 1960, a number of problems – some systemic, some specific to the United States – emerged. First, European countries and Japan recovered from the impact of the war and became more competitive and more assertive in their trade policies. They were prepared to continue cooperation with an

American-led system but demanded a voice in its direction. Second, the American people became increasingly sensitive to the inequities within their society, the persistence of poverty amid plenty. The Kennedy administration, faced with a serious balance-of-payments problem, a declining trade surplus, and demands for social justice at home, conceived a series of innovative steps to expand the economy, but a simultaneous increase in defense and foreign assistance spending precluded success. Keynesian methods of achieving full employment might well have succeeded in a quiescent world; added to the expense required to meet the challenge of a Khrushchev-invigorated Soviet Union, they meant excessive federal deficits, inflation, and a balance-of-payments deficit that threatened the stability of the international economic order established at Bretton Woods.

Lyndon Johnson was even more committed to social justice for his countrymen. His reforms rivaled those of Franklin Roosevelt's New Deal for boldness of vision and presidential skill in obtaining the necessary legislative action. But Johnson was also committed to winning the war in Vietnam and squandered billions of dollars in that benighted cause. A powerful president who dominated the executive branch and manipulated the legislative branch with ease, he lacked the strength and courage to tax the American people to pay for his Great Society programs and his war. The budget deficit grew, inflation increased, the rate of economic growth declined, and the domestic and foreign economic policies of the United States were left in disarray for Richard Nixon.

Nixon, Kissinger, and their aides much preferred to focus their attention and hone their skills on the pursuit of political and military advantage over their adversaries. But they were confronted with a politically damaging recession in 1969 and concluded that inflationary tactics, including devaluation of the dollar, were essential. The United States had run out of devices for maintaining the Bretton Woods system. The Germans and Japanese were resisting American pressure to revalue the mark and the yen, unwilling to allow the United States to devalue the dollar, and gold was leaving the country at alarming rates. The huge balance-of-payments deficit meant foreigners held more dollars than could be redeemed in gold. The system had always been costly to the United States. but it had borne the cost for political reasons, to enable its friends to reconstruct and to preserve vital security relations. By 1971, Nixon had decided the price was too high, the system too restrictive. He was confident that Germany and Japan would not stray and that the United States could change the rules and destroy the system at acceptable cost. Contrary to the commitment to convertibility, the president decreed that the gold would not be given in exchange for the excess dollars of countries with balance-of-payments surpluses. He placed a surcharge on import duties to meet protectionist demands in Congress and instituted wage and price controls in an effort to control inflation. Before the year was out, agreement was reached on a devaluation of the dollar. These steps, however disruptive of the international economic order, helped stimulate a boom in the United States in 1972, easing Nixon's path to reelection. Again, it should be noted that despite the decline of American economic power in the 1960s, the United States remained strong enough to determine the shape of the new international economic order. In order to increase its freedom of maneuver, the United States wrecked the system it had created.[14]

But in the new era that began in the 1970s, the United States no longer dominated the international financial system. In 1971, the United States recorded its first balance-of-trade deficit of the twentieth century. Increasingly, it required the acquiescence of Germany and Japan, German and Japanese capital, to maintain domestic prosperity and to project its military power across the world. Both countries became increasingly assertive, the Germans on monetary issues and the Japanese on trade. Gradually American leaders discovered they no longer had the freedom of action their predecessors had enjoyed in the quarter of a century following World War II. Increasingly, the United States needed foreign capital to maintain the living standards of its people and its influence abroad, and that capital did not come without strings. German and Japanese ideas about what the United States did at home and abroad had to be considered. If, as seemed likely, the United States became a debtor nation, it might have to defer to its creditors as France had had to defer to the United States to obtain needed funds in the 1920s.

The relative decline of American power had also been underscored in the oil crisis of the mid-1970s, induced by the Organization of Petroleum Exporting Countries (OPEC). Until then the United States

---

[14] See Joanne Gowa, *Closing the Gold Window: Domestic Politics and the End of Bretton Woods* (Ithaca, 1983); Robert Gilpin, *The Political Economy of International Relations* (Princeton, 1987), 139–41.

had controlled the world energy market as well as the monetary system. But as American automobiles and industry consumed more and more of the world's oil each year, American reserves declined. The United States, for the first time, became dependent on foreign suppliers. It could no longer use its own once vast petroleum reserves to keep world prices down, and to assure Americans an endless supply of inexpensive fuel. In the midst of the Arab-Israeli war of 1973, the presumably friendly shah of Iran extorted an enormous price increase while Arab suppliers withheld shipments, and the Saudis replaced Americans as the arbiters of world oil prices. Unable to assure its friends of essential supplies at affordable prices, the United States lost the ability to influence their policies, as was exemplified by American inability to prevent the Japanese from shifting from a pro-Israel to a pro-Arab policy in 1973.

The year Nixon resigned the presidency, 1974, was a particularly bad year for the American economy. Gerald Ford entered the White House confronted with a stagnant economy and a high rate of inflation, the unusual combination economists called stagflation. Ford and Kissinger found the American people much more concerned about jobs and the cost of living than competing with the Soviets on the periphery. With the collapse of the Saigon regime in 1975, there was a widespread unwillingness, in Congress and across the country, to throw scarce resources into endlessly draining, relatively unimportant, probably hopeless causes abroad. The war in Vietnam had denied Americans the Great Society Lyndon Johnson had promised. It was hard for them to imagine any place in the Third World that was worth a further lowering of their standard of living.

Kissinger was deeply troubled by the message that American ennui sent to the Soviets. He never doubted that the Soviets would seek any advantage they could; that an indication that the United States was withdrawing from the field would be perceived in Moscow as an opportunity to expand Soviet influence without risk. Détente depended on the stick as well as the carrot. Congressional action on trade and credit issues had left him little in the way of carrots. Now it began to appear that the administration lacked the support it required to continue three decades of containment. When in May 1975, Cambodian Communists seized an American vessel, the *Mayaguez,* the Ford administration reacted muscularly, sending in the Marines. The operation proved to have been unnecessary. The captives had been released before it began, and more lives were lost among the would-be rescuers than there had been prisoners. But Ford and Kissinger had demonstrated, to their satisfaction, that the United States was not to be trifled with.

Angola, an African nation in which the United States had little interest, emerged as the major point of contention in Soviet-American relations during the Ford administration. A bewildering array of indigenous groups, each with external sources of support, had been seeking to wrest independence from the Portuguese, who abandoned the field after their own revolution in the spring of 1974. As might be expected, there was a Marxist-Leninist organization, the MPLA, supported primarily by Cuba, with intermittent support from the Soviet Union, the Congo, Algeria, the Communist party of Portugal, and some Western European governments. A second group, the FNLA, won the support of an odd assortment of backers, including the CIA, Zaire, North Korea, China, Algeria, Morocco, Romania, Libya, India, several Western European governments, the Ford Foundation, the AFL-CIO, and, eventually, South Africa. A third important force, UNITA, also received aid from China and wooed South Africa. Tribal as well as ideological differences separated the Angolan revolutionary factions.[15]

In January 1975, the Organization of African Unity brokered an agreement among the three leading organizations: They would work together and with the Portuguese in a transitional government to which Portugal would transfer power in November. The Chinese, determined to prevent a regime friendly to the Soviets, moved first to strengthen the FLNA. The CIA followed suit. In due course the Soviets and Cubans stepped up their aid to the MPLA. By mid-1975, heavy fighting initiated by the FLNA had resulted in unexpected MPLA successes. A Soviet-supported Marxist-Leninist regime seemed likely to emerge in Angola.

Additional aid from the United States, China, Zaire, and South Africa enabled the opponents of the MLPA to regain the advantage by late September. A major South African intervention in October allowed the FNLA and UNITA to close in on the Angolan capital, still held by MPLA forces. In November, Cuba raised the stakes, sending combat

---

[15] Garthoff, *Détente and Confrontation*, 502–8, makes the tangle comprehensible, but Piero Gleijeses, *Conflicting Missions: Havana, Washington, and Africa, 1959–1976* (Chapel Hill, 2002), provides essential detail. See especially 235–54.

forces to assist the MPLA. Quickly, the MPLA turned the tide again, routing FNLA and Zairian troops in the north and halting the South African advance.

Unwilling to be tainted by association with South Africa, the Chinese withdrew from the Angolan tangle before the Cubans arrived in large numbers. Kissinger, however, was less interested in local issues, less concerned about alienating black Africa, and willing to ally with the devil to stop a regime friendly to the Soviet Union from controlling Angola. The decision to intervene in force appeared to have been made in Havana, but there was no reason to doubt that it pleased Moscow. Moreover, there was evidence of Soviet involvement in the airlifting and supplying of the Cuban troops. Angola was not important to the United States, but the Cubans and Soviets could not be allowed to act unopposed. The administration turned to Congress for more money for its Angolan revolutionaries.

To Kissinger's horror, Congress said no. In January 1976 it banned further covert aid to Angola. Congress was unwilling to step into another morass on the periphery. Money would not stop the Cubans and, as American prestige became more intensely involved in the struggle, American troops would be required. Not so soon after Vietnam; not in the midst of the domestic fiscal mess, which Kissinger did not deign to consider.

Freed of the risk of confrontation with the United States, the Soviets deepened their involvement and the Cubans sent more troops. Unable to count on American support, the South Africans abandoned the field. The People's Republic of Angola, beneficiary of South African hostility, quickly won recognition from other black African states and by March 1976 had reached agreements with Zaire and South Africa to relieve most of the external pressures on it. Soviet influence in Angola increased briefly, but the dominant foreign influence was Cuban. In 1977, Cuba and the Soviets backed different factions within the Angolan regime, with the Cuban-backed government forces prevailing over pro-Soviet dissidents – with the help of Cuban tanks. Neither Cuban- nor Soviet-backed members of the Angolan government could be restrained from reaching out to the West, including the United States, for trade and investments.[16]

---

[16] Odd Arne Westad, *The Global Cold War* (New York, 2005), 244.

The Soviets had gained little in Angola, but that was not Kissinger's perception. The victory of the Soviet-backed MPLA sharply reduced his tolerance for Soviet competition in the Third World. As long as the Chinese- and American-backed FNLA seemed likely to prevail, the Soviet role had not been troublesome. When the tide of battle shifted, the United States declared Soviet intervention unacceptable, inconsistent with détente. Efforts to persuade the Soviets to back off were ultimately unsuccessful, and the administration, for better or worse, lacked the means to respond more forcefully. Kissinger feared that the Soviets would be emboldened to further interventions, further demonstrations of their growing ability to project power abroad. Perhaps worst of all, he feared that Americans had lost the will to meet the Soviet challenge.[17]

To Brezhnev and his colleagues, Kissinger's strictures seemed the rankest hypocrisy. The American interpretation of the rules of détente allowed competition so long as it resulted in success for the Americans. Now that the Soviets were able to do what the Americans had been doing throughout the Cold War, the Americans declared such action unacceptable. They might make gestures toward compliance with American wishes, but there is no indication in the statements of Soviet leaders or in their actions in the Angolan situation that they were prepared to surrender in the contest for influence on the periphery.

The Soviets, moreover, were confronted by an additional challenge, that of the Chinese. Not only did they have to prove to themselves and the rest of the world that their country was a superpower as deserving of deference as was the United States, but they also had to demonstrate to Communists and radicals in and out of power all over the world that Moscow and not Beijing was their Mecca, that the Soviet Union would do more for them than would China. In the unlikely event that the Politburo had concluded that its potential gains in Angola were not worth the possible increase in Soviet-American tensions, Chinese involvement likely would have drawn the Soviets into the fray. Moreover, Chinese-American collusion in Angola seemed to touch a raw nerve among Brezhnev's colleagues. Too much had been invested

---

[17] William Hyland, *Mortal Rivals: Superpower Relations from Nixon to Reagan* (New York, 1987), 142–6.

in building Soviet military might to allow the Chinese and Americans to intimidate or outmaneuver Moscow.[18]

Finally, it is clear that as American willingness to use military power abroad declined, Soviet willingness increased. In part, as Kissinger feared, the Soviets perceived a clear field in Angola. Congressional action suggested there was little risk of confrontation. Like the Americans before them, the Soviets did not easily resist the opportunity to test their newly developed air- and sealift capabilities. The Soviet military was eager to experiment with new equipment and new techniques. Despite the evidence of how the cost of America's Third World interventions had eroded the power of the United States and contributed to its relative decline, the Soviets were determined to defy the lessons of history. Starting with a far weaker economic base, the Soviets wanted to believe that their great military power, the one area in which they excelled, would enable them to succeed where the Americans had failed, to gain advantage on the periphery.

In the central arena, Europe, détente held. Europeans, especially German leaders, were less concerned with Soviet-American rivalry in the Third World, and eager to take steps to reduce the likelihood of their home-lands' becoming battlegrounds for testing Soviet and American tactical nuclear weapons. Willy Brandt, chancellor of West Germany, had made enormous strides with his *Ostpolitik*. Trade burgeoned between Eastern and Western European countries. In 1970 West Germany and the Soviet Union signed a nonaggression pact. They declared the boundaries of Poland, the Soviet Union, and Germany, as determined by Churchill, Roosevelt, and Stalin at Tehran and Yalta during World War II, to be inviolate. In 1971, accord was reached on Western access to Berlin, to be guaranteed by the Soviets. By 1972, East and West Germany had recognized each other. Uneasy about the German initiatives but preoccupied by Vietnam, Nixon and Kissinger could do little but follow suit.

The Soviets pressed hard for détente with Western Europe. They sought technology not easily obtained from the United States and hoped to be able to drive a wedge between the Americans and their NATO allies. Brezhnev and his colleagues wanted formal acceptance by all European countries of their post-1945 borders and proposed a

---

[18] Garthoff, *Détente and Confrontation*, 527–30; Zubock, *Failed Empire*, 252–54.

conference from which they hoped to exclude non-European nations, most obviously the United States. By 1973, the Soviets succeeded in bringing about a Conference on Security and Cooperation in Europe but had to accept American participation – and that of Canada and the Vatican.

Two years of negotiations resulted in the Helsinki Agreements of August 1975, giving the Soviets the assurances they wanted on the European status quo. To get those assurances, the Soviets were forced to commit themselves to improve their record on human rights, specifically to allow the free movement of people and ideas. Were they to honor their Helsinki commitments, the political system from which Brezhnev and bloc leaders derived their power would be destroyed. Perhaps little of substance had been achieved, but like the American Declaration of Independence, the Helsinki Agreements established a standard toward which the signatories might strive and to which they might be held. They symbolized the extent to which the Iron Curtain had been penetrated from both sides.

Nixon and Kissinger remained apprehensive about the easing of tensions in Europe. They feared Europeans would relax their vigilance, that they would be unwilling to support military preparedness, that they might think the Cold War over and turn away from the United States. While Europeans were heartened by the Helsinki accords, the decision of President Ford to sign them was derided by his political opponents as evidence of his naïveté in foreign affairs. Ford, a popular Midwestern conservative, fought off the Reagan challenge from the right wing of his party and won the Republican presidential nomination in 1976 but lost the election to Democrat Jimmy Carter, whose views on most issues seemed vague and elastic. It was Carter who had to determine how the United States would respond to Brezhnev's opportunism in Africa, and whether efforts toward extending détente would continue.

The election of Jimmy Carter as president of the United States in 1976 illustrated the best and worst of the American political system. The American people were weary of the sacrifices demanded of them – the lives of their children spent senselessly in distant wars, the inroads of stagflation on their standard of living. Not unreasonably, they blamed their government, the people in control in Washington. And unlike their counterparts in the Soviet Union, China, and many other parts of the world, they had a remedy: They voted out their rulers and started fresh, with a new government headed by a man completely uncontaminated by previous contact with Washington and unassociated with any of the tired policies of the past. America would remake itself. A new president would remove all of the irritants and set the country back on course toward a liberal democratic Utopia.

Unfortunately, the new American president, however well he had once run the state of Georgia, was ill-prepared to manage the foreign policy of the world's greatest power. He was bright and he was able, but he had to learn on the job. In the nuclear age, in the volatile world of the late 1970s, it was terrifying to think that the man who had his hand on the levers of American power, the man responsible for American policy, had no experience in international relations. It was not a job for an amateur; it was not a time for an amateur. But Jimmy Carter was the people's choice.

The result was four years of disarray. A good and decent man, Carter was also sufficiently arrogant to think he could put aside the misguided efforts of his predecessors and start anew. Like Woodrow Wilson more than a half-century before, he denounced the selfish realpolitik of the preceding administration and proclaimed America's intention to return to its ideals. Insistence on respect for human rights would be the centerpiece of his administration's foreign policy. He was determined to alleviate tensions with the Soviets and to end the Cold War, but was slow to comprehend that his criticism of Soviet performance on human rights complicated his efforts. Eager to accelerate the arms control process, he disrupted it by putting aside proposals resulting from years of Soviet and American negotiations and substituting a more radical plan, the implications of which were unclear and were ultimately perceived as threatening by the Soviets. His principal advisers on foreign policy – Cyrus Vance, secretary of state, and Zbigniew Brzezinski, national security adviser – pulled him in opposite directions on Soviet issues in particular but on many others as well. The president attempted to construct a policy out of ideas offered by both and succeeded only in confusing friends and enemies alike, provoking contempt at home and abroad.

For Vance, the principal objective of American policy was to revive and strengthen Soviet-American détente, to work closely with the Soviets both to reduce bilateral tensions and to resolve some of the world's less tractable problems, like those of the Middle East. He was persuaded that beneath the geriatric leadership of the Brezhnev Politburo was a generation of Soviets free of Stalinist dogma, as eager as any American to end the Cold War and desperately anxious to modernize their country.[19]

Specifically, Vance sought further arms control agreement, a SALT II treaty, to slow and, if possible, reverse the arms race. Such an agreement might also serve to permit the United States to reduce the defense expenditures that strained the nation's resources and contributed mightily to inflation. He was prepared to accept a Soviet role in the Middle East, convinced that admitting the Soviets to partnership was the only way to persuade them to act responsibly, that giving them a stake in the peace of the region was the best way to stop malicious Soviet agitation of radical Arab forces. Vance was troubled by aggressive Soviet behavior in Africa but perceived no threat to any important American interests. In due course the men in the Kremlin would learn the lesson the United States had learned in Vietnam: The ability to project power on the periphery was double-edged, its exercise as likely to sap national strength as to increase it.

Vance was not particularly interested in China and apprehensive lest the Chinese manipulate the United States toward their own ends, exacerbating Soviet-American tensions to maximize China's room to maneuver. To Vance, the best hope for the future, for the world as well as for the United States, was to encourage the modification of Soviet behavior. Change would not occur overnight, but if détente were back on track, the next cycle of Soviet leaders might accelerate the process.

Brzezinski never doubted that the Soviet Union was central to American concerns. He did not believe, however, that solutions to the problem could be found in Moscow. He perceived no prospect for a voluntary improvement in Soviet behavior. The Cold War could be ended only with the defeat of one of the superpowers. To defeat the Soviet Union the United States had to strengthen itself and its allies and maintain relentless pressure on the Soviets. SALT II was less important than seeking strategic advantage over the Soviets, revitalizing NATO, enlisting the Chinese on the side of the United States, weakening Soviet control over Eastern Europe, promoting dissent within the Soviet empire,

[19] See Cyrus Vance, *Hard Choices* (New York, 1983).

and countering Soviet interventions anywhere in the world. He insisted that the competition between the United States and the Soviet Union was ordained by history and geography, as well as conflicting political cultures. The United States could only play to win.[20]

Vance was clearly right about the imminence of change in the Soviet Union. The forces Khrushchev had unleashed in the late 1950s, the reinvigoration of the social sciences, the serious scholarly study of the world, had proved their worth to the Soviet leadership. The "new thinking" leaking through the dikes of ideological dogmatism had increased from a trickle to a flood by the late 1970s. Nonetheless, the dikes held. Brezhnev and his colleagues in the top echelons of Soviet government remained largely impervious to the intellectual turmoil that Vance's advisers had noted. The party elders were not receptive to fresh ideas, new approaches. They held on to power and exercised it as they always had, and the Soviet people had no recourse. Vance's vision was probably not realizable in the 1970s.

Brezhnev perceived a United States weakened by Vietnam and Watergate, led by an irresolute and uninformed president. The moment was opportune for the Soviet Union to press its advantage, as it did in the fall of 1977, airlifting Cuban forces to the Horn of Africa and winning the allegiance of America's longtime Ethiopian ally. Odd Arne Westad called the Ethiopian operation "the most important Soviet-led military ... [action] outside the area of the Warsaw pact since the Korean War."[21] Brezhnev could only be heartened by the Communist seizure of power in Afghanistan in April 1978 and his Vietnamese protégés' easy victory over the Chinese-backed Khmer Rouge of Cambodia in December of that year. In January 1979, the shah of Iran, the American surrogate in the Middle East and Southwest Asia, fled his country, and the ensuing civil strife undermined the strategic position of the United States in the region. Even on the doorstep of the United States, first in tiny Grenada and then in Nicaragua, forces friendly to Cuba and the Soviet Union seized power.

From the perspective of the Kremlin, Carter had been ineffectual in responding to each of these situations. Soviet power could no longer be checked anywhere. The men of the Politburo were quite satisfied

---

[20] See Zbigniew Brzezinski, *Power and Principle* (New York, 1983).
[21] Westad, *Global Cold War*, 277.

with themselves and saw no need for new approaches. They ignored the probable repercussions of their policies on American behavior and functioned much as Brzezinski had anticipated. Forsaking their usual prudence, Soviet leaders undermined Vance and drove Carter into Brzezinski's arms.[22]

Although ground was lost in the all-critical effort to end the Cold War, the Carter administration enjoyed important successes in Latin America, the Middle East, and East Asia. Unfortunately, none of these successes could be achieved without affecting Soviet-American relations adversely. In 1977, Carter signed several treaties that ultimately would permit Panama to gain control over the canal, an eventuality to which some American conservatives were unalterably opposed. The administration won a bruising battle for ratification by the Senate, but the process cost it votes it would need for acceptance of the SALT II treaty. Some of the conservative senators who helped the administration on the Panama treaty would have to renew their conservative credentials by voting against arms control.

The Camp David accords – enormously important agreements between Israel and Egypt facilitated by Carter – angered the Soviets, who had been excluded from the process. Sadat had lost faith in the ability of the Soviets to aid his cause before the 1973 war and relied increasingly on American leverage with the Israelis. In 1977, aware that Carter needed help overcoming Israeli rigidity, Sadat heroically traveled to Israel to demonstrate to American friends of Israel, as well as Israelis, his willingness to live in peace with his erstwhile enemies. Carter succeeded in brokering the agreements by means of which Egypt regained its Sinai territory and, by making peace with Israel, by recognizing the state of Israel, broke the back of the Arab coalition against Israel.

Egypt's rapprochement with the United States and Israel deprived the Soviets of their most important friend in the Middle East. Exclusion of the Soviets, who were trusted by neither the Egyptians nor the Israelis, from the peace talks disparaged their claim to superpower status. The affairs of one of the most vital regions of the world were being arranged without them. Moscow did not sanction the accords and gave encouragement to those forces in the Arab world that continued to reject's Israel's right to exist. The odds on Israel's survival had

---

[22] Gelman, *Brezhnev Politburo*, 145–6.

increased greatly, but without at least a gesture toward Soviet interests in the region, there was little chance for an enduring peace. And again, Soviet support of Arab belligerence against Israel intensified anti-Soviet attitudes in the United States, creating a political climate unreceptive to the strengthening of détente. As long as the Soviet Union was excluded from the peace process, it would stir trouble in the Middle East. As long as it stirred trouble in the Middle East, it would be difficult to improve Soviet-American relations. Until Soviet-American relations improved, it would be difficult for the leaders in Washington to share influence in the region with the Soviets. It was a conundrum from which there seemed no escape short of surrender by the Soviets, for which the Politburo was not quite ready.

The long-overdue normalization of relations between the United States and the People's Republic of China was also one of Carter's accomplishments. Regrettably, the issue of when and how to achieve this goal was caught up in the Vance-Brzezinski rivalry and in the two men's conflicting view of how to cope with the Soviet Union. Vance was convinced that showing any kind of favoritism toward the Chinese would aggravate Soviet-American relations, that relations with China were less important than relations with the Soviets. Brzezinski, of course, demonstrated less concern for Soviet sensibilities and thought frequent jabs to the head reminded Soviet leaders of the need to conciliate the United States. Brzezinski prevailed.[23]

Chinese ends were not congruent with those of the United States. There was, to be sure, a shared interest in containing Soviet power, but the Chinese were apprehensive about improvement in Soviet-American relations. Historically, a weak China had used barbarians to control barbarians, and in the 1970s they perceived an interest in playing the Soviets and Americans off against each other. Deng Xiaoping, who emerged as China's leader in the late 1970s, was quick to recognize the Vance-Brzezinski rivalry and to use it to China's advantage. Eager to bloody the Vietnamese for challenging Chinese influence in Cambodia, Deng wanted an American connection that would neutralize the Soviets, reduce the possibility of Soviet intervention when China attacked Vietnam. Whenever and wherever they could, Chinese leaders

---

[23] Michel Oksenberg, "A Decade of Sino-American Relations," *Foreign Affairs* 61 (1982): 175–95; Harding, *Fragile Relationship*, 67–81.

attempted to stir trouble between the Soviet Union and the West. Deng was at least as successful at using the Americans as they were at using the Chinese.

Recognition in 1979 of the Beijing regime as the government of China was unquestionably sensible and an important achievement for American diplomacy. If, however, it was to be accomplished in a way that increased tensions with the Soviet Union, the one nation in the world with the capacity to destroy the United States, the price was too high. Whereas Vance was unappreciative of the opportunity for rapprochement with the Chinese, Brzezinski was indifferent to the cost of antagonizing the Soviets. Indeed he rarely missed an opportunity to taunt Moscow. But it was Brzezinski's approach that appealed to the American electorate, and to which Carter was drawn.

Despite Vance's opposition, Washington persistently signaled interest in strategic cooperation with the Chinese against the Soviets. When the Soviets reacted angrily, American critics of détente were appeased momentarily. On the other hand, if the American public was led to believe that getting tough with the Soviets was the appropriate course, there were men like Senator Henry Jackson (D.-Wash.) and Ronald Reagan who were better cast for the role of helmsman than was Jimmy Carter.

Carter's last effort to salvage détente came in 1979 when, despite anger at Chinese-American collusion over China's attack on Vietnam, the Soviets agreed to a summit meeting and the signing of the SALT II agreement. Certainly Vance was genuinely interested in regaining momentum toward accommodation with the Soviet Union, and Brzezinski thought that Brezhnev's willingness to meet Carter and sign the treaty was evidence of the success of his efforts to intimidate the Soviets. SALT II was not a great breakthrough in arms control, but most of the professionals who examined it thought it better crafted than SALT I and very much in the interest of the United States. The Soviets, for their part, had an intense need to reduce military expenditures. Although Brezhnev and the other party elders seemed unmindful of the alarms being sounded by Soviet midlevel analysts, the economy of their country was beginning to disintegrate and the cost of their empire was greater than their people could bear. At the meeting Carter embraced Brezhnev and managed not to berate him about human rights violations. Surprised, the Soviet leader declared that Carter was "quite a nice guy, after all."[24] Briefly, the possibility of revitalizing détente seemed to exist, but it was not to be.

Soviet actions in the Third World and the Kremlin's suppression of dissidents at home, combined with Carter's inept leadership, allowed Senator Jackson and other anti-Soviet elements in American society to seize the initiative. In late summer 1979, Frank Church (D.-Idaho), a senator friendly to détente, inadvertently doomed the SALT II treaty by calling attention to a Soviet combat brigade in Cuba and demanding its immediate removal. Church, widely considered too liberal for his constituents, was attempting to ward off conservative attacks in his fight for reelection. In fact, the brigade had been in Cuba for years with the acquiescence of the American government. When Carter, in response to the domestic political furor caused by Church's revelation, demanded that the Soviets withdraw their troops, it was Brezhnev's turn to be outraged. The Soviets had done nothing wrong. They had honored their promise not to reinforce their forces in Cuba. They were being asked to retreat from a position they had held since the early 1960s to assist the American president with his domestic political problems. They refused. Carter and the Soviets thus gave additional ammunition to the anti-SALT forces in the Senate.[25]

The issue of the Soviet combat brigade discovered in Cuba was quickly overshadowed by the hostage crisis in Iran that began in November 1979 and the Soviet invasion of Afghanistan in December. The shah of Iran, reestablished in power by the CIA-directed coup of 1953, had fled in January 1979, as forces hostile to his far from benevolent rule became increasingly threatening. Hopes for a moderate democratic successor regime were quickly buried by powerful Islamic fundamentalists who looked to the Ayatollah Khomeini as their leader. In November, Khomeini's followers seized the American Embassy and took those inside it hostage, ultimately holding fifty-seven of them for fourteen months, for the remainder of Carter's presidency. The inability of the Carter administration to obtain the freedom of the hostages, through negotiations or a bizarre rescue attempt, intensified public frustration with the president's leadership – or lack thereof. Gulliver tormented by the Lilliputians was not an image of their country acceptable to

---

[24] Zubock, *Failed Empire*, 258.
[25] Garthoff, *Détente and Confrontation*, 828–48.

Americans. They wanted their leader to act forcefully to command the respect due the world's greatest power. They could not understand why he could not get the Soviets out of Cuba, or the hostages out of Iran. They were ready to find someone who could – and would. The president had to run before the mob.[26]

In December, the Soviets gave Carter an opportunity to act assertively, to assume the mantle of greatness Brzezinski held out for him, at the cost of détente. In Afghanistan, the Communist regime that had come to power in April 1978 was disintegrating, partly under pressure of Islamic fundamentalist opposition, but largely because of ethnic factionalism within the Afghan Communist party. Soviet advisers and pressures had failed to ameliorate the situation. Unrest in a nation on its border, among people ethnically related to restive Soviet peoples in Central Asia, boded ill. The triumph of Islamic fundamentalism in Iran threatened Soviet interests as well as American. Whereas the American concern was primarily for control of Persian Gulf oil, the Soviets feared for the security of their border regions. Some analysts feared Afghan leaders would reprise Sadat's betrayal and turn to the United States. Few foresaw how intensely the international community would react, and fewer still anticipated the forceful American response. When political pressure failed, the Soviets resorted to force, another classic example of the arrogance of power. The mighty Red army, feared all over Europe and America, marched into Afghanistan to teach what Lyndon Johnson would have called a "pissant country" not to defy the will of a superpower. Again, Brezhnev and his colleagues underestimated the American reaction to steps they considered vital to their security.[27]

Carter responded vigorously. With striking hyperbole, he called the Soviet action the gravest danger to world peace since World War II. He imposed a grain embargo against the Soviet Union, infuriating American farmers. In due course he decided to have American athletes boycott the summer Olympics scheduled for Moscow, outraging the athletes and all those who considered athletics more important than politics. He declared the Carter Doctrine, a warning to the Soviets that the United States considered the Persian Gulf a vital interest and would

[26] Gary Sick, *All Fall Down* (New York, 1985), is the most useful starting point for the study of the Carter administration and Iran.

[27] Westad, *Global Cold War*, 316–26, is easily the best explanation of Soviet behavior in Afghanistan. See also Garthoff, *Détente and Confrontation*, 887–965.

not tolerate a Soviet advance toward the Gulf. Of greatest consequence, he called for an arms buildup in the United States to meet the new Soviet threat.

The Soviets were shocked by the forcefulness of Carter's response and were put on the defensive in the court of world opinion. They surrendered hope of cooperating with the Carter administration and hunkered down for a new era of confrontation. The war in Afghanistan drained resources from their already profoundly troubled economy.

The glorious achievement of parity with the United States, the exhilarating sense that the correlation of forces in the world favored the Soviet Union, the joy of traveling the road to world leadership, had hardly been savored before the foundations of the Soviet empire began to give way. The army, no matter how brutally it performed its duties, could not crush Afghan guerrilla forces, supplied primarily by the Chinese and Americans. The economy, ramshackle at best, could not stand the strain of subsidies to allies like Cuba and Vietnam, the price of empire. And now there was likely to be a new and costly arms race with the United States. Fearful of Soviet communism, Americans had long exaggerated the threat posed by the Soviet Union. In 1980, many Americans perceived the Soviet Union as on the offensive, poised to achieve its goal of world domination. Brezhnev and the other party ancients reveled in that vision, but the reality was a regime everywhere on the defensive.

The years 1969 through 1980 were years of erratic, halting steps by the superpowers toward the end of the Cold War. The euphoria of Nixon's openings to Moscow and Beijing in 1972, the widespread hopes for peace, were dashed in the closing months of the Carter administration. But the forces propelling the superpowers toward accommodation remained powerful. Foremost among them were the domestic economic realities from which no American or Soviet leader could escape. The empires built at such great cost in the years since World War II had placed unacceptable burdens on both societies. America's relative decline had begun in the 1960s, but the Americans had achieved a standard of living that remained out of the reach of the people of the Soviet Union. The agricultural and industrial foundation of American power remained stronger than anything the Soviet system could construct. The Soviets kept straining to equal, to surpass the United States, but what they succeeded in doing militarily, they could not accomplish in

Map 4. Soviet and Soviet-Bloc Military Presence, Circa 1985.

Legend:
- U.S.S.R. and allies
- Soviet-bloc military occupation
- Cuban combat units
- More than 1,000 Soviet-bloc military technicians
- Fewer than 1,000 Soviet-bloc military technicians
- Soviet naval access
- Soviet air-reconnaissance facilities

Map labels: Soviet Union, Mongolia, Afghanistan, India, Vietnam, Laos, Cambodia, Poland, Czechoslovakia, Hungary, Romania, Bulgaria, German Democratic Republic, Syria, Iraq, Yemen (Sana), Yemen (Aden), Egypt, Libya, Algeria, Mali, Niger, Guinea, Guinea-Bissau, Cape Verde, Equatorial Guinea, Sao Tome and Principe, Congo, Angola, Ethiopia, Zambia, Madagascar, Mozambique, Cuba, Nicaragua, Peru their consumer economy. The United States might be in decline, but the Soviet Union could not overtake it.

Neither Soviet nor American leaders were willing to surrender hegemonic visions, and the structure of their respective societies continued to erode. The competition continued into the 1980s. The strains were obviously greater on the Soviet side, and advocates of the "new thinking" in the Soviet Union knew the race could not go on much longer. Americans, however, were not willing to give up their nation's place in the sun, and their system was stronger, more flexible, their people living farther from the edge. Under the leadership of Ronald Reagan, the American people were prepared to mortgage the future of their children in a renewed effort to win the Cold War. Brezhnev's successors had nothing to mortgage. If wise leaders could not find a way to end the mutually debilitating confrontation, bankruptcy might.

8

IN GOD'S COUNTRY

If anyone ever doubted that America was God's chosen country, the events of the 1980s should have been reassuring. Electing Ronald Reagan, a onetime movie star, to lead them, to determine their future in a world of extraordinary complexity, with nuclear holocaust a hair's breadth away, was the ultimate act of faith by the American people. Their faith did not go unrewarded.

Reagan was a man of unusual charm, with an appealing self-deprecating sense of humor. He was a likeable man who shared the nostalgia many Americans felt for the days of American hegemony. He offered himself as their leader at a time when their economy was a shambles, when they were still heartsick from defeat in Vietnam and from the humiliation of the Iranian hostage crisis. Once in the White House, he restored the nation's confidence in itself and its future. He was the charismatic leader his people wanted. His impact was reminiscent of that of his early idol, Franklin Delano Roosevelt, who had assured hungry Americans, frightened by the grinding misery of the Great Depression, that they had "nothing to fear, but fear itself," that they had "a rendezvous with destiny."[1]

Unlike Roosevelt, Reagan knew little about the world in which the United States had long been the dominant power. He was uninformed – and not terribly interested. Details, such as the political orientation of various governments, bored and eluded him. Efforts by foreign policy specialists to explain were often futile. He ignored briefing books and dozed while the intricacies of military strategy were presented to him.

---

[1] Lou Cannon, *President Reagan: The Role of a Lifetime* (New York, 1991), is the most balanced study of Reagan as president.

He was generally uncritical of stories that fit his presuppositions and seemed to lack a capacity for analysis. And yet, most of those who worked with him as governor of California or president of the United States argued that he was not stupid. Lou Cannon, a reporter who followed him for much of his political career, wrote of Reagan having a different kind of intelligence, more common to actors than to lawyers and professors.[2]

Perhaps more troubling than the peculiarities of his mind was Reagan's disinterest in governing. He had wanted to be president, to provide his vision to Americans, to ride into Washington on his white horse and rescue his country. Once there he had little interest in how things were done. He did not know enough, or care enough, about how government worked to exercise his presidential powers. On most issues, he was quite content to delegate his authority, to let others make decisions and determine how they would be implemented. Once the script had been prepared by his advisers, he would perform for the public. His was an unusual conception of presidential power, but there were surely times when Jimmy Carter envied him.

Reagan was not without ideas relevant to foreign affairs, however many came from movies that he had seen or in which he had acted. He perceived a world in which the forces of good led by the United States were pitted against the "evil empire," the Soviet Union. The Soviet Union and its allies were adversaries with whom "we are at war," a war he intended to win. Opposition to the Soviets was the central focus of all he knew or thought about foreign policy. He contended that the Soviets had achieved military superiority in the 1970s as a consequence of détente, and he was critical of arms control agreements in general and Carter's SALT II accord in particular. The Soviets, he argued, had cheated on all those agreements; Soviet leaders would always lie and cheat. Confronted by such an opponent, the United States could depend only upon its military power. He was determined to rebuild that power, regain for the United States the capability to wage war successfully against the Soviets, to act with impunity against Soviet Third World clients, and to regain its status as the world's dominant military force. Not until then could the Soviets be expected to keep their agreements,

---

[2] See Cannon's fascinating application of the theories of Harvard psychologist Howard Gardner to his analysis of Reagan's mind in Cannon, *President Reagan*, 137–40.

if ever. He despised the Soviet political system and doubted whether the United States could ever reach an accommodation with it.

Despite the extraordinary military buildup over which he presided and the confrontational rhetoric for which he was notorious, Reagan had an intense emotional horror of nuclear weapons. He was appalled when he realized that American security was dependent on the concept of deterrence, on having a sufficient number of strategic nuclear weapons, deployed at sea, in the air, and on land, to deter a first strike by the Soviets. In theory, no matter how the Soviets attacked, American weapons sufficient to retaliate and destroy the Soviet Union would survive, and vice versa. The security of both superpowers had come to rest on the idea of Mutually Assured Destruction. A fraction of each side's strategic force would survive a first strike and destroy the other; there was, therefore, no point to an attack. Deterrence had been central to American defense strategy at least since the Soviets developed a credible strategic force in the 1960s, but it was not good enough for Ronald Reagan. He equated nuclear war with Armageddon, the destruction of the world. He wanted nuclear weapons eliminated rather than controlled. Short of their elimination, he wanted some means to prevent them from being used against Americans. In the 1940 movie *Murder in the Air,* Reagan, as Brass Bancroft, had protected an American secret weapon, an "inertia projector" capable of destroying enemy planes before they could reach their targets. He would have to do something like that again to stave off the apocalypse. Absent nuclear war, the strength of the American free-enterprise system would ultimately leave the Soviets light-years behind.

Once settled into the White House, Reagan and the men and women who accompanied him lacked a blueprint for action. Indeed his administration required two years to produce a document outlining its policy toward the Soviet Union. In 1981, the United States was slipping into the worst economic decline since the Great Depression. The president and his aides, like Herbert Hoover and Franklin Roosevelt in the early 1930s, were preoccupied with the domestic crisis. The Soviets and the rest of the world could wait.

In the interim, the president's rhetoric was inflammatory, but American actions were contradictory. Carter had imposed an embargo on grain sales to the Soviet Union as punishment for the Red Army's invasion of Afghanistan. Despite his vows to be much tougher with Moscow, Reagan's first major foreign policy act was to lift the ban. American farmers had voted for Ronald Reagan, and he had made promises to them, too. For all his ideological rigidity, Reagan had little trouble rationalizing compromises dictated by political exigencies, foreign or domestic. His determination to abandon SALT II evaporated when he discovered that the Joint Chiefs of Staff were quite content with its provisions and angered by his charges of American military inferiority. Reagan decided he could live with its provisions.

Similarly, the president found he could not so easily dispense with arms control negotiations. In response to European anxieties over new Soviet intermediate-range missile deployments in the late 1970s, Carter had agreed to station a new generation of American Pershing and cruise missiles in Europe in the 1980s. Unabashed by the threat their weapons posed to Western Europe, the Soviets were outraged by the threat the proposed American deployment constituted to them. They organized a major propaganda campaign against it among Europeans. Indeed, keeping the new American missiles out of Europe became the principal task of Soviet diplomacy in 1981 and 1982. To protect themselves from antimissile political activists, the European potential host governments needed to demonstrate a good faith effort to achieve security through arms reduction: They needed to have the United States negotiate with the Soviets for the removal or reduction of intermediate missiles from Europe prior to accepting the necessity of deploying new weapons. Reagan had no choice and he sent his negotiators to talk to their Soviet counterparts in what were known as INF (intermediate-range nuclear force) talks. Shortly afterward, Reagan was forced by Congress to back away from his refusal to resume strategic arms limitation talks (SALT). He disguised his retreat by calling these strategic arms *reduction* talks (START). His predecessors had been content to control the arms race by agreeing to limits on their new weapons. He claimed he would reverse the process by eliminating weapons.[3]

---

[3] Michael Mandelbaum and Strobe Talbott, *Reagan and Gorbachev* (New York, 1987); Raymond L. Garthoff, *Détente and Confrontation* (Washington, D.C., 1985), 1023; George P. Shultz, in his memoir, *Turmoil and Triumph: My Years as Secretary of State* (New York, 1993) testifies to the genuineness and intensity of Reagan's goal. James Mann, *The Rebellion of Ronald Reagan* (New York, 2009), 39–43, 46–51, 232–38, focuses sharply on his determination to abolish nuclear weapons.

The crisis in Poland in 1981 provided another example of Reagan being forced to retreat under pressure from his European allies. As the growing strength of Polish workers and intellectuals united in the Solidarity movement promised to sweep away the Communist regime, Soviet pressures prompted the Polish army to seize power. The United States responded with economic sanctions against Poland and the Soviet Union and insisted that its NATO allies follow suit. In particular, the Reagan administration demanded that Europeans stop assistance to the Soviet construction of a gas pipeline to facilitate the sale of Soviet natural gas to Western Europe. When the Europeans failed to respond to Reagan's satisfaction, American firms licensed in Europe were ordered by Washington to withhold essential parts, an act of dubious legality guaranteed to infuriate host governments. In the ensuing uproar, the United States retreated once more and the pipeline construction resumed.

Reagan seemed content to accelerate the arms race and bash the Soviets verbally. His secretary of state, the volatile Al Haig, wanted to demonstrate American resolve in other ways, by striking at Soviet friends around the world, particularly in Central America. Although Haig was reputedly desirous of turning Cuba into a parking lot, he focused his attention on El Salvador, where murderous right-wing army officers contended with leftist guerrillas across the helpless shell of a would-be democratic government. The leftists were receiving aid from the Sandinistas – who had wrested power from the Somoza family dictatorship in Nicaragua – and from Cuba. The rightists, despite their responsibility for the assassination of the popular and politically moderate Archbishop Romero and their complicity in the murder of American nuns, received aid from the United States. It was not a happy choice of fields for liberal democracy to contend against authoritarian socialism, but it was accessible, and American operations there were relatively inexpensive and risk-free. If American intervention in El Salvador was not especially troubling to Moscow, it did prove to the American Right that the Reagan administration's anticommunism would be demonstrated with more than words.

Further comfort to those whose mistrust of the Soviets knew no bounds came when the administration repudiated an informal agreement reached between Soviet and American arms control negotiators in July 1982. Paul Nitze – who had long since established his anti-Communist credentials as principal author of NSC-68 in the Truman era and as the driving force behind the Committee on the Present Danger, created to alert Americans to the threat Carter's arms control programs posed to their security – was the American negotiator. He and his Soviet counterpart went for a walk in the woods near Geneva, Switzerland, and worked out a compromise on intermediate missiles, to the chagrin of the White House, which wanted no agreement. Repudiation upset European leaders, but the president was spared substantial embarrassment by Soviet rejection of the arrangement.[4]

Reagan sent one further message to the world early in his administration. In a "don't tread on me" signature gesture, U.S. Navy pilots intercepted and destroyed two Soviet-built Libyan jets that dared to challenge them over the Gulf of Sidra, an area claimed by Libya. Carter may have been the sort of president who would turn the other cheek and invite disrespect from Third World countries; Reagan most definitely was not. American power would not be reined in. "Let friend and foe alike know that America has the muscle to back up its words," the president warned.[5] Additional evidence of Reagan's willingness to project American power came in 1982, when, against the advice of the secretary of defense, he ordered U.S. Marines to Lebanon in an attempt to create order out of the chaos resulting from the Israeli invasion of that benighted country.

Despite Reagan's hostile campaign rhetoric and anti-Soviet reputation, Soviet anger at Carter had been so great in 1980 that Soviet leaders had welcomed Reagan's election. They assumed that once in office Reagan, like Nixon, would shed his Red-baiting garb and work toward détente. The years of détente had been good for the Soviets, and they were unwilling to see that era end. They had been granted formal recognition of equality with the United States, had been able to expand their influence in the Third World, and, in the ABM treaty, had obtained a measure of restraint on the technological advantages of the Americans. Brezhnev, too enfeebled to devise a new policy, allowed the hope of renewed détente to obscure the reality that Reagan's approach would be radically different from Nixon's, an intensification of all the Soviets had disliked of Carter's confrontational policies of 1980. Brezhnev died

---

4 Strobe Talbott, *Deadly Gambits* (New York, 1984), 116–51.
5 Quoted in Garthoff, *Détente and Confrontation*, 1060.

in 1982, never to see a glimmer of hope that Ronald Reagan would accept accommodation with the Soviet Union.[6]

By the time of Brezhnev's death, surviving Soviet leaders recognized Reagan's intransigence and were ready to give up any expectation of working with the United States. They saw little choice but to wait him out, to hope that dissatisfaction with his belligerence, in both Europe and the United States, would bring a new, more reasonable American president in 1984. But of greater long-term consequence was evidence that the people to whom Yuri Andropov, Brezhnev's successor, looked for advice were beginning to recognize that Soviet actions contributed to American militance; that the Soviet military buildup in the 1970s and Soviet expansionist policies in the Third World might be perceived as threatening by the United States; that the Soviet quest for "absolute" security might have forced the United States to resume the arms race; that changes in Soviet behavior might be necessary to obtain the desired changes in American policy. And Andropov and his advisers, analyzing the results of Brezhnev's ineptitude, reviewing the strains on the Soviet economy, the costs of the war in Afghanistan and their overseas adventures, began to realize that their empire was overextended.[7]

Andropov, slowly dying of kidney failure, presided over the worst year in Soviet-American relations since the Cuban missile crisis of 1962. The Soviet Union's diplomatic offensive to prevent the deployment of new American intermediate-range missiles resulted in a humiliating failure. In the arms control negotiations, the United States offered only propagandistic proposals markedly disadvantageous to the Soviets. One by one the European governments that were to provide sites for the missiles overcame internal opposition and approved their installation. In November 1983, hoping to place blame on the United States, the Soviets walked out of the INF talks. They accomplished nothing.

Most threatening to the Soviet leadership was the apparent intention of the United States to begin a new high-tech race for defensive weapons. In March 1983, Reagan's interest in preventing the use of nuclear missiles led him to announce suddenly, with minimal warning to the secretaries of state and defense, that the United States would seek

---

[6] Seweryn Bialer and Joan Afferica, "Reagan and Russia," *Foreign Affairs* 61 (1982–3): 249–71.

[7] Mandelbaum and Talbott, *Reagan and Gorbachev*, 24–5; Bialer and Afferica, "Reagan and Russia."

to create a strategic defense system (SDI, or "Star Wars"). The idea had intrigued the president for years, and he was delighted when he found both scientists and military leaders who thought it feasible. Although those of his advisers who supported the plan saw it either as a bargaining chip to trade for Soviet arms reductions or as a limited antimissile defense to reduce the chance of a Soviet first strike, the president imagined a shield that would prevent any missiles from striking the United States. His conception may have been undiluted science fiction, but SDI came to be the critical element in arms negotiation for the remainder of his administration. Soviet scientists, like most American scientists, thought the idea preposterous, but Soviet leaders could not take the risk of ignoring it. SDI had to be stopped, or the Soviets would have to compete in its development, a task for which they were ill-equipped.

The worst political disaster of the year, the incident that probably had the most adverse effect on any movement toward Soviet-American accommodation, came late in the summer. On August 31, the U.S. government learned that a Soviet plane had shot down a Korean jetliner, KAL 007, en route from Alaska to Seoul. The crew and all passengers, including several Americans, were killed. The Soviets initially denied shooting the plane down and then charged that it was a spy plane. American intelligence intercepts determined that the plane had indeed strayed into Soviet airspace and that the Soviets had indeed mistaken it for a spy plane. Reagan, angered by the outrage, attacked the Soviets sharply, alleging falsely that they had knowingly fired on a civilian plane. In the context of Soviet-American tensions, and given the fact that the United States did fly spy planes in the area, the tragic Soviet action was understandable, perhaps even inevitable. Andropov's unwillingness to accept Soviet responsibility, to express regret for the tragedy, is less easily explained. Similarly, Reagan's deliberate abuse of the evidence to belabor the Soviets – who for years afterward persisted in believing that KAL 007 was being used by American intelligence – was needlessly inflammatory.

The principal American defeat of the year came in Lebanon, but the Soviets failed to gain from American blunders there. In June 1982, the Israelis had invaded Lebanon, with the acquiescence of Secretary Haig, who saw Israel as an American surrogate against the Soviets and their friends. The Israelis were determined to eliminate sanctuaries of the Palestine Liberation Organization (PLO) and to turn southern Lebanon into a buffer zone to shield Israel against Arab attacks. Syria, supplied with Soviet arms, failed to contain the Israeli advance.[8]

Reagan, like much of the world, was appalled by Israeli aggression and unmoved by Israel's insistence that it was acting defensively, clearing out terrorists. When the Israelis failed to prevent their Lebanese Christian allies from massacring Palestinians trapped in refugee camps, Reagan sent in the Marines to attempt to maintain order in Beirut. Slowly the Americans were drawn into the civil strife as various Lebanese factions, Muslim and Christian, backed variously by Syria, Israel, and Iran, struggled to control the country. One morning in October 1983, a terrorist with a truckload of explosives evaded American security, attacked the Marine barracks, and killed 241 Americans. The president then withdrew the remaining Marines to ships offshore.

American forces had been put in an untenable position in the midst of a war, and lives had been lost. Intervention had accomplished nothing. The Soviets, apprehensive about American and Israeli intentions, had avoided direct involvement but resupplied the Syrians, who became the dominant force in Lebanese politics. The Israelis, trapped in a quagmire, spent many months and many lives, Israeli as well as Arab, before extricating themselves. Lebanon ceased to exist as a viable country and the world's attention shifted elsewhere.

Two days after the American Marines were withdrawn from Beirut, American forces attacked the Caribbean nation of Grenada, ostensibly to rescue American medical students trapped between rival Marxist factions vying for control of the island. Vastly superior American forces overwhelmed local resistance, including that of several hundred Cubans and a handful of North Korean advisers. Pro-Western forces seized power. The Soviets, skeptical of Cuban testimonials on behalf of the self-styled Marxists of Grenada from the outset, did not attempt to counter the display of American force. But again, Reagan's signal to Andropov could not have been clearer: The eagle was screaming. American pressures on the periphery of the Soviet empire would increase.

SDI, the aftermath of the KAL 007 incident, the American use of force in Lebanon and against Grenada, the deployment of new missiles

---

[8] Garthoff, *Détente and Confrontation*, 1062; Douglas Little, *American Orientalism* (Chapel Hill, 2002), 246–8.

in Europe, all suggested to the Soviet leaders that a sharply increased level of confrontation was ahead for them and would continue as long as Reagan remained in the White House. The correlation of forces was shifting against them, and they prepared their people for a crisis. In fact, as Soviet apprehensions began to crystallize, George Shultz, who had replaced Haig as secretary of state in mid-1982, had already begun the process of moving the president toward a less apocalyptic vision of how to cope with his adversaries. More fortunate than Brezhnev, Andropov did catch a glimpse of a more hopeful relationship before he died in February 1984.

Shultz discovered that Reagan was interested in traveling to China and the Soviet Union. He indicated to the president that an improvement in relations would have to antedate a visit to either nation. Reagan remarked that he was not unwilling to reduce tensions. Shultz arranged for the president to have a surprise talk with the Soviet ambassador, Anatoly Dobrynin, in February 1983. Reagan demonstrated interest in a more constructive relationship. The Soviets responded by allowing a group of Pentecostal Christians who had taken refuge in the American Embassy in Moscow – and for whom Reagan had expressed concern – to leave the country in April. But distrust of Reagan was overwhelming in the Soviet leadership, and the remainder of the year provided little hope that he was changing. Still, Shultz pushed internally for conciliatory moves, arguing that the United States had recovered economically, was rebuilding militarily, and was in a strong position to negotiate. Shultz's hand was strengthened by polling data revealing that foreign policy was Reagan's one weak point with the electorate. In January 1984, Reagan made a relatively amiable speech about future Soviet-American relations and Shultz persuaded Soviet Foreign Minister Andrei Gromyko that the president was in earnest. Andropov responded with a secret letter manifesting interest in developing communications between the two leaders.[9]

The death of Andropov and his replacement by the ailing Konstantin Chernenko precluded any dramatic moves by Moscow. Reagan continued to offer friendly gestures, and efforts to resume arms control talks began, but no significant change in Soviet-American relations was

---

[9] Don Oberdorfer, *The Turn: From Cold War to the New Era: The United States and the Soviet Union, 1983–1990* (New York, 1991), 15–77; Shultz, *Turmoil and Triumph*, 358.

likely until the Soviets had a leader as strong as the American president. Shultz and Reagan turned their attention to the other corner of the strategic triangle, China.

The tensions that had developed in relations with China were partly a result of the inability of Reagan, prior to taking office, to understand that China had become a strategic asset to the United States. Chiang Kai-shek and "Free China" (i.e., the Republic of China on Taiwan) were important symbols to the American Right, and candidate Reagan had surrounded himself with men and women who saw Nixon's rapprochement with the People's Republic of China as a gross betrayal. Reagan talked of restoring recognition of the Taiwan regime, withdrawn when the Carter administration recognized Beijing in 1979. He frequently offered gratuitous remarks and gestures offensive to the government of Deng Xiaoping. Reagan's behavior aggravated disagreements over the continued sale by the United States of weapons to the Taiwan regime. The advantages Nixon, Ford, and Carter had gained by drawing China closer to the United States in opposition to the Soviet Union were in danger of evaporating.[10]

Vice-President George H. R. Bush and Secretary of State Haig had both traveled to China to reassure Chinese leaders of American interest in a cooperative relationship. The Chinese continued to separate themselves from the United States and to be unsupportive in public forums like the United Nations. In August 1982, an agreement on arms sales to Taiwan merely papered over unresolved differences. Shultz never shared the Kissinger-Brzezinski estimate of China's strategic importance, but he recognized the value of good relations, especially if tension could be reduced easily by muzzling the president. Gradually he brought Reagan to an understanding of the extent and value of Chinese-American collaboration, especially in gathering intelligence information about the Soviet Union. The president learned to swallow most of his notorious one-liners. In April 1984, Reagan visited China, his first foray into a Communist country. The Chinese greeted him with the extraordinary hospitality for which they are justly renowned, and they never had any trouble with him again. He enjoyed the trip and his reception enormously and came away with a more sanguine view of life in China

---

[10] Harry Harding, *A Fragile Relationship* (Washington, D.C., 1992), 107–19; Warren I. Cohen, *America's Response to China*, 5th ed. (New York, 2010), 225–9.

than was probably justified. Trade and cultural relations prospered. The political relationship never regained the closeness of the late 1970s, but with the resurgence of American power it was not likely to be as important again.

In November 1984, the American people once again chose Ronald Reagan to lead them. At the peak of his popularity and power, he turned to the Soviet Union to look for possible accommodation as the centerpiece of his second administration. Arms control negotiations began in Geneva in January 1985. In March, however, Chernenko died. Enter Mikhail Gorbachev, destined to become one of the most important political figures of the twentieth century.

Soviet leaders had realized since Brezhnev's dying days that their economy was in trouble, that their society was on the verge of crisis, that their system was not working. The research institutes of the Academy of Sciences had produced an avalanche of papers pointing to the need for reform and offering blueprints for change. Andropov had begun the process of reform, but his failing health precluded significant progress. Chernenko was less active. By March 1985, the Politburo was ready to select a young, vigorous man to lead the country. The goal was the modernization of the Soviet economy.

Gorbachev understood that to revitalize the Soviet economy, radical changes were probably necessary, but the fragility of his support in the Politburo, the resistance of the military and the civil bureaucracy, and the skepticism of ordinary Soviet workers required him to move slowly. The support of Soviet intellectuals was enormously helpful, but the Soviet Union of 1985 was not a state in which the power of the pen seemed likely to prevail.

Gorbachev and his wife had traveled in the West as tourists, and he had no illusions about the superiority of the Soviet model of development. He knew that apart from its great military power, conditions in the Soviet Union were more like those of a Third World country than like one of the developed societies of the West: It was "Upper Volta with missiles." He understood that to modernize, the Soviet Union could not just buy technology; it would have to accept some Western ideas and values as well. He would have to dismantle the Stalinist obstacles to Western civil society, to complete the task Khrushchev had begun. The job would have to be done with extraordinary care to avoid either a conservative backlash or a rush to democracy that would undermine the Communist party, which was, after all, the source of his power.

Modernizing and strengthening the Soviet Union would also be costly. Virtually the entire infrastructure was rotten or outdated and would have to be replaced. His colleagues, especially in the military, were greatly agitated by Reagan's SDI program and frightened by high-tech defensive equipment already a part of NATO's force structure. Where would they find the assets, material or intellectual, with which to compete? Gorbachev could ill afford to increase military expenditures.

Then there were Soviet commitments to the Third World, a tremendous drain on existing Soviet resources. One American analyst estimated the Soviets were spending $40 billion annually on their friends abroad.[11] Gorbachev and his advisers saw little economic, strategic, or ideological advantage deriving from the overseas commitments of the 1960s and 1970s. They were not only an extravagance, but they were also a major irritant in Soviet-American relations. Although some Soviet leaders still clung to the vision of their nation as the protector of socialist revolution against capitalist imperialism, Gorbachev was skeptical. He saw little potential for revolutionary change in the Third World. The experts to whom he turned for advice noted that in the 1980s most of the national liberation movements in the Third World were anti-Communist and anti-Soviet.[12]

Not least of his problems was the war in Afghanistan. It was expensive in both blood and rubles. It was increasingly unpopular at home. The Soviets had learned little from the American experience in Vietnam, but Afghanistan was teaching them firsthand how difficult it was to win or to extricate themselves from a civil war in an undeveloped country. Moreover, the invasion had brought upon them nearly universal condemnation, intensifying Soviet isolation. He had to find a way out.

In brief, Gorbachev needed a respite from the Cold War to be able to devote his energies and his nation's resources toward building a more modern, efficient Soviet state. He thought he could win one from the

---

[11] William Hyland, *Mortal Rivals* (New York, 1987), 227–60.

[12] Elizabeth K. Valkenier, "Revolutionary Change in the Third World: Recent Soviet Assessments," *World Politics* 38 (1986): 415–34; Seweryn Bialer, "The Soviet Union and the West: Security and Foreign Policy," in Seweryn Bialer and Michael Mandelbaum, *Gorbachev's Russia and American Foreign Policy* (Boulder, Colo., 1988), 457–91; Odd Arne Westad, *The Global Cold War* (New York, 2005), 364–95, details the evolution of Gorbachev's thinking about the Third World.

United States, from Ronald Reagan, archenemy of communism and the Soviet Union. First of all, Gorbachev was persuaded that the Soviet Union was secure from external threat. That much Brezhnev had willed to his successors. More nuclear weapons were unnecessary. More was not better: Soviet accumulation of missiles aroused apprehension in the United States, left American leaders feeling insecure, and triggered a new cycle in the arms race. Gorbachev was the first Soviet leader to understand the security dilemma, to understand that there could be no security for the Soviet Union without security for the United States. Second, he was aware that Reagan's first-term military expenditures had resulted in an intolerable deficit in the United States budget and that Reagan was unlikely to be able to maintain the pace of the arms race. The Americans would probably be receptive to Soviet overtures for an arms control agreement, for a mutual reduction of military spending. Finally, he recognized that the Soviet obsession with secrecy, initially born of the need to hide weakness, created anxieties abroad, because it allowed for exaggerations of Soviet military capabilities and misperception of Soviet intentions. He was ready to open up the society a little, even to consider the on-site inspections the Americans always demanded.[13]

Reagan and the rest of the world were not quite ready for the extraordinary course Gorbachev was about to undertake. Nor, as the Soviet leader's plans unfolded, were Americans sure that it was in the interest of the United States to help him to build a modern, efficient Soviet economy, a stronger Soviet Union. The skeptics waited. In the interim, Reagan persisted in his efforts to roll back Soviet influence. Implementation of the Reagan Doctrine, American assistance to forces attempting to overthrow Communist or pro-Soviet regimes in the Third World, intensified. The CIA had gone to war against the Sandinista regime in Nicaragua in 1982, beginning with the training and equipping of "contras," or, as the president preferred to describe them, "freedom fighters." Nicaragua was the central front in the campaign, but American aid in various forms went to opponents of the Soviet-backed governments of Afghanistan, Angola, Cambodia, and untold other

---

[13] Bialer, "Soviet Union and the West"; Valkenier, "Revolutionary Change in the Third World"; Celeste A. Wallander, "Third World Conflict in Soviet Military Thought: Does the 'New Thinking' Soviet Grow Prematurely Grey?" *World Politics* 42 (1989): 30–63.

distant lands. When Congress tried to restrain the executive branch, the president's aides raised money in the private sector and lobbied for financial support from wealthy friends abroad, such as the Saudis or the sultan of Brunei. Even the Israelis and ultimately the Iranians became involved as zealots in the National Security Council decided to sell arms secretly and illegally, with Israeli collusion, to the Iranians. The president's aides used the proceeds to support the contras, thus subverting the intent of Congress and the Constitution of the United States. Reagan seemed only vaguely aware of what was being done in his name but was to be weakened gravely when the Iran-Contra scandal became public knowledge in 1986.

The Soviets continued the struggle in Afghanistan, supported the Vietnamese in Cambodia and the Angolan government against its enemies, but backed off from sending MIGs to Nicaragua and suggested Cuban restraint as well. Gorbachev had higher priorities. He wanted an arms control agreement with the United States, and he wanted a meeting with Reagan to accelerate the process, to try to persuade the American president to give up the expensive fantasy of strategic defense. In November 1985, Reagan and Gorbachev traveled to Geneva for the first meeting between Reagan and a Soviet leader.

Reagan despised and mistrusted Communists and hated the "evil empire" in the abstract. But he responded differently to contact with people, with individual Soviet citizens, such as Dobrynin and Gromyko. In Gorbachev he found a man as personable and confident, as determined to protect his nation's interests, and as eager to avoid nuclear holocaust as he was himself. At Geneva, and in the meetings that followed, the two men found common ground. From time to time each grew angry or impatient with the stubbornness of the other, but the antagonism between them and their countries gradually diminished. Summitry, so often derided by professional diplomatists and scholars as sheer puffery, proved to be remarkably useful in the late 1980s. Reagan could not have come to trust Gorbachev had he not met him, argued with him, shared his hopes and fears.[14]

Little besides the establishment of a personal relationship resulted from the first meeting between Gorbachev and Reagan. The Americans

---

[14] Oberdorfer, *The Turn*, 139–54; Mann, *Rebellion of Ronald Reagan*, 57–9; Leffler, *For the Soul of Mankind* (New York, 2007), 381–5.

were not ready to take the dramatic Soviet proposals seriously, and Reagan left no doubt of his commitment to SDI. In the months that followed, however, Gorbachev electrified the world with the changes he began to institute in the Soviet Union and the ideas he was offering for ending the arms race. Most striking were his professed willingness to drop the rigid stance of his predecessors on intermediate-range missiles and to sign an INF agreement largely on American terms; his apparent willingness to accept limits on previously nonnegotiable intercontinental ballistic missiles, so beloved of the Soviet military and worrisome to their American counterparts; and his indications that he was also ready to adjust the balance of conventional forces in Europe, to redeploy Soviet forces from their traditional offensive posture, so threatening to the West, to a defensive one. He explained to the Soviet people that the struggle against capitalism was no longer decisive in world affairs and that a way had to be found to permit both the United States and the Soviet Union to feel secure, that the goal of the superpowers had to be common security. Gorbachev was prepared to take risks that appalled his military. He was determined to end the Western perception of a Soviet threat, to obtain an arms control agreement with Reagan, and to avoid a struggle for advantage in strategic defense.[15]

The American response had to be profoundly disappointing to the Soviet leader. In April, American planes attacked Libya with the intention of killing Qaddafi – the Libyan leader with whom the Soviets had ties – presumably in retaliation for Libyan complicity in a terrorist act in Europe. At approximately the same time, Reagan ordered the CIA to provide the Afghan resistance with Stinger shoulder-fired antiaircraft missiles, with which the Afghanis promptly began downing Soviet helicopters. The United States was increasing the pressure on Soviet friends in the Third World. And in May, Reagan announced that the United States would no longer be bound by the terms of the unratified SALT II agreement. As the Soviet leader waved the olive branch, seeking to shift to the defensive, the United States became more threatening.

At virtually the same time, late April 1986, the Soviet Union was devastated and Gorbachev distracted by a nuclear catastrophe, an explosion at the Chernobyl nuclear power plant. Soviet leaders handled

---

[15] Robert Legvold, "War, Weapons, and Soviet Foreign Policy," in Bialer and Mandelbaum, *Gorbachev's Russia and American Foreign Policy,* 118–19; Archie Brown, *The Gorbachev Factor* (Oxford, 1996), 212–51.

the crisis badly, and most Soviet citizens learned of the explosion and of the danger to them from foreign broadcasts. It took Gorbachev nearly three weeks to issue a statement – in which he petulantly rejected Western estimates of the magnitude of the disaster. The episode did little to encourage Western faith in the Soviet leader's promise to open his society, his talk of *glasnost*.

In August, another Cold War incident, a reminder that Stalinism was not dead in the Soviet Union, disrupted the Soviet leader's efforts to establish his credibility in the West. Gennadi Zakharov, a Soviet UN official, was arrested in New York in the act of purchasing classified documents. It was hardly a major incident. Indeed, there had been several more shocking revelations of American CIA, FBI, and military personnel betraying their country to the Soviets in 1986. But a week after Zakharov's arrest, Soviet authorities retaliated by framing Nicholas Daniloff, the highly respected Moscow correspondent of *U.S. News and World Report*. Americans were outraged, and movement toward a summit was temporarily derailed when Gorbachev brushed aside a letter from Reagan giving the president's personal assurance Daniloff was not a spy. Shultz and Eduard Shevardnadze, the Soviet foreign minister, struggled mightily before coming up with a formula that resulted in charges being dropped against Daniloff, and Zakharov being deported after pleading no contest to the charges against him.

By October, the two superpower leaders were in need of some dramatic breakthrough to enhance their domestic political fortunes. Gorbachev had little to show, at home or abroad, for his efforts. Reagan was beginning to lose his magic. The American people still loved him, but Congress cut his defense budget sharply and then overrode his veto of sanctions against the racist regime in South Africa. If the Democrats gained enough seats to take control of the Senate in the November election, his remaining two years in office would likely prove frustrating. His efforts to achieve an "October surprise," a triumph that would galvanize the electorate, by selling arms to Iran in exchange for the release of American hostages held by pro-Iranian terrorists in Lebanon, was floundering. Both Gorbachev and Reagan stood to benefit politically from a major agreement at their meeting at Reykjavik, Iceland.

Gorbachev had asked for the meeting, hoping that in direct talks with Reagan he could reach agreement on limiting SDI. He was prepared to offer major concessions. He whetted Reagan's interest by suggesting 50 percent reductions in strategic missiles over a five-year period, the removal of American and Soviet intermediate-range missiles from Europe, and the elimination of all ballistic missiles in ten years. He dropped a number of previous Soviet conditions for an agreement, even accepted SDI laboratory research. Reagan indicated his willingness to accept Gorbachev's proposals – until he understood that SDI testing would be limited to the laboratory.

Reykjavik collapsed over SDI, but it was apparent that SDI had motivated the Soviets to take the initiative in arms control. For the first time, it was evident that they were ready to move forward. Reagan's obstinance on SDI and his inability to comprehend some of the issues involved – as when he agreed to surrender the missiles on which European security arguably depended – muddied the waters temporarily, but the American negotiators sensed that historic agreements were virtually within reach.[16]

The next few months were difficult for Reagan. The Republicans did lose control of the Senate in the midyear elections, and the Iran-Contra scandal broke, revealing the president's willingness to enter into deals with terrorists, the disregard of his aides for the law, and the extent of his detachment from the operations of his government. Reagan never lost the affection of his people, but they came to hold a more realistic estimate of his limited competence. His presidency had lost its moorings in the early days of 1987. The president was adrift.

Gorbachev, on the other hand, had to drive harder and faster to stay in control of the apparatus of power in the Soviet Union. He had failed to achieve anything by insisting on halting Reagan's SDI program as a price for Soviet concessions. In February he proposed the elimination of intermediate-range missiles *without* mentioning SDI. Those of Reagan's advisers least amenable to an arms control agreement had the president respond to Gorbachev's offer favorably, contingent on the Soviets accepting highly intrusive verification procedures, which the Soviets had always rejected. The Americans were astonished and appalled when the Soviets proved amenable. It took several months of haggling, with Gorbachev fighting off opposition in Moscow, maneuvering constantly to strengthen his forces in the Politburo and the military, but in

---

[16] Mandelbaum and Talbott, *Reagan and Gorbachev*, 163; Shultz, *Turmoil and Triumph*, 773–7.

November Shultz and Shevardnadze reached agreement on verification procedures, and in December, Gorbachev went to Washington, where he and Reagan signed a momentous agreement (INF) to destroy more than 2,500 intermediate-range missiles. The arrangements for verification were so thorough that American officials became apprehensive about Soviet inspectors learning too much about what was going on in the United States.[17]

Signs that the Soviet Union was on a radically new course multiplied. At home, human rights abuses declined and political dissidents and Jewish would-be emigrants were released from exile or prison. The Russian Orthodox Church, with the support of the government, marked the thousandth anniversary of the introduction of Christianity into Russia. Churches were refurbished and reopened all over the country. Criticism of the Soviet system became more acceptable. Gorbachev chose the seventieth anniversary of the Bolshevik Revolution to denounce the Stalinist heritage and to praise some of Stalin's victims. Denunciation of the 1939 Nazi-Soviet pact surfaced in the Baltic republics. Gorbachev won approval for reforms that pointed toward a less centralized economy. And in foreign policy, the Soviets reached out to the Israelis and indicated their intention to withdraw their forces from Afghanistan.

In March 1988, Soviet troops began to pull out of Afghanistan. In May, they began coming back from Mongolia, and, incredibly, there was even talk of the Red army withdrawing from Eastern Europe. Also in May, Ronald Reagan traveled to Moscow to exchange ratifications of the INF treaty. Polls showed that only 30 percent of the American people still perceived the Soviet Union as an enemy, and Reagan readily acknowledged that it was no longer an "evil empire."

There can be no doubt that Mikhail Gorbachev had found, arguably had been forced upon, the path to ending the Cold War. His initiatives were beyond the imagination of his predecessors in the Kremlin and astonished his Western interlocutors. Indeed, many American leaders – Nixon and Kissinger foremost among them – and most of Reagan's advisers, Soviet specialists in the CIA in particular, remained mistrustful and warned Reagan against taking Gorbachev at his word. Prominent conservatives charged Reagan with appeasement. But Reagan was

---

[17] Oberdorfer, *The Turn*, 233–4.

convinced the Soviet Union was changing. He had faith in his own judgment and found in Gorbachev a man willing to meet him more than halfway. Without questioning the primacy of Gorbachev's role, prominent American scholars such as Melvyn Leffler and James Mann, neither of them associated with the Reagan claque, credit Reagan with the good sense to allow Gorbachev to succeed in ending Soviet-American tensions.[18]

In December, after the heir apparent, George Bush, was elected to succeed Reagan, Gorbachev flew to New York and before the United Nations announced that he would reduce Soviet forces by 500,000 – *unilaterally* – and that he would eliminate units then stationed in Germany, Czechoslovakia, and Hungary. The structure of the remaining elements of the Red army in Eastern Europe would be altered to put them on the defensive, eliminating the threat to the West. As further evidence of his good intentions, Gorbachev added Soviet pressure to that of the United States to persuade the Cubans to withdraw their forces from Angola. As he explained to President-elect Bush, the crisis within the Soviet Union left him no choice. The Soviets could no longer afford an empire.[19]

The collapse of the Soviet Empire came faster than anyone had imagined possible. The United States had little to do with conditions in Eastern Europe and within the Soviet Union as the dominoes toppled on the Kremlin. One after another, events the world's leading analysts considered inconceivable occurred. Freedom came to much of Eastern Europe, to much of the Soviet Union, the two Germanies were reunited – and one day, the Soviet Union disappeared. The Cold War was surely over, and the United States, greatly weakened, staggering, but still on its feet, claimed victory.

Gorbachev's domestic policies heartened reformers throughout the Communist world. In 1968, Brezhnev had crushed the Prague Spring and intimidated all movements toward "communism with a human face." Now it was the turn of the old-line Stalinists to tremble as the Kremlin encouraged emulation of Gorbachev's *glasnost* and *perestroika*. In March 1989, the Soviet Union conducted the freest elections in its history, and many Communist party regulars were defeated in the

[18] Leffler, *For the Soul of Mankind*, 464–6 ; Mann, *Rebellion of Ronald Reagan*, 342–6.
[19] Oberdorfer, *The Turn*, 294–318.

competition for seats in the Congress of People's Deputies. In April, Andrei Sakharov, the great Soviet physicist and Nobel Prize–winning symbol of the fight for human rights in the Soviet Union, freed by Gorbachev from exile, was chosen by the Academy of Sciences to sit in the Soviet Chamber of Deputies. It was not democracy, nor was democracy Gorbachev's goal, but the Soviet Union was changing, and the signals were clear. And to underscore the message, Soviet troops and tanks began to pull back from Poland, Hungary, and East Germany.

In May, Gorbachev traveled to Beijing to deepen the rapprochement he had effected with China. But he was upstaged by thousands of Chinese demonstrators, who, chanting his name, demanded political reform from their own leaders. They had assembled in the vast Tiananmen Square before he arrived and they continued their vigil after his departure, ignoring government demands that they disperse. The world, watching the demonstrations on satellite television, dared to imagine that the Chinese leaders might yield, that China too might be verging on a democratic revolution. But on June 4, the aging Chinese leaders responded with force, sending the People's Liberation Army to crush the people. Hundreds, perhaps thousands, died; and many more were imprisoned. China, the Communist nation whose successful economic reforms had won widespread admiration in the 1980s, would not join the march to freedom in 1990. Instead, the "Chinese solution" came to signify the choice of repression in response to the cries of the people.

The Communist governments of Eastern Europe were also forced to choose. In July, the communique issued after a meeting of Warsaw Pact nations declared that "there are no universal models of socialism." Gorbachev indicated that the Soviet Union would not interfere in Poland, where a resurgent Solidarity movement was on the verge of overwhelming the Communist regime, or in Hungary, where reform Communists were moving the economy away from socialism and opening the political system to opposition parties. In August, when the Communists of Poland reached out frantically to Gorbachev for help in salvaging their power, he advised them to let go.

As astonishing as the events in Poland were, East Germany provided yet greater drama. In September, Hungarian authorities made the critical decision to allow East German refugees to cross their borders to flee to the West, in violation of an agreement with the East German regime. A German appeal to Moscow was brushed aside. No new wall was built to contain freedom-seeking Germans. Gorbachev's spokesman reported that the Hungarian decision was not a Soviet concern. The Soviets would not interfere. The Hungarian Communists quickly transformed themselves into democratic socialists and opened the floodgates for East Germans to pass through. Massive demonstrations swept East Germany. Hundreds of thousands of Germans took to the streets demanding democracy, freedom, and unification with West Germany. Erich Honecker, the German Communist leader, chose to emulate Deng Xiaoping. He would replicate Tiananmen in Leipzig if necessary. But his subordinates rejected the order to turn their guns on their own people. The regime was forced to open the gates of the Berlin Wall in November, and that hated symbol of the Cold War, of the division of Germany and of Europe, was destroyed. The Soviet Union did not interfere.

Soon the Czech people were back in the streets. The Communist regime evaporated. Alexander Dubcek, leader of the 1968 liberalization, returned and was elected chairman of the national parliament. The dissident playwright Vaclav Havel, released from prison only months earlier, was elected president. In Bulgaria and Romania, the people also rose against their Communist rulers. In Romania, the Communist dictator, Nicolae Ceausescu, attempted the Chinese solution. Although the people did not prevail over the party apparatus, Ceausescu and his wife were executed as an earnest of the new regime's allegedly reformist intentions.

The Soviet sphere of influence in Eastern Europe, conceded by Roosevelt at Yalta, long perceived as Moscow's most vital interest, had vanished. In Poland, Hungary, Germany, and Czechoslovakia, the people had freed themselves, but it was Gorbachev who had opened the door to freedom by signaling his willingness to see the old-guard party leadership replaced. To be sure, he had not anticipated the utter rejection of the Communists, most likely assuming that reformist Communists like himself would prevail. But he made no effort to resist radical change until it began to threaten the very survival of the Soviet Union.[20]

Across the vast Soviet empire, ethnic tensions were common. Racial, linguistic, and religious differences had been submerged in a harsh

---

[20] Brown, *The Gorbachev Factor*, 247–51; see also Timothy Garton Ash, "1989!" *New York Review of Books*, November 5, 2009, 4–8.

minorities policy through which little more than lip service was paid to the multiplicity of existing cultures. Conflicts arose from time to time and were suppressed more or less ruthlessly by the Soviet leaders. As Gorbachev attempted to open Soviet society, to give a degree of legitimacy to pluralism, long smoldering separatist movements as well as interethnic violence erupted. The Baltic republics – Estonia, Latvia, and Lithuania – comprised a special problem. They had enjoyed independence between World Wars I and II but were occupied and then annexed by Stalin as part of the agreement with Hitler in 1939, the notorious Nazi-Soviet nonaggression pact. By 1989, discussion of the pact was no longer forbidden and the Soviet government admitted its culpability – or rather Stalin's. The obvious next step was for the Baltic peoples to denounce the pact and demand their independence. Here Gorbachev drew the line: If the Baltic republics were allowed to claim their independence, how could Ukraine, Georgia, or any of the other republics with strong separatist movements be denied? Gorbachev might well have paraphrased Winston Churchill: He had not become president of the Soviet Union to preside over its demise.

As Gorbachev attempted to threaten and cajole the Baltic republics into remaining part of the Soviet Union, complications with the United States arose. There were substantial and vocal Lithuanian, Latvian, and Estonian populations in the United States. There were still Americans who mistrusted the Soviets. The use of force against the Baltic republics would undermine much of the goodwill Gorbachev had generated and bring considerable anti-Soviet pressure to bear on George Bush, who had proved much more tentative in his acceptance of the new Soviet image than had Reagan. Gorbachev's attempt to hold on to the Baltics without alienating the United States was probably doomed from the outset by the intransigence of the Lithuanian independence movement and the anti-Lithuanian belligerence of Russian elements in the Soviet military.

For a year, amid this incredible turmoil, amid the dissolution of the Soviet Empire and the unraveling of the Soviet Union itself, Gorbachev tried with minimal success to reach out to the new American president. He indicated his willingness to effect disproportionately large cuts in Soviet conventional forces to highlight the absence of any hostile intent. Shevardnadze went fishing in Wyoming with Bush's secretary of state, James Baker, and bared his heart, admitting Soviet wrongs and errors,

promising to do the right thing. Gorbachev expressed the desire to integrate the Soviet Union in the world economy, to join GATT (the General
Agreement on Tariffs and Trade) and the IMF, to accept the offer Stalin
had rejected in 1945. Bush temporized. Finally, in December, the two
men met at their first summit, in Malta.

Bush seized the initiative and assured Gorbachev of American support. The essential gesture from Bush was his indication that he was
ready to begin negotiations on a Soviet-American trade agreement
without restrictions on most-favored-nation treatment. The United
States would support various Soviet efforts to participate in the international economic order. The economic warfare that had begun in the
1940s would end in 1990. And the United States was also ready to
respond to Gorbachev's desire for rapid progress in arms control and
force reductions. In turn, Gorbachev stressed his desire for partnership
with the United States: The Soviets now *wanted* an American presence
in Europe, most likely to contain the Germans. It was not quite a resurrection of the grand alliance of World War II, but the United States and
the Soviet Union had ceased to be enemies.[21]

Tensions over Germany and the Baltic republics continued into 1990.
Neither the United States nor the Soviet Union was eager to confront
a unified Germany, but they lacked the power to resist the *Anschluss*.
The economic and political power of West Germany dictated the timing
and the terms of unification. Helmut Kohl, West Germany's chancellor,
dominated the process and forced the pace. He allowed the Big Four –
Britain, France, the Soviet Union, and the United States – to participate
in discussions of the external modalities and gave appropriate assurances of satisfaction with Germany's existing borders. The Germans
also indicated their willingness to provide the Soviets with desperately
needed economic assistance. Reluctantly, Gorbachev accepted first
reunification and then participation of a united Germany in NATO. The
question of independence for Estonia, Latvia, and Lithuania continued to be troublesome, but Bush, understanding Gorbachev's dilemma,
the mounting pressures on him from the military and ultranationalists,
restrained his criticism. Gorbachev, appreciating the demands on Bush,
did what little he could to minimize the irritation.

---

[21] Oberdorfer, *The Turn*, 374–83; George Bush and Brent Scowcroft, *A World Transformed*
(New York, 1998), 161–74.

The decisive test, which the new Soviet-American relationship passed successfully, came in the confrontation with Iraq that began in August 1990 with Iraq's invasion and occupation of Kuwait. Haltingly, but conclusively, the Soviet Union abandoned its longtime Arab ally and aligned itself with the United States. The Soviet-armed and -trained Iraqi army was left to confront and be decimated by the full fury of the United States and its European and Arab allies. Even George Bush, who prided himself on his lack of the "vision thing," was inspired to promise a New World Order.

For Gorbachev, the end of the Cold War brought a well-deserved Nobel Peace Prize, but the great statesman won little honor at home. Neither his diplomatic exploits nor his *perestroika* put food on the plates of his people, or did anything to alleviate the miserable economic conditions of the Soviet people. Buffeted from the right and the left, he sailed first one way and then the other, in a desperate and ultimately unsuccessful effort to ride out the storm. In August 1991, he was deposed in a coup led by conservatives and held prisoner in the Crimea. A few days later, the coup leaders found the military unwilling to crush a few thousand demonstrators who had rallied around Boris Yeltsin, a onetime Gorbachev supporter who had come to personify the demand for more radical change. Gorbachev returned to Moscow, but events had passed him by. Communism, however reformist, was finished in the Soviet Union. Indeed, the Soviet Union was finished. The Baltic states immediately declared and achieved their independence, without resistance from Moscow. One after another, the constituent republics declared their independence, the Communist party was outlawed, and Gorbachev had no empire, no country, and then no government to rule. Before the year was out, Boris Yeltsin, popularly elected president of the Russian Republic, moved into the Kremlin and Gorbachev was forced into early retirement. On December 31, 1991, the Soviet Union officially ceased to exist, succeeded by a loosely organized Commonwealth of Independent States.[22]

The United States of America was the only superpower to survive the Cold War. It had triumphed economically, ideologically, and politically.

[22] Archie Brown and Lilia Shevtsova, eds., *Gorbachev, Yeltsin, Putin: Political Leadership in Russia's Transition* (Washington, D.C., 2001), 22–43.

It had been spared the ultimate military test of a direct confrontation, probably nuclear, with its principal adversary. Curiously, few Americans stopped to celebrate. They found, in fact, that the quality of their lives was declining rather than improving. Their economy, the envy of the Soviet Union, Eastern Europe, and the Third World, was a mess. They were confronted with an industrial infrastructure and transportation system in decay, a corrupt banking system that had cost thousands of people their life's savings, massive unemployment, and widespread homelessness. The Reagan administration, in its effort to expand American military power without asking the American people to pay for it, had run up an incredible deficit, leaving the government without the means to respond to the economic crisis at home or the needs of its less fortunate constituents. Once the nation upon which the world depended for investment capital, the world's leading lender, it had become in 1985 the world's leading debtor, dependent on Japan, Germany, and Arab oil-producing states. It had to solicit donations from foreign governments to finance the war against Iraq in 1991. It could no longer provide sufficient aid to needy countries abroad or necessary services for its own people. Voter apathy eroded the value of its electoral system. Racism simmered just below, barely below, the surface and boiled up explosively with painful frequency. And as a portent for the future, international tests showed American children far behind most Western European and Japanese children in their mastery of math and science skills.

Some analysts, most notably Paul Kennedy and David Calleo, had suggested that the United States was in decline, that it suffered from imperial overreach or, at the very least, a lack, among its leaders, of the political will or courage to ask the people to make the sacrifices necessary to rebuild the nation for their children and their children's children.[23] But the United States had won the Cold War: It was still number one.

---

[23] Paul Kennedy, *The Rise and Fall of the Great Powers* (New York, 1987); David P. Calleo, *The Imperious Economy* (Cambridge, Mass., 1982).

9

AMERICA AND THE
WORLD, 1945–1991

The era herein reviewed began in the closing months of World War II and ended with the disappearance of the Soviet Union. The central thread in the tapestry of the international politics of the time was the Soviet-American confrontation. In 1945, the Soviet Union and the United States, allied in the war against the Axis powers, crushed their enemies and emerged from the war triumphant, each with only the other remaining as a credible adversary. The next forty-five years constituted what John Lewis Gaddis has called the "Long Peace," as the two great empires competed without direct conflict between them.[1] And then the Soviet empire collapsed and was gone.

The period was also striking because of the disintegration of all of the pre–World War II colonial empires and the appearance of scores of newly independent states in Africa, Asia, and Latin America. As each of these new nations struggled to define itself, to search for some modicum of wealth and power, it contributed another ripple to the tides of world affairs, sometimes barely perceptible, often so evident as to force one or both of the great powers to change course. There was too much turmoil in the world for any country, even one as powerful as the United States, to exercise hegemony. And along the way the locus of power shifted, as Chinese military strength developed and as Japan, South Korea, and the ASEAN states demonstrated their economic vitality. The reemergence of Japan and Germany as major forces in the world and the solidifying of the European Community were also important currents precluding superpower complacency.

[1] John Lewis Gaddis, *The Long Peace* (Oxford, 1987).

Ideologically, anticommunism was the engine that drove American action, just as hostility to what they perceived as capitalist imperialism energized Soviet leaders, few of whom still dreamed of a socialist Utopia. As Soviet power grew in the 1950s, 1960s, and 1970s, so did American fears of communism. With the opening of Soviet society in the late 1980s, even ideologues like Reagan were prepared to cooperate with the former "evil empire." With the collapse of the Soviet state in 1991, American leaders lost their compass and sailed, bewildered, in search of a new heading. What remained of the Soviet hierarchy, in Russia and other former Soviet republics, had a surer sense of what it sought: the course to capitalist development. An era that began with Stalin's rejection of Bretton Woods, of the invitation to participate in GATT, the IMF, the World Bank, ended with his heirs begging for membership, at a time when aspirants to lead the United States were talking of abandoning the liberal international economic order.

And, perhaps most incredibly, a time that began with the United States as the greatest economic power the world had ever seen, extending its largesse to former enemies as well as allies, using its enormous wealth to buy friends in the struggle against the Soviet Union, ended with the United States as the world's largest debtor nation. Embattled American diplomatists, assigned to protect uncompetitive industries, devoted their energies to persuading Japan to limit its exports to the United States and to demanding that the Japanese open their doors to imports. And the president was reduced to begging other nations to finance his foreign policy goals.

How does one explain the menacing posture the United States and the Soviet Union adopted toward each other in the late 1940s and sustained until the late 1980s? The answer has three parts, found by pursuing three intersecting lines of inquiry. First, there was the determination of American leaders to accept what they saw as the responsibilities of power, to lead the world, to create a new world order. Second was the qualities of the two states – the excesses of civil society in one (the powerful-state, weak-government pattern in the United States) and the absence of it in the other (the all-powerful Stalinist government). Third was the security dilemma.

Without the American determination to provide world leadership, it is difficult to conceive of a Cold War. Had the United States chosen to pursue a version of the "continentalism" advocated by some intellectuals in the 1930s or the autarky advocated by others in the 1960s, the dynamics of the postwar world would have been very different. But a generation of American leaders had concluded that it was American shirking of responsibility after World War I that had allowed for the temporary ascendency of Adolf Hitler and the Japanese militarists, for the Great Depression, and for World War II. Conscious of Santayana's dictum about those who forget the past being doomed to repeat it, they learned the lessons of the historians and began to apply them in the mid-1940s.

Their goal was to create a world order conducive to the interests of the United States, in which the wealth and power of the United States would grow, in which the values Americans treasured would be carried around the world. Specifically, they planned for a liberal international economic order based on free trade and stable currency exchange rates that would provide prosperity for all peoples. The world they envisaged had no place for militarism; military power would be largely irrelevant. The kind of international system of which Richard Rosecrance has written, where economic prowess rather than brute force prevails, is close to what they had in mind, although it was American economic prowess, not German or Japanese, that they envisaged.[2]

The Bretton Woods agreements were designed to implement that vision. The agreements were unquestionably intended to serve the long-term interests of the United States, but it also was widely believed, at home and abroad, that the United States was taking a responsible and generous position that would benefit those nations that participated in the system, that accepted American hegemony.

The Bretton Woods agreements are also useful as an illustration of the strong-state, weak-government notion. They were designed by the men who controlled the apparatus of government in 1944 not only to serve American interests abroad but also to preempt special-interest groups of the sort that often prevent the leadership from pursuing its conception of the national interest. The executive branch of the government in 1944 was committing the United States to a particular economic regime before the opposition (primarily protectionist and functioning primarily through Congress) could act. In wartime, the executive tends to have much greater leeway to impose its will, and students of contemporary

---

[2]   Richard Rosecrance, *The Rise of the Trading State* (New York, 1986).

American affairs will note how often the executive attempts to simulate wartime conditions to claim powers it could not otherwise exercise.

The Soviet decision not to participate in the Bretton Woods system was not perceived at the time as a serious blow. The British were the key foreign players in the world economy. But when it came to strategic planning, which President Roosevelt controlled more closely, it was evident that the Soviet Union was important. Between the United States and the Soviet Union there had been a generation of enmity, largely ideological, but the two nations had no vital interests in conflict. They shared an interest in pacifying Germany and Japan, and Roosevelt had few reservations about conceding to the Soviets a sphere of influence in Eastern Europe.

The issue of the Soviet sphere in Eastern Europe provides another illustration of how the structure of the American government placed restraints on even a strong president and, equally important, how the brutality of the Stalinist system precluded an acceptable solution. Roosevelt had no problem resolving the matter of conflict between the Polish right to self-determination and the Soviet right to security in favor of the Soviets. The Poles had done little to commend themselves in the 1930s. They had flirted with Hitler, persecuted Jews, and seized a part of Czechoslovakia after Munich. Soviet power was essential to victory over the Nazis and would be essential for maintaining world peace after the war. But because of the nature of the American political system, Roosevelt needed some help from Stalin. He needed Soviet gestures toward the cherished principle of self-determination, and he needed to have Soviet influence in Eastern Europe generally and in Poland in particular to be exercised magnanimously (as the Americans would exercise theirs in Germany, Italy, and Japan, which were, after all, defeated enemies). But, just as the exigencies of the American system demanded a benign Soviet domination of Poland, the exigencies of the Stalinist system precluded it.

At the end of the war, Soviet suspicion of American intentions, combined with awareness of superior American power and the memory of Western hostility to the existence of the Soviet state, drove Stalin and his colleagues to take steps to enhance their security. These steps aroused apprehension in Washington in 1946, as the security dilemma – the notion that an increase in one state's security automatically decreases that of another – began to affect strategic thinking. Initially divided in their estimates of Soviet intentions, American leaders, troubled by Soviet behavior, reached a consensus on the need for policies to demonstrate the nation's will to protect its interests. These policies were perceived as threatening by the men in the Kremlin. Although each state conceived of its own actions as defensive, each was alarmed increasingly by the maneuvers of the other. Every wary step triggered a response that heightened the sense of menace felt in both capitals.

After the 1946 elections, Truman's foreign policy advisers emphasized the collapse of European power and the importance of the United States filling that vacuum. They saw the disinclination of Congress and the American people to concern themselves with world affairs, the desire to demobilize and consume, as the principal obstacles to assuming the responsibility of world leadership – a conflict between the perceptions of the international relations elite and popular pressures (again the strong-state, weak-government paradox). They also warned of the unexpected difficulty of Europe with postwar recovery. Marshall, Acheson, Harriman, Will Clayton, and Kennan did not fear Soviet attack on the United States or Western Europe but rather the collapse of Western European societies unable to recover from war damage, subverted by local Communists.

Their task was to convince a hostile, budget-cutting Congress to finance the reconstruction of the economies of America's competitors in order to oppose an imperceptible threat. They had to persuade the American people to make new sacrifices after so recently persuading them that joining the United Nations would spare them international concerns. They chose to use the idea of a Soviet threat to dominate the world. They did not see such an attack coming; they were not preparing for war. But they saw the Soviets as expansionist, opportunistic, reaching beyond their security needs. The Middle East – specifically Greece – and Western Europe were in danger of being subverted by indigenous Communist forces. Only the United States could stop them, if it had the will.

This, of course, is the context for the Truman Doctrine and the Marshall Plan. In the weak-government paradigm, the president's authority is contested constantly by Congress, especially when the two branches of government are controlled by different parties. Certainly this tension is what the framers of the American Constitution intended as a check on executive power. In practice, Congress members who

have been elected on the basis of issues peculiar to their home dis-
tricts respond more readily to the demands of domestic special-interest
groups than to the imperatives of foreign policy. To focus congressional
attention on foreign affairs and attain their objectives, presidents and
their retainers may contrive an international crisis. Often in domestic
affairs, almost always in foreign affairs, a sense of crisis will result in
legislative deference to the president, to an enhancement of executive
power, to an imperial presidency. In 1947, the Truman administration
misled Congress and the American people by exaggerating the Soviet
threat, in order to enable the president to gain congressional and public support for aid first to Greece and Turkey and then to Western
Europe.

There may have been no other way to get money from the
Republican-controlled Eightieth Congress. Truman and his advisers obtained the funding they wanted and provided the foundation
for an extraordinary level of material prosperity for all who accepted
American hegemony. In the process, however, they strengthened forces
at home hostile to the New Deal and to the dream of social democracy,
and they gave renewed hope to the supporters of Chiang Kai-shek.

And once again the security dilemma came into play. Although the
Marshall Plan may have been conceived defensively, to protect Western
Europe from possible communist subversion, it was perceived by Stalin
as a threat. He responded "defensively," by consolidating his control
over Czechoslovakia and the rest of Eastern Europe, provoking new
fears in the United States. With memories of the Grand Alliance fading
rapidly, there seemed no way either the Soviet Union or the United States
could enhance its security without undermining that of the other.

In June 1948, Soviet imposition of the Berlin blockade increased anxieties. Stalin was trying to prevent the creation of a German state capable of challenging Soviet dominance in Eastern and Central Europe,
of reversing Soviet gains since 1945. This confrontation was unlike
earlier disagreements between the Soviet Union and the United States.
American action was not merely irritating; it was fraught with danger.
Stalin consequently risked more in trying to deflect the Americans from
their course. He failed and had to acquiesce in the inevitable revival of
German power, supported by the United States.

American leaders, denying any animosity toward the Soviet Union,
perceived the confrontation differently. They had conceded the

requirements of Soviet security and offered the Soviets a role in the new international economic order. The Soviet response had been hostile, aggressive, ominous. The men in Washington suspected the Soviets of attempting to dominate the Eurasian landmass; they had to be stopped before they threatened the security of the United States. The problem of perception was complicated by the Stalinist system. It was difficult to trust the Soviet government, because it was closed, secretive, brutal toward its own people and the others it dominated – because of Stalinism.

After the Berlin blockade, relations between the United States and the Soviet Union were clearly adversarial. And yet the two countries were not quite enemies. They had avoided bloodshed, and no critical issues remained to divide them. None of their vital interests were in conflict. American security and that of its allies were assured by the preponderance of American power. The United States was uninterested in pressing its advantage any further, nor is there any evidence to indicate that Stalin feared an American offensive against his Eastern European buffer. The division of the European continent may not have satisfied the leadership in Washington or Moscow, but it was bearable. A return to the level of amity achieved during the war years, permitting attention to pressing domestic problems, was conceivable. But it did not happen.

Stalin was ready to consolidate his gains, accept the status quo of 1949, and promote peaceful coexistence. His maneuvers had stiffened American resolve and increased rather than lessened the danger to his regime. War with the United States had no appeal to him. But even peaceful competition meant the Soviet Union would strive for equality with the United States, demand respect as a superpower, remain mistrustful of American intentions, and compete for control of the periphery.

The structure of the international system, nominally bipolar, continued to frame Soviet-American relations. By 1949, the two governments had gained considerable experience contending with each other. In Europe, the United States had drawn the line and Stalin had accepted it as consistent with the existing correlation of forces. Continuing Soviet efforts to compete for power and influence, however, and the decline in America's relative power as the rest of the world began to recover from the impact of the war, proved intolerable to Truman's advisers. They were profoundly troubled as they watched decolonization and pressures for it loosen Western control over the periphery, and they determined to prepare for the worldwide struggle to come.

The principal obstacle to American preparedness, as perceived by Dean Acheson and Paul Nitze, had been Truman's determination to hold down defense spending. The president's parsimony was supported by Congress and public opinion. Change followed the Soviet A-bomb test in 1949. The loss of the nuclear monopoly forced the United States to reconsider the size and deployment of its conventional forces. In January 1950, Truman approved the development of the H-bomb and the review of policy that emerged as NSC-68, both with the intent of maintaining American superiority.

With evidence that the Soviets had acquired a nuclear capability, a new cycle of anxiety began. Soviet leaders could not accept a permanent American monopoly of nuclear weapons. Perhaps their apprehension over the Marshall Plan was unjustified, but there was nothing unreasonable about their fear of Germany or of NATO, or about their decision to arm against the threat they perceived. But increments to Soviet power and improvements in Soviet security threatened American security and interests. Certainly the Soviet acquisition of nuclear power constituted such a threat.

The United States and the Soviet Union engaged in a systemic rivalry after World War II. To paraphrase the historian Melvyn Leffler, both sides acted prudently.[3] Friction was predictable as they competed. The principal surprise was probably the extent to which the United States asserted its interests across the globe, in the Middle East, and ultimately in Africa and Southeast Asia as well. This is easily attributable to a sense of mission, Wilsonian internationalism, or perhaps, more simply, a conviction that the time had come for the United States, as the world's greatest power, to behave responsibly and benevolently, to create and oversee the new world order. The United States was, after all, far and away the world's greatest power. It alone could afford the short-term sacrifices necessary to gain broad acceptance of its hegemony.

One problem with the Pax Americana was the circumscribed role it allowed the Soviet Union. Contempt for the Soviet system, for Stalinism,

---

[3] Melvyn P. Leffler, *A Preponderance of Power* (Stanford, 1992).

contributed to American unwillingness to contemplate partnership. The historic experience with the Stalinist regime precluded trust. But the Soviets were far too strong to tolerate American dominance any longer than forced to.

The fact that the competition became hostile and evolved into the Cold War is attributable principally to the nature of the Soviet regime – a powerful and vicious dictatorship, a ruthless totalitarian state that terrified its own people and all who came under its control, a closed society whose secretiveness precluded verification of agreements. Like most revolutionary regimes, the Soviet Union was slow to learn the value of traditional diplomatic procedures, of civility in discourse. Communication was difficult, and suspicion was always close to the surface.

But the American political system also contributed mightily to the problem. To serve the national interest as they conceive it, presidents and their foreign affairs advisers appear to have two choices. First, and apparently the choice of Roosevelt, Johnson, Nixon, Reagan, and Bush, they can ignore congressional and constitutional restraints and do what they think right, being as devious as necessary to get the job done. Or, second, they can persuade Congress and the people of the wisdom of the course chosen. The latter approach also allows two further choices. Presidents can tell the people the truth, as Jimmy Carter promised to do, or they can tell them something "clearer" than the truth, as Dean Acheson had Harry Truman do, and as he believed all great teachers do. In this context, articulating something clearer than the truth meant magnifying the Soviet threat, and the Soviet role in events with undesirable outcomes – to the delight of anti-Communist ideologues, who then argued, if the Soviet threat was so great, why had Truman not done more? The exaggerated view of the Soviet threat took root, came back to haunt Truman, Acheson, Kennan, et al., and seems to have been internalized by some of the mythmakers themselves.

The security dilemma, ostensibly a product of the systemic rivalry, was aggravated by the American sense that the United States posed no threat to anyone, was acting in the best interests of all, and that any state, specifically the Soviet Union, that enhanced its own military position was preparing to take hostile action. Kennan occasionally, unlike most others, was able to conceive of Soviet actions as defensive responses to the disposition of American power.

In the years when the United States enjoyed a monopoly or a pre-ponderance of nuclear power, Stalin's natural prudence was rein-forced by a disinclination to invite the use of such weapons against the Soviet Union. Truman and Eisenhower were unquestionably willing to resort to nuclear blackmail against the Soviets or the Chinese, but recommendations for preemptive strikes against one or the other of the Communist giants emanated primarily from the lunatic fringe and never received serious consideration in the White House. The United States enjoyed the status quo: It would not start a war against a major power. Its historic traditions militated against (although they did not prevent) acts of aggression, as did the image it hoped to convey to the rest of the world.

As the Soviets developed their nuclear capability and the necessary delivery systems, civilian theorists in Moscow and Washington con-cluded that war was unwinnable. Khrushchev understood that Leninist concepts of international relations were irrelevant in the age of the hydrogen bomb, that the bomb did not observe class principles. The initiator of a nuclear war, whether it ultimately won or lost, would have to endure a retaliatory strike of unacceptable magnitude. All of its cities might be destroyed in a few hours, perhaps in a matter of min-utes, with scores of millions of almost immediate deaths. Avoiding war, deterring an enemy strike, rather than fighting became the mission of Soviet and American strategic forces. The Soviets did not actually have a second-strike capability until the 1960s, but Eisenhower was also a pru-dent man. Subsequent Soviet-American summitry and then arms con-trol negotiations, promoting a sense that the two nations could resolve their differences peacefully, helped preclude direct confrontation.[4]

It must not be forgotten, however, that the Soviet-American Cold War was responsible for millions of deaths. Walter LaFeber noted that 21.8 million people died of war-related causes between 1945 and 1990, most of them as surrogates for one or the other superpower or at the receiv-ing end of arms provided by one of the superpowers.[5] The Korean War was probably the most dangerous of the wars on the periphery. Civil strife escalated into an international conflict and very nearly a world

---

[4] See Gaddis, *The Long Peace*, and especially Robert Jervis, *The Meaning of the Nuclear Revolution* (Ithaca, 1989).

[5] Walter LaFeber, *America, Russia, and the Cold War, 1945–1990*, 6th ed. (New York, 1991), 335.

war. Approving Kim Il Sung's design for attack was Stalin's most serious miscalculation of the postwar era. Truman's decision to send American forces across the thirty-eighth parallel was equally misguided.

For Americans, Vietnam was the most grievous of its many interventions in the Third World, bringing incredible misery to the Vietnamese people, weakening further an already faltering American economy, and undermining the willingness of many Americans to support further adventure in the guise of exercising the responsibility of world leadership. In Afghanistan, for the first time, Soviet troops were bloodied as they tried to control an unruly neighbor. But for every American or Soviet soldier who was killed in combat, perhaps as many as two hundred Africans, Asians, Central Americans, and Middle Easterners died in these wars. Millions more suffered human rights abuses in the Soviet empire and in countries like Chile, El Salvador, Guatemala, Iran, and South Korea, where the United States supported brutal regimes as bulwarks against communism.

Almost always internal or regional issues precipitated the struggle in the Third World, and one or the other superpower intervened, posing a perceived challenge to the credibility or resolve of the other and intensifying the misery of the local people. Rarely did these conflicts threaten the vital interests of either the Soviet Union or the United States. The superpowers simply would not tolerate indigenous challenges to the status quo unless the challengers were likely to align with their side. With less risk of provoking a nuclear exchange, intervention was always tempting. More often than not the superpowers underestimated the autonomy of countries like Cuba, or Israel, or Korea, or Vietnam and feared the machinations of their major adversary. Washington and Moscow developed elaborate rationales, such as the notorious "domino theory," to explain why it was necessary to expend lives and dissipate their wealth in some distant benighted land.

And then it all came to an end – not the turmoil in the Third World, for sure, but the will and capacity of the superpowers to attempt to control the world. The Americans, staggering since the late 1960s, held on longer. The Soviets, after a furious flurry of activity in the late 1970s, collapsed in the mid-1980s. Changes in Soviet society, Gorbachev's reforms, modifications of Soviet military doctrine – and, more important, Soviet military posture – provided the United States with a desperately needed respite. The Americans no longer had the financial means necessary to respond to every test of their resolve, and the collapse of the Soviet Union allowed them to claim victory before their own society was strained beyond bearable limits. Finding a credible enemy, a potential threat so grave as to sustain the enormous military establishment of the United States, was not conceivable in the 1990s. So weakened was the victor that even with Soviet support, the United States needed German and Japanese money, Saudi and Kuwaiti funds, to underwrite its forces in operations against Iraq in 1990 and 1991.

Much of the change on the international scene was related only marginally to the Cold War. Most significant was decolonization, the end of the European empires, and the emergence of scores of new nations, each seeking to modernize as rapidly as possible, to gain a share of the wealth and power so long enjoyed exclusively in the metropoles. World War II was the catalyst, weakening the imperial powers, awakening the colonials. In some instances, Cold War tensions affected the pace and the price of winning freedom and attaining its rewards. Sometimes the Cold War helped Third World peoples such as the Egyptians, who, in the absence of superpower competition, might have been ignored, but who were able to manipulate the anxieties in Moscow and Washington to their advantage. Sometimes, superpower-supported internal strife delayed development, as in Angola, or brought widespread misery and death, as in Vietnam and Afghanistan.

Another disruptive legacy of World War II was the state of Israel, an effort to do justice to the Jewish people, victims of the world's earlier indifference and persecution, who had suffered horribly at Hitler's hands. But the Jewish return to their ancient homeland displaced thousands of Palestinian Arabs, who did not move aside voluntarily. The Palestinians and their Arab neighbors fought war after war against the Israelis, and again both sides manipulated the superpowers. The Soviets, eager to disrupt the British position in the Middle East, contributed to the victory of the Jewish settlers with a critical shipment of Czech weapons in 1948. Beginning with an arms deal with Egypt, the Soviets shifted sides in the mid-1950s and supplied the radical Arab states with sophisticated military equipment and advisers until 1990. In the 1960s, the United States, after an initial effort to remain aloof, was drawn by primarily domestic political considerations into becoming Israel's principal backer. As the Soviets aided the Arabs, Israel was seen increasingly as an American surrogate against Soviet surrogates in the region. The end of Soviet assistance to the Arabs in 1990 soon diminished the intensity of American support for Israel, but Arab-Israeli tensions continued without the backdrop of the Cold War.

At the end, Germany and Japan had reemerged as major forces in the world, the nations of Eastern Europe had regained their freedom, some of the Soviet republics seceded from the Soviet Union, and the rest struggled to define their new identities. Ethnic tensions long suppressed by communism exploded into civil strife reminiscent of the early years of the twentieth century. The Cold War was over, but the world would not know peace.

The United States in the 1990s was a land very different from what older Americans remembered of 1945. The lot of minorities – Catholics, Jews, African Americans, Hispanics, and Asian Americans – and of women was greatly improved. There remained enormous room for progress, but American society was vastly more open, unimaginably more open than it had been in 1945. Some of the change had been set in motion by the ideals for which Americans had professed to be fighting in World War II. Some – for example, the improved status of Catholics in American society – might be attributed to the Cold War, as the Catholic church had long been in the vanguard of anticommunism, and Cardinal Spellman of New York and Senator Joseph McCarthy of Wisconsin provided Catholic folk heroes in the anticommunist crusade. The election of John F. Kennedy to the presidency in 1960 put an end to the Catholic issue in American politics.

The distribution of wealth in America left much to be desired and seemed to be heading in the wrong direction in the 1980s and early 1990s. Much of the maldistribution – the fact that the most affluent 1 percent of the American people controlled more of the nation's wealth than did the bottom 90 percent – was simply in the nature of the capitalist system. But the enemies of New Deal efforts to redistribute wealth more equitably among the American people had succeeded in using the Cold War to crush progressivism in the United States. And the Reaganomics of the 1980s had used defense spending, the rebuilding of American military power for the Cold War, as a means of manipulating the federal budget to enhance the fortunes of the already very rich.

When historians of the twenty-first century look back on the Cold War era, at its impact on the world in which they live, they are less likely to be struck by the death and destruction facilitated by the superpowers than by the influence of American culture, the success of the American model. The obvious manifestations will be the McDonald's, Pizza Huts, and Kentucky Fried Chicken franchises found all over the world, the blue jeans and rock and roll. More significant will be the computers and fax machines that facilitate global interdependence. And not least will be the heightened concern for human rights, the hope for governments that rule by law – governments of the people, by the people, and for the people – and illusions about the miracles that a market economy will bring.

Of course, the United States of the 1990s had been influenced notice-ably by its intense encounters with the outside world during the Cold War years. The percentage of Asian Americans had risen greatly, as increased contact had brought Koreans, Vietnamese, and Thais, as well as Indians, Pakistanis, and Chinese, in large numbers to the United States. The new immigrants contributed enormously to the broadening of American culture – to conceptions of art and food and beauty. They staffed the nation's hospitals and universities, as well as its groceries and restaurants. To a country fearful of losing the work ethic, they brought new vitality.

Economically, the interdependent liberal world order, facilitated by the leadership and foresight of Americans in the 1940s, had come into existence. The United States no longer had the wealth with which to dominate that order, and many members were temporizing about meet-ing their obligations – but there were as many nations outside clam-oring to get in. Learning to share power with Japan, the European Community, even ASEAN, proved difficult for the United States, but there were no viable alternatives.

Politically, militarily, the United States in the early 1990s was more secure than at any time since World War I. Terrorism would continue, was indeed unstoppable, but however angrily, Americans could tolerate that level of violence. The global concerns of the Cold War era, justified by the existence and threat of the Soviet Union, were shrinking rapidly. Interest in black Africa, South America, South Asia, rarely intense, all but evaporated. But there was no returning to the Atlanticism of pre–Cold War American leaders. People like Dean Acheson, George Ball, and George Kennan had tried to focus American attention and power on Europe, the Middle East, and Japan, seeing little of importance in the rest of the world. They calculated that with control of sufficient oil and with the industrial power of Western Europe, Japan, and the United States, the United States would prevail in any competition short of nuclear holocaust. In the 1990s, men and women who thought like Acheson, Ball, and Kennan would include the need to attend to all of East Asia, noting the resurgence of China and the economic power of Taiwan, Hong Kong, ASEAN, and South Korea.

Given the quality of the leaders they chose in the 1960s, 1970s, and 1980s – people who abused the nation's power and mishandled its economy – the Americans people had much for which to be grateful in the 1990s. They had nonetheless survived. There were no external dangers. Most of them were eating. They were no longer the wealthiest people in the world, but the top was still within reach if they were willing to work for it and were able to find leaders who would demand the appropriate sacrifices. And despite the many failings of the United States, there was no doubt that the world, for all its misery, was a better place than it would have been without American resistance to Joseph Stalin's vision.

PART II

AFTER THE COLD WAR

10

THE NEW WORLD ORDER

For more than four decades, the lodestar of American foreign policy had been opposition to the Soviet Union and its allies. With the end of the Cold War, the disintegration of the Soviet Union, and the emergence of an infinitely more cooperative Russia, the men and women in Washington who were responsible for shaping relations with the rest of the world, with ensuring the nation's security, scoured the compass in search of a new guiding principle. They never found it.

From 1989 to 1992, dozens of analysts in the universities and research institutions across the country were also asking what the world would be like after the Cold War. They wondered what role the United States should play. In the absence of a superpower rival, should it or the United Nations serve as the world's policeforce? As indicated in the principal American journals of world affairs, foreign policy specialists were divided on all questions. There was no consensus to inform policymakers.[1]

George H. W. Bush, although more experienced in world affairs than most American presidents, never had a vision of the role the United States would play in the years ahead. He and his secretary of state, James Baker, were superb problem solvers, not given to long-range planning. Several midlevel officials, most notably Francis Fukuyama and Paul Wolfowitz, foresaw an opportunity for the United States to hasten what they imagined to be the inevitable process of creating a liberal democratic world order. Fukuyama, sometime member of the State Department's Policy Planning Staff, gained fame among the foreign policy elite for his essay and subsequent book contending that the

---

[1] Warren I. Cohen, *America's Failing Empire* (Oxford, 2005), 38–55.

world was moving inexorably toward democratic societies with market economies.[2] Wolfowitz, then undersecretary of defense, urged that the promotion of democracy be a high priority. But Brent Scowcroft, Bush's national security adviser, perceiving himself as a Kissinger-style "realist," concentrated on relations with major powers and was unsympathetic to the views of Fukuyama and Wolfowitz, especially when their cohort focused on regions he considered of little importance. Richard Cheney, secretary of defense, was an old-fashioned nationalist who favored exercising presidential and state power without restraint.

The earliest test had come in 1989 when Deng Xiaoping's minions brutally suppressed protestors in China's Tiananmen Square, crushing the reform movement. Bush, who had served as liaison officer in Beijing 1974–5, kept policy toward the People's Republic in his own hands. He considered China to be an important strategic partner of the United States, and he and Scowcroft were determined not to allow the massacres that occurred there to disrupt the relationship. Forced by public outrage to impose sanctions on China, he nonetheless sent Scowcroft on a secret mission to assure Deng of Washington's continued friendship – an assurance belied by the necessity of keeping the mission secret and by the outrage that exploded when word of it leaked out months later. Presumably, Bush and his advisers, not wholly persuaded of Gorbachev's good intentions, discerned a continuing need to avoid antagonizing the men in Beijing. The atrocities perpetrated by the People's Liberation Army in the vicinity of Tiananmen Square – and elsewhere in China – occurred, after all, several months before Eastern Europeans liberated themselves, before the Berlin Wall came down. And the United States had condoned comparable brutality by friendly states throughout the Cold War.

Before the year was out, *after* the Wall had been breached and Eastern Europeans had cast off their communist dictators, however, Bush did appear to strike a blow for democracy. In Panama, Manuel Noriega was no longer useful to the CIA. Kept on the payroll despite the objections of the Department of State and the National Security Council, despite indications he was guilty of drug trafficking, money-laundering, and perhaps murder as well, the Agency protected him. His assistance

---

[2] Francis Fukuyama, "The End of History?," *National Interest* (Summer 1989) 16: 3–18; *The End of History and the Last Man* (New York, 1990).

in the struggle against the Sandinistas in Nicaragua had been his "get out of jail free" card, but Baker was preparing to disband the contras in exchange for a Sandinista pledge to hold elections. Noriega resisted suggestions that he step aside to allow democracy to prevail in Panama and his men began harassing Americans, indeed killing an American military officer.

A few days before Christmas, in a reprise of earlier U.S. interventions to overthrow Central American governments of which Washington did not approve, Bush sent in 27,000 troops to eliminate the Noriega regime and to capture Noriega. Few analysts accepted the contention that the U.S. government was concerned with Noriega's criminal activities or the desire to revive democracy in Panama. Noriega had defied Bush, leader of the free world, and American inaction had prompted questions in the media about Bush's resolve, the "wimp factor." There was nothing quite like a major – and successful – military operation to dispel any concerns about the president's manhood or willingness to use deadly force. But there was still no indication that the Bush administration was doing anything more than responding to ad hoc situations – or that the president felt a need for some guiding principle.

Since the hostage crisis in Tehran in 1979, the United States had been openly hostile to the Iranian government. Unfortunately it could not be disposed of as readily as Noriega's regime or as easily as the Eisenhower administration helped dispose of an earlier Iranian government in 1954. Washington settled for efforts to contain its influence, and the Reagan administration did not hesitate to assist the vicious Soviet-backed Iraqi dictatorship of Saddam Hussein when it engaged in a long war with Iran in the 1980s. But when that war ended in 1988, Saddam's actions became increasingly irritating. His rhetorical belligerence toward Israel and Kuwait worried the National Security Council, but in 1989 the president was preoccupied with the Baltic challenge to Gorbachev and that issue's potential to disrupt Soviet-American relations.

In July 1990, ignoring warnings and pressures from Washington, Iraqi forces began to mass along the Kuwaiti border. Assuming Saddam was bluffing, the United States did not indicate to Baghdad what action it might take if the Iraqis actually invaded Kuwait. When the invasion came, Bush was shocked and determined not to allow this act of aggression to go unpunished. If there was to be a new and peaceful world order with the end of the Cold War, Iraq would have to be stopped. Increasingly, the president equated Saddam with Hitler, the invasion with unchecked German and Japanese actions in the 1930s. If Saddam were allowed to succeed in Kuwait, Saudi Arabia likely would be next – and then he would seek dominance over the entire Arab world and its oil. Bush prepared for a crusade against evil and to preserve the flow of oil. Many Americans, however, including Colin Powell, chairman of the Joint Chiefs, saw no compelling reason for the United States to ride to the rescue. Some thought sanctions would suffice to bring about an Iraqi pull-back. Others perceived no need for American lives to be risked to protect the profits of the oil companies.

Once the president decided to act, he and Secretary Baker managed affairs magnificently. They persuaded the Saudis to allow American troops to be stationed on their sacred soil to deter an attack. They succeeded in having the United Nations Security Council approve an economic embargo against Iraq. They won the support of the Soviets – despite opposition from the Soviet military. An American military buildup in the region was set in motion. Bush personally contacted leaders of other nations to gain support for the military action he anticipated. But he also needed money. The Reagan era deficits had left the country unable to finance a war. Bush wrung the funds he needed out of Germany, Japan, and Saudi Arabia. Perhaps most impressive was the administration's success in keeping Israel from responding to Saddam's missile attacks after the war began.

Congress proved more difficult. Bush wanted congressional approval of military action, and there was strong opposition, especially from Democrats. Secretary of Defense Cheney argued against seeking either UN or congressional backing, insisting the president needed neither. But Bush followed Baker's advice to obtain a UN-supported coalition that would assuage congressional concerns about American unilateralism.

In late November 1990, the Security Council voted to allow members to use "all necessary means" to liberate Kuwait. In the wake of the UN mandate, Congress gave its approval, and when Iraq did not withdraw by the stipulated date of January 15, 1991, the United States commenced savage air attacks that lasted more than a month. Iraq's infrastructure was devastated, and tens of thousands of Iraqi civilians were killed despite the use of "smart bombs" designed to hit specified targets. Defiantly, Saddam promised his people victory in "the mother of all battles."

On February 23, coalition forces, numbering more than half a million, attacked. It took less than forty-eight hours to eliminate organized Iraqi resistance. Kuwait was liberated quickly, and Iraqi army survivors fled toward Baghdad. Expecting Saddam to be overthrown as a result of his defeat, Bush called a halt to the fighting exactly one hundred hours after the ground offensive began. American forces had lost only 146 lives, and neither Bush nor any of his senior advisers saw any point in risking additional American lives by driving on to Baghdad. Moreover, there was no UN mandate to invade Iraq. Mission accomplished.

Although he publicly defended administration policy, Wolfowitz was profoundly dissatisfied. He thought the cease-fire had come too soon, leaving Saddam in power, his elite Republican Guard forces intact. He still had his programs to create weapons of mass destruction, and there was no reason to assume his regime's human rights abuses or hostility to Israel would subside. When Shiites in the South and Kurds in the North rose against Saddam, Wolfowitz would have supported them. He understood that the odds were poor, but he perceived an opportunity for democracy to flower in Iraq. His superiors, on the other hand, feared successful rebellions would fragment the country to Iran's advantage and allowed Saddam to crush the rebellions, establishing "no fly" zones to limit the mobility of Saddam's air force only after thousands of rebels had been killed. American leaders had no interest in occupying Iraq and bearing the burden of nation-building. The balance of power in the Gulf had been preserved: No hostile power controlled the region's precious oil. The president and his military commanders were content to bask in the glory of their impressive victory.[3]

But what next? If democracy was going to spread, there seemed little likelihood of the United States serving as its handmaiden. The overthrow of democratically elected President Jean-Bertrand Aristide in Haiti in September 1991 was further evidence that the administration would do little to further the vision of Fukuyama and Wolfowitz. Although Baker conceded the United States had an interest in the restoration of democracy in Haiti, he argued it was not a vital interest. Force was not justified. To be sure, the administration went through the motions of condemning the coup and persuading the Organization of

---

[3] James Mann, *Rise of the Vulcans: The History of Bush's War Cabinet* (New York, 2004), 192–93.

American States (OAS) to impose a trade embargo, but it preferred the maintenance of the military junta to the restoration of Aristide, viewed by many conservatives as a dangerous radical. It did nothing to facilitate his return. Perhaps more embarrassing for the moral standing of the United States, it forcibly returned Haitians who sought refuge on America's shores – or interned them at Guantanamo.

Of perhaps greater consequence was the administration's unwillingness to cope with the crisis in the Balkans as Yugoslavia disintegrated. By the spring of 1991, it was evident that Croatia and Slovenia, two of the six republics of the federation, were preparing to secede, encouraged by Germany. It was equally clear that Serbia, driven by the demagoguery of its leader, Slobodan Milosevic, would attack both republics if they declared independence. In June, Baker made a perfunctory trip to Belgrade, advised the Croat and Slovene leaders against independence, and chastised Milosevic for human rights abuses, specifically against Kosovars of Albanian ethnicity. Baker expressed the hope they could resolve their differences peacefully and left, fully expecting to be ignored. A few days later Croatia and Slovenia declared independence, and on the next day Serbia attacked.

Bush and Baker decided that Yugoslavia was a problem best left to the Europeans and were delighted when the European Community attempted to mediate, with the support of the UN Security Council. The German government chose to preempt the results of mediation by recognizing the independence of Croatia and Slovenia in December, and the remainder of the European Community fell in line in January 1992. A cease-fire arranged that month left Serbia in control of considerable Croat territory. American leaders saw no need to become involved.

Serb behavior began to trouble European observers. There were indications of what came to be called "ethnic cleansing," the killing and forced deportation of non-Serbs in territory that came under Serb control. Men and women who had admired the beauty of the historic city of Dubrovnik were appalled when the Serbs shelled it needlessly. And then came the horrors of Serb atrocities in Bosnia.

Bosnia-Herzegovina, the most ethnically diverse of the Yugoslav republics, also chose to withdraw from the federation. Bosnia contained substantial numbers of Croat Catholics and Serb Orthodox Christians, but a plurality of Muslims. Croats and Serbs, without putting aside hostility toward each other, agreed to divide Bosnia between them. The

Map 5. Breakup of the Yugoslav Republic, Circa 1993.

Muslims constituted a temporary obstacle, which the Serbs had no intention of tolerating. Hoping to preserve the territorial integrity of Bosnia, the United States joined the European Community in recognizing its independence in April 1992, and the UN sent a peacekeeping force.

Milosevic, however, was determined to seize control of Bosnia and used Bosnian Serb fighters, supported by irregulars from his own forces, to achieve his ends. The Serbs launched major offensives against majority Muslim towns, raping and murdering innocent civilians everywhere they went. The UN peacekeepers proved hopelessly inadequate, and Bosnia became a humanitarian nightmare. The Security Council imposed an economic embargo on Serbia, to no avail.

In Washington, there was a growing sense that the United States, the world's greatest power, had a responsibility to stop the Serbs. Wolfowitz pressed hard for American intervention to stop what he perceived as genocide. Scowcroft, too, was deeply troubled by the horror stories coming out of Bosnia. But Baker, Cheney, and Powell were opposed to becoming involved militarily, arguing that there was no threat to America's national interests. The Air Force chief of staff brushed aside the question of whether the national interest was at stake, insisting that the United States was obligated to act and contended he could do the job with airpower alone. Bush concluded that Baker, Cheney, and Powell were right. As Baker famously phrased their conclusion, the United States "had no dog in this fight."

Within the administration – and outside, among those Americans who followed world affairs – pressure mounted for action against Serbia. Over the objections of Cheney and Powell, Bush decided to approve the use of force to deliver humanitarian relief to the besieged Bosnian capital of Sarajevo. Insisting that American action be part of a multilateral UN operation, he won congressional approval. The Serbs backed off, allowing the relief supplies to be delivered. But as evidence of Serb atrocities against Muslims mounted, support grew for a more aggressive American response. The most popular proposal was for lifting the arms embargo to allow the Bosnians to obtain weapons with which to defend themselves and to bomb Serb positions to level the playing field. But Bush was not prepared to push any further against the advice of Cheney and Powell. Moreover, he was aware that the electorate thought he was more interested in foreign affairs than in repairing the American economy. He did not order American forces into action, and the horrors in Bosnia intensified.[4]

The administration had decided initially to stand clear of the Arab-Israeli tangle. Baker's predisposition to avoid any diplomatic effort on that issue was reinforced by Nixon's warning that no good could come it. One president after another had failed to persuade the Israelis to abide by UN resolution 242, which called upon them to surrender the land occupied after the Six-Day War in exchange for peace treaties that

---

[4] Samantha Power, *A Problem from Hell: America and the Age of Genocide* (New York, 2002), 252–74.

would constitute Arab recognition of Israel's right to exist – the "land for peace" formula. Bush and Baker had no expectation of greater success than their predecessors, but they were angered, especially by Israel's persistent building of settlements in Arab East Jerusalem and amidst Arab populations of the West Bank and Gaza.

Their attempts to convince the Israelis to stop the settlements were ignored. There seemed no point in arousing the anger of pro-Israel groups in the United States if nothing could be accomplished. The administration would have left matters alone had it not been for a promise made to Gorbachev in return for his support during the run-up to the Gulf War.

Bush and Baker had offered Gorbachev a role in the search for peace in the Middle East. Working together rather than supporting opposing forces in the region, perhaps they could bring an end to the hatred their Cold War rivalry had exacerbated. Despite reservations elsewhere in the administration, Baker chose to honor the commitment and began discussions with Arab and Israeli leaders in the spring of 1991. Both the Saudis and Jordanians had been astonished by Israel's restraint during the Gulf War, and King Hussein of Jordan was clearly ready for peace with Israel. The Saudis, Egyptians, and Arab states of the Gulf quickly agreed to participate in the conference Baker proposed. Syria, Israel, and the Palestinians, however, tested his diplomatic skills – and patience.

Somehow, Baker managed to get all the players to the conference table in Madrid in October 1991. Agreement after hard-won agreement unraveled, but he stayed with it and prevailed. It was an extraordinary performance. Gorbachev and Bush personally hosted the opening ceremonies, and for a brief moment, there was hope of peace between Israel and the Arabs. For the first time, Israelis and Palestinians sat together and negotiated. But, as the historian Douglas Little has written, the conference proved anticlimactic: "[N]o deals were struck, no wrongs were righted, and no land changed hands." Nonetheless there were promising signs of flexibility on both the Israeli and the Palestinian sides.[5] And renewed pressure by the Bush administration contributed to the demise of Yitzhak Shamir's Likud coalition and his replacement by Yitzhak Rabin, who agreed to stop building settlements and proved open to territorial compromise.

---

[5] Little, *American Orientalism*, 267–8, 298–99.

And then there was North Korea, a perennial problem that persisted even with the end of the Cold War. In the mid-1980s, satellite photos had indicated that the North Koreans were building a nuclear reactor at Yongbyon. Even before Reagan left office, the intelligence community reported its conclusion that Pyongyang was attempting to develop nuclear weapons. Bush and Baker inherited the situation and hoped to win assistance from China and the Soviet Union to persuade Kim Il Sung to cease his efforts. The possibility of Chinese cooperation was one reason Bush was reluctant to react strongly against the Tiananmen massacres, but Beijing was not interested in dealing with the issue as it coped with world opprobrium. The Soviets were more responsive, but when Gorbachev decided to establish diplomatic relations with South Korea in September 1990, Moscow lost what little leverage it had with Kim.

North Korea had signed the Nuclear Nonproliferation Treaty (NPT) in 1985 as a price for obtaining a Soviet promise to provide light water reactors for civilian power use. It had failed, however, to sign a required safeguard agreement with the International Atomic Energy Agency (IAEA). Pyongyong insisted there could be no inspections in North Korea while it was threatened by American nuclear weapons, especially those based in South Korea. Both the American ambassador in Seoul and the military commander of U.S. forces in Korea, backed by the Department of Defense, recommended removal of the weapons to facilitate negotiations, but Scowcroft was unwilling. He persuaded Bush that removal would give the North Koreans something for nothing. The intelligence community warned that Kim might have his weapons by the mid-1990s, but the administration, divided on the issue, preoccupied with Soviet, Chinese, and Iraqi affairs, did nothing.[6]

In a very different context, in an attempt to gain an important arms control objective before Gorbachev lost control in Moscow, Bush announced that the United States would remove all of its overseas-based tactical nuclear weapons, anticipating Soviet reciprocity. At the same time, he quietly approved the removal of all nuclear weapons from South Korea, allowing the president of South Korea to declare his country nuclear free in December 1991. The Bush administration simultaneously indicated its willingness to have the high-level meeting Kim wanted.

[6] Don Oberdorfer, *The Two Koreas* (London, 1998), 249–80.

Kim's regime was in economic trouble. The Soviets had abandoned it. The Chinese, eager to expand ties with Seoul, might withhold aid if Kim failed to show flexibility. Desperate for help, he looked to South Korea and the United States as well as to China for possible economic assistance. His representatives met with their South Korean counterparts and quickly reached agreement on a nonaggression pact and a ban on the processing of uranium. After persuading the South Koreans to cancel the intimidating U.S.-ROK Team Spirit military exercise, the North Koreans made the concession most important to Washington: They agreed to sign the safeguards agreement with the IAEA and to allow inspection of the Yongbyon facility. But the Americans offered no economic aid in return, merely insisting upon an end to Pyongyang's nuclear program as well as the IAEA inspections.

From North Korea's perspective, the situation deteriorated rapidly. IAEA inspectors found discrepancies between what Pyongyang declared and what they found on the ground. The American and South Korean presidential elections of 1992 allowed no room for tolerance of North Korean transgressions. South Korea urged the United States to stiffen its approach to the North. In particular, its military asked to resume the Team Spirit exercise, and Cheney authorized the operation without consulting the Department of State. Kim's overtures had gained nothing and his nuclear ambitions had been exposed.[7]

Kim had hidden his efforts to develop nuclear weapons from his friends as well as his enemies. He had ordered activities in violation of his government's commitments under the NPT, lied in response to suspicions voiced, gambled on his ability to deceive the inspectors – and lost. He broke off talks with the South on all issues, refused to allow inspections at Yongbyon, and waited to see how the Bush administration would react.

Focused on his campaign for reelection, Bush chose not to respond during the campaign. Tensions between the IAEA and Pyongyang intensified in November 1992, but having failed in his bid to remain in the White House, Bush left the problem to his successor.

The Bush administration, to paraphrase Dean Acheson, was "present at the creation" of the post–Cold War world. On its watch, the Cold War

---

[7] Michael J. Mazarr, "Opportunity Seized: Preventive Diplomacy in Korea," in Bruce W. Jentleson, *Opportunities Missed, Opportunities Seized: Preventive Diplomacy in the Post-Cold War World* (Lanham, MD, 2000), 297–99; Oberdorfer, *Two Koreas*, 273.

ended, the Soviet Union collapsed, and Germany reunified. It played a secondary role in these great events but played it well. Nixon, in particular, criticized Bush for not giving more aid to Gorbachev and Yeltsin, but Reagan had emptied the Treasury and Bush had little leeway. Helmut Kohl needed no help and managed German reunification brilliantly, on terms with which Washington was quite content.

The two interventions the president ordered – Panama and Iraq – went well. The administration's basic goals, elimination of Noriega and the liberation of Kuwait, were attained with minimal American casualties – the sine qua non of public approval of military operations. Panama disappeared from Washington's horizons. Unfortunately, Saddam Hussein did not. But criticism of Bush's decision not to send troops on to Baghdad, not to rescue rebellious Shiites or Kurds, struck no chord with the American people.

Bush's handling of a number of other issues was more contentious. His response to the Tiananmen massacres, to the "Butchers of Beijing," outraged men and women who demanded that their country's foreign policies reflect its ideals as well as its interests. Similarly, Bush's unwillingness to intervene in Yugoslavia to stop Serb atrocities disappointed millions of Americans who believed the United States was obligated to prevent genocide.

Nonetheless, on the whole the president scored well with his people for his leadership efforts in foreign affairs. They faulted him, on the other hand, for his failure to bring the country out of economic recession – and his campaign for reelection was hurt by the third-party candidacy of Ross Perot, a wealthy Texas businessman who condemned Bush's efforts to bring Mexico into the North American Free Trade Agreement (NAFTA). Perot referred to a "giant sucking sound," which he declared to be caused by American jobs being drawn into the cheap labor market south of the Rio Grande. Even a desperation move to provide jobs in Texas and California by selling F-16 fighter planes to Taiwan failed to save Bush. He doubted the wisdom of the sale, fearing it would undermine his efforts to preserve what was left of the relationship with China, but, trailing in the polls, he took the risk. As he anticipated, he infuriated the Chinese – and lost the election anyway.

After the election, Bush made one more foreign policy decision that had unimaginable consequences. He sent American troops into Somalia. Hundreds of thousands of Somalis were dying as a result of civil strife.

Strategically located on the Horn of Africa, the country had been of interest to both superpowers during the Cold War, but with the collapse of the Soviet Union few in Washington or Moscow thought the country of much importance. Among those few were the Africanists in the State Department, who called for humanitarian assistance in cooperation with the UN. American television began to show images of starving Somalis, producing what came to be called the "CNN effect," the ability of television reporters to force Washington to attend to crises it preferred to ignore. Bush authorized the airlift of food under UN auspices. His advisers hoped that humanitarian aid to Somalia might deflect complaints about the administration's refusal to aid Bosnia.

Supplies were insufficient, however, to alleviate the misery of the people of Somalia. Despite the opposition of the CIA, the Pentagon, *and* the Africanists at the State Department, Bush sent in a major American force as part of a multilateral operation to stop food theft and oversee the equitable distribution of aid. Neither Cheney nor Scowcroft was enamored of the plan, but the president was being pushed by Congress and public opinion. He assumed the troops would be withdrawn in a matter of weeks, and sending them would – and did – save tens of thousands of lives. Unfortunately, intervention did not stop clan warfare in Somalia, and the troops were still on the ground when Bush's successor took the oath of office.

And Washington still lacked a vision for its foreign policies in the post–Cold War world. Toward the end of the administration of George Herbert Walker Bush, there were no imminent threats to the security of the United States. Its apparent victory in the Cold War allowed the American people to conclude that foreign affairs were no longer important and they were entitled to a "peace dividend." The country no longer needed a president who focused on external events: It could afford to elect a small-state governor who promised to focus his attention on domestic affairs. Arkansas's William Jefferson ("It's the economy, stupid") Clinton was the man they chose.

Although he had graduated from Georgetown University's School of Foreign Service and interned for the Senate Foreign Relations Committee, Clinton had little interest in foreign policy. Before taking office, he remarked to Lee Hamilton, then chair of the House Foreign Affairs Committee, that no one in America but a handful of journalists cared about foreign relations. For the next several years, Clinton's inattention frustrated those of his advisers with foreign policy responsibilities. He never developed a useful working relationship with Warren Christopher or Lee Aspin, respectively his first secretaries of state and defense – and neither of them provided strong enough leadership of their agencies to compensate. Clinton ended the presidential practice of receiving daily briefings from the director of the CIA. At the urging of Tony Lake, his national security adviser, he agreed to have weekly meetings with these senior officials but postponed them as often as not. Other than on trade issues, his staff found it difficult to engage him.

Clinton's relations with the Pentagon were especially poor. He was often derided as a "draft dodger" for avoiding service in Vietnam. His desire to allow gays to serve openly in the military was opposed by Colin Powell, his inherited chairman of the Joint Chiefs. The usually politic Powell was disturbed sufficiently to undermine the president publicly. Aspin's incompetent administration only aggravated the problems. It was not until William Perry took over from Aspin, playing much the same steadying role George Shultz had played in Reagan's administration, that military-civilian relations functioned effectively again.

There were three men who, sharing his priorities, had easy access to the president: Samuel "Sandy" Berger, Lake's deputy and ultimate successor at the National Security Council; Ron Brown, secretary of commerce; and Mickey Kantor, who served as U.S. Trade Representative (USTR). All three were intensely concerned with trade issues, opening foreign markets to American exports and opening doors for American corporations to avail themselves of the cheap labor and natural resources of less-developed countries.

Three others were able to gain Clinton's attention and further their agendas through personal ties and force of personality. Strobe Talbott had been close to Clinton for many years and initially was named special ambassador. A prominent journalist with exceptional knowledge of Russian affairs, Talbott won the president's support for efforts to assist the Russians toward developing a democratic government and a market economy. The other two – Madeline Albright and Richard Holbrooke – were enormously successful at attracting media attention, overshadowing Christopher and Lake. Albright, before succeeding Christopher at State, served as ambassador to the UN and worked to reinvigorate the organization and strengthen American ties to it. Her banner line was "assertive multilateralism" – which did not prevent her from describing the United States as the "indispensable nation." The notoriously aggressive Holbrooke served briefly as ambassador to Germany and then as assistant secretary of state for European and Canadian affairs. He was unquestionably the right person to handle Slobodan Milosevic when Clinton finally decided to take on the Serb leader.

And then there was Winston Lord, a Kissinger protégé who had served as Bush's ambassador to China. Lord was disappointed and angered by Bush's management of Chinese-American relations, especially on issues of human rights. He was troubled sufficiently to advise Clinton on policy toward China in the 1992 election campaign and was rewarded with appointment as assistant secretary of state for East Asia and the Pacific. Aware of Lord's outrage at the Tiananmen massacre, Chinese leaders were uneasy about his presence in the administration. They need not have worried. Although with the end of the Cold War there was no longer a strategic reason for appeasing China, for Clinton the expansion of trade took precedence over human rights – and Ron Brown, rather than Lord or anyone else in the national security hierarchy, had Clinton's ear on policy toward China.

Clinton was no less determined to maintain American preeminence in world affairs than Bush and his advisers had been. He differed from them in devaluing military power and perceiving the principal threat in economic terms. This was probably most evident in his administration's approach to the Japanese-American relationship. Fears of German economic power had receded in the wake of Kohl's enormously costly effort to integrate East Germany, but Japan remained of grave concern to analysts in and out of the government.

In addition to Ezra Vogel's classic *Japan as Number One*, Samuel Huntington, his influential Harvard colleague, sounded the tocsin, arguing that the Japanese were practicing economic warfare, attempting to use their economic power to replace American influence in the world. Huntington was troubled by American dependence on Japanese exports and capital and suspected that Japanese agents were buying elections and scholars in the United States. Should they prevail, he warned, the world would be more violent with "less democracy and economic growth."[8]

---

[8] Vogel, *Japan as Number One* (Cambridge, 1979); Huntington, "Why International Primacy Matters," *International Security* 17 (Spring 1993): 68–83.

Clinton chose to minimize the Japanese-American security relationship, widely considered to be the keystone of American strategy across the Pacific, and took the offensive in trade relations. For roughly three years, Mickey Kantor threatened and cajoled the Japanese in a modestly successful effort to get them to liberalize their trade practices. The struggle to open Japanese markets was hardly new, but during the Cold War trade had been subordinated to security concerns. Putting economic concerns first, Clinton not only rattled the Japanese but also worried American specialists concerned with maintaining the strength of the alliance in the face of an unfriendly China and North Korean provocations.

If additional evidence of Clinton's priorities were necessary, he offered it with his willingness to challenge major interests in the Democratic party by fighting for ratification of NAFTA. One concept with which both the president and Vice-President Al Gore were enamored was "globalization." To them this meant the spread of "market democracy." To the American Federation of Labor and Congress of Industrial Organizations (AFL-CIO), it meant the loss of jobs, specifically to Mexico in the case of NAFTA. Most congressional Democrats opposed NAFTA, but Clinton pushed on, winning only because of strong support from Republicans. It is unlikely that any other foreign policy issue engaged him comparably in the early years of his presidency.

There were other situations, nonetheless, to which the president had to respond. When Clinton was inaugurated, there were 30,000 American troops on the ground in Somalia. As president-elect, Clinton had defended Bush's humanitarian intervention, but once in office, his attention was elsewhere. Months passed before he was forced to focus on events there. In the absence of presidential leadership, his foreign policy apparatus functioned poorly.

The initial success of the UN mission to Somalia had led, perhaps inevitably, to mission creep. Having saved hundreds of thousands of lives by establishing order sufficient to allow the distribution of food, the UN determined to pacify the warlords who had brought chaos to the country and to reconstruct the failed state. Confident that this task could be accomplished easily, the administration reduced American forces to 4,000, and command of these troops and all others present was passed to a UN commander (a retired American naval officer).

In June, however, the forces of Mohammed Farah Aidid, the most powerful Somali warlord, ambushed a UN patrol and killed twenty-four

Pakistani peacekeepers. UN forces proved inadequate to capture Aidid, and Albright persuaded the president to send in Rangers and Delta Force commandos. The mission could hardly remain "humanitarian" as attacks against Aidid's forces intensified. The efforts of Robert Oakley, former American ambassador to Somalia, to negotiate with Aidid were brushed aside by Boutros Boutros-Ghali, the UN secretary-general, who was determined to punish the offending warlord.

The president and his national security adviser offered no direction, content to leave control of the Somali venture to the troops in the field – until disaster struck in October, when two American Black Hawk helicopters were downed by Aidid's forces. Unknown to UN or American analysts at the time, Aidid's fighters were receiving training from Al Qaeda, a terrorist organization, evidence of whose activities was beginning to appear in various parts of the Muslim world, from East Africa across the Middle East to South Asia.[9]

Eighteen U.S. soldiers were killed in the Black Hawk disaster, a captured pilot was mistreated by the Somalis, and the body of one casualty was dragged in front of television cameras. Suddenly a horrified American public found Somalia on the map, and a president, awakened to realities there, angrily demanded that his aides clean up the mess. He wanted out of Somalia as quickly as possible short of further humiliation of the United States. Both Congress and the media agreed. If the people the United States and the UN were trying to help were shooting at their would-be saviors, it was time to get out.

Clinton accepted the advice of his foreign policy team to disguise the retreat by first reinforcing American troops in Somalia. They hoped this action would demonstrate to the world that the United States could not be intimidated by some tin-pot warlord. Oakley was reenlisted to resume negotiations with Aidid and succeeded in gaining the release of the captured pilot. Then Clinton ordered the withdrawal of American forces, and Somalia ceased to be of interest to the public and the media in the United States.

To adversaries of the United States elsewhere in the world, the retreat from Somalia after the "Black Hawk down" incident suggested that the

---

[9] Derek Chollett and James Goldgeier, *America Between Wars: From 11/9 to 9/11* (New York, 2008), 74.

sole remaining superpower could be outmaneuvered simply by killing a few American soldiers – or merely threatening to do so. This was quickly apparent in Haiti. Clinton had been critical of Bush's policy of forced repatriation of Haitian refugees, but he reneged on his promise to reverse Bush's policies and paid little attention to that benighted country's woes. There was no interest in the United States in accepting tens, perhaps hundreds, of thousands, of Haitians alleged to be preparing a mass exodus in celebration of Clinton's election.

Officially, Washington continued to demand the restoration of Jean-Bertrand Aristide to his presidential office, but the reality was much different. Too many powerful elements in the U.S. government, not least the CIA, the Department of Defense, and Jesse Helms (R.-N.C.), chair of the Senate Foreign Relations Committee, preferred the military junta that had overthrown him in 1991. Aristide was a defrocked priest, a preacher of liberation theology, who outraged American investors by threatening to double the minimum wage in Haiti. Bush and his advisers had been uninterested in seeing him return to power in Haiti.

In contrast, Clinton's advisers, specifically Lake, Talbott, and Albright, stressed the fact that Aristide had won an overwhelming victory in a fair election. The junta was thwarting the will of the Haitian people. Diplomatic efforts to arrange for Aristide's return failed when the junta reneged on a deal. It had no intention of relinquishing power.

In October, the Haitian generals demonstrated what they had learned from events in Somalia. They had agreed to allow a small group of American and Canadian military trainers to land in Haiti to work with local security forces. When the American ship carrying the troops attempted to dock, it was challenged by a mob brandishing guns and chanting "Somalia." Unprepared to land under fire, the ship sailed away. Unwilling to risk the lives of its troops, the United States retreated – and did nothing to relieve the humiliation.

Economic sanctions accomplished nothing, and the flow of Haitian refugees, most caught and returned to Haiti, increased. Human rights groups and the Congressional Black Caucus intensified their efforts on behalf of Haitians, pressing the administration to act. Lake and Talbott called for an invasion, unsettling to an increasingly risk-averse Pentagon. But in July 1994, the Organization of American States called for the use of force to restore Aristide to his presidency. The UN

Security Council, prompted by Albright, authorized a "coalition of the willing" to invade Haiti.

Polls showed the American public opposed to the operation, and Congress followed the people. Clinton insisted he had the constitutional authority to send in the troops. In September, when the operation was ready, the junta blinked. The generals invited Jimmy Carter, accompanied by Colin Powell and former Georgia senator Sam Nunn, to come to Haiti to find a peaceful resolution. Clinton gave them one day, accepted several brief delays as the junta stalled, and then told Carter the invasion would commence in thirty minutes. The junta folded and coalition forces landed unopposed the next day. In the absence of casualties, debate over the wisdom and constitutionality of Clinton's decision evaporated quickly.

Humanitarian intervention, without a strong case for serving the national interest, had limited popular appeal in the United States. Clinton, ever attuned to winds of public opinion, grew more resistant to the use of force, even less interested in foreign policy problems that were unrelated to economic issues. He vacillated in response to the crisis in Bosnia and refused to intervene when confronted with genocide in Rwanda. In fact, in what was probably the most reprehensible moment of his administration, the United States obstructed UN efforts to save hundreds of thousands of lives in Rwanda. Somalia was doubtless in his thoughts in both crises.

Like Bush, Clinton was content to leave peacemaking in the former Yugoslavia to the European Union (EU) and the UN. But neither organization was prepared to intervene forcibly to stop the fighting and ethnic cleansing. Their mediators had failed to halt the bloody test of wills between Serbs and Croats but had managed in 1992 to come up with a peace plan that preserved a semblance of Bosnian independence but left Serbs in control of two-thirds of the country. It was the best arrangement the Bosnian Muslims could obtain in the absence of foreign intervention on their behalf. Clinton was not willing to send American troops to drive the Serbs out of Bosnia, but he also was unwilling to endorse the EU-UN plan, which clearly rewarded the aggressor.

Lake was eager to intervene on humanitarian grounds and pressed Clinton, who was troubled by the evidence of atrocities and who spoke out against ethnic cleansing but remained unwilling to act. The Pentagon provided the principal opposition to American involvement, its leaders convinced that airpower alone would not stop the Serbs. Fearing a Vietnam-like quagmire, the Joints Chiefs were adamantly opposed to sending in ground troops. Albright outraged Colin Powell by voicing her contempt for the generals who had claimed to have a superb military and were averse to using it and risking casualties.[10]

Lake, Albright, Talbott, Holbrooke, and Gore persuaded Clinton to consider the strategy known as "lift and strike" that Bush had rejected. Clinton sent Christopher to Europe to sound out NATO allies but found no interest. He allowed himself to be persuaded that strife in the Balkans was rooted in ancient disputes, that atrocities were part of Balkan culture – and beyond the ability of the United States to bring to an end.[11]

While the administration dithered and Clinton hoped the war in Bosnia would be forgotten by the public, the story was kept alive in part by the extraordinary efforts of Christiane Amanpour, a CNN television journalist. Appalled by the atrocities, she was convinced stopping the Serbs was a moral duty. CNN had great credibility in the United States and abroad, and many other reporters picked up on her stories.[12] Several Foreign Service officers continued to demand action from within the State Department or resigned in protest against inaction. Much as Clinton tried, the continuing horrors in the Balkans could not be ignored forever.

As the Bosnian Muslims in particular, but Serbs and Croats as well, died by the thousands, an even greater tragedy was developing in Africa, in Rwanda, where the United States had no interest whatever. Civil war simmered between Hutus and Tutsis, but the tiny UN force sent to contain it proved inadequate. The United States had reduced its contribution to peacekeeping operations and attempted to prevent the UN from intervening in areas where Washington had little or no interest. Another of the lessons of Somalia.

In April 1964, the massacres began. Hutu soldiers murdered all of the moderate Rwandan politicians, including the prime minister. They

---

[10] Jeffrey Record, *Making War, Thinking History: Munich, Vietnam, and Presidential Uses of Force From Korea to Kosovo* (Annapolis, 2002), 113–20; Colin Powell, *My American Journey* (New York, 1995), 576.

[11] Warren Christopher, *In the Stream of History* (Stanford, 1998), 347 and David Halberstam, *War in a Time of Peace* (New York, 2001), 228 refer to the influence of Robert Kaplan's *Balkan Ghosts*.

[12] Halberstam, *War in Time of Peace*, 265–66.

seized the fifteen peacekeepers at her home, released the five Ghanaians, and butchered the ten Belgians – assuming correctly that Belgium would withdraw its troops, as the Americans had in Somalia.

Over the next hundred or so days, 800,000 Tutsis and moderate Hutus were massacred by Hutu militants – an unquestionable case of genocide. According to the Genocide Convention that the UN had adopted in 1948 and the United States ratified belatedly in 1988, the nations of the world were obliged to intervene to stop genocide. But the Clinton administration, unwilling to act, refused to acknowledge that genocide was occurring. Washington rejected all requests to reinforce the peacekeepers and blocked UN efforts to send more troops. The most powerful country in the world, led by an administration that prided itself on its commitment to protect human rights, did nothing to stop the slaughter. Clinton did not call a single meeting of his senior advisers to consider an American response. The president and his senior advisers were unwilling to risk American lives in a country few Americans could find on a map. The results were catastrophic – for the Tutsis of Rwanda.[13]

Serb determination to eliminate the Muslim population of Bosnia was not dampened by either the inability of the UN or the unwillingness of the United States to act in Rwanda. But there seemed no way to engage the president or to awaken the Pentagon from its Vietnam-inspired nightmares. Discouraged, Talbott decided it was time for strong medicine: He arranged to bring the abrasive and overbearing Holbrooke back to Washington to take charge of European and specifically Balkan affairs, to the dismay of the leadership at the Pentagon, State Department, and National Security Council.

Returning to Washington in September 1994, Holbrooke demanded that NATO bomb the Serb "fuckers." Albright, Lake, and Gore were ready, but Clinton was not; nor were European leaders. The Serbs murdered and raped thousands more, harassed UN peacekeepers and concluded no one had the will to stop them. In July 1995, they pushed aside a handful of Dutch peacekeepers at Srebrenica and systematically murdered 7,000 Muslims who had taken refuge there. At last the monstrous behavior of the Bosnian Serb military forced a NATO response. France pressed for action, and Clinton, who remained unwilling to send

[13] Power, *Problem from Hell*, 334–35, 358–66, 382–85.

American troops, agreed to Holbrooke's demand, and NATO carried out a massive three-week bombing campaign that won the attention of Serb leaders. At almost the same time, encouraged by Holbrooke and the American ambassador, Croatia began a ground offensive, driving the Bosnian Serbs out of territory they had taken from Croats and Muslims.

Flying to Yugoslavia, Holbrooke took charge. Milosevic stopped pretending he had no influence with Bosnian Serbs. Aware that the tide had turned against him, he agreed to negotiate. Holbrooke won a cease-fire in September and arranged a meeting in Dayton, Ohio, where he bullied Milosevic and the Croatian and Bosnian leaders into accepting a settlement. The Holbrooke plan called for the division of Bosnia on de facto ethnic and religious lines, similar to the UN-EU plan Clinton had rejected in 1993 – although the Serb share of Bosnia was reduced significantly, and the semblance of a unified Bosnian state was retained.

Unhappily for Clinton, he was called upon to deploy 20,000 American peacekeepers to Bosnia, a use of American forces opposed by most Americans, including many members of Congress, where the Republicans had won control in the 1994 by-elections. Clinton assured the country there would be no mission creep, as in Somalia, and that the troops would be brought home after one year – an unlikely prospect that did not materialize. Fortunately, he was supported by Senator Robert Dole (R.-Kans.), his likely Republican opponent in the next presidential election, who helped win Senate approval.

Only the presence of NATO troops in Bosnia prevented the Bosnian Serbs from overturning the Dayton agreement. But the NATO commanders failed to arrest those Bosnian Serb leaders who had been indicted as war criminals for the atrocities they had carried out or ordered. It was not until General Wesley Clark, who had been with Holbrooke in Bosnia in 1995, took over the NATO command in 1997 that vigorous efforts to enforce the Dayton accords began.

Unfortunately, the United States was not quite free of Milosevic and Yugoslav problems. To the delight of his Serb supporters, Milosevic had revoked the autonomy of Kosovo, a Yugoslav republic inhabited primarily by Albanian Muslims and a territory of great historic significance to Orthodox Christian Serbs. Fears that he intended to drive the Muslims out of Kosovo had elicited warnings from both Bush and Clinton. Throughout the Bosnian crisis, Kosovo was relatively quiet. In the late 1990s, however, the Kosovo Liberation Army (KLA) emerged as the dominant force in the Muslim community, and it attacked Serb police and vandalized Orthodox churches and cemeteries, deliberately provoking Milosevic. KLA leaders anticipated NATO support when the Serbs attacked, but Washington considered the KLA a terrorist organization and was unsympathetic to its goal of an independent Kosovo.

When the inevitable Serb retaliation commenced, Albright, now secretary of state, feared Albania or Macedonia or Greece or Turkey might intervene, destabilizing the region. She warned Milosevic against ethnic cleansing, but to little avail. In early 1998, the president was coping with revelations about his affair with a White House intern and was even further removed from foreign policy concerns than usual. It was a job for Holbrooke, and Albright sent him to Belgrade, where in October 1998 he succeeded in persuading Milosevic to halt the repression.

The respite lasted only a few months. In January 1999, Serb irregulars and police massacred dozens of Kosovar villagers. Clinton and his advisers could not escape memories of Rwanda and Srebrenica: The United States could not stand aside again. Once again, the Pentagon resisted intervention, and once again, Albright led the demand for action. She staged a conference in France at which the KLA was forced to agree to disarm if the Serbs would withdraw most of their forces from Kosovo, restore a degree of autonomy, and accept NATO peacekeepers. But even the threat of NATO airpower could not induce Milosevic to accept the terms, and in March, NATO began to bomb Serbia.

Clinton undermined the effort to restrain the Serbs by declaring that he would send no ground troops. Undeterred by the bombing, buoyed by indications no NATO troops would intervene, anticipating Russian support, Milosevic ordered a massive offensive that drove more than a million Kosovar Muslims from their homes, many, if not most, seeking refuge in Albania and Macedonia. The humanitarian disaster had begun.

General Clark antagonized his superiors in the Pentagon by calling for the use of attack helicopters, even ground troops if necessary, to stop the Serbs. Permission was denied. Instead he intensified bombing of Serbia, inflicting immense suffering on Serbian civilians. It took eleven weeks of devastating attacks and evidence that the Russians were not riding to the rescue before Milosevic abandoned his offensive and accepted the terms he had been offered in February. Thousands of Kosovars and Serbs had died – but not a single American.

American reluctance to use its power in Somalia, Haiti, Rwanda, Bosnia, and Kosovo reflected what the Air Force historian Jeffrey Record called "force protection fetishism," wherein the military's mission is subordinated to avoiding casualties.[14] Based on the lessons they drew from the war in Vietnam, senior military officers mistrusted civilian leaders generally – and Clinton in particular. Having avoided military service himself, Clinton hesitated sending others into battle. But it was painfully clear that if the United States did not act forcefully, no other state would. Certainly the UN lacked the means: It had no armies of its own. More appalling was the performance of Europe. Even in Bosnia, where the European Union might have been expected to lead, to demonstrate that Europe could manage its affairs without the United States, all the European states abdicated responsibility, docilely tolerated atrocity after atrocity. Perhaps the United States was in fact "the indispensable power." Perhaps Europeans had drifted into a Kantian conception of a world in which force was no longer required – and would henceforth be geopolitically irrelevant.[15]

Largely due to Strobe Talbott's influence, Clinton focused frequently on relations with Russia. Efforts to continue Gorbachev's reforms accelerated under the leadership of the mercurial Boris Yeltsin, with whom Clinton met in April 1993 to underscore his support. But Yeltsin faced opposition at home, where many people were being hurt by the changes being implemented. The Russian parliament, the Duma, proved recalcitrant, and when Yeltsin tired of legislative restrictions on his power, of hostile and violent street demonstrations organized by his enemies, he sent in tanks to fire on the parliamentary building, which the offending legislators were using as their headquarters – an action that might have been considered undemocratic and excessive.[16]

Nonetheless, the Clinton administration continued to support Yeltsin, convinced that he alone of potential Russian leaders was committed to reforms deemed essential to Russia's liberalization and integration into Europe. Moreover, Yeltsin's Russia promised to be friendly to the United States and supportive of American foreign policy. His erratic behavior and other transgressions would have to be tolerated.

---

[14] Record, *Making War, Thinking History*, 142.
[15] Robert Kagan, *Of Paradise and Power* (New York, 2003).
[16] Lilia Shevtsova, *Yeltsin's Russia: Myths and Reality* (Washington, D.C., 1999), 81–85.

A critical question for American officials and public intellectuals in the 1990s – and after – was what to do with NATO, an organization once viewed as a means of containing German as well as Soviet power during the Cold War. Some, Albright and Holbrooke most prominent among them, advocated expansion of NATO to protect the new democracies of Central and Eastern Europe from a resurgent Russia; others, to prevent a united Germany from dominating Europe again. For Clinton there were potential domestic political advantages to NATO expansion: bipartisan support for the idea in Congress and the votes of Americans of Czech, Hungarian, Polish, and Slovak ancestry.

There was also a powerful argument against NATO expansion: the strong probability that it would anger Russia and undermine efforts to maintain Russian-American cooperation in world affairs. Talbott, wanting to build a strong relationship between NATO and Russia first, opposed expansion. George Kennan called the offer of membership to the Czech Republic, Hungary, and Poland the most fateful error of the post–Cold War world. The Pentagon resisted, fearful of being called upon to defend a region beyond the traditional scope of American power. Secretary of Defense William Perry was sufficiently troubled to consider resigning.[17]

Clinton's new chairman of the Joint Chiefs, General John Shalikashvili, came up with an idea that eased many of these concerns. He proposed creation of a Partnership for Peace, a relationship with NATO that every nation in Central and Eastern Europe – *and* Russia – would be invited to join. NATO members would not be required to defend these partners. Yeltsin seemed pleased by the concept and untroubled by Washington's intent to expand NATO.

Suddenly, in November 1994, the Russians reversed course. Yeltsin denounced the Partnership for Peace and the expansion of NATO as a threat to Russia and warned that a "cold peace" was descending upon Europe. Yeltsin's supporters had been defeated badly in the parliamentary elections of December 1993, and his political advisers argued that NATO expansion was angering the Russian people. There were indications that even those most supportive of the new Russian-American relationship perceived the United States as taking advantage of Russia's weakness. Defense specialists in the Duma worried also about American

---

[17] Chollett and Goldgeier, *America Between Wars*, 124.

plans for national missile defense and demanded revision of the START II arms limitation agreement. It was time for Yeltsin to play to his domestic audience, to force the Americans to treat Russia with a little more respect.

In fact, Washington no longer perceived any need to defer to Russian sensibilities. As the sole remaining superpower, acting in what the commentator Charles Krauthammer called the "unipolar moment," the United States was prepared to act unilaterally.[18] The Russians might be consulted, they were welcome to come along, but they could deter American action no longer. When Clinton and his advisers asked for Russian cooperation, they were looking for a compliant junior partner.

Mounting pressure from extremist nationalists led Yeltsin to his disastrous decision to use force in 1994 in an attempt to crush a separatist movement that emerged in Chechnya, a primarily Muslim Russian republic in the Caucuses. Long hostile toward Russians, not least because Stalin had deported them during World War II, Chechens sought greater autonomy after the collapse of the Soviet Union. Their provocations in 1994 were met by an invasion of Russian troops and bombing of Chechen cities. Clinton called the war an internal Russian affair and continued his support of Yeltsin, hoping the rebellion could be suppressed quickly with a minimum of bloodshed. It was not to be.

Within a month, it was evident that the Chechens were not going to collapse in the face of the Russian army attack. It was also apparent that Russian troops were poorly trained and led and were behaving brutally toward people who were still Russian citizens. Atrocities against civilians mounted, as did the casualty rate among the invaders. Anxiety grew in Washington and in the capitals of former Warsaw Pact nations – although Helmut Kohl was the first to condemn Russian actions. Clinton flew to Moscow in May 1995 to celebrate the fiftieth anniversary of the German surrender that ended World War II in Europe. He complained to Yeltsin about the human rights violations in Chechnya of which the Russian army was accused. Yeltsin was unresponsive on that issue but agreed to sign the Partners for Peace agreement. Clinton did not come home empty-handed, but the war in Chechnya went on until opposition to the casualties among their children fighting there led the Russian people to demand an end. A peace

---

[18] Krauthammer, "The Unipolar Moment," *Foreign Affairs* 70 (1991): 23–33.

agreement was reached in August 1996, although Russian troops did not withdraw until mid-1997.

Yeltsin continued to try to win support from both the United States and the Russian people, telling each what he thought they wanted to hear. He fought his war in Chechnya and made anti-Western speeches at home. Privately he assured Clinton and Kohl of his continued intention to cooperate, to integrate Russia into Europe. But pandering to the electorate did not spare Yeltsin's followers, who were routed by Communists and extreme nationalists in the parliamentary elections of 1995. Polling in the single digits, Yeltsin faced a grim future, but Clinton's advisers, fearing a return to power of the Communist Party, could muster no alternative to backing him. Supported by the West and the "oligarchs" – the robber barons who accumulated great wealth in the privatization of Soviet state-owned assets – Yeltsin won an easy second-round victory in the 1996 presidential election, which some observers suspected was rigged.

Less than a year later, Russia signed an agreement with NATO that all but made it an honorary member of the Western alliance. Two months later, the Czech Republic, Hungary, and Poland were invited to join NATO, to the dismay of the Russian military establishment. Despite efforts by Clinton and Yeltsin to paper over their differences, Russian officials were not willing to accept a unipolar world in which Russia was expected to play by Washington's rules while the United States did as it pleased. They were angered by U.S. intrusions into Russia's historic sphere of influence, not least by American efforts to exploit Caspian Sea oil and gas. Yeltsin continued to favor integration and perceived a need for Western aid, but the Russian foreign policy elite insisted on a multipolar world in which Russia remained a great power.

In August 1998, the Russian economy collapsed, the ruble was devalued, and Moscow defaulted on loan repayments to the IMF. The last of the liberal reformers considered responsible for the troubles were fired and Yeltsin's new administration rejected the so-called Washington Consensus. Rapidly privatizating state-owned property, abolishing price controls, lowering trade barriers, allowing foreign investment, and counting on the market to solve all problems and provide economic growth had not worked. The results had been chaotic, bringing misery to millions through the undermining of social welfare while jobs were lost and real wages declined. Analysts in Europe and the United States questioned whether Russia would stay on the path to democracy, a market economy, and cooperation with the West.

Economic liberalization did not end entirely; nor did Russian efforts to strengthen democratic institutions. Yeltsin remained determined to integrate Russia with the West, but it was apparent that he was weakening, physically as well as politically. Trying desperately to retain his grip on power, Yeltsin fired his prime minister in August 1999 and replaced him with Vladimir Putin, an unknown former KGB agent. Putin quickly indicated he had little interest in political democracy. He demonstrated distaste for opposition politicians and a free press. He resumed forceful, brutal military action against Chechnya. And the Russian public responded favorably. Putin appealed to Russian nationalism and pride, and the people were willing to tolerate the deterioration of their newfound freedoms in exchange for an increase in their sense of security. Four months later, Yeltsin astonished the world by stepping aside and anointing Putin as his successor. And Putin wasted little time setting a course to counter American influence everywhere in the world. Clinton's critics suggested he had "lost" Russia.

And then there was China, ruled by the "butchers of Beijing." In the campaign of 1992, Clinton and Lord had promised a stiffening of sanctions against China, but it was not to be. Those eager to punish China, both conservatives and liberals, called for withdrawing most-favored-nation status (MFN) from its exports to the United States. Without MFN status, Chinese exports to the United States would be subject to tariff rates higher than those of other nations, putting China at a competitive disadvantage. Bush had blocked such sanctions. Clinton was expected to approve them.

Clinton's ultimate concern, however, was reviving the American economy. A trade war with China would not stimulate economic growth or put Americans back to work. It might cost tens of thousands of jobs. So he temporized, persuading his supporters in Congress to delay legislation to eliminate MFN for China while he tried to get the Chinese to release political prisoners, respect Tibet's cultural heritage, stop jamming Voice of America broadcasts, and stop selling missiles to Iran and Pakistan. In May 1993 he renewed MFN conditionally: China would have a year to improve its behavior.

American corporations trading with China undertook a major lobbying campaign to prevent conflict. In addition to the economic arguments they raised, "realists," most notably Henry Kissinger, argued that the strategic relationship with China was too important to jeopardize by pressing human rights matters that they considered less important. The issue crystallized in August 1993, when the administration denied licenses for the sale of satellites to China in retaliation for Chinese missile sales to Pakistan. The Chinese turned to European suppliers, and representatives of the affected American companies, including major donors to Clinton's political campaigns, demanded waivers. Clinton then made an extraordinary decision: He took the authority on the licensing of technology sales to China away from the departments of State and Defense and gave it to the Department of Commerce. Henceforth commercial rather than political or military considerations would be privileged.

Incredibly, lobbyists for the business community and other opponents of sanctions argued that the results China's critics desired – democracy in China and respect for human rights in Beijing – would be brought about by increased trade, preaching what the historian and foreign affairs analyst James Mann has called "The China Fantasy."[19] Presumably trade would strengthen the private sector, and China's nascent middle class would then demand a share in governing the country. One day China would be a middle-class democracy, just like America.

The claim that MFN would lead to democracy in China won few converts among human rights advocates or on the anticommunist right. But other arguments for avoiding confrontation with China, for continued "engagement," had merit. Economic warfare between the United States and China would harm the American economy and reverberate throughout the world economy. Admired reformers in Hong Kong, struggling to secure democracy before the Chinese takeover scheduled for 1997, warned their cause would be hurt by the elimination of MFN for China. And the strategic reasons for restoring a working relationship with the Chinese government could not be ignored. China could obstruct American efforts in the UN. It could use its influence to avoid a crisis over North Korea's nuclear program. Conceivably, Beijing

---

[19] Mann, *The China Fantasy* (New York, 2007).

could be persuaded to cease its own contribution to nuclear and missile proliferation.

Deng Xiaoping and his advisers saw no need to make any concessions to the Americans. They concluded Washington was bluffing. Good communists that they were, they were confident that American businessleaders, desperately eager for a larger share of the market in China, would force Clinton to grant another renewal of MFN. When Secretary of State Warren Christopher flew to Beijing to see what concessions the Chinese would offer in return, he was treated with contempt. Dissidents were rounded up on the eve of his arrival, and his scheduled meeting with President Jiang Zemin was canceled. He met instead with Li Peng, widely despised even in China as one of the architects of the Tiananmen massacres. Li informed Christopher that the Chinese embassy in Washington had reported that Clinton would renew MFN no matter what China did. Clinton offered Christopher no support and did not bother to attend the meeting at which his secretary of state reported on his mission. Few were surprised when Clinton abandoned his expressed concern for human rights and extended MFN to China without conditions in the spring of 1994.

In time, the memory of Tiananmen faded in the American imagination. The Chinese government continued to deny its people political, intellectual, and religious freedoms. It continued to repress minorities, most obviously Tibetans, and to commit a myriad of other human rights abuses. These transgressions had little impact on American policy toward China. On the contrary, officials in Washington stressed the improvement in the quality of life of ordinary Chinese citizens as a result of Deng Xiaoping's reforms.

Trade between the United States and China grew rapidly in the mid-1990s, and the PRC became an increasingly important American trading partner. The Chinese, however, exported far more than they imported, creating a serious balance-of-trade problem for the United States. Tensions grew over Beijing's restrictive trade practices, use of prison labor, and currency manipulation, but these were trivial compared to those that exploded over Taiwan in 1995 and 1996.

Taiwan was evolving into a democratic state and in March 1996 was scheduled to hold the first direct election for president that the Chinese people had ever known. The ruling Kuomintang, party of Chiang Kai-shek, no longer exercised absolute power. Chiang's son, Ching-kuo, before his death, had allowed an opposition party, the

Democratic Progressive Party (DPP), to emerge, and its popularity with the Taiwanese majority native to the island – and its call for independence from China – threatened the Kuomintang and Lee Teng-hui, Ching-kuo's designated successor. Lee, also a native Taiwanese, concluded that being more assertive internationally and hinting none too subtly that he, too, favored independence, would be good politics.

American specialists on Taiwan affairs recognized the changes and understood the desire of the island's political elite for an international role commensurate with Taiwan's de facto independence. In Washington the dilemma was to find a way to adjust to these changes without provoking Beijing, without violating the principle of one China, which had been accepted by every administration beginning with that of Richard Nixon. Only a few senior officials from Taiwan had been allowed to visit the United States after derecognition in 1978, attracting little media attention.

In 1994, President Lee forced the issue by requesting a visa to stop over in Hawaii en route to Central America. The request was denied, but as a sop, Lee was offered a reception in a transit lounge. Angered by the gesture, Lee commenced a strikingly successful lobbying effort with Congress. Since 1948, only Israel had been more successful than Taiwan in manipulating the American government. The Senate soon passed a resolution calling for the State Department to issue visas to Taiwan officials, and Lee's lobbyists demanded that the administration grant him a visa to attend a reunion at Cornell, where he had earned his doctorate. The administration refused and assured Beijing Lee would not be allowed to enter the United States.

But Lee prevailed. In May 1995, the House of Representatives voted 396–0 to demand a visa for Lee, and the vote in the Senate was 97–1. Taiwan's lobbyists had performed well, but the key to their success was the democratization of Taiwan, assuring support across the political spectrum rather than only from the aging cadre of right-wing supporters of the elder Chiang. Delight in the political evolution of Taiwan combined with anger at Beijing's human rights abuses won support for Taiwan – and Lee's visa request. Clinton surrendered and allowed Lee to visit Cornell in June 1995.

Chinese leaders were outraged and a major diplomatic crisis ensued. They recalled their ambassador to the United States and refused to accept the credentials of the newly appointed American ambassador.

They broke off the "cross strait" dialogue they had been having with Taipei, the most promising venue for peaceful reconciliation. In a temporarily successful effort to intimidate the people of Taiwan, the People's Liberation Army (PLA) conducted exercises in the Taiwan Strait, firing nuclear-capable missiles into the sea north of Taiwan. Support for independence declined on the island and its stock market fell sharply, as did the value of its currency.

Rising tensions won Clinton's attention, and his advisers had him write to Jiang Zemin, inviting him to Washington and assuring him the United States would oppose Taiwan's independence and admission to the UN. The letter ended the crisis. The American ambassador was received in Beijing, and the Chinese ambassador returned to Washington.

The Clinton administration also protested against the PLA exercises, reminding the Chinese of American insistence on the peaceful resolution of the issues between Taiwan and China. But relieving American concerns was not a high priority in Beijing. In February 1996, the PLA began massing troops across the Strait from Taiwan. In March, just before the presidential election, the PLA bracketed the island with missiles, demonstrating its ability to devastate Taiwan without invading. Again, Taiwan's stock market fell, an expression of public fears.

Clinton's advisers understood that the United States had to respond to the challenge. Lake warned a senior Chinese diplomat that military action against Taiwan would have "grave consequences." Lest the Chinese dismiss the warning as mere words, Clinton ordered two carrier battle groups to the vicinity of the island. Taiwan went ahead with its election, and Lee Teng-hui won a decisive victory. The PLA troops concluded their exercises and returned to their barracks. The American warships sailed away without firing a shot. Another phase of an apparently unending crisis was over.

The Chinese-American partnership of the late Cold War era had ended with the Tiananmen massacres of 1989. Efforts to accommodate China's power, by Clinton as well as Bush, had not been reciprocated. Friendly relations were not likely, given the enormous gap between the values of the American people and of the Chinese leaders and in the absence of a shared enemy such as the Soviet Union had been. Nonetheless, China's capacity for jeopardizing American interests around the globe demanded that Washington find the path toward a decent working relationship. The two governments had to accept their differences, cooperate when possible – and avoid confrontation when it was not. Clinton called for "comprehensive engagement," and Jiang, despite intense internal opposition, especially from the PLA, concluded a working relationship with the United States was in China's interest as well. Washington and Beijing agreed to exchange presidential visits. Jiang came to the United States in 1997, and Clinton returned the visit in 1998. Little of substance came of the trips, but the two leaders had achieved a modus vivendi that eased tensions between their countries for almost a year.

The quiet interlude in Chinese-American relations ended abruptly in May 1999 amid NATO's bombing of Serbia in an attempt to stop ethnic cleansing in Kosovo. The Chinese had opposed the bombing as an illegal sidestepping of the UN Security Council, where they had veto power. Sensitive about the possibility of foreign intervention to protect Tibetans or Uighurs from Chinese oppression, Beijing opposed Kosovo operations as interference in the internal affairs of a sovereign state. And then in May, NATO accidentally bombed the Chinese embassy in Belgrade, killing three Chinese. The Chinese government rejected American explanations and encouraged its people to believe the attack had been deliberate. Outraged demonstrators besieged the American embassy in Beijing and set fire to the home of the American consul general in Chengdu. The incident triggered an explosion of discontent with Jiang's policy of accommodation with the United States.

For the next several months Jiang's critics enjoyed unusual access to the media. He came under enormous pressure, especially from the PLA, to end strategic cooperation with Washington. He bought off the PLA with promises of funds for military modernization and rode out the storm. By the end of summer, the debate had ended and no policy change was instituted.[20]

The debate within the American foreign policy elite went on without resolution. On one side were men and women who perceived China as the next great threat to the nation's security, supported by those troubled by China's human rights record. They were unable to devise a policy that would force Chinese leaders to be more responsive to their

[20] David Finkelstein, *China Reconsiders Its National Security: "The Great Peace and Development Debate of 1999"* (Alexandria, Va., 2000).

concerns. On the other side were those whose eagerness to trade with China overrode any anxieties about security or human rights issues. They perceived no alternative to continued engagement with a government that frequently behaved reprehensibly. It would not be the first time American leaders chose strategic partnerships with distasteful regimes – Mao Zedong's China, for example. As the world entered the twenty-first century, Americans were stuck with engagement in the fond hope China would become more humane at home and more cooperative in its international relations.

One obvious hedge against a potentially hostile China was the alliance with Japan. In 1995, with the American economy booming and the Japanese economy obviously weakening, the Clinton administration eased its trade pressures. Secretary of Defense Perry and Joseph Nye, the Harvard political scientist serving as assistant secretary for international security, were able to make the case for more attention to security affairs. The initial purpose of the alliance – defense of Japan and containment of the Soviet Union – was redirected toward maintaining peace and stability in the Asia-Pacific region. The principal American concerns were North Korean nuclear weapons and tensions in the Taiwan Strait. The Japanese were improving their defensive capabilities and in 1997 Tokyo joined Washington in issuing new Guidelines for U.S.-Japan Defense Cooperation. The new guidelines extended the range of cooperation from defense of Japan to undefined "surrounding areas," a deliberately ambiguous reference to North Korea and Taiwan. In 1999 the Japanese Diet authorized logistical support for the United States if Americans became involved in a war in East Asia outside Japan. With the rise of Chinese power and the threat from North Korea, the Japanese were being forced to contemplate revision of Article 9 of their constitution, in which they had renounced any right to go to war.

There were a host of seemingly lesser issues that forced themselves on the attention of Clinton's foreign policy advisers – and occasionally gained the president's attention as well. Saddam Hussein's Iraq continued to be an annoyance, with his ceaseless pinprick challenges to the United States. The Gulf War and the UN economic sanctions that followed meant that Iraq, a third-rate power at its peak, was significantly weaker than in 1990, but Saddam seemed irrepressible. In 1993, a report of an Iraqi plot to assassinate former president Bush, visiting Kuwait, reached Washington. Clinton was persuaded to strike Baghdad with cruise missiles – which had the virtue of avoiding American casualties – but his critics were contemptuous of what they considered an inadequate response to a major provocation.

France and Russia, eager to resume trade and investment ties, did what they could to subvert the sanctions regime. Saddam maneuvered ably along the fracture lines between the United States and the others. When he sent troops into Kurdish-held territory in violation of the 1991 settlement, the United States appealed unsuccessfully for UN action, ultimately firing off a few more cruise missiles to no effect. When he obstructed the work of UN inspectors assigned to assure the Security Council that he had destroyed all of his weapons of mass destruction (WMDs), Clinton tried to intimidate him by sending an aircraft carrier to the Persian Gulf and strengthening American ground forces in the region. But efforts to obtain new sanctions against Iraq were thwarted by the French, Russians, and Chinese, and support for the sanctions was eroding even in the United States.

Within the Clinton administration, Berger, who succeeded Lake as national security adviser, and Albright were most supportive of military action against Saddam, but they could not muster adequate support at home or abroad. Regime change was desirable, but they concluded containment was their only option. Wolfowitz, however, had another idea. Insisting that Saddam had to be overthrown, he persuaded a Republican-controlled Congress to give $97 million to the Iraqi opposition, which, presumably with American air support, would overthrow Saddam. It was a plan reminiscent of the disastrous Bay of Pigs operation the CIA launched against Castro in 1961. Clinton's foreign policy advisers ridiculed the idea, arguing that the Iraqi National Congress had more support in Washington than in Iraq, but his political advisers persuaded him to sign the bill into law.

In December 1998, as Saddam continued to obstruct UN inspection teams and Clinton faced impeachment for lying about a sexual liaison in the White House, the administration launched a new and sustained air and missile attack on Iraq. Critics suspected Clinton of attempting to divert attention from his peccadilloes, to rally the public around the flag. They may have been right, but there is no doubt that Saddam, perceiving a weakened president, had been provocative. The American military action had no noticeable impact on either the impeachment proceedings or Saddam.

Iraq was a threat to its neighbors, to American interests in the Persian Gulf, and to the international system many people throughout the world had hoped would emerge with the end of the Cold War. But the United States, the greatest power the world had ever known, seemed helpless to cope with a tin-pot dictator ruling over a Third World country with a decrepit military force. The Clinton administration could only hope that at some point Saddam would be sufficiently provocative to persuade the French and Russians of the need for sharp reprisals – or that the Iraqi people would rise against him. Wolfowitz was dismissive of both possibilities and in the election campaign of 2000 he was prominent among advisers to the Republican candidate. He and other such advisers were vehement in their criticism of Clinton's failure to get rid of Saddam.

Clinton vacillated in his approach to Iran over the years of his presidency. Tehran continued to be hostile to the United States, and there was increasing evidence that it was seeking a nuclear weapons capability as well as supporting Hamas and Hezbollah, both frequently engaged in acts of terrorism. Initially, the administration worked toward isolating Iran, attempting with minimal success to deny it loans, investments, and arms supplies. Great Britain alone among America's friends and allies supported Washington. Lake, Christopher, and Albright pressed Clinton for a more aggressive sanctions regime, but the CIA contended that Iran was not as much a threat to U.S. interests as were Iraq, Libya, China, and North Korea. Analysts in and out of the government argued that Iran's economic difficulties and its declining oil production capability indicated it was not likely to make trouble for its neighbors.

The Republican seizure of control of Congress after the mid-term elections of 1994 precluded any effort to reach out to Tehran. Republican congressional leaders demanded tougher policies toward "rogue" states. The American Israel Public Affairs Committee (AIPAC), the powerful pro-Israel lobby, called for a ban on all commercial contact. Clinton ran before the wind and endorsed a complete economic boycott. Congress followed with legislation mandating sanctions against foreign countries that contributed to the development of Iran or Libya, angering allies that objected to being coerced into supporting an American policy they deemed counterproductive.

Domestic critics of efforts to isolate Iran included former national security advisers Brent Scowcroft and Zbigniew Brzezinski, but Clinton was not willing to battle the Republican Congress until May 1997, when the Iranian people elected Mohammad Khatami, a reformist cleric, as their new president. It was evident that the Iranian people wanted to change course and as hostility toward Khatami's Iran eased at home – and in Israel – Clinton's advisers reconsidered rapprochement.

Khatami had considerable success moderating Iran's behavior. Support for terrorism and assassination of exiled dissidents declined. Tehran ratified the Chemical Weapons Convention, ostensibly surrendering one WMD option. In an interview with CNN, Khatami expressed regret for the Carter era hostage crisis and called for cultural and educational exchanges with the United States. But although Clinton took several steps to relax tensions, including easing sanctions and recognizing the legitimacy of the Iranian government, Khatami, restrained by Ayotollah Ali Khameni, the nation's ultimate power, was unable to move any closer to the Americans.

State-supported terrorism was not the only form of terrorism the United States faced in the post–Cold War era. In 1995, a member of the home-grown lunatic fringe bombed a federal building in Oklahoma City, killing 168 people. But increasingly, the threat came from foreign nonstate actors with grievances rooted in the Middle East. American backing of Israel was one source of anger at the United States. Support for authoritarian Arab leaders such as the Saudi royal family or Egypt's Hosni Mubarak was another. Probably the strongest grievance was the perception in the Muslim world of a Western assault, presumably led by the United States, on Islamic values.

U.S. forces were frequently sent abroad to protect American interests or what were perceived as those of the international community: peace, stability, the free flow of commerce, including oil. In foreign cities and ports, they became targets. Reagan sent marines to Lebanon, and 241 of them were killed when a suicide bomber drove a truck into their barracks in 1983. In 1996, terrorists killed 19 and wounded 240 American troops sleeping in Khobar Towers in Saudi Arabia. In 2000, the *U.S.S. Cole* was attacked in Yemen, resulting in the deaths of 17 sailors.

Comparable dangers faced American diplomats. In the worst episode, in August 1998, the American embassies in Nairobi, Kenya, and Dar es Salaam, Tanzania, were struck by car bombs almost simultaneously, injuring a total of 5,500 people, mostly Kenyans and Tanzanians. Over 200 died in Nairobi, as did 11 others in Dar es Salaam.

But staying home was not adequate protection. In 1993, terrorists struck in New York City, exploding a car bomb under the World Trade Center, killing five and injuring hundreds of others. The World Trade Center survived the attack, and the responsible terrorists were captured before they could execute the attacks they planned on the UN building and the Lincoln Tunnel, but the vulnerability of ordinary Americans was evident. Military bases and embassies might be shielded by increased security, but it would be extraordinarily difficult to guard against attacks in civilian settings.

All of the men involved in the 1993 attack on the World Trade Center were Muslims from the Middle East, led by an Egyptian cleric. In the course of the investigation, American officials learned that the group's activities had been financed by a multimillionaire Saudi businessman, Osama bin Laden. Bin Laden was probably also responsible for the attack on U.S. forces in Saudi Arabia in 1996. Often in the 1990s he raged against the presence of non-Muslims on Saudi soil, insisting their presence was an offense against Allah. And in 1998, he called for a jihad against the Jews and the "crusaders," his pejorative term for Westerners in the Middle East.

Bin Laden considered American actions in the region, even the liberation of Kuwait, a declaration of war against Islam. Killing Americans and their allies, wherever they could be found, was the sacred duty of every Muslim. Relatively few Muslims agreed that the Koran called for terrorism, for the murder of innocent bystanders, but implementation of bin Laden's vision did not require many. Even the Pentagon, representing the most powerful military the world had ever known, could not devise a strategy for deterring nonstate actors.

Inevitably the United States tried to capture or kill bin Laden. Once, American intelligence tracked him to Sudan but failed to close a deal with a Sudanese government that appeared willing to turn him over. When Sudan was forced by the UN to expel him, he fled to Afghanistan, where he collaborated with the country's Taliban rulers and ran training camps for terrorists. Clinton authorized the launching of cruise missiles against one such camp, and the CIA ran a covert operation with Ahmed Shah Massoud, a famed Afghan guerrilla, hoping to capture bin Laden, but he remained out of reach. Reports that his men were working with diverse weapons of mass destruction worried counterterrorism specialists in the United States. The initiative rested with bin Laden, and an attack on an American city could come at any time.

North Korea provided a very different kind of threat. There was no doubt about the existence of its nuclear weapons program. Bush's success in getting Pyongyang to accept IAEA inspections proved more apparent than real: The North Koreans attempted to conceal their plutonium holdings, and in March 1993, as the Clinton administration prepared to cope with the issue, Pyongyang announced its intent to withdraw from the nonproliferation regime it had accepted in 1985. Neither Clinton's hints of economic aid to the famine-ravaged country nor efforts to negotiate with it brought satisfactory results. Pyongyang raised hopes of a resolution and then dashed them, repeating the process while continuing efforts to develop nuclear weapons. By the end of 1993, the CIA estimated North Korea had sufficient plutonium for at least one bomb, possibly two.

The inability of the Clinton administration to resolve the issue prompted former government officials, most notably Brent Scowcroft, to demand military action to eliminate the threat. The U.S. air force was prepared to turn North Korea into a "parking lot." Some experts warned, however, that there was no certainty that air strikes would destroy underground or unknown sites. Others worried about what North Korea would do to South Korea if attacked.

With the possibility of war increasing, in June 1994, Kim Il Sung, North Korea's "Great Leader," invited Jimmy Carter to Pyongyang, relishing the visit of a former American president. Clinton was not pleased, but he and his advisers, not wanting to risk the domestic political ramifications of appearing to impede a peace effort, gave their approval. Carter persuaded Kim to agree to freeze his nuclear program before negotiations began. The North Koreans pledged not to refuel their Yongbyon reactor or to produce any more plutonium. In July 1994, instead of sending bombers, Clinton sent a delegation to Pyongyang to negotiate. Chalmers Johnson, a leading specialist on Asian affairs, called the apparent breakthrough "a cardinal achievement of U.S. diplomacy and successful nuclear blackmail."[21]

Despite Kim's sudden death, negotiations continued, resulting in the Agreed Framework. North Korea agreed to continue the freeze and

[21] Johnson, "Korea and Our Asia Policy," *National Interest*, 41 (Fall 1995): 66–77.

dismantle its nuclear program in stages. In return, the United States pledged to assist Pyongyang in obtaining light-water reactors, not easily used to produce weapons-grade plutonium – and to provide fuel oil to replace energy lost when the existing reactors were shut down. The crisis passed – for the moment.

When the Republicans gained control of Congress in the 1994 elections, implementation of the agreement was not assured. Republican leaders agreed with analysts who charged Clinton with having bribed a brutal and untrustworthy regime. The U.S. did not fulfill its end of the bargain, and there was no reason to doubt that the issue of North Korea's nuclear weapons would rise again, precipitating yet another crisis.

After the struggle over NAFTA and despite Clinton's eloquence on the subject of globalization, there was a growing sense among many Americans – and others in the international community – that the world economic system benefited capitalists at the expense of workers and the environment. Trade unquestionably contributed an increasing percentage to the nation's gross domestic product, but that provided little gratification to the hundreds of thousands of Americans who lost well-paying jobs to low-wage workers abroad.

Skepticism about NAFTA intensified with the collapse of the Mexican peso in 1994. Robert Rubin, who had become secretary of the treasury in 1995, took charge and concluded Mexico needed a $40 billion stabilization loan. His warning that inaction would result in millions of additional illegal immigrants did not move the Republican Congress, which refused the appropriation. Undeterred, he found the money elsewhere, and the loan succeeded in stabilizing the Mexican economy. Within a year, Mexico registered a trade surplus and was able to begin paying off its debt. Not coincidentally, Wall Street bankers, whose loans to Mexico had been speculative, were bailed out as well.

In 1997, an enormous financial crisis began in Asia, again revealing the dark side of globalization and raising questions about Washington's insistence on the free flow of capital as well as trade. It started with a speculative run on Thailand's currency. The Thai government allowed the baht to float against the dollar and it dropped sharply, leaving the country unable to pay off its short-term debt to foreign banks. The International Monetary Fund came up with a stabilization package to which the United States did not contribute directly, angering the Thais and the financial ministries of other Southeast Asian countries affected. From Washington came disparaging remarks about "crony capitalism," while Indonesia and South Korea slipped into serious trouble. None of these countries had regulatory institutions strong enough to control the movement of capital in and out of their territories. The Americans stood by as the authoritarian Suharto government in Indonesia collapsed, but they did aid South Korea, where democracy seemed to be taking root.

Serious doubts about the wisdom of open capital markets were expressed by prominent economists and by George Soros, who had gained his great fortune as a currency speculator. But the United States continued to push for greater openness in Asia, part of the American mission to re-create the world in its own image. Asia survived, but skepticism about Washington's approach intensified.

Ireland and Israel, in contrast to Thailand or Indonesia, were countries whose affairs were followed closely by millions of Americans and often affected domestic politics. Both had Clinton's attention: He recognized the importance of Irish and Jewish voters and believed they were committed, however blindly, to the goals of Irish nationalists in Northern Ireland and of Israeli expansionists.

In 1992, Clinton bid for Irish votes by promising a visa to Gerry Adams – leader of Sinn Fein, political arm of the Irish Republican Army – and by criticizing Britain's human rights record in Northern Ireland. Clinton promised to pursue peace between Catholics and Protestants in that troubled part of the British empire. He waited until after the British government and the IRA agreed to a cease-fire that would allow Sinn Fein to participate in negotiations over the future of Northern Ireland before approving a visa for Adams in early 1994 – yielding to pressure from senators Ted Kennedy (D-Mass.) and Pat Moynihan (D-N.Y.).

Adams met with senior White House officials, set up an office to raise funds in the United States, and was even invited to the White House for St. Patrick's Day festivities. There could be no doubt of the legitimacy granted Sinn Fein in Clinton's America. Ultimately of greater importance, however, was the appointment of former senator George Mitchell as Clinton's special representative on the Northern Ireland issue. Mitchell spent much of the next three years chairing talks between Sinn Fein and the Protestant Irish Unionists and in 1998, his efforts contributed to a precarious agreement between Irish nationalists and unionists on the governance of Northern Ireland. Clinton's Irish policy was clearly successful.

Coping with Israel and its neighbors proved a more daunting challenge. Christopher flew to Damascus more than twenty times in a vain effort to broker peace between Syria and Israel. Yitzhak Rabin, the Israeli war hero and prime minister, offered to return the Golan Heights, taken from Syria during the Six-Day War of 1967, in exchange for a peace treaty, but the Syrians were unresponsive.

At home Israel had to cope with the Palestinian intifada, an armed uprising of Palestinians in the occupied territories of Gaza and the West Bank that began in 1987. In 1993, in secret negotiations in Oslo, Israelis and Palestinians reached an agreement on principles for the resolution of their differences on the basis of land for peace. In exchange for an end to the intifada, Israel would gradually turn over control of the West Bank and Gaza to a Palestinian Authority. The agreement was signed in Washington. The U.S. then persuaded forty-five other countries to pledge $2.5 billion in development aid for the Palestinians. With assistance from the Clinton administration, Israel proceeded to sign peace agreements with Jordan, Morocco, and Tunisia, each receiving substantial incentives. Optimism about a comprehensive Arab-Israeli peace grew.

And then came one of those moments that force scholars to evaluate the role of the individual in history. In November 1995, Rabin, vilified by Israelis who opposed yielding any of the lands conquered in 1967, was murdered by a right-wing Israeli Jew. His death proved an enormous setback for the peace process. In 1996, despite obvious American efforts to bring about a different outcome, Benjamin Netanyahu and his Likud party, opponents of the Oslo Accords, won control of the Israeli government. Apprehension spread throughout the Arab world and in Washington. These fears proved justified. Determined to heighten tensions, Palestinian radicals, engaged in a symbiotic relationship with the Israeli Right, terrorized Israel with suicide bombings.

Netanyahu resisted intense pressure from Washington to continue on the course Rabin had set. He knew he could count on the Israeli lobby and supporters in the U.S. Congress to prevent the Clinton administration from punishing him. The peace process came to a halt. To Netanyahu's surprise, Clinton pushed harder, risking the alienation of the strong support he received from the American Jewish community. He became deeply engaged in efforts to end the Israeli-Palestinian conflict. Unfortunately, cooperation from the principal parties was minimal. The Israelis continued to build settlements in the West Bank, and the Palestinians persisted in acts of violence against Israelis.

Hope reemerged in May 1999, when the Israeli electorate turned against Likud, allowing Ehud Barak, the Labor party candidate, to become prime minister. Barak seemed much like Rabin, a tough military man, less ideological than Netanyahu. Apparently having decided that peace in the Middle East would be his foreign policy legacy, Clinton pressed Israelis and Palestinians to resolve the issues that continued to divide them. It was quickly evident that he was more eager for negotiations than either of the adversaries.

In July 2000, after Barak had been in office for more than a year, during which American diplomats shuttled between him and Yasir Arafat, the PLO leader, Clinton invited the two men to Camp David. At great risk to himself, physically as well as politically, Barak grudgingly accepted an American proposal to give Palestinians authority over parts of East Jerusalem. It was not a sufficient concession for Arafat, who needed much more to compensate for the concessions he was asked to offer on the Palestinian right of return – the right of those who fled or were driven out of Palestine in 1948 to reclaim land and homes in what was now Israel. The negotiations failed.

However disheartened, Clinton kept trying to achieve peace in the Middle East before he left office. But in September, a second intifada began, provoked by Ariel Sharon, an Israeli politician even more belligerent than Netanyahu. Clinton persisted until the end of the year, but both Israelis and Palestinians turned down a fresh American proposal on December 30. For Clinton the game was over. A few weeks later, Barak's Labor party was badly defeated, and Sharon, the man most dreaded by Palestinians and most feared by peace advocates around the world, was Israel's new prime minister.

Clinton also tackled two remnants of the Cold War: relations with Vietnam and Cuba. One important success in his first term was the establishment of diplomatic relations with Hanoi. Carter's efforts had been put aside to focus on rapprochement with China, and Reagan had shown no interest. Bush was preoccupied first with ending the Cold War and then with teaching Iraq that aggression would not be tolerated in the new world order. But there were compelling economic and strategic reasons for Clinton to establish a working relationship with Vietnam.

Hanoi indicated its willingness to help resolve the POW/MIA issue by assisting in efforts to account for missing Americans. The business community in the U.S. pressed for trade opportunities, and Clinton lifted the trade embargo in 1994. With essential support from prominent Vietnam War heroes, most importantly Senator John McCain (R.-Ariz.), who had spent more time in Vietnamese prisons than any other living American, Clinton gave official recognition to Hanoi in July 1995. Vietnam was about to be incorporated into the global economic system.

Improved relations with Cuba proved elusive, not least because Castro was not interested. But Cuba was also a third rail of American politics because of the power of the anti-Castro Cuban-American National Foundation (CANF) – and the heavy concentration of Cuban-American voters in Miami. Clinton recognized the need to pander to them.

Cuba was in serious economic trouble at the end of the Cold War, having lost the subsidies, especially cheap oil, that the Soviet Union had provided since the days of Khrushchev. The quality of life deteriorated sharply in the early 1990s for most Cubans. Castro's response was to relieve tensions by encouraging emigration to the United States, but Washington reneged on an agreement to issue twenty thousand visas annually. The Americans had no interest in easing Castro's problems, but the result was large-scale illegal immigration, Cubans on boats and rafts risking their lives to get to Florida, where any who reached land were granted asylum automatically.

In 1994, after consultations with CANF, Clinton increased the pressures on Castro, prohibiting remittances from Cubans in America to their relatives in Cuba – an important source of hard currency for the regime. He also reduced flights between Miami and Havana and increased anti-Castro broadcasts to Cuba. None of these measures proved effective. Cubans in the United States found new ways to send money back to relatives and demanded the restoration of flights to Havana.

Conditions in Cuba improved in 1995, thanks to the exodus of thousands of the discontented as well as continued remittances and a new emphasis on tourism. Specialists in the State Department perceived signs of Castro's opening the economy a little, easing off on repression. The American business community was eager to get into

Cuba, offering the familiar argument that increased commerce would lead to a more open Cuban society, perhaps even democracy. The UN criticized the American embargo, and even Cuban-Americans began drifting away from CANF's hard line. But any hopes of reconciliation between Washington and Havana were blasted in February 1996, when Cuban fighter planes shot down two unarmed aircraft flown by members of Brothers to the Rescue, a Cuban exile group that tried to help Cubans risking their lives as they attempted to sail to the United States on makeshift boats. In response to the public outcry, Clinton, up for reelection, signed a bill stiffening sanctions.

It was evident that Castro and the hard-liners in America thrived on each other's belligerency. Owen Harries, a leading conservative analyst, noted that whenever Castro was in trouble, he manipulated a crisis that provoked a tough American response, which enabled him to blame Cuba's troubles on Washington or Miami and rally his people behind him. Harries dismissed Castro as a "squalid local tyrant," no longer capable of harming U.S. interests. He argued that ending efforts to isolate Cuba, depriving Castro of an American threat, would force him to open Cuban society.[22] Clinton lacked the political courage to follow Harries's advice.

Clinton and his foreign policy advisers did not lack a vision for the post–Cold War world. They were determined to expand the community of free-market democracies. But the president kept his promise to focus on domestic affairs, and his principal appointees for foreign affairs lacked the charismatic personalities essential to compensate for a disengaged president. There were no Achesons or Kissingers among them.

The American role in the world was further circumscribed by the election of a nativist Congress in 1994, riddled with people who boasted that they had no passports and had never traveled abroad. These were the legislators who were responsible for the U.S. failure to pay its dues to the UN, who delayed ratification of the Chemical Weapons Convention, finally passed in 1997, prevented acceptance of an international ban on the use of antipersonnel mines that were killing and maiming thousands of innocent civilians in various parts of the world,

[22] Harries, "An Offer Castro Couldn't Refuse – or Survive," *National Interest,* 44 (Summer 1996): 126–28.

defeated the Comprehensive Test Ban Treaty intended to end testing of nuclear weapons, and intimidated the Clinton administration to the point where it refused to sign the treaty to establish the International Criminal Court and did not submit the Kyoto Treaty on global warming to the Senate.

And the American people, never known for a deep interest in foreign affairs, were content. With the end of the Cold War, there was little desire for an activist foreign policy.

In 2001, the "Vulcans" took charge, with their own sense of the role the United States would play in the world.[23] The new president, George W. Bush, and his foreign policy team had been sharply critical of Clinton's management of international affairs. They held him responsible for the alleged decline of American military power and pledged to rebuild it. They were contemptuous of humanitarian interventions and nation-building efforts. They dismissed Clinton's attempts to resolve the Israeli-Palestinian conflict as a waste of energy and ridiculed his "pin-prick" retaliations against Iraqi provocations. China, they insisted, was a strategic "competitor," not the strategic partner Clinton had claimed. They portrayed the Agreed Framework with North Korea as submission to blackmail. They contended that Clinton had been too cozy with Yeltsin, too accommodating to Russia. Most of all, they were skeptical of efforts to work through the UN or to accept international agreements that limited America's freedom of action.

The incoming Bush team was well aware of the threat posed by terrorists but focused on state-supported terrorism. It was determined to deal with rogue states, especially those such as Iraq that were believed to possess or be developing weapons of mass destruction. Al Qaeda was not considered a high-priority concern, despite the urgency perceived by specialists on counterterrorism at the National Security Council and the CIA.

Unlike his father, the younger Bush had a vision of his country's place in the post–Cold War age. Like Woodrow Wilson, he was determined to use the power of the United States to promote American values as well as interests, to spread democracy around the world. Bush, however, did not share Wilson's belief in the importance of international institutions to accomplish his goals. On the contrary, he was an assertive nationalist,

[23] Mann, *Rise of the Vulcans*, ix–xix.

determined to shed restraints on the use of American power – and he assembled a superb group of foreign policy specialists to advise him.

The central figure among the Vulcans was Condoleezza Rice, a specialist on Soviet affairs, much admired by Brent Scowcroft and George Shultz. It was Rice with whom Bush was most comfortable, and as national security adviser she had an office in the White House and easy access to the president. She was an exceptionally able analyst and articulator of administration policy, but it was soon apparent that she was unable to harness the rest of the president's team, least of all Donald Rumsfeld, a late choice for secretary of defense, and his protégé, Dick Cheney, the vice-president. One commentator referred to her as "a marble caught between two elephants."

Another Vulcan was the widely admired Paul Wolfowitz. His reputation as an indifferent administrator denied him the top post at the Pentagon, but he was named deputy secretary of defense. Although he had been involved in East Asian affairs for much of his career, his writings in the 1990s suggested that his focus in the Bush administration would be the Middle East. He was determined to bring about regime change in Iraq, confident that deposing Saddam Hussein and replacing his tyrannical rule with a democratic state would be the answer to the region's woes. Democracy, he was convinced, would then spread to nearby states, serving the interests of the United States and its friends in the Middle East.

But the appointment that gave the most credibility to the Bush team was that of the highly respected Colin Powell. Among the many important posts he had held were national security adviser to the president and chairman of the Joint Chiefs of Staff. Had he chosen to run for office, he might well have been a nominee of either party for president or vice-president. Largely unnoticed was the fact that Powell was not part of Bush's inner circle. And unforeseen was his inability to direct the course of policy in the years that followed. Frustrated and unwanted, he resigned at the end of Bush's first term.

Ultimately, it was not Powell or any of the Vulcans who dominated the policy process through the Bush presidency, but rather Vice-President Cheney, the consummate Washington insider. He had served in Congress, as White House chief of staff, and as secretary of defense. He knew where the levers of power were and how to use them. He was more involved in foreign policy than any prior vice-president. He set up his own national security council, and key positions throughout the national security bureaucracy were filled by people associated with him.

Soon after the Bush team settled into its offices, the first crisis hit, triggered by the collision between an American spy plane (EP-3) and a Chinese interceptor off the coast of China on April 1, 2001. Confident that they had a better approach than Clinton to managing relations with China, they had determined to confront the Chinese at the first opportunity, acting as necessary to demonstrate that the United States would not allow China to challenge American influence in East Asia or its preeminence in the world. They would remind Beijing that the United States looked to Japan and South Korea as its true strategic partners across the Pacific. Bush signaled the new approach by deliberately excluding Chinese president Jiang Zemin from the list of leaders to whom he placed courtesy calls when he took office.

In the collision the Chinese plane fell into the sea and the pilot was killed. The American plane made an emergency landing on China's Hainan Island where the crew was detained. Beijing demanded an apology for the incident. Bush and Cheney reacted instinctively by trying to intimidate China. In Congress there was talk of war or other means of forcing the Chinese to release the crew and return the plane. To the astonishment of the administration, the Chinese were unresponsive: No senior Chinese official would take calls from Washington or meet with the American ambassador in Beijing.[24]

A little of the humility Bush had promised during the election campaign proved necessary. After a few days the Chinese accepted an American expression of regret for their pilot's death and for the American crew's failure to obtain clearance before landing on Chinese territory – short of the apology for the mission and collision that Beijing had demanded. The crisis passed, and Bush learned that China was too strong, too important to be ignored – and too proud to be dictated to by the American superpower.

Toward Russia, the Clinton administration had despaired when Yeltsin self-destructed and waited watchfully, intensely wary of Putin. Rice, the most knowledgeable of the Bush team still saw Russia as a

---

[24] Ivo H. Daalder and James M. Lindsay, *America Unbound: The Bush Revolution in Foreign Policy* (Washington, D.C., 2003), 67–69.

potential threat. Cheney had only grudgingly conceded that the Cold War was over. The consensus among the president's advisers was that the United States should use its overwhelming power to force Moscow to accept decisions it would not like, including further NATO expansion and the building of a national missile defense system.

Bush and Putin met in June 2001 and appeared to like each other. Powerless to stop the Americans from abrogating the ABM treaty or going forward with NATO enlargement, Putin yielded gracefully. He gave no ground, however, on the matter of Russian assistance to Iran's nuclear program, an important source of income. Overall, Bush was pleased with the encounter, and Russia dropped off the administration's agenda.[25]

Having resolved problems with China and Russia, troubled by a decline in his approval ratings, Bush turned to domestic affairs. His foreign policy team planned its strategy for challenging rogue states, specifically Iraq, Iran, and North Korea – the "axis of evil." In August 2001, however, Richard Clarke, the National Security Council's specialist on counterterrorism, warned his superiors that Osama bin Laden and his al Qaeda operatives were planning to attack the United States.[26] Clarke was convinced that the threat was urgent, but none of the president's advisers was persuaded. Al Qaeda was not a high-priority issue. And the president was more concerned with Saddam Hussein, who had tried to kill his father.

Much of that changed on September 11, 2001.

---

[25] Mann, *Rise of the Vulcans*, 288; Daalder and Lindsay, *America Unbound*, 64.
[26] CNN.Com/2004/ALLPOLITIKS/04/10/Bushbriefing (accessed 3 May 2010).

II

THE "WAR" AGAINST TERRORISM

On September 11, 2001, after the twin towers of New York's World Trade Center came crashing down, Americans could no longer be complacent about the outside world. Osama bin Laden's men, seizing control of commercial airliners, had flown suicide missions against the symbols of American financial power and against the Pentagon, symbol of the nation's military might. A fourth attack was thwarted over Pennsylvania, sparing Capitol Hill or perhaps the White House. More than three thousand Americans died in the attacks. Bin Laden had demonstrated that the United States, the lone remaining superpower, was not invulnerable.

When Bush met with his advisers to determine his response, Cheney, Rumsfeld, and Wolfowitz urged him to invade Iraq. Wolfowitz was certain Iraq was involved in the attacks. But Bush couldn't wait the months until an invasion could be readied. He had to act immediately, and all available intelligence pointed to bin Laden, operating out of Afghanistan, under the protection of the Taliban, a radical Islamist force that controlled most of the country. Iraq could wait while the Taliban and bin Laden received a demonstration of American power.[1]

Leaders across the globe promised their support, including Russia's Putin and China's Jiang. The UN condemned the attacks, and NATO, for the first time, invoked its mutual defense clause. Many nations offered help. Democrats and Republicans in Congress united to give

[1] Brian Urquhart, "A Cautionary Tale," *New York Review of Books* (June 10, 2004), 8–19; James Mann, *Rise of the Vulcans: The History of Bush's War* (New York, 2004), 302–3; Ivo H. Daalder and James M. Lindsay, *America Unbound: The Bush Revelation in Foreign Policy* (Washington D.C., 2003), 99.

the president a free hand to fight the war he declared on terrorism – and his popularity with his people soared as they rallied 'round the flag.

When the Taliban refused to turn bin Laden over to the United States, Americans went to war against the Taliban regime, with a mandate from the UN and British troops alongside. Powell gained the critical support of Pakistan, long the principal backer of the Taliban. But in general, offers of assistance were brushed aside. Rumsfeld resisted creation of a broad coalition. He wanted complete freedom of action: There should be no expectations of consultations with other nations – or of the multilateralism he despised.

Given the military's continued aversion to risking casualties, the Pentagon's war plan stressed technology over combat troops. When airpower and high-tech devices proved insufficient, the United States recruited the troops of the Northern Alliance (Afghan forces hostile to the Taliban) and prevailed quickly. Unfortunately, Taliban and al Qaeda leaders escaped into the mountains. At this point, American tactics failed disastrously. U.S. forces were too few to cut off escape routes into Pakistan, and American commanders were reluctant to assign their troops the dangerous task of pursuing Taliban and al Qaeda fighters into the caves and passes they had chosen for their last stand. The Afghan warlords upon whose troops the Americans depended were satisfied at driving the Taliban out of territories they coveted and gave up the chase. Bin Laden and Mullah Omar, the Taliban leader, slipped away, to plague the United States and its friends in the region for years to follow.

The American victory over the Taliban had been easy, but it was not clear anything enduring had been accomplished. Disdainful of peacekeeping operations and nation-building, the Bush administration all but abandoned Afghanistan as Bush, Cheney, and Rumsfeld returned their attention to Iraq. The American-backed government of Hamid Karzai proved unable to assert its authority outside Kabul. Regional warlords, once driven out by the Taliban, ruled much of the country, and gradually Taliban and al Qaeda fighters came out of hiding to attack American and allied troops and foreign aid workers remaining in the country. Little progress had been made in the war against terrorism.

In the months that followed the 9/11 attacks, the Bush administration alienated a world that had been largely sympathetic and supportive in response to the attacks. It brushed aside most offers of assistance, perceiving the battle in Afghanistan as an American war, when it could have assembled a broad coalition of states that recognized that terrorism was a threat to all societies, not only American. The administration's refusal to treat captives as prisoners of war, entitled to the safeguards of the Geneva Conventions, troubled people everywhere. Insisting that those who opposed the invasion were "illegal combatants," Bush's aides shipped many to the American naval base at Guantanamo, Cuba, where they were denied legal counsel and where some claimed to have been tortured. In the view of the president and his advisers, the need to protect their nation's security freed them from observing its international obligations.

Bush's first State of the Union address to Congress in January 2002 redirected the country's focus in the war on terror from al Qaeda to the need for regime change in rogue states, specifically Iraq, Iran, and North Korea. He warned that these three were seeking weapons of mass destruction that they might make available to terrorists. The United States was determined to prevent that from happening. At West Point a few months later, the president declared his intent to take preemptive action if necessary to prevent another terrorist attack. He told his audience that the world's most powerful nation intended to remain the world's most powerful nation in perpetuity, acting as necessary to stifle any challenge.[2]

In September, the administration issued its congressionally mandated statement on *National Security Strategy,* stressing the points Bush had articulated at West Point. Echoing the words of Woodrow Wilson as understood by neoconservative intellectuals, the document declared that the United States would use its power to promote democratic values worldwide. Unlike Wilson, the Bush administration contemplated using unilateral military force to remake the world. The doctrine was perceived widely as a revolution in American foreign policy.

Although the administration hoped to intimidate all three of the states Bush named as the "axis of evil," the principal target was Iraq. Most of Bush's advisers assumed that lesser threats in the region would fall into line as soon as the United States demonstrated its resolve in the Middle East. Iran and North Korea posed far more complex problems – and neither was as vulnerable to American power as was Iraq. Presumably

---

[2] Daalder and Lindsay, *America Unbound,* 120–2.

they, too, would be chastened by a demonstration of American military prowess.

In fact, Iran had already signaled its interest in rapprochement, and both Powell and Rice, supported by Scowcroft, favored engagement with the reformist Khatami government. Tehran shared American hostility toward the Taliban and was at least as eager as Washington to crush Saddam Hussein. When al Qaeda struck the United States on 9/11, Iranian leaders condemned the attacks. Iran seized several al Qaeda operatives and facilitated American-led operations in Afghanistan. Unpublicized talks between Iranian and American diplomats suggested that the years of enmity that had begun with the Islamic revolutionaries' seizure of the American embassy in 1979 might end.[3]

Cheney and Rumsfeld, however, insisted that the United States seek regime change in Tehran. They received strong support from neoconservatives with ties to the Israeli Right. Ariel Sharon, Israel's prime minister, contended that Iran was the major threat to the peace and security of the Middle East – and no one denied that the Iranian government supported anti-Israeli terrorists. When Bush declared Iran to be a member of the "axis of evil," he indicated that Cheney and Rumsfeld had prevailed in the policy debate. Washington was not interested in engagement. His speech undermined the efforts of Iranian reformers and prompted Tehran to intensify its efforts to obtain a nuclear deterrent.[4]

The administration was similarly conflicted over policy toward North Korea. Cheney and Rumsfeld opposed engagement and urged the use of force if Pyongyang failed to comply with American demands. Powell argued for a continuation of Clinton's approach but failed to persuade the president, who openly expressed his contempt for Kim Jong Il, who had succeeded his father as leader of the North Korean regime. The South Koreans, Japanese, and Chinese waited in vain for a constructive suggestion from Washington. And, like the Iranians, the North Koreans responded by accelerating their nuclear weapons development program.[5]

[3] John Newhouse, *Imperial America: The Bush Assault on World Order* (New York, 2003), 4.

[4] Guy Dinmore, "Washington Hardliners Wary of Engaging with Iran," *Financial Times* (March 17, 2004): 7.

[5] Michael O'Hanlon and Mike Mochizuki, *Crisis on the Korean Peninsula* (Washington, D.C., 2003), 14–15; Joel S. Wit, Daniel B. Poneman, and Robert L. Gallucci, *Going*

Specialists in Korean affairs, both in and out of the government, insisted on the urgency of resuming a dialogue with Pyongyang. Its nuclear program threatened American interests in East Asia, and fears mounted that it might sell nuclear materials to bin Laden or other terrorists. It seemed a more immediate threat than Iraq. How could the Bush administration justify its plans to attack Iraq on the grounds that it *might* have a nuclear weapons program when it was doing nothing about North Korea, which had an advanced program – and quite possibly already had several bombs?

The option of fighting a preventive war against North Korea, of overthrowing the Kim regime before it could damage American interests, was discounted as too risky. North Korea had an enormous army and countless missile launchers within range of Seoul. If attacked it could devastate South Korea. It could strike Japan and, conceivably, even the United States. Cheney and Rumsfeld, deeply engaged in planning the invasion of Iraq, acquiesced to a limited diplomatic effort to persuade Pyongyang to back down. When that failed, Bush signaled a major policy shift. In January 2003, on the eve of war with Iraq, he declared that the U.S. had no intention of attacking North Korea and would consider offering economic assistance and a security agreement if Pyongyang would dismantle its nuclear program. The Americans were even willing to talk to the North Koreans, as urged by Seoul and Tokyo. Critics accused the Bush team of adopting a Clintonesque policy of doing nothing and hoping Kim's evil regime would fade away. But the president was determined to keep the focus on Iraq and received strong support from like-minded neoconservatives.

There was another issue that begged resolution before the United States invaded a Muslim nation: the Arab-Israeli conflict. Whatever progress had been made in Israeli-Palestinian negotiations during the closing days of the Clinton administration vanished with the election of Ariel Sharon as Israeli premier in February 2001. No Israeli was feared and hated more by the Palestinians. No Israeli was perceived as more hostile to their aspirations, more ruthless in his determination to crush them. Terrorist attacks against Israel increased. Neither Sharon nor Arafat

Critical: The First North Korean Nuclear Crisis (Washington, D.C., 2004), 377–8; Mann, *Rise of the Vulcans*, 277–81.

seemed interested in working toward a peaceful settlement. Bush saw no point in launching a major effort to resolve the conflict.

The al Qaeda attacks on the United States in September 2001 forced the administration to reconsider. All of Bush's advisers understood that the Israeli-Palestinian struggle was an essential part of the politics of the Middle East, but were uncertain as to how to proceed. Instinctively, Bush sympathized with the Israelis, equating terrorist attacks on Israel with terrorist attacks on the United States. Israeli fears that 9/11 would undermine American support proved unfounded. Although Bush appealed to Arab opinion by becoming the first American president to support explicitly the creation of a Palestinian state, the U.S.-Israeli relationship grew stronger. Despite the ruthlessness with which Sharon responded to terrorist atrocities, Bush labeled him a man of peace.[6]

In April 2002, after Cheney's efforts to win Arab support for regime change in Iraq foundered because of American support of Israel, Powell tried his hand with Arafat and Sharon, but he, too, had little credibility as a neutral mediator. Both Arafat and Sharon knew Powell had no authority to put pressure on the Israelis – certainly not in an election year in the United States, when there was much to be lost by appearing to be anti-Israel. Moreover, Rumsfeld and Wolfowitz insisted that Sharon's crackdown on the Palestinians was a legitimate response to terrorism. The administration failed to restart the peace process, confirming the majority view on Bush's foreign policy team that it was a hopeless cause. Bush abandoned Powell's attempt at being evenhanded and announced the United States would not support statehood for the Palestinians until they had a new and democratic leadership. And the planning for war with Iraq continued.[7]

Although Scowcroft and James Baker, the *elder* Bush's principal foreign policy advisers, opposed a new war with Iraq, Cheney, Wolfowitz, and several prominent neoconservative public intellectuals, notably Richard Perle, pressed for action. Frustration with Saddam's games and erosion of the sanctions regime designed to contain him had made the idea of regime change popular across the American political spectrum. Atrocities

---

[6] Mark Lynch, "Taking Arabs Seriously," *Foreign Affairs* 82 (September/October 2003): 81–94; Shibley Telhami, "The Ties That Bind: Americans, Arabs, and Israelis after 9/11," *Foreign Affairs* 83 (March/April 2004): 8–12.

[7] Mann, *Rise of the Vulcans*, 322–7.

committed against Iraqi Shiites and Kurds rallied human rights advocates to the cause of intervention. The Democratic party opposition seemed cowed by the president's soaring popularity after 9/11 and fearful of being perceived as hindering the fight against terrorism.

Cheney emerged as the most strident advocate for war, contending that Saddam had weapons of mass destruction that he was preparing to use against the United States and its friends. He had to be stopped. The State Department's Bureau of Intelligence and Research (INR) was skeptical of Cheney's sources in the Iraqi exile community, but he and Rumsfeld brushed aside its doubts and set up a competing intelligence unit in the Pentagon, which confirmed reports of Saddam's WMDs. Years later it became apparent that one Iraqi source, code-named Curveball, was utterly unreliable, and another, Ahmed Chalabi, leader of the exile group Cheney, Wolfowitz, and Perle most admired, appears to have had ties to Iran, the nation most likely to gain from an American defeat of Saddam's military. But they were telling the war hawks what they wanted to hear.[8]

Within the administration, Cheney was also the strongest advocate of unilateral action by the United States and for ignoring the U.S. Congress and the UN. His interpretation of presidential power precluded the necessity of legislative consent in matters of foreign affairs. He opposed seeking authorization for war from the UN Security Council, fearful of having restraints imposed on the exercise of American power and insisting the United States did not require international approval to defend itself. But Bush was persuaded that public support for war would be stronger if Congress and the UN approved.

Cheney, Rumsfeld, and Wolfowitz, perhaps deluded by Chalabi, were convinced that Saddam's forces could be defeated by relatively few Americans, perhaps half the number the army chief of staff and outside experts called for. They also assumed American troops would be welcomed as liberators by the Iraqi people and that Chalabi could install a democratic government quickly. They did not anticipate a need for a large U.S. force to stabilize the country, and they brushed aside the

---

[8] National Intelligence Council, "Iraq's Continuing Program for Weapons of Mass Destruction" (NIE, October 2002). See 8–9 for INR's "Alternative View," www.dni/gov/nic/special_keyjudgments.html, accessed July 19, 2010; Bob Droggan and Greg Miller, "Curveball Debacle Reignites CIA Feud," *Los Angeles Times*, April 2, 2005; Peter Beinhart, *The Icarus Syndrome: A History of American Hubris* (New York, 2010), 321, 344, 360–1.

State Department's elaborate plans for postwar Iraq. Prescient critics warned that the Pentagon was not prepared for victory.[9]

Those of Bush's advisers who argued for preventive war against Iraq varied in their reasoning. Some were genuinely fearful of Saddam's alleged weapons of mass destruction. Some were eager to spread American power and values in the Middle East. Control of Iraqi oil does not appear to have been a high priority of any of them, but all were aware that it would be a useful side effect. Interest in Iraq and its neighbors had always been rooted in awareness of the importance of access to the region's oil.

Humanitarian concerns were also peripheral but unquestionably sincere. Saddam was a brutal tyrant, and his people would benefit enormously from his departure. Bush listened to the arguments and found them persuasive. Most of all, he was enamored of the Wilsonian vision of spreading democracy. Aware that many analysts and Republican conservatives preferred a policy more immediately related to the national interest, the administration chose the WMD issue as the rationale for war it presented to the public.

In September 2002, Bush appeared before the UN General Assembly to warn against Saddam's weapons of mass destruction. He urged the UN to pass a resolution demanding that Saddam allow the UN inspectors he had expelled to resume their work. Next, Bush turned to Congress and requested authorization to use force against Iraq. Although there was strong opposition from Senate Democrats, all those with presidential aspirations voted in favor of the resolution. The debate in the United States was over.

Throughout the fall, thousands of American troops were deployed to the vicinity of Iraq, mostly in Kuwait. Saddam determined that it was in his best interests to invite the UN inspectors to return: Coercive "diplomacy" had worked. French, German, and Russian leaders imagined that there would be no need for military action. In November the UN Security Council unanimously demanded that Iraq surrender all weapons of mass destruction – without authorizing the use of force if Saddam failed to comply. Bush, however, concluded that the UN resolution gave legitimacy to the invasion of Iraq the Pentagon was

---

9 Kenneth M. Pollack, "Next Stop Baghdad?" *Foreign Affairs* 81 (March/April 2002): 32–47; Philip H. Gordon, *Survival* 45 (Spring 2003): 155–66; Jack Snyder, "Imperial Temptations, *National Interest* 71 (Spring 2003): 29–40.

planning. On January 11, 2003, Rumsfeld told the Saudi ambassador that war was certain. Powell, who had reservations, was not informed until later.[10]

In Baghdad, Saddam toyed with the inspectors, cooperating minimally at first and then, after they reported his failure to comply with their demands, relaxing restrictions on their access. And they found no evidence of WMDs or programs to produce them. In Washington there was palpable disappointment. The troops were in place, and the Pentagon was eager to invade Iraq before spring, before the desert heat became a problem. But across Europe there was strong opposition to war. British prime minister Tony Blair urged Bush to try again for UN authorization. In February, Powell, who had more credibility abroad than anyone else in the administration, was sent before the UN to obtain the necessary resolution.

Powell presented an impressive case for the existence of WMDs in Iraq and won over many skeptics in the United States – although not in his own Bureau of Intelligence and Research. He failed, however, to win the necessary support in the Security Council. Bush, Cheney, Rumsfeld, and Wolfowitz did not expect to win UN approval and saw no need for it. To meet the domestic political needs of Blair, their principal foreign supporter, they allowed Powell to try a little longer before abandoning the effort. In the absence of backing from other Western European states, Rumsfeld dismissed America's longtime allies as "Old Europe," where the will to fight had evaporated.[11]

By the eve of the war, the administration had succeeded in persuading more than half of the American people that Saddam had been involved in the 9/11 attacks on the United States. The time had come for vengeance. Undeterred by antiwar demonstrations across the globe, the world's most powerful nation, equipped with extraordinary military technology, began Operation Iraqi Freedom, an invasion of a Third World country possessed of a decrepit military armed with obsolete Soviet weapons. The outcome was never in doubt.

---

[10] Bob Woodward, "Behind Diplomatic Moves, Military Plan Was Launched," *Washington Post*, April 18, 2004.

[11] See Robert Kagan, *Of Paradise and Power: America and Europe in the New World Order* (New York, 2003), for an elegant discussion of a Europe that has moved "beyond power," becoming irrelevant to American efforts to maintain strategic stability in the rest of the world.

Islamists across the Middle East, including several who had condemned al Qaeda's attack on the United States, called upon Muslims to launch a jihad against the Americans. Great Britain provided major support, and a number of other states including Australia, Spain, Poland, and a few client states, sent token forces to join the U.S.-led "coalition of the willing." It took but three weeks for coalition forces to reach Baghdad, and only three more before President Bush, standing on the deck of the *U.S.S. Abraham Lincoln,* declared victory. It was May 1, 2003.

It was quickly apparent, however, that defeat of the Iraqi army had been easy compared to managing the postwar situation. American forces in Baghdad were unprepared for the chaos that followed the destruction of Saddam's regime. There were too few troops to stop widespread looting or to provide security for the people of the city. Hospitals, museums, libraries, public buildings generally were ransacked. Thugs ran rampant, robbing and raping. Residents of Baghdad were left without basic necessities: water, electricity, jobs. The mood in the city turned ugly as the joy of men and women delivered from tyranny faded when confronted by the incompetence of their "liberators."

The Pentagon named Jay Garner, a retired general who had managed an Iraqi Kurd refugee crisis in 1991, to run the new civilian administration. By the time he and his team arrived, two weeks after Baghdad fell to coalition forces, the looting had spun out of control. Garner and his team lacked the means for establishing order and were overwhelmed by the situation. In the north, Kurds, who had enjoyed considerable independence before the war, established their control – a state within a state. In the south, the power vacuum was filled by militia forces commanded by Shiite religious figures, eager to lead the country as soon as coalition forces left. But in Baghdad and central Iraq, in the "Sunni Triangle," forces hostile to the United States, including some affiliated with al Qaeda, generated massive unrest. The American military, using overwhelming firepower in its effort to crush the resistance, killed and wounded many innocent civilians, exacerbating Iraqi anger against coalition forces.

It was obvious that the assumption that a quick victory would be followed almost immediately by the establishment of a friendly Iraqi government, permitting a rapid reduction of American forces, was a fantasy. The United States would have to occupy Iraq until the security of its people could be assured and reconstruction was under way – precisely the kind of nation-building the Bush team abhorred. Garner was replaced by L. Paul Bremer, a former diplomat, who became de facto dictator of Iraq, although his writ carried little weight outside the compound in which his Coalition Provisional Authority was housed.

One Bremer dictate proved disastrous: the precipitous disbanding of the Iraqi army. Iraqi police and security forces vanished. The Pentagon had underestimated the number of troops necessary to maintain order, and attacks on coalition forces occurred daily. President Bush was contemptuous of the insurgents: He said, "Bring 'em on." But Americans in Iraq were being killed in increasing numbers, and many at home were reminded of the Vietnam quagmire. The media in the United States began to portray the Bush team as bumblers. It was evident that achieving American goals in Iraq would require more time, money, and troops than anticipated.

The administration was also in trouble at home because of its failure to find weapons of mass destruction, the threat from which it had used to justify going to war. Searches of suspected sites and interrogation of Iraqi officials led nowhere. Questions arose about the quality of intelligence reports used to justify the attack. In his January 2003 State of the Union speech, Bush had claimed that the Iraqis had attempted to buy uranium for nuclear weapons, but the allegation proved false. A scandal over "cooked intelligence" broke in London, and in the United States there was a growing sense that the administration had "cherry-picked" intelligence to suit its preferred course of action.[12] There were no WMDs in Iraq: They probably had been destroyed, however grudgingly, in compliance with UN demands. Apparently, Saddam had chosen to maintain the charade that he still had WMDs in order to intimidate his enemies, especially Iran.

By the summer of 2003, as casualties mounted, it was evident that the U.S. military was facing intensified guerrilla warfare. In addition to the ubiquitous IEDs (improvised explosive devices), rocket, mortar, and sniper fire, car bombs, and suicide bombers appeared with increasing frequency. Evidence mounted of the presence of non-Iraqi jihadis and U.S. intelligence reported that volunteers for jihad were streaming across the Muslim world, eager to confront Americans readily accessible in Iraq.

---

[12] Ewen MacAskill and Richard Norton-Taylor, "10 Ways to Sex Up a Dossier," *The Guardian*, September 27, 2003.

Symbolic of the inability of coalition forces to contain the insurgency was the bombing of UN headquarters in Baghdad in August, killing the UN special representative, the widely admired Sergio Vierira de Mello. The attack caused various countries and nongovernmental organizations to cancel or delay plans to aid in the reconstruction of Iraq.

Public opinion polls in the United States showed declining support for the war – and declining approval of the president's leadership. Neoconservatives criticized the administration for failing to devote adequate resources to the democratization of Iraq. In Great Britain, opposition to the war soared and Blair was castigated for supporting Bush. Nowhere on the horizon could Washington find military, political, or financial assistance. In November, the administration promised to end the occupation and transfer sovereignty to an Iraqi government on June 30, 2004, following the drafting of a constitution and election of a national assembly, but the insurgency continued unabated.

The idea of creating a transitional government and restoring a semblance of sovereignty to the Iraqis was challenged immediately by various Iraqi factions. The Kurds, having enjoyed virtual autonomy since 1991, told Bremer they would not surrender their power and freedom to the proposed new government. Former exiles, operating in the Iraqi Governing Council, were insistent upon retaining what little power they exercised. Grand Ayatollah Ali Sistani, the most widely respected Shiite cleric, feared the new constitution would violate Islamic law, demanded direct elections managed by the UN, and mustered 100,000 supporters for a peaceful march in Baghdad. American authorities in Iraq and Washington yielded to Sistani's demands and hoped to finesse the challenges from the Kurds and the former exiles.

None of these political maneuvers brought peace to Iraq. On March 2, 2004, insurgents attacked Shiite mosques in Baghdad and Karbala, killing nearly two hundred worshipers. A year after the war began, Iraqi civilians were being killed almost daily by suicide bombers and assassins. Hundreds of thousands of Iraqis were out of work. Crime was rampant. The supply of electricity was uncertain. For all of their tribulations, the Iraqis blamed the United States. Most were grateful to be rid of Saddam, but they had no love for their new "oppressors," the occupation forces, and were eager for them to be gone.

The Bush administration was just as eager to withdraw from Iraq. The president had focused his reelection campaign on his leadership in the war on terror. The fact that things were going badly in Iraq – as well as in the forgotten war in Afghanistan – was apparent every day in the world's media. Hundreds of American troops had been killed, and thousands more wounded, in the months *after* Bush declared victory. The president and his advisers were desperately eager to find a face-saving way out.

In April, the administration was shaken by revelations of the horrors inflicted on Iraqi prisoners at Abu Ghraib by American guards. The photos of prisoners being tormented and humiliated, beaten, forced to simulate sexual acts, attacked by dogs, piled naked in human pyramids were aired by CBS – and spread quickly around the world: American soldiers photographing each other grinning while abusing prisoners, bringing the blessings of democracy to the Middle East. The abuse had been reported months earlier, and nothing had been done to stop it. Investigative reporters and congressional hearings revealed that the administration had deliberately evaded the Geneva Conventions and allowed mistreatment of POWs in its quest for actionable intelligence.

By May an air of defeatism had settled over Washington. Neoconservatives such as William Kristol remained convinced the United States could prevail in Iraq if it used sufficient power, but senior military officials warned the country was on the road to defeat – and blamed Rumsfeld and Wolfowitz. Kristol's colleague Robert Kagan called the administration clueless. It had no idea of how to get the violence in Iraq under control, no idea of how to achieve its goal of transforming Iraq into a democratic state with a free-market economy. The dream of sparking democratic reform throughout the Middle East was all but forgotten.[13]

Despite the nominal transfer of power to an Iraqi regime on June 30, despite major American concessions of power to that government forced by the UN, despite the departure of Bremer, the insurgency intensified. Polls showed that only 2 percent of Iraqis had a favorable view of the occupation. In the United States, public approval for the war and the president's job performance dropped sharply. William F. Buckley, doyen of American conservatives, declared, "If I knew then what I know now about what kind of situation we would be in, I would have

---

[13] Kagan, "Lowering Our Sights," *Washington Post*, May 2, 2004.

opposed the war."[14] Across the political spectrum, demand for an exit strategy grew.

Americans had come to realize that the war in Iraq had been a war of choice, not of necessity. They had learned that when Bush decided for war, Saddam no longer had weapons of mass destruction and that his regime posed no imminent threat to the United States or its friends in the region. It was equally apparent that there had been no link between Iraq and the al Qaeda attacks on the World Trade Center and Pentagon. Bush and his advisers had deluded themselves on the issue of WMDs and misled the American people on Saddam's ties to bin Laden. Defeat of Iraq had done nothing to diminish the threat of terrorism.

On the other hand, despite Cheney and Rumsfeld's contempt for humanitarian interventions, the overthrow of Saddam's brutal regime was a great blessing to the Iraqi people, a great victory for human rights. The world had one less vicious tyrant. But the administration would not have spent scores of billions of dollars, as well as the lives of so many young Americans, to improve the human rights situation in Iraq; nor would it have found much congressional or public support for such a venture. Even the grand vision to which Bush succumbed – the neoconservative dream of creating a democratic Middle East – would not likely have been marketable without the illusion of an imminent threat to American security.

Despite widespread unhappiness with the administration's foreign policies, the war in Iraq in particular, Bush, insisting he had set the Iraqis on the path to freedom and democracy, was reelected in November 2004. There would be no change of course: The president was not look-ing for a graceful way out.

The January 2005 Iraqi election allowed some to imagine that they saw the proverbial "light at the end of the tunnel." Eight million Iraqis risked their lives to vote for a national assembly that would draft a new constitution. There could be no doubt that they had been inspired by the opportunity, and Bush, quite reasonably, claimed vindication. As expected, a religious Shia slate with ties to Iran won, but with only 48 percent of the vote, much less than anticipated. The party of Ayad Allawi, a secular Shiite and former CIA asset appointed interim prime

---

[14] Quoted by David Kirkpatrick, "National Review Founder Says It's Time to Leave the Stage," *New York Times*, June 29, 2004.

minister in 2004, received 14 percent – more than expected, thanks apparently to covert support from the United States. But Sunnis, who dominated the insurgency, did not participate, a fact that boded ill for the future.

It took the Iraqis three months to turn the election results into a government – from which Alawi was excluded. Sectarian divisions remained and intensified, and the rule of law was absent. Violence increased in Iraq, as did calls for withdrawal in the United States. In Washington there was a vigorous debate about strategy, with the Pentagon considering troop reductions and general agreement on training Iraqi security forces, to whom responsibility for maintaining order might be transferred. But many analysts argued against withdrawal, some – especially neoconservatives – insisting *more* rather than fewer American ground troops were needed.

In October 2005, an Iraqi referendum endorsed the new constitution and in December there was another general election, in which Sunnis decided to participate and thereby strengthened their position in the national assembly. But the basic sectarian divisions persisted with Shiite leaders, enjoying power and control of oil revenues, less willing to negotiate a compromise than were the Kurds and Sunnis. As Iraqi leaders of all persuasions perceived the Americans eager to go home, the fighting on the ground became more a struggle for power among Iraqis than an anti-American insurgency. Indeed, there were indications that some Sunnis were prepared to turn against the insurgents if assured of a long-term American presence as a hedge against Shiite domination. Most commentators contended that an American withdrawal would mean full-scale civil war, disastrous for the region as well as for Iraqis.

In November 2006, dissatisfaction with Bush and the situation in Iraq – where more than two thousand Americans had been killed – resulted in the Democrats' winning of control of both houses of Congress. At home and abroad, the vote was perceived as support for withdrawal. In December, the Iraq Study Group, a bipartisan panel of respected elders appointed by Congress, cochaired by James Baker and Lee Hamilton, issued its report. Much like the "wise men" who told Lyndon Johnson it was time to end the war in Vietnam, the group declared the situation in Iraq to be deteriorating and contended that the troops and resources dedicated to Iraq were needed in Afghanistan.

Among its recommendations the group called for turning authority in Iraq over to local elites.

Support for maintaining the existing approach to Iraq was virtually nonexistent. The Shiite leaders, Prime Minister Nouri Al-Maliki and Ayotollah Sistani, were unable to rein in the Shia militias engaged in bloody ethnic cleansing. Maliki and his colleagues in the ruling coalition were unwilling to make concessions to the Sunnis and Kurds, concessions that might stabilize the situation. Most analysts argued for withdrawal if the Shia-dominated Iraqi government failed to make progress toward reconciliation. But several neoconservatives, most prominently Frederick Kagan of the American Enterprise Institute, an important Washington think tank, continued to argue for more American ground forces. Senator John McCain of Arizona, a leading contender for the Republican presidential nomination, called upon the administration to send 100,000 more troops to bring peace and order to Iraq. Even General Anthony Zinni, a highly respected critic of the decision to go to war in Iraq, supported the idea of sending more troops over the next six months.[15]

Kagan and General Jack Keane, former vice chairman of the JCS, persuaded Cheney that an increase in combat troops might succeed. Bush, angered by the Iraq Study Group's account of his failures in Iraq, dismissed its recommendations as coming from people whose powers had peaked when they served his father more than ten years before.[16] In January 2007, he announced plans to augment American forces in Iraq by at least 20,000, the beginning of what came to be called "the surge." A few weeks later, General David Petraeus, arguably the army's leading authority on counterinsurgency, was appointed to command the Multi-National Force, Iraq.

To the relief of most Americans and Iraqis, the level of violence in Iraq declined over the next year. The additional troops provided more security for the people, but, as Fareed Zakaria, a prominent foreign affairs analyst, noted, the key was Petraeus's skill at finding Iraqi allies, especially among the Sunnis. Al Qaeda fighters were concentrated in heavily Sunni Anbar province. The Iraqi army, composed primarily of Shiites and Kurds, was neither welcome nor effective there. When his

[15] Robert Kagan and William Kristol, "Bush's Iraq Legacy," *Weekly Standard,* November 20, 2006; Kagan and Kristol, "It's Up to Bush," *Weekly Standard,* December 18, 2006.
[16] Steve Coll, "His Way," *New Yorker,* December 25, 2006, 43.

efforts to persuade Shiite leaders in Iraq to reconcile with the Sunnis failed, Petraeus won over Sunni sheiks in Anbar, providing them with money and training to turn against al Qaeda. Together, the Americans and the Sunnis of the "Awakening" produced order in Anbar, decimating al Qaeda's forces – and the Sunnis no longer demanded American withdrawal from Iraq.[17]

Combined with the decision of Muqtar al Sadr – the Shiite cleric whose Mahdi army had tormented Americans, Sunnis, and fellow Shiites – to call a truce in August 2007, the surge and the Sunni Awakening allowed the United States to withdraw troops at a measured pace. By the spring of 2008, although the number of Americans killed in Iraq hit four thousand, a Pew poll found 48 percent of Americans believed the military effort was satisfactory. Iraq began to fade from the front pages and as an issue in the forthcoming presidential election. And the neoconservatives claimed success: Iraq, they contended, was now a stable country whose representative government controlled its territory and was oriented toward the West, an ally against militant Islamism.[18]

But there were shadows that could not be ignored. Sectarian tensions did not disappear. Indeed, government forces began attacking members of the Sunni Awakening, and tensions rose along the Kurdish-Arab border, where territory and oil rights were still disputed. Government troops also attacked Sadr's Mahdi army, raising fears he would end the truce he had called. Negotiations were not going well between Maliki, Bush, and their representatives over a status of forces agreement to cover American troops in Iraq after the UN mandate expired in December 2008. On the one hand, Maliki's regime needed an American military presence to avoid civil war, perhaps to survive; on the other, he was up for reelection and had at least to appear to drive a hard bargain. And Barack Obama, leading in the polls as the American presidential election loomed, was insisting that Iraq was not central to the war on terror and that if elected, he would withdraw American troops in sixteen months.

Shortly after Obama won the election, the Bush administration agreed to pull American troops out of Iraqi cities and towns by June 2009, and out of Iraq completely by December 31, 2011 – a deadline few commentators took seriously. For Bush and Cheney, however, time

---

[17] Fareed Zakaria, *Newsweek*, November 12, 2007.
[18] Frederick Kagan, "How We'll Know When We've Won," *Weekly Standard*, May 5, 2008.

ran out in January 2009. Responsibility for managing the war in Iraq and the war against terror now belonged to Barack Obama.

After 9/11, Bush focused sharply on his "war against terrorism." By 2003 he had sent American forces to fight Islamic terrorists in approximately fifty countries around the world. The need for cooperation against terrorists led the United States to overlook the human rights transgressions of its friends in Central Asia, especially Uzbekistan, of the Russians in Chechnya, and of the Chinese in Tibet and Xinjiang. It had little choice but to cozy up to General Pervez Musharraf and the Pakistani military, condemned by Washington when they overthrew a democratically elected government in 1999.

While the administration struggled with the occupation of Iraq, it lost ground in its efforts to maintain pressure on North Korea and Iran, the other two members of the president's "axis of evil." Both were determined to have nuclear weapons capability, perhaps for national status or as credible deterrents against the threat of an American preemptive strike. Cheney and other advocates of regime change prevented meaningful negotiations with Pyongyang, and Washington eventually was forced to accept the fact that North Korea was a nuclear power. Iran made several overtures to the administration in the wake of 9/11, but Cheney and Rumsfeld prevailed again over those such as Powell and Rice who were interested in engagement. Unable to strike a deal, the Iranians accelerated their nuclear program.

To the surprise of a world unaccustomed to Chinese foreign policy initiatives, in April 2003 China stepped into the vacuum created by the unwillingness of the U.S. to address the nuclear crisis in Korea. Washington had given Beijing the opportunity to supplant American influence in Northeast Asia, and the Chinese seized it. Using their leverage with Pyongyang, reliant on China for food and fuel, they won North Korean assent to six-nation talks, an American demand, and obtained U.S. agreement to meet one-on-one, a North Korean demand. The initial talks failed, however, and further Chinese compromise proposals were rejected by the president at Cheney's instigation. Despite some apparent progress in June 2004, both Bush and Kim Jong Il appeared to be stalling to await the outcome of the American presidential election.

Conservative critics warned that time was running out to check the North Korean nuclear program. They argued that North Korea had been cheating on the Clinton administration's Agreed Framework since 1997, had voided that agreement, withdrawn from the Nuclear Nonproliferation Treaty, and expelled the IAEA monitors because the regime wanted nuclear weapons. But they offered no policy options and little hope of resolving the crisis.[19] They were pleased when in 2005 the Treasury Department sanctioned a Macao bank alleged to be laundering funds Pyongyang had gained from illegal activities – and appalled when Treasury was forced to back off by the State Department.

Rice had taken over as secretary of state in Bush's second administration and was immediately more assertive and more effective than she had been as national security adviser. Outmaneuvering Cheney and Rumsfeld, she and Christopher Hill worked out a tentative accord with Pyongyang in September 2005, but they were undermined by the Treasury initiative that gave the North Koreans an excuse to back away. Rice's support in the administration frayed when North Korea tested an underground nuclear device in October 2006, but she and Hill persisted. Finally, in February 2007, after Rumsfeld was gone and Cheney's office was preoccupied with the criminal investigation of Louis Libby, his chief of staff, they persuaded Pyongyang to freeze the reactor at Yongbyun again and to readmit the IAEA inspectors. But by then North Korea was a declared nuclear power, with eight to ten more nuclear weapons than it had when Bush took office in 2001. North Korea was one more major unresolved issue to be left to his successor.[20]

Similarly, the unwillingness to engage Iran precluded any improvement in relations between Tehran and Washington. In May 2003, after the defeat of Saddam's forces but before it was evident that the aftermath would be disastrous, the Bush team was startled by a new Iranian initiative. Ayatollah Ali Khameni's representative proposed ending Iran's support of militant Palestinian groups such as Hamas and Islamic Jihad and converting Hezbollah into a strictly social and political organization. Tehran was willing to recognize Israel and a separate Palestinian state. In return, Khameni wanted the United States to guarantee Iran's

[19] Nicholas Eberstadt and Joseph P. Ferguson, "The North Korean Nightmare: It's Later Than You Think," *Weekly Standard*, August 30, 2004.

[20] Michael J. Mazarr, "The Long Road to Pyongyang: A Case Study in Policymaking without Direction," *Foreign Affairs* 86 (September/October 2007); Nicholas Eberstadt, "What Went Wrong: The Bush Administration's Failed North Korea Policy," *Weekly Standard*, January 26, 2009.

security and remove economic sanctions. Once again, Cheney and Rumsfeld and their neoconservative supporters insisted on regime change. Flushed with victory in Afghanistan and Iraq, they were convinced of the imminent collapse of the Islamic Republic.

Iran grew stronger and more hostile to the United States in the remaining years of Bush's presidency. American forces had pushed aside the Taliban, a source of irritation to Iran, and eliminated Saddam Hussein's regime, the most immediate threat to Iran. In August 2005, Iranians elected Mahmoud Ahmadinejad president, and he proved to be exceptionally belligerent and provocative. Relations with the West deteriorated rapidly. He was a Holocaust denier who insisted that Israel had to be destroyed, and his ascendance raised fears that the Israelis would launch a preemptive strike against Iran's nuclear facilities. A controversial National Intelligence Estimate in November 2007 suggested the Iranians had stopped development of nuclear weapons in 2003, but there was little doubt they were still progressing toward that capability. Ignoring sanctions and threats from the Bush administration, lying to IAEA inspectors, the Iranians had installed 7,200 centrifuges and produced more than a ton of low-enriched uranium by the time the president left office.[21] Another potential crisis left to his successor.

In addition, there was the perpetual Israeli-Palestinian conflict, from which the administration preferred to remain disengaged. Neither Arafat nor Sharon was interested in a reasonable solution, and peace would not come before both men were off the stage, if then. Sharon and his advisers were confident they could ignore American complaints about their policies. They knew Bush would be running for reelection in 2004 and would not want to alienate Israel's American supporters – Christian evangelicals as well as Jewish Zionists.

Sharon surprised the world in December 2003 by announcing his intention to withdraw unilaterally from the Gaza strip and parts of the West Bank. He would not negotiate with Arafat and would draw the lines where he pleased and retreat behind them. Settlements on the other side of the line would be abandoned, an idea that infuriated Israeli settlers and most members of his own party, the right-wing Likud. Part of the West Bank would be annexed to Israel, outraging many Palestinians

[21] National Intelligence Estimate, "Iran: Nuclear Intentions and Capabilities," www.dni. gov/press_releases_2007.htm (November 2007), accessed July 21, 2010; Roger Cohen, "The Making of an Iran Policy," *New York Times*, August 2, 2009.

and their supporters in the Arab world. But Sharon won the endorsement of President Bush, and Israel dismantled its settlements and withdrew from Gaza in 2005.

In April 2004, Bush announced a major shift in American policy. For the first time since the Six-Day War, the American government stated that it did not expect Israel to return to its pre-1967 borders and it approved Israel's policy of denying Palestinian refugees the right of return. The administration did urge Sharon to begin dismantling the West Bank settlements, to no avail. Few in the United States were willing to press the point before the election. Both Democratic and Republican politicians pledged their undying support for Israel, and there was less questioning of Israeli policy in the United States than there was in Israel. After the election, Rice made several attempts to broker a peace deal between the Israelis and Palestinians, but after Arafat died and Sharon suffered a stroke, neither side had a government strong enough, confident enough, to reach an agreement.

Nothing Israel or the PLO said or did stopped harassment by Hamas from Gaza or Hezbollah from Lebanon. In 2006 Hamas kidnapped a young Israeli soldier, and Hezbollah began rocket attacks on border towns and followed with a strike against Humvees on the Israeli side of the border. Israel struck back harshly against Hezbollah, and war ensued, with Hezbollah sustaining severe losses but able to deny the Israelis a decisive victory. Hamas, which seized control of Gaza in June 2007, began pummeling southern Israel with rockets in December 2008. After retaliating with air strikes that killed many civilians, Israel sent ground troops into Gaza in January 2009. It was too late for the Bush administration to act – had it wished to – and too soon for the incoming Obama administration.

As Bush and his foreign policy team prepared to leave office, the critical issue in Afghanistan remained the lack of security. Karzai, whose corrupt regime frustrated Washington, exercised little control outside Kabul. Training of a national army proceeded slowly, suggesting it might be another decade before it would be ready to relieve coalition forces. It was outnumbered and outgunned by warlord forces and constantly under attack by Taliban raiders, with both groups financing their forces by expanding the drug trade. Patience with Karzai and the war was evaporating in NATO capitals, and there were serious doubts as to how long troops would be kept there. The Dutch withdrew combat forces in mid-year, 2010. Americans, exhausted by the war in Iraq, devastated at home by a severe recession, had little interest in pouring more blood and treasure into Afghanistan. What little hope remained for success there – and that would be defined far short of the creation of a liberal democracy – depended upon how long the United States and its allies would continue to work toward providing security and on the reconstruction of the country.

Much also depended on developments in Pakistan, whose security forces provided the principal support for the Taliban prior to 9/11 and remained reluctant to see it eliminated. The Pakistani military remained focused on its unending struggle against India and imagined that having pawns in Afghanistan gave it strategic depth. After al Qaeda's attack on the United States, Washington demanded that Musharraf choose sides – and he chose to align Pakistan with the American cause, a decision unpopular with a majority of his people. There was always the danger that he would be killed or overthrown and Pakistan would dissolve into chaos.

Probably the greatest American fear was that the Pakistani government would lose control of its nuclear arsenal. Pakistan had never signed the Nuclear Nonproliferation Treaty and in 1998 had tested its weapons and become a declared nuclear power. In 2004 Abdul Qadeer Khan, the scientist Pakistanis considered a national hero for making their country a nuclear power, confessed to having assisted Libya, Iran, and North Korea in their programs. After a public apology, he was pardoned immediately by Musharraf. The obvious point – that he could not have carried out his operations without the complicity of the Pakistani military – was not addressed. That terrorists might gain access to Pakistan's nuclear weapons with or without the complicity of Khan or the Pakistani military led some analysts to argue that Pakistan – rather than Afghanistan or Iraq or Iran or North Korea – was the most dangerous country in the world.

Unrest in Pakistan intensified over the next several years, and opposition to Musharraf's rule provoked street demonstrations and led ultimately to his departure from office in August 2008. He was replaced, however, by a weak civilian government headed by the widower of Benazir Bhutto, who had been assassinated by terrorists while campaigning in December 2007. The last months of the Bush administration were marked by mass-casualty terrorism in Pakistan's major cities and a notable increase in American predator strikes against presumed al Qaeda and Taliban redoubts on the Pakistan side of the border with Afghanistan, generating more anger toward the United States among Pakistanis.

Relations between Washington and New Delhi were among the few bright spots in American foreign affairs in the early years of the twenty-first century. Throughout the Cold War, India had been an irritating critic of the United States and had developed close ties to the Soviet Union, belying its nominal nonaligned status. In the early 1990s, however, Indian leaders decided to liberalize their economy and open it to foreign investment, resulting in rapid growth and India's emergence as an important economic power on the world scene. Gradually it became an important commercial partner of the United States, with two-way trade soaring between 2004 and 2008.

In the closing years of the Clinton administration, American support of India against Pakistan had convinced New Delhi that rapprochement with the United States was in India's national interest. Improvement in relations between the world's two largest democracies was also facilitated by the existence of nearly three million Indian Americans and the lobbying activity of the U.S.-India Political Action Committee.

The Bush administration was no less interested in nurturing Indian-American relations. The two countries shared a common interest in fighting Islamic terrorists – demonstrated by their joint response to the November 2008 terrorist attacks in Mumbai – and anxiety about the rise of Chinese power, evidenced by India's participation in military exercises with the United States and Japan. Perhaps most striking was the civil nuclear agreement signed by Washington and New Delhi in 2008, despite India's refusal to sign the Nuclear Nonproliferation Treaty – a major departure from long-standing American policy.[22] Strengthening strategic ties between India and the United States may prove to be the most positive legacy of Bush's foreign policy.

The record in Latin America was mixed as that part of the world rarely succeeded in gaining Washington's attention. After 9/11, the administration was preoccupied with its war on terrorism, in which Latin America

---

[22] Evan Feigenbaum, "India's Rise, America's Interest," *Foreign Affairs* 89 (March–April 2010): 76–91.

was not a major concern. It did pander to the Cuban vote in Florida with actions hostile to Fidel Castro's government, and it engaged in frequent unpleasantries with Hugo Chavez in Venezuela, who found countless ways to bait his target in Washington. The principal American activity in the region was in Colombia, source of most of the cocaine used in the United States.

Outside of Afghanistan and the Middle East, Colombia was the top recipient of security assistance from the United States. Washington spent billions on what Congress called "The War on Drugs and Thugs," but the violence within the country and the drug traffic to meet American demand barely slowed. Suggestions that development aid might be more effective were brushed aside. The argument that reduction of demand for drugs in the United States was urgent was never denied, but no effective action was taken.

Problems with Haiti continued long after the Clinton administration returned Aristide to power. Aristide's presidency proved as disappointing as his most vociferous American critics had anticipated. He was guilty of demagoguery and provided his people with neither good government nor satisfactory economic development. His term as the first democratically elected president of Haiti expired in 1996, and he stepped down – only to be reelected in November 2000.

The Bush administration was unfriendly from the outset, and lobbyists close to it encouraged Aristide's opponents to resist his rule. As his policies grew more erratic, the support he had enjoyed from Haiti's masses eroded. Calls for his resignation increased, as did political violence. Early in 2004, rebellion threatened the overthrow of Aristide's government, prompting fears in Washington of a flood of Haitian boat people to Florida. Powell flew to Haiti and persuaded Aristide to leave. Immediately after his departure, the UN authorized a peacekeeping mission to Haiti. A semblance of order was restored, but with little promise that anything would be done to improve the lot of the long-suffering Haitian people.

Brazil posed a very different set of problems. In 2002, Brazilians elected Luiz Inacio Lula da Silva, a well-known leftist, as their president. In these post–Cold War days, amid Bush's war on terrorism, Washington reacted calmly. Even Brazil's vote in the Security Council against the Anglo-American resolution on Iraq provoked no public anger. Indeed, it was evident that Bush was courting "Lula" in 2003, inviting him to the White House in June despite his opposition to the invasion of Iraq, despite his friendship with Chavez and the Castros. Brazil was clearly the most important state in South America, and Lula was committed to democracy and promised economic policies American analysts perceived as responsible. But trade issues provoked open friction. Lula was skeptical of the elder Bush's call for a Free Trade Area of the Americas (FTAA). He wanted the United States to be more receptive to Brazil's agricultural exports, especially ethanol – and he was leery of opening his country further to American investments. The FTAA talks collapsed in 2003, but trade between the two counties soared nonetheless.

Lula and Bush continued to seek ways to strengthen the relationship between Brasilia and Washington. There were reports that Lula, despite his leftist ideology, favored Bush over John Kerry in the American presidential election of 2004 – fearing as did all those dependent on exports to the United States for their prosperity – that the Democrats would be protectionist. Despite minimal progress on key issues that divided them, Bush and Lula edged toward increased cooperation. In 2006 there were reports of closer military ties, and in 2007, on a visit to Brazil, Bush signed an ethanol agreement that did less to help the Brazilian industry than the hoped-for reduction in the American tariff might have. But also in 2007, the United States and Brazil commenced an Economic Partnership Dialogue, indicating the importance the United States placed on Brazil as a trading partner. Two more of these meetings were held in 2008. Before Bush left the White House, Americans were the main investors in Brazil as well as Brazil's main trading partner. The two countries had clearly avoided a dangerous confrontation.

Most disappointing of the Bush administration's relationships in Latin America was that with Mexico. Although Mexico had become the second-largest trading partner of the United States, thanks to NAFTA, and there appeared to be a close personal tie between Bush and Vicente Fox, the Mexican president, disagreements over the immigration issue proved impossible to transcend. Relations were briefly quite chilly when Mexico refused to support the Anglo-American resolution in the Security Council intended to legitimize the invasion of Iraq, but the two leaders papered over their differences in 2004. Immigration reform was postponed indefinitely, the victim of popular anger in the United States at the presence of large numbers of illegal migrants in the country.

In July 2003, Bush traveled to Africa, ostensibly to boost the fight against the AIDS epidemic that was ravaging the continent. Africa had little strategic value to the U.S. after the Cold War but provided 20 percent of American oil imports – a figure expected to rise over the next decade. American business leaders had invested billions in West Africa, and the president was persuaded it would be useful to show the flag – and to demonstrate humanitarian as well as economic concerns.

While Bush was in Africa, a brutal civil war raged in Liberia, a nation with links to the United States that dated back to the early nineteenth century, when American black nationalists had established a colony there. For much of its subsequent history, the country had been ruled by Liberians of American descent. During the Cold War, the United States had provided substantial aid to the Liberian government, although the various regimes in Monrovia were undemocratic, often vicious. After the Cold War, Washington lost interest in Liberia and withdrew support. It had no commodity of importance to the United States, no useful bases. The country's weak economy grew worse, and in 2000 a rebellion took root.

By July 2003, the country was a humanitarian disaster and pressure built for American intervention to stop the carnage. But U.S. forces were stretched thin in Iraq and Afghanistan, and the task was left to West African troops as peacekeepers. Demonstrating its concern, the Bush administration sent 2,000 American marines to the coast of Liberia to provide support for the peacekeepers. It would neither lead nor send troops ashore. Happily for all concerned, the war wound down in August.

Although the administration was similarly unwilling to use American power to stop ethnic cleansing in Sudan, its performance compared favorably to that of the rest of the developed world. Civil strife between the primarily Arab Muslim north and the largely black Christian south had begun on the eve of independence in 1955. By the 1990s, nearly two million Christians had been killed and American evangelicals worked desperately to help the victims and stop the fighting. Clinton was never engaged, but Bush took up the cause on the eve of 9/11. Bush sent a representative, who pressed successfully for peace talks between the Arab Muslim government and the black Christian rebels of southern Sudan late in 2003. But the government, as it eased its raids in the south, began bombing its people in Darfur, in western Sudan. The regime also armed Arab tribesmen, called *janjaweed,* to raid villages in

Darfur, killing the men and raping the women. The people of Darfur were almost all Muslims, but they, too, were black and viewed with contempt by Arabs. The government was determined to drive them out of the country – and the rest of the world seemed unconcerned.

Months passed before the UN humanitarian coordinator labeled events in Darfur "ethnic cleansing." Bush quickly condemned the attacks and demanded that Khartoum stop abetting them, but there was no letup. In the spring of 2004, the American media began to focus on the atrocities, and in July a congressional resolution called the killings "genocide." The Bush administration contributed $200 million in relief aid to Darfur refugees but was unable to get the UN Human Rights Commission to issue a strong denunciation on the horrors. It received virtually no support from Europe. Hostile to the Bush team for its past unilateralism and self-righteousness, the other major powers did not rally to America's side, even in so worthy a cause. Bush had forfeited Washington's right to lead – and the people of Darfur were paying the price. Even after Omar al-Bashir, Sudan's president, was accused of crimes against humanity and war crimes by the prosecutor of the International Criminal Court, no action was taken against him. The United States, having never accepted the jurisdiction of the court, could hardly complain.

After 9/11, Russia faded from the view of the Bush administration until the brief war between Russia and Georgia in August 2008. Colin Powell expressed unhappiness with the fact that Putin and his comrades from the former KGB were eliminating opposition and silencing critics, but his colleagues had more immediate worries than the gradual reversal of democratic reform in Russia.

Moscow had been uneasy about Washington's unilateralism and Bush's doctrine of preventive war. Putin and his colleagues were profoundly displeased by the continued eastward expansion of NATO, questioning why NATO even needed to exist after the Cold War. They perceived American promotion of democracy in Ukraine and Georgia, American support of the Orange and Rose revolutions, respectively, in those countries, as an attempt to undermine Russia's influence in its "near abroad." But Bush's foreign policy team tended to dismiss Russia as a declining power whose complaints were unworthy of concern.

Buoyed by American support, failing to appreciative its limits, Mikheil Saakashvili, the American-educated president of Georgia, decided to

attack a break-away province that had come under Russian protection. Apparently welcoming the provocation, Russia struck back forcefully, bombing Georgia and defeating the Georgian military quickly and
easily. Putin told French president Nicolas Sarkozy that he wanted to
"hang Saakashvili by 'the balls.'"[23]

Washington responded with verbal support for Saakashvili and
acceptance of his claim that his country was the victim of Russian
aggression – that the Russians had attacked first. The facts that Russia
was spoiling for a fight and that Russian forces behaved brutally once
on Georgian soil must be acknowledged, but the evidence that Georgia
provoked the assault cannot be ignored. Nonetheless, the Bush administration jeopardized its chances for a cooperative relationship with
Russia by condemning Moscow's actions and resuming its efforts to
link Georgia to NATO.

China, on the other hand, had to be treated with respect and, occasionally, even deference. It had become the engine of economic growth
in East Asia, its military power surging, and it was poised to challenge
American political and strategic influence in the region. Chinese foreign
policy was becoming less passive, and its diplomats increasingly skillful.
China's leaders and foreign policy intellectuals were transcending the
victim mentality prominent in the last half of the twentieth century and
beginning to accept for their country the role of a great power.

Most of the issues between the two countries proved manageable.
Knowledgeable Americans remained troubled by human rights violations in China, but for the most part the Bush administration muted its
criticism, privileging economic and strategic issues. Concerns about the
erosion of the freedoms promised to the people of Hong Kong also were
expressed quietly, to the dismay of Bush's neoconservative supporters.
Of course, the one major flashpoint – the Taiwan Strait – allowed for
no complacency, if only because it was not a bilateral issue. As often as
not, it was the Taipei government that stirred the pot.

Troubled by the PLA's preparations to attack Taiwan and the missile buildup in China across the Strait from Taiwan, Bush warned
that the United States would defend the island against an unprovoked
attack. "Unprovoked," however, was subject to interpretation, and

---

[23] Quoted in Thomas de Waal, "Missiles Over Tskhinvali," *National Interest* 107 (May/
June 2010): 89.

Chen Shui-bian, Taiwan's president and leader of the pro-independence Democratic Progressive Party, kept trying Beijing's patience with gestures and rhetoric designed to win more international space for Taiwan. The Chinese contended that American arms sales encouraged Chen's troublesome behavior.

Although Bush was uneasy about being perceived as betraying democratic Taiwan, the United States needed a good working relationship with China. In December 2003, to the dismay of Taiwan's leaders and the American friends of Taiwan, Bush publicly warned Taiwan against taking unilateral action toward independence. Most striking was his decision to issue the warning in the presence of Chinese premier Wen Jiabao. Analysts in Taiwan feared abandonment.

There was little doubt that Washington as well as Beijing hoped to see Chen defeated in Taiwan's March 2004 presidential election. The Kuomintang party of the late Chiang Kai-shek and Chiang Ching-kuo was perceived as less likely to be provocative. But Chen won a narrow, disputed victory and trimmed his sails a bit, leaving Bush and Hu Jintao, China's new president, to await his next sally. Washington counseled China to be patient and did what it could to rein in Chen, but Beijing, especially the Chinese military, never believed the Americans were doing enough.

Chen's rhetoric, used by the PLA to justify its belligerent posture, kept the embers burning uncomfortably close to the Taiwan powder keg. If the PLA attacked across the Strait, would the United States come to Taiwan's defense? For years, American policy had stressed "strategic ambiguity," trying to keep both Beijing and Taipei guessing as to what the American response would be. If it was clear that the United States would defend Taiwan, American leaders feared Chen or others on the island would behave dangerously, sparking an attack from the mainland. On the other hand, if it seemed certain the United States would not defend Taiwan, most analysts assumed there would be no restraints on the PLA. To the national security elite in both Beijing and Washington, it was apparent that the Taiwan Strait was the most dangerous place in the world – the only place in the world where two great nuclear powers might stumble into war.[24]

---

[24] Nancy Bernkopf Tucker, *Strait Talk: United States-Taiwan Relations and the Crisis with China* (Cambridge, Mass., 2009), esp. 253–72.

Despite their sharp differences over Taiwan, human rights, Chinese currency manipulation, and violations of intellectual property rights, leaders in both China and the U.S. wanted desperately to find a basis for a good working relationship. Late in September 2005, Robert Zoellick, then deputy secretary of state, called upon China to become a "responsible stakeholder" in the international system. It was a role Chinese analysts believed their country was ready to play. It was time for China to stop whining about the "century of humiliation" at the hands of the imperialists and accept the responsibilities of great-power status.

Chinese interest in being perceived as acting responsibly in world affairs did not extend to assisting in Western efforts to contain Iran's nuclear ambitions. Iran was too important a source of China's oil supply. In January 2006, Zoellick flew to Beijing, where the Chinese rebuffed him on sanctions against Iran and on a series of economic issues that were roiling American domestic politics.

In April 2006, Hu Jintao visited Washington and met with Bush. Both understood that their countries' economies were intertwined and recognized the enormous value, strategically as well as economically, of maintaining good relations. Hu intended to continue Jiang Zemin's grand strategy, and Bush had learned the importance of winning some level of support from China. Many international problems could not be resolved without help from Beijing. Differences had to be subordinated to joint management of the threats from terrorism and nuclear proliferation. Analysts in both countries wrote of maturing Chinese-American relations. In December 2006, Bush declared the relationship the "best ever."

Although Congress persisted in expressing displeasure about currency manipulation, China gave a little ground on other economic issues, allowing greater access to its domestic market and stiffening its effort to stop violations of intellectual property rights. Beijing was more cooperative with American attempts to deal with Iranian and especially North Korean nuclear problems. And the PLA assured Americans that there was no need to fear China's military modernization – that it might take a hundred years to equal American military power.

In the United States, men and women troubled by China's continuing human rights violations, its repression of Tibetans and Uighurs, its support for the genocidal Sudanese government, the brutal Burmese junta, and Robert Mugabe's vicious regime in Zimbabwe, expected their government to press their concerns. But for the Bush administration – and the majority of the national security elite – these issues were negligible when weighed against the need for China's help in dealing with North Korea: "Realism" prevailed over "idealism." The consensus in Washington was that engagement had been a tremendous success.

The election of Ma Ying-cheou, the Kuomintang candidate, as president of the Republic of China in 2008, came as a tremendous relief to both the American and Chinese governments. Ma, a graduate of Harvard Law School, favored improved relations with the mainland. Tensions in the Strait were greatly reduced. American military analysts perceived the PLA relaxing its offensive posture, putting aside plans to invade Taiwan.

For the United States, 2008 was also a presidential election year. The Chinese, having declared Bush a "lame duck" after the 2006 midterm elections, waited uneasily for the outcome. Little progress was made on bilateral issues that divided the two countries. Immediately after the election, in December 2008, both the Chinese ambassador in Washington and the Chinese State Council's principal spokesman on foreign affairs spoke of the mutually beneficial relationship and the importance of maintaining course, but they laid down markers for the incoming administration: Stay away from China's "core" interests in Taiwan and Tibet – and avoid protectionism.

Bush had begun his presidency with a superb foreign policy team, highly intelligent and experienced men and women, comparable to John F. Kennedy's best and brightest. And like Kennedy's team, the Bush team advocated policies that took the nation to the brink of disaster. In the course of their obsession with Iraq, they alienated many of America's friends in the world and mired the U.S. military in a quagmire of their own creation. When Bush left the White House in 2009, the United States was held in lower esteem by other nations and peoples than at any time in the twentieth century.

With its armed forces bogged down in Iraq and most of the rest of the world mistrustful of American claims and motives, the Bush administration was unable to cope with the more serious nuclear weapons challenges posed by North Korea and Iran. Preemption or preventive war was not feasible. China became the dominant player in the standoff with Pyongyang, and the European Union and the IAEA negotiated with an evasive Tehran.

Also damaging to the security of the United States, if less immediately so, was the unwillingness of the Bush team to confront long-term threats to the environment. The administration consistently catered to the interests of domestic constituencies that opposed regulation, even if based on international agreements premised on the assumption that clean air, clean water, and other environmental protection measures are a public good. The president was personally committed to using American wealth to stop the spread of AIDS, especially in Africa, but only a fraction of the funding he promised was forthcoming.

Across the world, the actions and rhetoric of the Bush administration turned public opinion against the United States. Resentment was strongest in Muslim countries because of policies that were viewed as hostile to Islam: indifference to the plight of Palestinians evidenced by Bush's reference to Sharon as a man of peace and the invasion of Iraq in the absence of the WMDs the Bush team had used to justify the attack. Public opinion polls nearly everywhere revealed a perception that the United States was itself the greatest threat to world peace. Despite the end of the Cold War, American defense spending remained enormous, reputedly as much as that of the next dozen nations combined. There seemed to be no force on earth capable of restraining Washington. There was an extraordinary erosion of "soft power," the admiration of American values and what America had once stood for. And then Bush went home to Texas, as the nation's economy collapsed.

On January 25, 2009, Barack Hussein Obama, the Hawaiian-born son of a white American mother and a black Kenyan father, was sworn in as president of the United States. The country was sliding into the worst recession since the Great Depression of the 1930s. The battle against al Qaeda and the Taliban in Afghanistan was going badly. Iraq appeared relatively stable, but with little prospect of becoming the peaceful democracy Americans yearned to leave behind. North Korea continued to flex its nuclear muscles, and Iran continued on its devious path toward becoming a nuclear power, thwarting American efforts in Iraq as best it could. And these were only the more obvious problems the new administration would be forced to confront.

The Cold War was becoming a distant memory, but Russia and China continued to frustrate Washington in its efforts to promote democracy and support human rights around the world – and the two countries undermined the sanctions regime the U.S. hoped would restrain Iran. The standoff between Israel and the Palestinians continued to fester, with Hezbollah in Lebanon and Hamas in Gaza, both backed by Iran, outdoing Israeli settlers in provocations. But Obama's supporters, relieved to be rid of Bush and Cheney, imagined that he would make it all right. As testimony to worldwide expectations of the new American president, he was awarded the Nobel Peace Prize in 2009, largely on the promise of his rhetoric.

Two striking appointments headed Obama's foreign affairs team: Hillary Clinton as secretary of state, and Robert Gates as secretary of defense. Clinton had been Obama's principal rival in a bitterly contested battle for the Democratic presidential nomination, and Gates had succeeded Rumsfeld as Bush's secretary of defense. Of the two, Gates had by far the most experience in foreign affairs, having served previously on the NSC and as director of the CIA. James Jones, a relatively unknown general, led the NSC, and Dennis Blair, former CINCPAC, became director of the Office of National Intelligence – a position that had proved thankless under his three predecessors (and in which he lasted hardly more than a year). Obama filled most of the other key positions with men and women who had gained experience in the Clinton administration.

Just as Bush had been determined to demonstrate that he was not Clinton, the Obama administration promised change from the Bush era. In the election campaign, Obama had faulted Bush's war in Iraq and insisted that as president he would reemphasize the battle against al Qaeda and the Taliban in Afghanistan. American combat forces would be withdrawn from Iraq in 2010. Once in office, Obama reached out to the Muslim world with a moving speech delivered in Cairo. He insisted that the United States was not hostile to Muslims, quoted from the Koran, and called for respect for human rights and democracy. He offered Iran and North Korea the opportunity to negotiate an end to their pariah status – and to their nuclear weapons programs. He signaled to both Russia and China a desire to avoid adversarial relations and stepped into the morass of Israeli-Palestinian relations, eager to bring peace to the region. Not even the brutal junta that ruled Burma was judged unworthy of an overture.

Conditions in Iraq, though far from optimal, allowed the Obama administration to proceed with plans to withdraw most combat troops in 2010. Approximately 45,000 armed men and women remained to

Map 6. United States and Allied Forces in Iraq and Afghanistan, Circa 2010.

provide training for the Iraqi army and a degree of security. A reasonably democratic election to the national legislature, held in January 2010, resulted in a near tie between the two leading parties and their allies – and a stalemate that persisted for months before the selection of a prime minister. Violence persisted, usually Shia attacks on Sunnis and vice versa, but with occasional fraternal warfare among Shiite factions and with al Qaeda – echoes of the past. But American attention had shifted elsewhere.

"Elsewhere" was primarily to the domestic economy as the country was wracked with massive unemployment amid a painfully slow and uncertain recovery. But Clinton, Gates, and their colleagues remained focused on Obama's foreign policy agenda, headed by the war in Afghanistan, which had become "Obama's war." American troop levels in the country increased, efforts to win the support of the Afghan people intensified, but the resurgence of the Taliban continued. Dissatisfaction with Karzai's corrupt government and his outrageous manipulation of the results of the 2009 election soared, as did tensions between Karzai and the American diplomats who tried to work with him – including the redoubtable Richard Holbrooke. In 2010, the highly respected General David Petraeus, who had overseen the surge in Iraq, took command of NATO forces in Afghanistan, allowing a modicum of hope for a minimally acceptable outcome in the foreseeable future. Support for the effort was eroding in the United States as well as among NATO allies, which began to withdraw their troops. American troop reductions, well under way in Iraq, would begin in Afghanistan before the next presidential election. Pakistani intelligence forces (ISI) continued to play a double game, providing some assistance to the NATO effort – and protecting Afghan Taliban leaders, whom they saw as a strategic asset against India. Indeed, when Osama bin Laden was finally found in 2011 – and killed by U.S. Navy SEALs – he was living comfortably in a Pakistani military garrison town. Suspicion pervaded the ranks of American officials and foreign affairs observers that the ISI was complicit in sheltering him there.

Many analysts argued that ending the Israeli-Palestinian standoff constituted the key to peace in the Middle East. Muslims throughout the world often pointed to U.S. support of Israel as the source of their anti-Americanism. The Obama administration committed itself to bringing the two sides together, appointing George Mitchell, who had brokered peace in Northern Ireland for the Clinton administration, to the lead role. Unfortunately, Hamas, controlling Gaza, demonstrated no interest, and the Palestinian authority on the West Bank was too weak to make peace with Israel without concessions that the right-wing Likud government of Israel would not grant. Pressure on Israel to stop building settlements on Palestinian land gained little for the United States – and convinced most Israelis that Obama was hostile to them. In 2010, Washington pushed the Palestinians into new direct talks with Israel that failed to achieve any progress. Mitchell resigned in frustration, and in 2011 Israeli prime minister Binyamin Netanyahu, confident of support among the American people and their representatives in Congress, was openly dismissive of Obama's efforts.

The most dramatic developments in the Middle East occurred without American agency, in some instances to the dismay of American policymakers. In 2011, the "Arab Spring," an apparent democracy movement, surprised the world, beginning with the overthrow of a dictatorial and corrupt Tunisian regime. Quickly the movement spread throughout the region to Egypt, Bahrain, Yemen, Libya, and Syria. Washington's Egyptian ally, Hosni Mubarak, found himself under intense pressure to resign. In Bahrain, headquarters of the U.S. Fifth Fleet, the ruling class was threatened, and in Yemen, where the unpopular president claimed to be assisting the United States against al Qaeda, protestors filled the streets. Hesitantly, Obama moved to support the demonstrators, uncertain as to who they were and how their success would affect American interests in the region. Washington advised Mubarak to step aside: Eventually he did. The Bahrain authorities were asked to refrain from violence: They did not. No one in the administration seemed to know what to do about Yemen, where al Qaeda was stronger than in Afghanistan or Pakistan – and where the peaceful resolution of tensions in the capital was unlikely.

Obama had less difficulty responding to rebellion in Libya. Muammar al-Qaddafi had long been an irritant to the United States, and Washington, supported by NATO, used indiscriminate attacks on civilians by Qaddafi's forces as justification for bombing their positions. But unwilling to risk involving his country in a third war, Obama quickly passed the lead to NATO. Libya was soon wracked by civil war, with neither rebels nor loyalists able to strike a decisive blow. American and NATO aid to the rebels, including recognition of their leadership as the legitimate government, prevented Qaddafi's brutal attacks from overwhelming them.

Syria, despite the difficulties it had posed for American interests in the region, prompted a more complicated response. If the regime of Bashar al-Assad were overthrown by persistent demonstrations against it, Syria's ties to Iran might be weakened and its threat to Lebanon diminished. But there might also be sectarian violence, and Assad's successors might be even more hostile to their neighbors. As Americans are wont to do, the administration called for reform, for an end to authoritarianism, some movement toward democracy. Assad offered verbal gestures toward a more open society. His security forces, however, did not hesitate to kill protestors. Belatedly, Obama perceived that the Syrian government, in its ruthless suppression of its people, had lost its claim to legitimacy. He called for Assad to step aside. Instead the regime intensified its efforts to crush the revolt.

In none of the uprisings in the Arab world was the role of the United States decisive – and only in Libya could it be called significant. Obama's hesitation to endorse the stated goals of the protestors did not go unnoticed. The enormous prestige he had won in the Arab world with his 2009 Cairo speech quickly diminished. Faith in the American commitment to democracy, never great, all but vanished. And yet there was little the United States could do. Few Americans called for military action – and more thought he had gone too far in Libya. If democracy was to come to the Arab world, it would have to be fought for and won by Arabs.

Obama's foreign policy team reached out to the Russians and Chinese with mixed results. Relations with Moscow were to be "reset," and Obama and Dmitri Medvedev, Russia's new president, developed a relationship that offered some promise of cooperation. Putin, however, remained the most powerful force in Russian politics and resumed the presidency in 2012 after a flawed election. He never wavered in his determination to resurrect his country's great-power status and its influence in the former Soviet republics. Cooperation with the United States was not high on his list of priorities. Nonetheless, Russia and the United States signed a new strategic arms limitation treaty (START) in 2010.

The Chinese were even less responsive. The men and women who oversaw relations with China in the Obama administration began by signaling that they would not press Beijing on human rights and would defer to Chinese sensitivity on meetings with the Dalai Lama. Anticipating reciprocity from the Chinese, they were profoundly disappointed. As the Chinese economy quickly recovered from the recession while the American economy continued to founder, Chinese arrogance became increasingly blatant. The United States, they posited, was in decline. It was acting from weakness. By contrast, China's rapid rise demonstrated that its form of government, its economic management, would provide a superior model for the future. Beijing yielded little on any of the issues that divided it from Washington and became increasingly bellicose in its warnings to the United States on Taiwan and in its expansion of its "core" interests in East Asia. Analysts at the Pentagon worried about the rapid modernization and strengthening of the Chinese military and the threat it posed to American interests in the western Pacific. But the military power of the United States was likely to be sufficient to deter a confrontation for decades to come, and the relative calm in the Taiwan Strait appeared to defuse a dangerous situation. Nonetheless, in 2012, the Obama administration announced that it was strengthening its defensive position across the Pacific, "pivoting" (presumably from the Middle East) toward East Asia. A small contingent of American Marines was stationed in Australia while diplomatic efforts in the region reinforced ties to friendly countries, and opened new possibilities with Burma as Burmese leaders hedged against their overbearing Chinese neighbor.

In 2012, the most ominous challenge to American foreign policy came from Iran, whose leaders had dismissed Obama's overtures. Neither the United States nor Israel was willing to countenance an Iranian nuclear weapon. Tehran appeared determined to develop at the very least the capability to assemble a bomb quickly. Obama saw Iran's activities as undermining his commitment to nonproliferation and unsettling the entire Middle East. Israel, in the face of Iranian denials of the Holocaust and promises to destroy the Jewish state, perceived a threat to its very existence. If sanctions imposed by the UN and Western powers failed – and the willingness and ability of China and Russia to dilute them could not be overestimated – Israel or the United States might attack Iran's known nuclear facilities. The outcome of such an attack would likely be devastating for the whole region and probably beyond.

As Obama's 2012 campaign for reelection began, many of those in the United States and abroad who had cheered his 2009 ascension to the presidency were disappointed. He had failed to pacify Iran or North Korea or bring peace to the Middle East. His war in Afghanistan seemed endless, and suicide bombers still ravaged Iraq and seemed more active than ever in East Africa. The Chinese were behaving badly, the Russians hardly less so. The economy staggered along. The best that could be said was that he was not Bush, and he remained relatively popular in much of the world. Clearly, he could not walk on water.

The election of a Republican-controlled House of Representatives in 2010 resulted in a dysfunctional government, soon focused on reducing the national deficit rather than on economic growth and job creation. Obama seemed incapable of doing what was necessary for the economy. Therein lay a graver danger to the interests and standing of the United States than that posed by terrorists or any foreign power. If the country could not respond adequately to an economic crisis at home, it could hardly expect the rest of the world to look to it for leadership.

In the 1990s, with the Cold War as history, American leaders and the foreign affairs elite searched for some concept to replace containment as a focus for American policy. Neither the administration of George H. W. Bush nor that of Bill Clinton could provide a satisfactory guiding principle. Then 9/11, the al Qaeda attack on the World Trade Center, appeared to resolve the issue: For the foreseeable future, the U.S. would be engaged in a "war on terror." Toward that end, hundreds of thousands of American troops were shipped to Iraq and Afghanistan in a seemingly endless and conceivably losing battle against men and women hostile to the U.S. and the values of the American people.

The world after the Cold War posed no existential threat to the United States, but there were more than enough challenges to American interests to keep its foreign policy specialists gainfully employed. The critical variable was the domestic situation: Could the political deadlock be overcome? Could the economy be revived? Would Washington be able to cope with environmental concerns? Soon after the end of the Cold War there had been much talk of America's decline, of the rise of trading nations such as Japan and Germany. But the American economy soared, and American military power helped sustain the nation's preeminence. Before the end of the first decade of the twenty-first century, however, fear of decline resurfaced as the economy neared collapse and the much-vaunted military remained mired in Afghanistan.

Much was made of China's rise, as it surpassed Japan to become the world's second-largest economy, en route to overtaking the United States. And Chinese arrogance, mirroring American triumphalism after the Cold War, boded ill for American interests in East Asia, if not everywhere. Would the United States rebound again? Would it regain the soft power lost by the Bush administration's unilateralism? Could it ever again serve as a political and economic model for rising powers across the globe? No matter how the questions are answered in the coming decades, the United States will remain central in world affairs, its actions – and inactions – continuing to have enormous impact on whatever new international system emerges. There is no other state willing and able to provide for the common good as the United States has – most of the time – since 1945.

BIBLIOGRAPHIC ESSAY

Perhaps the most important point to be apprehended by the student of the history of international relations in the Cold War era is that the documentary record remains incomplete, that American and British archival material is being released thirty years after the events at best. Moreover, there is evidence indicating that the integrity of the American record has been compromised. Other materials – Chinese and Soviet, for example – are being released very selectively, often to privileged nationals. Little was seen by Western scholars before the mid-1980s – and not much more has been seen since. For up-to-date information about the availability of documents, see the websites of the Cold War International History Project and the National Security Archives, two national treasures.

A second point worth noting is that enormously important work, much of it theoretical, has been done by political scientists and political economists. In particular the work of Robert Gilpin, Robert Jervis, Peter J. Katzenstein, Robert O. Keohane, Stephen D. Krasner, and Jack Snyder provides valuable guides to an understanding of what happened and why – and what is likely to happen tomorrow. See, for example, Gilpin, *The Political Economy of International Relations* (Princeton, 1987); Jervis, *Perception and Misperception in International Politics* (Princeton, 1976); Katzenstein, ed., *Between Power and Plenty* (Madison, 1978); Keohane, *After Hegemony* (Princeton, 1984); Krasner, ed., *International Regimes* (Ithaca, 1983); and Snyder, *Myths of Empire* (Ithaca, 1991).

The standard survey of American foreign policy since 1945 is Walter LaFeber, *America, Russia and the Cold War*, the tenth edition of which was published in 2008. Of enormous value are the essays collected by Melvyn P. Leffler and Odd Arne Westad for their three-volume *Cambridge*

History of the Cold War (Cambridge, 2009). The *Journal of Cold War Studies* provides new revelations in every issue. And *Diplomatic History* always has a new and often important contribution to some episode from the American involvement in world affairs after 1945.

1. AT WAR'S END: VISIONS OF
A NEW WORLD ORDER

Robert Dallek, *Franklin D. Roosevelt and American Foreign Policy, 1932–1945* (New York, 1979), remains the most useful introduction to FDR's thoughts on world affairs. The quest for a liberal international economic order can be followed from the 1920s through the 1940s in Michael J. Hogan, *The Marshall Plan* (Cambridge, 1990). Richard N. Gardner, *Sterling-Dollar Diplomacy,* expanded edition (New York, 1969), and Alfred E. Eckes, *A Search for Solvency* (Austin, Tex., 1975), are important to an understanding of the Bretton Woods agreements. The British perspective is most accessible in the relevant chapters of Roy F. Harrod, *The Life of John Maynard Keynes* (New York, 1951). Gabriel Kolko, *Politics of War* (New York, 1968), offers the least flattering evaluation of American ends leading up to Bretton Woods.

John Lewis Gaddis's classic *United States and the Origins of the Cold War, 1941–1947* (New York, 1972), captures Roosevelt's sinuous path toward the goal of maintaining the Grand Alliance after the war. Herbert Feis, *The China Tangle* (Princeton, 1953), is still the best introduction to American problems with wartime China. See also Michael Schaller, *The U.S. Crusade in China, 1938–1945* (New York, 1979). The most balanced account of Chiang Kai-shek's wartime diplomacy is John W. Garver, *Chinese-Soviet Relations, 1937–1945* (New York, 1988). Two very different efforts to read Stalin's mind are William O. McCagg, Jr., *Stalin Embattled, 1943–1945* (Detroit, 1978), and William Taubman, *Stalin's American Policy* (New York, 1982). Gar Alperovitz, *Atomic Diplomacy: Hiroshima and Potsdam,* expanded and updated edition (New York, 1985), is the best-known indictment of Truman's use of the atomic bomb against Japan, but see J. Samuel Walker, "The Decision to Use the Bomb: An Historiographical Update," *Diplomatic History* 14 (1990): 97–114. Roosevelt's decisions on whom to share the bomb's secrets with and whom to withhold them from can be followed in Martin J. Sherwin,

A World Destroyed (New York, 1975). Two excellent volumes on the subsequent importance of nuclear weapons are Gregg Herken, *The Winning Weapon* (New York, 1980), and Robert Jervis, *The Meaning of the Nuclear Revolution* (Ithaca, 1989).

2. ORIGINS OF THE COLD WAR

The American domestic context is portrayed vividly in Eric Goldman, *The Crucial Decade – and After, 1945–1960* (New York, 1960), and with more concern for women and minorities in William Chafe, *The Unfinished Journey* (New York, 1986). H. Bradford Westerfield, *Foreign Policy and Party Politics* (New Haven, 1955), remains the best account of how partisan politics contributed to the shaping of the Soviet-American relationship. The single most important study of Truman's foreign policy is Melvyn Leffler's magisterial *A Preponderance of Power: National Security, the Truman Administration, and the Cold War* (Stanford, 1992). Deborah Welch Larson, *Origins of Containment* (Princeton, 1985), provides a fascinating psychological study of how the policy toward the Soviet Union developed. Foreign economic policy is traced by Robert A. Pollard in *Economic Security and the Origins of the Cold War, 1945–1950* (New York, 1985). Richard M. Freeland argues persuasively the relationship between *The Truman Doctrine and the Origins of McCarthyism* (New York, 1972). Joyce and Gabriel Kolko offer a densely written but otherwise engaging Marxist analysis in their *Limits of Power* (New York, 1972). Joseph M. Jones, *The Fifteen Weeks* (New York, 1955), is the standard work on the evolution of the Truman Doctrine and the Marshall Plan by a participant.

The Wise Men (New York, 1986), by Walter Isaacson and Evan Thomas, is a highly readable examination of the thought and interactions of six major policymakers, but Dean Acheson's own *Present at the Creation* (New York, 1969) is still essential. There are too many books about George Kennan, whose own elegant writing and occasional profundities have led historians to exaggerate his importance. See, for example, Walter L. Hixson, *George F. Kennan: Cold War Iconoclast* (New York, 1989), and Anders Stephanson, *Kennan and the Art of Foreign Policy* (Cambridge, Mass., 1989). The most recent is John Lewis Gaddis' monumental *George F. Kennan: An American Life* (New York, 2012).

Lawrence Kaplan's *NATO and the United States* (Boston, 1988) is particularly helpful on the origins of NATO. European perceptions and activities are best explored with Geir Lundestad, "Empire by Invitation? The United States and Western Europe, 1945–1952," *Journal of Peace Research* 23 (1986): 263–77. See also Alan S. Milward, *The Reconstruction of Western Europe, 1945–1951* (Berkeley, 1984), and Anton W. dePorte, *Europe Between the Superpowers,* 2d ed. (New Haven, 1986). Wolfram F. Hanrieder, *Germany, America, Europe: Forty Years of German Foreign Policy* (New Haven, 1989), offers a wealth of information and insights for the entire postwar period. Marshall D. Shulman, *Stalin's Foreign Policy Reappraised* (New York, 1966), suggests Stalin was seeking to retreat from confrontation on the eve of the Korean War. Valuable insights into policies of the Soviet leader can be found in Vladislav Zubock and Constantine Pleshakov, *Inside the Kremlin's Cold War: From Stalin to Khrushchev* (Cambridge, Mass., 1996), and Zubock's *A Failed Empire: The Soviet Union in the Cold War from Stalin to Gorbachev* (Chapel Hill, 2007).

Marc S. Gallicchio, *The Cold War Begins in Asia* (New York, 1988), looks at American fears of Soviet influence in East Asia in 1945. See also his *The Scramble for Asia: U.S. Military Power in the Aftermath of the Pacific War* (Lanham, Md., 2008), which portrays the aspirations of some American leaders. Steven I. Levine, *Anvil of Victory* (New York, 1987), explains the American response to Communist successes in Manchuria in 1946. The major works on relations with China are Dorothy Borg and Waldo Heinrichs, *Uncertain Years: Chinese-American Relations, 1947–1950* (New York, 1980), and Nancy B. Tucker, *Patterns in the Dust* (New York, 1983). See also Robert J. McMahon, "The Cold War in Asia: Toward a New Synthesis," *Diplomatic History* 12 (1988): 307–27, for a superb overview, especially of work at variance with the prevailing Tucker-Cohen thesis. For Japan, see Michael Schaller's *The American Occupation of Japan* (New York, 1985), John Dower's *Empire and Aftermath* (Cambridge, 1979), *Embracing Defeat* (New York, 1999), and Carol Gluck's discussion of the issues and literature, "Entangling Illusions – Japanese and American Views of the Occupation," in Warren I. Cohen, ed., *New Frontiers in American–East Asian Relations* (New York, 1983), 169–236. The early American involvement in Southeast Asia is most accessible in Gary Hess, *The United States' Emergence as a Southeast Asian Power, 1940–1950*

(New York, 1987). See also Robert J. McMahon, *Colonialism and the Cold War: The United States and the Struggle for Indonesian Independence, 1945–1949* (Ithaca, 1981), on Indonesia.

3. THE KOREAN WAR AND ITS CONSEQUENCES

Bruce Cumings, *The Origins of the Korean War,* 2 vols. (Princeton, 1981, 1990), is essential reading for the serious student of the war. James Matray, *The Reluctant Crusade* (Honolulu, 1985), and Burton I. Kaufman, *The Korean War* (New York, 1986), are more accessible. William Stueck, *The Korean War: An International History* (Princeton, 1995), is the broadest, most inclusive study to date. Rosemary Foot, *The Wrong War* (Ithaca, 1985), and *A Substitute for Victory* (Ithaca, 1990), are major contributions to understanding American strategy during the war and in the peace negotiations. Allen S. Whiting's classic *China Crosses the Yalu* (Stanford, 1960) should be supplemented by Zhang Shuguang, *Deterrence and Strategic Culture* (Ithaca, 1993), which relies heavily on recently released cables exchanged between Mao and Stalin. Sergei N. Goncharev, John W. Lewis, and Xue Litai, *Uncertain Partners: Stalin, Mao, and the Korean War* (Stanford, 1993), Chen Jian, *China's Road to the Korean War: The Making of the Sino-American Confrontation* (New York, 1994), and Zubock's *Failed Empire* provide essential insights into Soviet and Chinese decision making.

Three important articles are Okonogi Masao, "The Domestic Roots of the Korean War," in Akira Iriye and Nagai Yonosuke, eds., *The Origins of the Cold War in Asia* (New York, 1977), 299–320; James I. Matray, "Truman's Plan for Victory: National Self-Determination and the Thirty-Eighth Parallel Decision in Korea," *Journal of American History* 66 (1979): 314–33; and Robert Jervis, "The Impact of the Korean War," *Journal of Conflict Resolution* 24 (1980): 563–92.

4. NEW LEADERS AND NEW ARENAS
IN THE COLD WAR

Eisenhower "revisionism" was a growth industry for historians in the late 1980s and early 1990s, as archival material for the 1950s was declassified. Richard A. Melanson and David Mayers, eds., *Reevaluating Eisenhower* (Urbana, Ill., 1987), is a convenient place to start. Ronald W. Preussen, *John Foster Dulles* (New York, 1982), is the best of the current biographies. Richard H. Immerman, ed., *John Foster Dulles and the Diplomacy of the Cold War* (Princeton, 1990), contains a number of superb essays. Immerman's own book, *The CIA in Guatemala* (Austin, Tex., 1982), is a very good account of how Eisenhower got things done, as is Fred I. Greenstein, *The Hidden-Hand Presidency* (New York, 1982). Burton I. Kaufman, *Trade and Aid: Eisenhower's Foreign Economic Policy* (Baltimore, 1982), delivers what it promises. Odd Arne Westad, *The Global Cold War* (Cambridge, 2005), demonstrates how the Soviet-American confrontation spread to the Third World.

Warren I. Cohen and Akira Iriye, eds., *The Great Powers in East Asia, 1953–1960* (New York, 1990), includes the perspectives of British, Chinese, Japanese, and Soviet, as well as American, scholars. The Chinese essays are especially interesting. Simei Qing, *From Allies to Enemies: Visions of Modernity, Identity, and U.S.-China Relations, 1945–1960* (Cambridge, Mass., 2007), is an important guide to understanding both American and Chinese policies in that era. Akira Iriye and Warren I. Cohen, eds., *The United States and Japan in the Postwar World* (Lexington, Ky., 1989), has substantial material on the 1950s, from Japanese and American scholars, economists, and political scientists as well as historians. Nancy Bernkopf Tucker's *The China Threat* (New York, 2012) offers the final word on American policy toward China in the Eisenower years.

Robert J. McMahon is thoughtful as always in "Eisenhower and Third World Nationalism: A Critique of the Revisionists," *Political Science Quarterly* 101 (1986): 453–73. On the Eisenhower administration and Castro, see Richard E. Welch, Jr., *The Response to Revolution: The United States and the Cuban Revolution, 1959–1961* (Chapel Hill, 1985). Stephen Rabe, *Eisenhower and Latin America* (Chapel Hill, 1988), is cast more broadly. Diane Kunz, *The Economic Diplomacy of the Suez Crisis* (Chapel Hill, 1991), provides a fresh approach to a battered subject. The single most important volume on the Suez crisis is W. Roger Louis and Roger Owen, eds., *Suez 1956* (New York, 1989). John C. Campbell, *Defense of the Middle East* (New York, 1960), is still useful for understanding the designs of the Eisenhower administration in the region, but Peter L. Hahn's *The United States, Great, Britain, & Egypt, 1945–1956* (Chapel Hill, 1991) and *Caught in the*

Middle East (Chapel Hill, 2004) mine more recently available sources. Howard Palfrey Jones, Eisenhower's ambassador to Indonesia, relates the pathetic tale of being undermined by Washington and especially the CIA in his efforts to woo Sukarno in *Indonesia: The Possible Dream* (New York, 1971). George M. Kahin, *Intervention* (New York, 1986), is excellent on Indochina.

Useful works on the Soviet side include Adam Ulam, *Expansion and Coexistence* (New York, 1974), William Zimmerman, *Soviet Perspectives on International Relations, 1956–1967* (Princeton, 1969), and Bruce D. Porter, *The USSR in Third World Conflicts* (Cambridge, 1984), as well as Zubock's *Failed Empire,* cited earlier. William Taubman's *Khrushchev: The Man and His Era* (New York, 2003) is essential reading.

5. CRISIS RESOLUTION

Thomas Paterson, ed., *Kennedy's Quest for Victory* (New York, 1989), is the best place to start the study of the early 1960s. Warren I. Cohen, *Dean Rusk* (Totowa, N.J., 1980), is more revealing than Rusk's own story, *As I Saw It* (New York, 1990). See Gordon Chang, *Friends and Enemies* (Stanford, 1990), for some especially provocative suggestions on Kennedy's policy toward China.

The Berlin crisis has not received as much recent attention as has the Cuban missile crisis. It can be studied in Philip Windsor, *City on Leave* (London, 1963); Jean Edward Smith, *The Defense of Berlin* (Baltimore, 1963); Robert M. Slusser, *The Berlin Crisis of 1961* (Baltimore, 1973); and Jack M. Shick, *The Berlin Crisis, 1958–62* (Philadelphia, 1972). See also the relevant portions of Alexander L. George and Richard Smoke, *Deterrence in American Foreign Policy* (New York, 1974), and Wolfram F. Hanrieder, *Germany, America, Europe: Forty Years of German Foreign Policy* (New Haven, 1989).

The history of the missile crisis has benefited enormously from a series of conferences involving American, Cuban, and Soviet participants. It is apparent the world was even closer to nuclear war than we had imagined previously. See James G. Blight and David A. Welch, *On the Brink* (New York, 1989), and Raymond L. Garthoff, *Reflections on the Cuban Missile Crisis,* rev. ed. (Washington, D.C., 1989). See also Leycester Coltman, *The Real Fidel Castro* (New Haven, 2003).

6. AMERICA'S LONGEST WAR

An unusually wide range of documentation has been available on the war in Vietnam since the Pentagon Papers were first published in 1971. The U.S. Department of State Historical Office subsequently accelerated publication of the relevant volumes of the *Foreign Relations* series.

George Herring, *America's Longest War,* 4th ed. (New York, 2002), remains the single most valuable book on the war in Vietnam. Frederik Logevall, *Choosing War* (Berkeley, 1999), is a superb study of the decisions that led to America's massive intervention. In *On Strategy* (Carlisle Barracks, Pa., 1981), Harry Summers explains how the war could have been won. Other books of interest include Gabriel Kolko's dense *Anatomy of a War* (New York, 1985) and Timothy J. Lomperis's *The War Everyone Lost – and Won* (Baton Rouge, 1984). Marilyn B. Young, *The Vietnam Wars, 1945–1990* (New York, 1991), is a powerful statement by a leading historian and antiwar activist. Lomperis, *Reading the Wind* (Durham, N.C., 1987), is a valuable analysis of the fictional and memoir literature. See also Katherine Kinney, *Friendly Fire: American Images of the Vietnam War* (Oxford, 2000). Ilya V. Gaiduk, *Confronting Vietnam* (Washington, D.C., 2003), reveals the Soviet role from 1954 to 1963, and Qiang Zhai, *China and the Vietnam Wars, 1950–1975* (Chapel Hill, 2000) provides important insights into Beijing's efforts.

7. THE RISE AND FALL OF DÉTENTE

The single most valuable book for the Nixon, Ford, and Carter years is Raymond L. Garthoff, *Détente and Confrontation* (Washington, D.C., 1985). Although ruthless editing might have produced a better book at half the length, it is a gold mine of information provided by a thoughtful midlevel participant. Henry Kissinger's two-volume memoir, *The White House Years* (Boston, 1979) and *Years of Upheaval* (Boston, 1982), is self-serving but nonetheless essential reading. Walter Isaacson, *Kissinger* (New York, 1992), provides a reasonable corrective. William Hyland, *Mortal Rivals: Superpower Relations from Nixon to Reagan* (New York, 1987), is a useful study by another midlevel participant.

The complex character of Richard M. Nixon is deciphered only in Garry Wills, *Nixon Agonistes* (Boston, 1970). Good critical accounts of the Nixon-Kissinger years are provided by the journalists Tad Szulc,

The Illusion of Peace (New York, 1979), and Seymour Hersh, *The Price of Power* (New York, 1983), the latter probably a trifle severe for the taste of most readers.

Zbigniew Brzezinski, *Power and Principle* (New York, 1983), is informative, especially of the author's efforts as national security adviser to usurp power once reserved for the secretary of state. For ego, the memoir rivals Kissinger's – but lacks the self-deprecating wit that was always Henry's charm. Instead of Carter's memoir, look to Gaddis Smith, *Morality, Reason and Power* (New York, 1986), for an understanding of Carter's foreign policy efforts. Cyrus Vance tells his own story in *Hard Choices* (New York, 1983).

Given the limited documentation available, Soviet-American relations are covered surprisingly well. Robert S. Litwak, *Détente and the Nixon Doctrine* (Cambridge, 1984), neatly indicates the contrasting expectations each side had of détente. Joseph S. Nye, Jr., *The Making of America's Soviet Policy* (New Haven, 1984), contains several useful essays. Harry Gelman, *The Brezhnev Politburo and the Decline of Détente* (Ithaca, 1984), is vintage Kremlinology. The Soviet thrust in the Third World characteristic of the late 1970s is analyzed nicely in Rajan Menon, *Soviet Power and the Third World* (New Haven, 1986), and Jerry Hough, *The Struggle for the Third World* (Washington, D.C., 1986). David Holloway, *The Soviet Union and the Arms Race*, 2d ed. (New Haven, 1984), focuses on the other critical issue in Soviet-American relations in the 1970s. Melvyn P. Leffler, *For the Soul of Mankind: The United States, the Soviet Union, and the Cold War* (New York, 2007), and Zubock, *Failed Empire*, are especially good on the Brezhnev years.

For Sino-American relations, see Harry Harding, *A Fragile Relationship: The United States and China Since 1972* (Washington, D.C., 1992). John W. Garver, *China's Decision for Rapprochement with the United States, 1968–1971* (Boulder, Colo., 1982), is interesting and suggestive. Nancy Bernkopf Tucker, *Strait Talk: United States-Taiwan Relations and the Crisis with China* (Cambridge, Mass., 2009), provides the definitive analysis of the Taiwan issue. See also Michel Oksenberg, "A Decade of Sino-American Relations," *Foreign Affairs* 61 (1982): 175–95. The Chinese perspective is offered in David Shambaugh's fascinating analysis of the views of China's foreign policy elite, *Beautiful Imperialist* (Princeton, 1991). See also Chen Jian's

Mao's China and the Cold War (Chapel Hill, 2001). William B. Quandt, *Decade of Decisions: American Policy Toward the Arab-Israeli Conflict, 1967–1976* (Berkeley, 1977), and Gary Sick, *All Fall Down* (New York, 1985), are excellent on Arab-Israeli relations and the collapse of the American position in Iran, respectively. On Iran, see also James A. Bill, *The Eagle and the Lion* (New Haven, 1988). Oksenberg, Quandt, and Sick all served on the National Security Council. For economic issues, especially the collapse of the Bretton Woods system, Joanne Gowa, *Closing the Gold Window: Domestic Politics and the End of Bretton Woods* (Ithaca, 1983), and Robert Gilpin, *The Political Economy of International Relations* (Princeton, 1987), are most helpful.

8. IN GOD'S COUNTRY

The journalist Lou Cannon has been studying Ronald Reagan for a very long time, and his *President Reagan: The Role of a Lifetime* (New York, 1991) is the most knowledgeable and the best-balanced biography. Another journalist-cum-historian, Don Oberdorfer, has written a valuable portrait of Reagan's metamorphosis from apocalyptic horseman to Gorbachev's partner in the quest for peace. See his *The Turn: From Cold War to the New Era: The United States and the Soviet Union, 1983–1990* (New York, 1991), based heavily on interviews with George Shultz. Shultz's own memoir, *Turmoil and Triumph: My Years as Secretary of State* (New York, 1993), is also useful. Leffler's *For the Soul of Mankind* and James Mann's *The Rebellion of Ronald Reagan* (New York, 2009) are superb on Reagan's transformation. See also Michael Mandelbaum and Strobe Talbott, *Reagan and Gorbachev* (New York, 1987), and Talbott, *Deadly Gambits* (New York, 1984). A very thoughtful, accessible overview of the Reagan years is Robert W. Tucker, "Reagan's Foreign Policy," *Foreign Affairs* 68 (1989): 1–27.

The role of the Bush administration in ending the Cold War is most accessible in James A. Baker III, *The Politics of Diplomacy* (New York, 1995), and George Bush and Brent Scowcroft, *A World Transformed* (New York, 1998).

The Soviet side of the 1980s is approached most easily through Seweryn Bialer, *Politics, Society, and Nationality Inside Gorbachev's Russia* (Boulder, Colo., 1989), and Seweryn Bialer and Michael Mandelbaum, *Gorbachev's Russia and American Foreign Policy* (Boulder, Colo., 1988).

See especially articles by Robert Legvold and Bialer. The articles in Marshall D. Shulman, ed., *East-West Tensions in the Third World* (New York, 1986), are also helpful; see the essays by Elizabeth K. Valkenier, Donald S. Zagoria, and Frances Fukuyama in particular. Jack F. Matlock, *Autopsy of an Empire: The American Ambassador's Account of the Collapse of the Soviet Union* (New York, 1995), delivers on the promise of its title. Archie Brown, *The Gorbachev Factor* (Oxford, 1997), is elegantly written, insightful, and accessible.

The historical context for American policy toward Central America is provided by Walter LaFeber, *Inevitable Revolutions* (1984). For a more contemporary focus see Nora Hamilton et al., *Crisis in Central America* (Boulder, Colo., 1988); Mary B. Vanderlaan, *Revolution and Foreign Policy in Nicaragua* (Boulder, Colo., 1986); Robert A. Pastor, *Condemned to Repetition* (Princeton, 1987); and Tommie Sue Montgomery, *Revolution in El Salvador,* 2d ed. (Boulder, Colo., 1990).

9. AMERICA AND THE WORLD, 1945–1991

In addition to works already mentioned, see Paul Kennedy, *The Rise and Fall of the Great Powers* (New York, 1987); David P. Calleo, *The Imperious Economy* (Cambridge, Mass., 1982); Richard Rosecrance, *The Rise of the Trading State* (New York, 1986); and John Lewis Gaddis, *The Long Peace* (Oxford, 1987).

10. THE NEW WORLD ORDER

Baker's *Politics of Diplomacy* and Bush-Scowcroft, *World Transformed,* are useful introductions to the Bush administration's activities beyond its dealings with Moscow. Lawrence Freeman and Ephraim Karsh, *The Gulf Conflict, 1990–91: Diplomacy and War in the New World Order* (Princeton, 1993), and the relevant chapters in Gary R. Hess, *Presidential Decisions for War* (Baltimore, 2001), are excellent on the Gulf War. For a brief discussion of Bush's mishandling of the Tiananmen massacre, see Warren I. Cohen, *America's Response to China,* 5th ed. (New York, 2010), and the oral histories of James Lilley and Winston Lord in Nancy Bernkopf Tucker's *China Confidential* (New York, 2000). On the search for a new role for the United States in the post–Cold War world, see the relevant chapter in Warren I. Cohen, *America's Failing Empire* (Oxford, 2005), and Ronald Steel, *Temptations of a Superpower* (Cambridge, Mass., 1995).

Warren Christopher's *Chances of a Lifetime* (New York, 2001) indicates his priorities as Clinton's secretary of state, 1993–6. Thomas Lipman, *Madeleine Albright and the New American Diplomacy* (Boulder, Colo., 2000), is best on her service as ambassador to the UN during Clinton's first term. Michael Dobbs, *Madeleine Albright: A Twentieth Century Odyssey* (New York, 1999), captures the woman and her life story. William Hyland, *Clinton's World: Remaking American Foreign Policy* (Westport, Conn., 1999), is an unflattering analysis. Derek Chollet and James Goldgeier, *America Between the Wars: From 11/9 to 9/11* (New York, 2008), is the best book to date on the policies of the Clinton era. The Russian side of those years can be found in three excellent studies: Michael Mandelbaum, ed., *The New Russian Foreign Policy* (New York, 1998), Lilia Shevtsova, *Yeltsin's Russia: Myths and Realities* (Washington, D.C., 1999), and Archie Brown and Lilia Shevtsova, eds., *Gorbachev, Yeltsin, Putin: Political Leadership in Russia's Transition* (Washington, D.C., 2001). For relations with China, see David M. Lampton, *Same Bed, Different Dreams* (Berkeley, 2001), and Robert Suettinger, *Beyond Tiananmen: The Politics of U.S. Chinese Relations, 1989–2000* (Washington, D.C., 2003). For Japan, Michael Armacost, *Friends or Rivals: The Insider's Account of U.S. Japan Relations* (New York, 1996), remains useful. Samantha Power, *"A Problem from Hell": America and the Age of Genocide* (New York, 2002), has blood-curdling accounts of events in Rwanda, Bosnia, and Kosovo.

The essential book on the backdrop to the Bush administration's foreign policy is James Mann, *Rise of the Vulcans: The History of Bush's War Cabinet* (New York, 2004). Also very useful is the volume by Ivo H. Daalder and James M. Lindsay, *America Unbound: The Bush Revolution in Foreign Policy* (Washington, D.C., 2003). Among the conservative critiques of neoconservative influences on Bush's policies, the most temperate is probably Stefan Halper and Jonathan Clarke, *America Alone: The Neoconservatives and the Global Order* (Cambridge, 2004). See also Glenn Kessler, *The Confidante: Condoleezza Rice and the Creation of the Bush Legacy* (New York, 2007).

11. THE "WAR" AGAINST TERRORISM

The story of 9/11 and its aftermath is obviously incomplete. An excellent book with which to begin is Lawrence Wright's *The Looming Tower: Al Qaeda and the Road to 9/11* (New York, 2006), to be accompanied by Richard Clarke's *Against All Enemies* (New York, 2004). Steve Coll's *Ghost Wars* (New York, 2004) is excellent on the early efforts in Afghanistan. Seth Jones, *In the Graveyard of Empires* (New York, 2009), does justice to what followed. To understand why so many members of the foreign policy elite accepted the decision to attack Iraq, start with Kenneth Pollack, *The Threatening Storm: The Case for Invading Iraq* (New York, 2002). For events subsequent to the invasion, see Thomas Ricks, *Fiasco: America's Military Adventure in Iraq* (New York, 2006), and George Packer, *The Assassin's Gate: America in Iraq* (New York, 2005).

For a superb analysis of China's grand strategy, see Avery Goldstein's *Rising to the Challenge* (Stanford, 2005). Russian strategy is best understood after reading Robert Legvold, ed., *Russian Foreign Policy in the 21st Century & the Shadow of the Past* (New York, 2007).

To appreciate the problems that the Obama administration was forced to address on the day it took office, David Sanger's *The Inheritance: The World Obama Confronts and the Challenges to American Power* (New York, 2009) is the best place to start. James Mann's *The Obamians* (New York, 2012) examines the administrator's performance through 2011.

INDEX